POWER AT THE PENTAGON

POWER

PENTAGON

By Jack Raymond

Harper & Row, Publishers

New York, Evanston, and London

FIRST EDITION

LIBRARY OF CONGRESS CATALOG CARD NUMBER: 63:20297

C-O

To my wife

Contents

Acknowledgments

To my wife, who listened to me read every word of the manuscript through several revisions and displayed excellent judgment as well as remarkable patience; Ted Slate, librarian of the *New York Times,* Washington Bureau, who traced some of the most obscure references imaginable; Elizabeth White Beverly, who typed the manuscript under forced draft. I found important material in *Air Force and Space Digest,* magazine of the Air Force Association; *Army,* magazine of the Association of the United States Army; *U.S. Naval Institute Proceedings,* and the files of the *Army-Navy-Air Force Journal, New York Times,* Washington *Post,* Washington *Star* and *Editorial Research Reports* and *Congressional Quarterly.* I also used, in revised form, articles I wrote for the *New York Times, New York Times Magazine,* the *Reporter* magazine and *Look.*

Preface

This book deals with the fact that twenty-five years ago our country had a handful of military, little more than a Swiss Guard; now we maintain the most powerful armed forces in history. In World War II our military officers received unusual responsibilities in Government, industry, diplomacy, science and human relations, which they carried out magnificently for the most part. At the same time our civilian industrialists, lawyers, scientists and teachers were handed responsibilities in national strategy under the disciplines of military requirements and they, too, left little to be desired. Victory in World War II was blurred by the "cold war" that followed and we further expanded American military power in the interests of national security. As we increased our military power to secure our nation, however, we also devoted ourselves increasingly to securing that military power. In the process, we altered some of our traditions in the military, in diplomacy, in industry, science, education, politics and other aspects of our society. We placed tremendous peacetime authority in the hands of our defenders, military and civilian. That is what this book is about.

It is not a history, although I have drawn from history to provide background for the present; it is not an analysis, although I have sought to explain some things I have been asked about in my occupation as a reporter. There certainly are more scholarly and detailed presentations of the special subjects included herein. But this is an effort to bring the whole into focus for the average citizen, who does not normally read books on defense affairs. Perhaps my occupation best characterizes this product. It is an attempted report on something that affects all our lives—the huge, persistent American military effort and its nexus of power at the Pentagon.

JACK RAYMOND

Washington, D.C.

POWER AT THE PENTAGON

I

——————————————————————— ☆

America's Military Posture

I

"Propaganda of a certain kind has spread the news that the Pentagon is a hive of warmongers where secret plots are brewed and where fabulous sums are put at the disposal of a gang of anti-communist fanatics."

　　　　—JEAN DE MADRE, NATO newsletter,
　　　　December, 1962

"The Pentagon, headquarters of the Department of Defense, is the world's largest office building."

　　　　—Pentagon pamphlet, April 1, 1960

The fabulous Pentagon, headquarters of the United States armed forces, sits on the Virginia side of the Potomac river outside the District of Columbia, on what was during the early thirties a wasteland of swamp, dumps and automobile graveyards known as "Hell's Bottom." Construction of the building was begun when America was still at peace, five months before Pearl Harbor. It was completed sixteen months later, in January, 1943, after the United States forces had helped turn the Nazi tide in North Africa, the Russians had already turned it at Stalingrad, Roosevelt and Churchill were agreeing at Casablanca on the goal of unconditional surrender, and in the Far East Guadalcanal was being painfully recovered.

The ground breaking for the Pentagon took place August 11, 1941. But the date of the cornerstone laying was not recorded. There was no ceremony, possibly because General Brehon Somervell, the Army Chief of Engineers, did not want to draw any more attention to it than was necessary. The project was being ridiculed as "Somervell's Folly." Critics thought the Pentagon building was unnecessary, too big and too expensive. According to J. Peter Hauck, of the John McShain Company, one of the contractors, the cornerstone was set in place in the early fall of 1941, on a Friday, a beautiful, sunny day, the kind that warms and lights up Washington in autumn.[1] Hauck made it a point to watch the job done by two specialists in stone setting. Two stories of the building already were up over the Mall Entrance, then known as the North Entrance.

On the following Sunday, Hauck encountered General Somervell and his two daughters as they entered the partly completed structure. General Somervell stopped on the concrete steps to look at the huge marble stone that bore his name along with those of other officials, headed by President Franklin D. Roosevelt. The general said to Mr. Hauck, "I see you've got it in." Mr. Hauck agreed with a nod. The Army general and his daughters then proceeded into the building and Hauck went to his office in town. That was all. Hauck learned afterward the workmen, not entirely devoid of sentiment, conducted a mock rite of their own. Perhaps on some future anniversary a sentimental Army public relations officer will organize a belated cornerstone ceremony to dedicate the building formally to ever-lasting peace.

The Pentagon was from its conception a matter of bitter controversy. Opponents of a new Army headquarters (the Pentagon was originally intended only for the old Department of War and not for the Navy) said it could not be put up in time to do any good during the war crisis that required a headquarters expansion. Some saw the whole idea of a new, larger headquarters as just another effort at "empire building" by the military. The chairman of the

Senate Military Affairs Committee warned that if so huge a building as contemplated by the Army were constructed on the Virginia side, the city of Washington "may be a ghost city after the war."[2] To mollify these critics, Army sources spread the word that the structure could afterward be used as a veterans hospital or school, or as a repository for government archives.

A mighty battle then ensued over the location. The Army originally proposed a site adjoining Fort Myer and Arlington Cemetery on the Virginia side of Memorial Bridge. This brought a scream of disapproval from the chairman of the District of Columbia Fine Arts Committee. He told the Senate Appropriations Committee that the proposed office building, with its "ugly vents and pipes" at the "very portals of Arlington Cemetery" would be a "blight upon the landscape."[3] President Roosevelt intervened in favor of the present location on the flats further down the river bank. According to one report, Mr. Roosevelt "smilingly" reminded General Somervell, a proponent of the Fort Myer site, that the President was Commander in Chief. The original site, however, dictated the ultimate famous design. Army architects, who had been given "a long weekend" to come up with drawings, took their inspiration from the fact that the roads in the area formed a rough pentagon. When the site was moved the design was retained. In addition, for sound professional reasons, it was felt that a building closely approximating a circle would provide the most space in a low-lying structure—mandatory because of nearby National Airport. The fortress-like appearance appealed to the military.[4]

Critics of the proposed military headquarters building next raised the question of money. President Roosevelt got the Army to shave its estimated cost figure from $35 million to $31 million. But it was evident before the Pentagon was completed that it was costing more than original estimates. Representative Engel of Michigan, in a lengthy speech in the House in October, 1942, reported with satisfaction that he had visited the new place and found no "unnecessary architectural features such as statues and fountains." He said there was evidence of "waste and extravagance" nevertheless. He predicted that the ultimate cost of the Pentagon would be double the original estimate, or about $70 million.[5] The Pentagon finally cost about

$83 million—"still cheaper than a battleship," one newsman observed cheerfully.

What took the edge off the criticism was the speed with which the new headquarters became serviceable. The first occupants, civil service workers and uniformed officials of the Army Ordnance Corps, moved into the partly completed structure on April 30, 1942, eight months after the ground-breaking. Already there was parking space for eight hundred cars (ultimately there would be room for ten thousand cars). Reporters who visited the site during the construction work wrote with awe of the building that was a mile in perimeter. The Pentagon finally was declared completed January 15, 1943.

In contrast with the forebodings of waste and extravagance, Washington took pride in the Pentagon's size and its fine accommodations. The Army had been housed for twenty years in the Munitions Building, a long, squat, three-story, concrete building on Constitution Avenue. Aligned with it was a similar three-story building housing the Navy Department. As the Army expanded its headquarters, it had moved into a new office building, a block north, on Virginia Avenue, which was rather modern in design for the old city. Some complained the new building looked like a theater. Secretary of War Henry L. Stimson was reported to have snorted in disdain over the luxurious appointments and decided to stay in the Munitions Building. After the Army moved into the Pentagon, the State Department inherited the Virginia Avenue building and subsequently added to it. The new entrance really did look like a theater.

At the Pentagon, whatever his personal feelings, Secretary Stimson had a private dining room, kitchenette, bath and emergency living quarters adjoining his office. General George C. Marshall, the Army Chief of Staff, also had a comfortable suite. "Before the reader gains a wrong impression of these office comforts, it is well to point out that their purpose and object is strictly utilitarian and time saving," the reporter for the Washington *Star* observed. "Both Mr. Stimson and General Marshall are among the most overworked officials in war-maddened Washington—and time saving is an element of utmost importance to the furtherance of war plans."

The building was officially named the Pentagon on February 19, 1943. Shortly afterward, the Navy, despite the reluctance of many of its workers, accepted the invitation of the War Department to join in the use of the Pentagon. Some recalcitrant members of the Navy Department composed this ditty:

> Carry me back to Old Virginny.
> That's where the Army and Navy have to go;
> That's where the roads are a mess in springtime;
> That's where the tombstones are heavy with snow.
> Carry me back to the Pentagon building—
> Five sides instead of the four that make a square.
> Carry me back to Old Virginny.
> 'Cause that's the only way
> You'll get me there.

Neither the Army nor the Navy got its entire headquarters staff into the new building. Despite the space for 27,000 workers, the Pentagon proved too small almost from the beginning. The real Navy "invasion" did not take place until after the war, in 1947, when the Unification Act created a third service, the Air Force, and former Secretary of the Navy James V. Forrestal took over as the first Secretary of Defense. In 1963 Congress appropriated money for the construction of another Pentagon—a "little Pentagon" it was to be called, although it would not have the same unique design.

By now, however, the Pentagon has taken on a meaning beyond architectural uniqueness. It has become the word symbol of American military power and direction. In this military nerve center decisions are made each day to order the push of buttons, the telephone calls, the coded radio messages, the signals fanning out to more than 2,700,000 men and women in the uniforms of the Army, Navy, Air Force and Marines, in camps and bases throughout the world. For in the 1960s the United States can show off a global military garrison of almost indescribable power with an arsenal of nuclear warheads counted in the "tens of thousands." Hundreds of land-based, nuclear-armed, intercontinental ballistic missiles cover the American landscape. The force set for 1965 is seventeen hundred ICBMs, each capable of rocketing through space for distances up to nine thousand miles and delivering hydrogen bombs with "pinpoint" accuracy—that is, an accuracy factor of less than two miles.

More than five hundred long-range jet bombers are ready at all times to take off within minutes of an alert signal and fly nearly half-way round the world and back without refueling. Each warplane can deliver at least one twenty-megaton bomb—one thousand times more powerful than the twenty-kiloton bomb that pulverized Hiroshima. The Air Force possesses also more than fifteen hundred "obsolescent" jet bombers that can carry out similar missions with the aid of remarkable mid-air refueling tanker planes. To be certain of immediate response, a certain number of flight crews sit in their planes at the end of runways. Those away from the field maintain contact as teams, even visiting the barber or going to the movies in pairs and keeping their automobile wheels turned away from the curb to permit speedy getaway.

The Polaris fleet is being expanded to forty-one boats. Each of these atomic submarines carries sixteen nuclear-tipped missiles. These can be dispatched from beneath the surface of the sea in undisclosed hiding places from the Polar icecap to the Persian Gulf. Giant aircraft carriers, one of them atomic-propelled, serve as mid-ocean bases for fighter bombers while atomic-powered attack sub-marines and amphibious ships, laden with Marines, carry out con-stant patrols in the vicinity of known trouble spots.

The American armed forces are designed to carry out a strategic policy of so-called "flexible response," to cope with big and little wars. "We have chosen not to concede our opponents' supremacy in any type of potential conflict, be it nuclear war, conventional war-fare, of guerrilla conflict," President Johnson said in his Budget Mes-sage to Congress, January 21, 1964. The United States' chief rival, the Soviet Union, also possesses sizable armed forces and missile and airplane fleets armed with nuclear weapons, but President John-son stated a fact when he said the United States has "the most formidable defense establishment the world has ever known." The managers of that establishment are in the Pentagon.

II

> "In the Councils of Government we must guard against the acquisition of unwarranted influence—whether sought or unsought—by the military-industrial complex."
>
> —DWIGHT D. EISENHOWER

There are three main entrances to the Pentagon—the River Entrance overlooking the Potomac, which is used by most high officials and their visitors; the Mall Entrance, next to it, facing north, which is also used by high officials and distinguished visitors; and the huge unnamed entrance, facing south, at which buses and taxis unload employees and ordinary visitors in a tunnel from which narrow staircases lead into the building's lobby or Concourse. This is a vast arcade, as crowded and bustling as a railroad station. And, in fact, there is a ticket counter where rail and plane tickets can be purchased. The crowds in the Concourse swarm in and out of great passageways that lead into the Pentagon proper. The Concourse has a bookstore, bank, post office, barbershop, department stores, laundry and dry cleaning stores, florist, bakery, drugstore, candy stores, baggage lockers, Western Union telegraph office, optometrist, photo supply shop, newsstand, jewelry store, shoe repair shop, pharmacy and medical and dental clinics.

Not surprisingly, many of the shoppers and browsers are in uniform, some of rather high rank. An ordinary visitor finds himself staring at the generals and admirals, wondering which of them are famous. There are myriads of colonels. What *are* so many officers doing here? Why aren't they somewhere with the troops? A large bulletin board opposite the post office indicates how transient are their assignments in the Pentagon. Hand printed with military neatness on white index cards are these notices: "For sale: 1959 French Fiat. Highest bidder. Owner suddenly transferred." Or: "Wanted: Used German language records," Or: "Lost: Small Japanese doll, in North parking area, has sentimental value only." Or: "For sale: 3 bedroom house, lovely garden, convenient to schools. Must sell quickly. Owner going overseas."

At the Information Desk a clerk issues cards with a floor plan of the Pentagon and pencils a simple route through the famous maze. Yet the huge building, with its unique, five-sided perimeter, is quite easy to get around in. Each floor is formed of five concentric rings, connected by ten spokelike corridors. The rooms are numbered according to a simple plan. The peculiar design of the Pentagon, however, its many stairways and escalators, its walled-off corridors and narrow passageways leading to huge basements have prompted jokes about visitors getting lost in the building. One durable story is of the young lady who rushes up to a guard and asks help in getting a taxi. She explains she is about to have a baby. Chided by the guard for entering the building with delivery time so near, she explains, "But I wasn't that close when I came in." Another story is of the Western Union boy who enters the Pentagon to deliver a message and by the time he can find his way out again he is a full colonel. But the jokes have never obscured the awesome function of the building or the responsibilities of its inhabitants.

The biggest desk in the biggest office in the Pentagon, on the third floor of the outer ring, over the Potomac River Entrance, with a good view of capital Washington, is the nine-by-five-foot solid-walnut desk that was made for American World War I hero General of the Armies John J. "Black Jack" Pershing. That desk, now used by the Secretary of Defense, is the government power center in the Pentagon. In the American tradition, a civilian occupies it. As an appointee of the President and ranking member of the President's Cabinet, he is a political person who needs never have experienced a day in uniform. Indeed, the law which created the office of Secretary of Defense expressly forbids career military men from being appointed to it.[6] The same law provides that a *civilian* Secretary of Defense serve as the principal adviser to the President in all defense matters. Thus the Secretary of Defense, and not any of the military Chiefs, the professionals at arms, is a member of the National Security Council. The Secretary of Defense can be influenced by the generals and admirals and at times he speaks for them, but he is in the Pentagon to carry out the policies and decisions of the President.

At the same time, despite the elaborate machinery of civilian control at the Pentagon, its prevailing image is of the generals and admirals, especially the Joint Chiefs of Staff. The uniformed Chiefs are political as well as military choices. They have arrived at the top in a process that puts great store in seniority and successful command experience. But they are appointed by the President for more than military considerations, as when in 1953 President Eisenhower swept out all the members of the Joint Chiefs of Staff. Eisenhower candidly explained that he wanted to emphasize his Administration's new approach.[7]

The Joint Chiefs of Staff, leaders of the military hierarchies, form a peculiar organization of military professionals, a corporate body with double loyalties. Four of the five men who comprise the Joint Chiefs—the Chief of Staff of the Army, the Chief of Staff of the Air Force, the Chief of Naval Operations and the Commandant of the Marine Corps—are at the same time ranking heads of their respective services and members of the single consultative body. The fifth man is the chairman, drawn from one of the services, but with no single service responsibility of his own.

All but the chairman thus wear "two hats." They have all-service duties in formulating strategic and logistic plans, reviewing force levels or service requirements for all the armed services and directing the activities of the unified, joint and specified commands—such as the Strategic Air Command or the American forces assigned to the Atlantic Pact in the European Command. They give military advice to the President and the National Security Council. But they are responsible as well for the administration and operations of their own individual services.

They are military planners, administrators and operators, and yet they move no troops except on the authority of civilian officials. The JCS chairman, who wears the uniform of one of the services, is a legal anomaly who has no command. The chiefs are served by a staff of high-ranking officers, but they are legally dependent upon the judgment of the civilian Secretary of Defense, over whose head they may appeal only to the President and Congress.

The unparalleled size and diversity of American military operations, the vast armies, the fleets of airplanes, warships and missiles can hardly be envisioned in the atmosphere of the office of the Secretary of Defense, although it is appropriately huge. To reach the great Pershing desk requires several long strides from the door. On the wall table behind the desk chair, the white telephone to the White House immediately catches the visitor's eye. There is also a red telephone that connects, through the command post in the basement, to the military commands across the world. It is linked also to the extraordinary "hot line" to Moscow that was arranged as a consequence of the Cuba crisis. This permits swift Soviet-U.S. communication in the event of a new crisis. A blue telephone provides the Defense Secretary quick communication with high-ranking assistants. Some landscape paintings adorn the high-ceilinged walls. A portrait of James V. Forrestal, the first Secretary of Defense, hangs on the wall directly behind the incumbent Secretary's chair, as if looking over his shoulder.

The mood of the office may vary according to the personality of the Secretary of Defense, but the atmosphere is always suffused with the grim knowledge that its occupant can make life-or-death decisions for America. Some Secretaries of Defense, notably Charles E. Wilson, who had been president of General Motors Corporation, treated the job like a production and management problem. He regarded strategy as something to be fought out between the military professionals and the policy-makers at the White House and State Department. Others, notably James V. Forrestal and Robert A. Lovett, regarded their responsibilities in broad policy perspectives and placed great reliance on the professional skills of the military. Some of the subordinate civilian secretaries were chosen for purely political reasons, others for their civilian expertise.

None of the Secretaries of Defense ever grabbed the job by the scruff of the neck and caused quite the commotion that Secretary Robert Strange McNamara, the brilliant young Ford Motor Company executive, precipitated with his "human IBM" approach. A pleasant, amiable man, McNamara turned out to be a determined, intellectually arrogant administrator who believed no problem was beyond analysis and probable solution.

A private elevator takes the Secretary of Defense to the National Military Command Center in the basement of the Pentagon. The Center is the nucleus of a labyrinth of soundproof rooms built with walls of acoustic tile, connected by a narrow, dead-end corridor, including rooms within rooms. It is served by a subbasement, world-wide communications room that operates twenty-four hours a day. The Center consists of four adjacent rooms, each with special armed guards at the doorways. Visitors, including the Secretary and the military Chiefs, gain admittance only after careful scrutiny. A camera and television eye record the scene while the guard examines face and credentials. The guard then presses a buzzer that unlocks a giant oaken door. A general officer is always on duty.

The main room is the green-carpeted conference briefing room. In the center is a large brown conference table, ellipse-shaped with the ends squared off. Each position at the table is equipped with an individual communications keyboard, telephones and switches. There, sitting in chairs of red leather and wood, the military and civilian officials can confer with commanders all over the world. They can talk by radio with pilots in flight. They can talk to ships at sea.

One wall of the main conference room is covered by a screen for rear-view projection of maps, status reports and intelligence pictures. Two walls consist of sliding panels with maps. These indicate the disposition of forces. The fourth wall has a line of twelve clocks that provide world-wide time coverage. On the same wall, four loud-speakers can be connected to incoming radio or telephone. This permits commanders in the field to address everyone in the room.

Two television screens occupy a corner. These display the latest data from North American Air Defense Command headquarters in Colorado Springs, from Strategic Air Command headquarters in Omaha (each with a huge underground command center head-quarters of its own) and from other command posts around the world. They display also, when connected for this purpose, the pictures received from radar screens the size of football fields in Alaska, Greenland and Scotland—major elements of the Ballistic Missile Warning Systems. Two stands, for ordinary maps and charts, occupy another corner. One wall has a special board with a battery of colored lights to indicate the readiness status of various commands. Behind the table positions are chairs for the aides, or "Indians" as the Chiefs call them.

Immediately next to the main conference room and overlooking it from a glass-fronted balcony is the communications center. It is packed with radio, telephone and teletype machines. There are "secure" military lines. These are in military hands at all points. In addition, the Chiefs use ordinary, open, commercial communications lines. A terminus of the "hot line" link to Moscow is in this room. The other terminus is in the Kremlin. Arrangements have been made for immediate notification of the President, the Secretaries of Defense and State, and the chairman of the Joint Chiefs of Staff should it bring a message. A bank of pneumatic tubes brings messages from other communications centers in the Pentagon. Special switchboards for interoffice communicators link the familiar office "squawk boxes." There are batteries of telephones, colored red, white, blue and black, according to their purpose. Thus the civilian and uniformed chiefs of the American military establishment exercise their "command and control" over the mighty and numerous United States armed forces throughout the world.

The Cuba crisis of 1962, precipitated when the Soviet Union secretly installed nuclear missiles and bombers in Cuba and was exposed, afforded some idea of the efficiency and power of the American armed forces. From the Command Center in the Pentagon, under direction of the President and the Secretary of Defense, emanated orders that sealed off Cuba with squadrons of destroyers, aircraft carriers, antisubmarine ships and picket planes. The United States' own ballistic missiles and bombers were placed on "maximum alert" and aimed at the Soviet Union; Army, Marine Corps and other Air Force and Navy units were shifted to combat positions, while radar networks backed by missile and aircraft interceptors were activated from the Polar skies to the Caribbean. Not since the Korean War had the country's military power been so flexed. More important, America demonstrated not only that she had the power but that she would not hesitate to use it. The Soviet Union, on President Kennedy's demand, withdrew its missiles and bombers, although continuing to strengthen Cuba militarily. While Soviet support of Cuba continued to pose a serious problem for the United States and Latin America, the Cuban military crisis faded in intensity. Aerial and sea surveillance of the island continued, adding yet another standing military operation to the United States' commitments all over the world.

In Korea more than a decade after America's "nastiest" and most unpopular war, some forty thousand United States troops still man dug-in positions along the demilitarized zone bordering Communist North Korea. Known as the "forgotten front," Korea produces occasional clashes and casualties.

There is another grim military commitment in the steaming jungles and cold mountains of South Vietnam. It is a clumsy and endlessly frustrating war, absorbing more than fifteen thousand of the very best men that the United States can muster. Pentagon officials have expressed the hope of withdrawing most of these men by 1965, but have made it clear that many Americans will have to stay on the scene to help train the South Vietnamese in their struggle against Communist insurgents. Technically, the Americans do not engage in battle, although they fly transport planes and helicopters and "fire back when fired upon." Such direct support has resulted in American casualties.

In Europe, meanwhile, America's heaviest commitment continues. More than 400,000 Americans, organized as the bulwark of the Atlantic Pact forces, are still there nearly twenty years after the end of World War II. Army troops, some of them armed with atomic bazookas, man an Allied defense line across the ancient invasion route from the Fulda Gap in the north to the Austrian Alps where the borders of Czechoslovakia, Austria and Germany meet. Airmen are on continuous alert with squadrons of bombers, fighter-bombers and troop transports. Men of the Navy—most of them attached to the carrier-based Sixth Fleet in the Mediterranean—share in America's support of Allied defenses opposite the Communist Iron Curtain.

It is apparent that both Western Europe and the United States have become restive over the American military presence on the Continent. This is expressed in European demands for more of a say in the strategy of deterrence and United States efforts to reduce the costs of the overseas military posture. But there appears to be no way out. Despite shifts in the alliance's military positions and money-saving reorganizations in the American troop disposition, United States forces stay on.

Elsewhere, outside the glare of international attention, American boys are stationed in remote places from Pole to Pole, on virtually every parallel line in both hemispheres, in virtually every longitudinal zone. To help contain the threat of the Communist drive for world power, America spends nearly 10 percent of her Gross National Product for defense and, continuing to draft her youth for military service, maintains vast armies and navies for a police patrol of the world.

The Pentagon presides over a complex of planes, ships, tanks, military bases, research laboratories, arsenals, quartermaster depots and shipbuilding yards comprising capital assets valued at more than $150 billion. In early 1964, despite many "deactivations," there were 6,700 separate military installations in the United States and abroad. "Defense" costs the American people more than $51 billion a year—nearly a billion dollars a week. Almost half the total goes to pay salaries and maintain the forces. Slightly more than half goes to the defense industries in the form of procurement contracts. To the average citizen these big numbers must be abstractions. What is the difference between a million dollars, a billion dollars and fifty billion dollars? How does one differentiate between a mountain, a high mountain and a very high mountain? President Eisenhower once tried to put it this way: "The cost of one modern heavy bomber is this: It is a modern brick school in more than 30 cities. It is two electric power plants, each serving a town of 60,000 population. It is two fine, fully equipped hospitals. It is some 50 miles of concrete highway."[8] But what average citizen ever tried to build a school or equip a hospital?

The tremendous American military establishment has undoubtedly deterred the Communist leaders of Europe and Asia from open aggression. It has given comfort to people in the shade of the Communist menace from Berlin to Bangkok. But the vast military effort has also stirred uneasiness. A British historian has observed that the Pentagon has taken its place "alongside the Elders of Zion, the Freemasons, 'world finance' and the like, in the Pandemonium of the worshippers of the 'conspiracy theory' of history."[9] Two American journalists have written a best-selling novel, dramatizing in fiction fears of a coup in which American military leaders attempt to usurp the civilian authority because of dissatisfaction with a disarmament "deal" with the Soviet Union.[10] Another best-selling novel dramatizes the possibility of an accident in the communications apparatus that could unintentionally dispatch nuclear bombers on a mission to wipe out Moscow.[11] Behind the rash of books and articles is the disturbing idea that the people of America—and the world—are somehow caught helplessly in fateful decisions made each day by war-minded soldiers with great technical power and authority.[12] Some Americans look about them and see in other lands, where military men assumed power, evidence of danger to their own beloved country.

Fear of and aversion to military influence are rooted deep in American traditions and can be traced to the English Civil War. The English immigrants, especially the Puritan colonists, remembered with loathing the story of Cromwell and his New Model Army, which emerged as the prototype of a "standing army."[13] When England pressured the colonies to quarter a standing army as a protection following the French and Indian Wars, it became a cause of the Revolution. The writers of the Declaration of Independence complained that King George had "affected to render the military independent of and superior to the Civil Power." The Continental Congress drove the philosophy home in 1787 with these words: "Standing Armies in time of Peace are inconsistent with the principles of republican Governments, dangerous to the liberties of a free people and generally converted into a destructive engine for establishing despotism."[14]

The attitude of many persons of that era—and many persons more than 170 years later—was reflected in the Senate debate of 1790 when William Maclay of Pennsylvania opposed Secretary of War Knox's request for an increase in his forces from 840 men and 46 officers to a militia six times that number. Said Maclay: "Give Knox his Army and he will soon have a war on hand."[15] A year later, President Washington announced "offensive operations" against the Indians.

Throughout American history the people have appeared to prefer ill-preparedness for war to the burden and purported dangers of maintaining a large peacetime military establishment. The War of 1812 led to the decision to have permanent military forces. But despite the victory in the Mexican War and Commodore Perry's show of force against Japan, the military never earned widespread acclaim in this country. The Civil War left the country in a state of shock. This most terrible of American wars produced more battle heroes and sagas than any other. Yet its contribution to the American pacifist sentiment outlasted even the Theodore Roosevelt period of navalism. After World War I, a wave of disillusionment swept the country. As late as 1941, with Europe and Asia aflame, the Chief of Staff of the Army found it prudent to conclude his testimony in behalf of a large Army budget with this reassurance: "In conclusion let me state with all the sincerity of which I am capable that there is no group today in America who view the possibilities of war with more horror, and consider the large appropriations involved with more reluctance than do the officers of the General Staff. There is no thought in our minds to seize upon the dilemma of this tragic world situation as an opportunity to aggrandize the Army."

World War II, in contrast with World War I, enhanced the role of the military in American society. The postwar years dominated by the tensions of the "cold war," also gave a military slant to American diplomacy. This was further underscored by the prominence of former officers in government, education, science and industry. The war had served to broaden and advertise the talents of military men. Arthur A. Ekirch, Jr., of American University in Washington, D.C., wrote: "In the process of two world wars, militarism as a 19th Century Prussian phenomenon, replete with brass bands and an arrogant officer class, has been superseded by the French Revolutionary variety of total militarism. To the old French Revolutionary *levée en masse* has been added the enormous productive capacity of modern industrialism and the incessant propaganda of the masses. With the power of the military extended to all phases of national life, its contrast and conflict with the civil authority has also become less apparent. In other words, military power is able to dominate civil authority to the point where the latter becomes a willing dupe of military men, overwhelmed by their prestige, and confused as to the validity of the experts' opinions on the questions of larger policy. The threat of militarism, therefore, seems to be far greater today than it was a hundred years ago when the chief dispute between the military and the civilian authority was over the size of the standing army."[16]

Harold Laski, the British economist, pointed to the possibility "that in the United States as elsewhere, the technological implications of modern warfare may make possible a new type of militarism unrecognizable to those who look for its historic characteristics. . . . Anyone who thinks for one moment of the effort involved in building the atomic bomb will not find it difficult to realize that in the new warfare, the engineering factory is a unit of the army and the worker may be in uniform without being aware of it. The new militarism may clothe itself in civilian uniform; and, if the present relations of production are maintained, it may be imposed upon a people who see in its development no more than a way to full employment."[17] The growing enforcement of Pentagon security regulations at thousands of defense plants, with millions of workers subject to security clearances, has underscored Laski's warning.

America's fears over the implications of the "new warfare" came out forcefully in President Dwight D. Eisenhower's remarkable farewell address to the nation, January 17, 1961. Eisenhower introduced a new colloquialism, "the military-industrial complex." The old soldier, who had held the highest military and civilian commands of his country, and whose best friends were industrialists, observed that America was "the strongest, the most influential and most productive nation in the world." While "understandably proud," the people should nevertheless realize that in addition to the danger of a hostile ideology abroad, there were other threats, "new in kind and degree."

Until World War II, President Eisenhower pointed out, the United States had no armaments industry. American makers of plowshares could, with time and as required, make swords as well. "But," he went on, "we can no longer risk emergency improvisation of national defense. We have been compelled to create a permanent armaments industry of vast proportions. Added to this, three and a half million men and women are directly engaged in the defense establishment. . . . Now this conjunction of an immense military establishment and a large arms industry is new in the American experience. The total influence—economic, political, even spiritual—

is felt in every city, every State House, every office of the Federal Government. We recognize the imperative need for the development. Yet we must not fail to comprehend its grave implications. Our toil, resources and livelihood are all involved; so is the very structure of our society.

"In the councils of Government, we must guard against the acquisition of unwarranted influence, whether sought or unsought, by the military-industrial complex. The potential for the disastrous rise of misplaced power exists and will persist. We must never let the weight of this combination endanger our liberties or democratic processes. We should take nothing for granted."

General Eisenhower thus eloquently focused attention not on the ancient bugaboo of military dominance in a direct sense, but on the subtle dangers posed by the changing times. As he explained at a farewell press conference a few days later, he was not thinking so much of willful misuse of power. He was thinking, he said, of "an almost insidious penetration of our own minds that the only thing this country is engaged in is weaponry and missiles—and I'll tell you we just can't afford that."

II

─────────────────────────────────── ☆

On the Eve of World War II

"As Commander in Chief of the Army and Navy of the United States it is my Constitutional duty to report to the Congress that our National Defense is, in the light of increasing armaments of other nations, inadequate for the purpose of national security and requires increase for that reason."
— PRESIDENT FRANKLIN D. ROOSEVELT,
Message to Congress, January 28, 1938

"The recommendations made by me in the foregoing message were but the beginning of a vast program of rearmament."
— Notation by PRESIDENT ROOSEVELT in
Public Papers of President Franklin D. Roosevelt, 1938 Volume, pp. 68-71

In the 1960s the United States possessed the most powerful military forces on earth. But twenty-five years earlier, on the eve of World War II, the Chief of Naval Operations feared that the Navy, whose slogan was "Second to none," was in fact "approaching inferiority in defensive power";[1] and the Army Chief of Staff complained that the Army already was suffering from "marked inferiority in strength."[2]

America did not spring to arms with these warnings. But the year 1938 in which they were issued in support of the President did, in retrospect, mark the "beginning of a vast program of rearmament," as Mr. Roosevelt afterward confirmed. Authorizations were approved by Congress for a huge shipbuilding program. Plans were laid for the creation of a tremendous airplane industry. More significantly, the worried President began successfully breaking down the nation's pacifist-isolationist mood, although he had to go slowly because of nationwide fears of involvement in war. Military leaders were apprehensive of attracting attention to their responsibilities. For example, a small group of Army and Navy junior officers, including the subsequently famous head of the Selective Service System, Captain Lewis B. Hershey, was studying techniques of military conscription. They were under admonition from their superiors, however, to hold their meetings in secret, lest these conferences be interpreted as a preparation for war rather than an exercise in professional caution.[3]

Still fresh in the minds of American military authorities, moving warily in an atmosphere of pacifism and isolationism, was an experience of 1915. After World War I broke out in Europe, President Wilson reacted violently to a news story reporting that the Army General Staff was "preparing a plan in case of war with Germany." The President threatened immediate relief of every officer in such duty. He calmed down only after General Bliss explained to the Commander in Chief the responsibility of the General Staff.[4] President Roosevelt was more sophisticated. But even he sought to save money by cutting the size of the Army officer corps through forced retirements. On the list of those scheduled to be retired as "over age in grade" were Lucius D. Clay, Leslie R. Groves, Alfred M. Gruenther, James A. Van Fleet, J, Lawton Collins and Matthew B. Ridgway.

The nation as a whole opposed any military preparation and steadfastly refused to believe that the world would be enveloped in war. A Gallup poll in January, 1937, showed only 15 percent forecasting war in Europe, 85 percent saying there would not be a war. As late as May, 1939, 68 percent said "No war," 32 percent predicted war. In those days, although battles raged in Spain and China, the "average American regarded marching troops as he did the parade of some foreign society. He felt himself a spectator—not a member of the lodge."[5] The President cautiously pursued a "both sides of the coin policy." On the one hand, he delivered a scathing indictment of the dictatorships. He characterized their policies as diseases and called for a quarantine. The "quarantine speech," delivered in Chicago late in 1937, aroused a storm of protest from the isolationists. The President then pulled back. By the end of the year, in a beautiful semantical concession, he was described as viewing the world situation in a mood of "watchful isolation."

That the United States was not already at war with Japan seemed only less remarkable, however, than American willingness to ignore insult and injury in the *Panay* incident. On December 12, 1937, the United States gunboat *Panay* was evacuating American refugees in the Asian war and escorting American merchant vessels up the Yangtze River. The gunboat was marked with two American flags. Japanese aviators, under instructions to keep the river "clear" for attacks upon the Chinese, suddenly bombed and sank the *Panay* and three oil tankers. They killed three, wounded seventy-four and strafed survivors struggling to get ashore. There was a temporary wave of United States indignation over the incident, but most Americans were determined to regard the attack as an accident. Secretary of State Hull demanded an apology and indemnity. The Japanese deliberately waited until December 14, the deadline, before apologizing and eventually did pay an indemnity.[6]

What was the United States doing in China anyway? Since the early twenties, the War Department had been trying to get State Department consent to the withdrawal of the Fifteenth Infantry, the Old China Regiment, from Tsientsin in northern China. Army leaders, short in manpower, wanted to reduce their commitments. They insisted that conditions had changed since the original garrison had been established in the wake of the Boxer Rebellion. But every Secretary of State from Charles Evans Hughes to Cordell Hull insisted upon the presence of American forces there. Mr. Hull said they constituted a "psychological influence of a reassuring and stabilizing character"; that is, they were a deterrent to Japanese molestation of the American Embassy, citizens and business enterprises.[7] The Army claimed that the garrison was at the mercy of any aggressor and must either be strengthened or removed. Strengthening was out of the question, especially after the Japanese began the Asian war with their attack upon Chinese troops at Marco Polo Bridge in 1937. In February, 1938, orders finally were issued to pull the Fifteenth out of China. By March it was out, after twenty-seven years of garrison duty. The protection of American interests was left to the Marines.

One of the last American soldiers to leave China was a tall, dark, spindly first lieutenant, Earle G. "Buzz" Wheeler, who was stationed at Tsientsin, near where the Japanese had established one of their big supply bases. Wheeler, who was to become Army Chief of Staff under President Kennedy twenty-five years later, stood reveille with his men. He could see the Japanese planes take off from the city airdrome on their bombing and strafing missions. As part of their intelligence operations, he and his fellow officers counted the bombers, the hospital and supply trains, the artillery pieces and the swarms of Japanese troops. Among these troops were many Korean conscripts in Japanese uniforms. Many of the Americans had never seen Koreans before. What impressed Wheeler and the other American officers was the "arrogance" of the Japanese.

One day, dressed in mufti, he crossed the river to the Japanese part of Tsientsin. There in the main square, he saw some five hundred Chinese coolies, herded under guard of Japanese soldiers wearing bayonets in their belts and wielding small clubs. A Japanese officer suddenly appeared and shouted an order for a certain number of the Chinese to join a work detail. Whereupon the guards cut into the herd and began flailing the nearest Chinese over the head and shoulders, sectioning off the desired number. Wheeler never forgot "this elevating sight."[8]

Otherwise, service in China had not been bad. Tsientsin was a city of 839,000, eighty-seven miles south of Peking on the Peking-Mukden line of the Chinese Government railroad. This was about 175 miles north of Chinwangtao, the port of call for Army transports. The garrison had relatively modern facilities in the foreign "concessions" and some first-class hotels. The troops were quartered in barracks. The officers had good clubs. There were several good movie houses, a country club and golf course available to all grades and ranks. A racing club and excellent race tracks were the scene of spring and fall meetings. There were international competitions in baseball, football, hockey and Rugger. Tsientsin was a desirable overseas Army post in those days, something like Germany in the post-World War II occupation.

So it was with regret mixed with relief that the Old China Infantry came home in 1938. When Wheeler and his fellow officers arrived in the United States, they were convinced that their country must inevitably clash with the Japanese. As they pulled into San Francisco Harbor, however, they were disturbed to see a ship taking on scrap iron for Japan. "None of us predicted a Pearl Harbor, but we took a grimmer view than the men at home," Wheeler recalled many years later. "The people in the United States seemed to have no idea what was going on. Our minds and our memories were filled with the sights of arrogant Japanese officers and their triumphant armies, behaving as though they expected to own everything."

In Tokyo, Ambassador Joseph C. Grew "remembered the Maine" and thought that the United States would declare war over the sinking of the *Panay*. He had with him in the embassy a young captain, Maxwell D. Taylor, assistant military attaché, who was assigned to research in the tactics of the Japanese Army. "It was pitiful how little we knew about the Japanese Army," Taylor recalled twenty-five years later when he was chairman of the Joint Chiefs of Staff.[9] Taylor was eminently qualified for his Tokyo assignment. He was fluent in Japanese. He had completed the staff course at Fort Leavenworth in 1935, when he was immediately ordered to Japan as a language officer. For nearly two years, he devoted himself almost exclusively to the Japanese language. In the late spring of 1937, he was assigned to a Japanese guard artillery regiment and remained with it through the summer. Such accommodation was not uncommon. The tradition of military exchanges was also adhered to by Nazi Germany.

Taylor next served as aide to General Joseph Stilwell, who was following the Japanese armies in China. As the climate of war grew more intense, Taylor returned to the embassy to prepare a handbook on Japanese Army tactics. While the Japanese had permitted American observers on the battalion and regimental levels, there was little information available on higher staff work. Taylor went to the neighborhoods of principal military schools and bought all the study materials he could find in the shops. There were several unofficial manuals available, prepared by professionals. These manuals did not have the problems that were being studied in the schools, but they were devised as study aids for diligent students. Taylor accumulated about eighty basic map problems, staked them out and matched conventional Western thinking against the Japanese techniques. It was a fascinating military exercise. Taylor recalled that when Pearl Harbor came, his was the only manual of its type available to the American Army. "And then of course," he reminisced ruefully, "it was immediately invalidated when both the enemy army and our own were faced with the truth in battle. Neither of us behaved according to the book."

When Captain Taylor returned to Washington and staff service at the Army headquarters in the Munitions Building, his head was full of Army plans to cope with a surprise Japanese attack on the Philippines. With growing Japanese military power, the defense of the Philippines was an American military preoccupation. In Manila, January 1, 1938, Manuel Quezon announced that General Douglas MacArthur, the former American Army Chief of Staff who had been seconded to the Philippines as military adviser and was due to retire from active service, had agreed to stay on to head the Philippine armed forces with the rank of field marshal. MacArthur's acceptance of the title caused a personal dispute between him and his aide, Lieutenant Colonel Dwight D. Eisenhower. General MacArthur had brought the balding, reddish-haired, younger man with him from Washington as a major in 1935. When MacArthur asked Eisenhower whether he should accept the grandiose title, the rather homespun Kansan said, "No." Whereupon General MacArthur imperiously accused his aide of being "small-minded."[10]

Those were busy days for Eisenhower. He was instrumental in founding a Philippine Military Academy, modeled after West Point. Working on the defense of the Philippines, he developed a doctrine that "a war of relentless attrition, of resistance from the water's edge to the farthermost retreat left available to the defending army, is the purpose . . . of any military unit that finds itself in the situation that faces the Philippine Military Establishment." The strategy that MacArthur later employed for the defense of the islands against Japan—including the retreat to Bataan—was worked out in detail during Eisenhower's assignment. It was during his years in Manila that Eisenhower first gained his reputation for "diplomacy." He and Mrs. Eisenhower lived in the Manila hotel. Their suite, overlooking Manila Bay toward Corregidor, was a favorite gathering place for American officers and Filipino politicians. Eisenhower "smoked like a furnace" in those days.[11]

One of the young officers stationed with a Philippine Scout Regiment was First Lieutenant James M. Gavin. He had been assigned there in 1936, after the usual routine of maneuvers and postgraduate schooling that followed his graduation from West Point in 1929. Recalling the "rather prosaic life" of an infantry lieutenant in those years, General Gavin—who rose to lieutenant general and Ambassador to France—later provided a good picture of prewar military life:

The marksmanship season, maneuvers, winter schools, spring training, civilian components and CMTC followed each other as night followed day. The Army was small and the public showed even smaller interest in it. After all we had just ratified the Kellogg-Briand Peace Pact of 1928, outlawing war as an instrument of national policy. There was never going to be another war. If we were training for anything, it was for a war that would never come. I, at times, bemoaned our fate with my contemporaries. We, the unfortunate ones, who were destined to go through life without hearing a hostile shot. How wrong we were!

The drill days were rather short and there was an abundance of time for extra-curricular activities. I should have spent more time on my books, but tennis, golf and riding offered too much competition. But I liked troop duty and I liked being with the troops. The long night marches, the sudden skirmishes, and maneuvers, all were teaching me things I would have to draw upon if war came. . . . Several times we rehearsed the withdrawal to the Bataan peninsula. We then maneuvered, falling back as we anticipated the World War II pattern of fighting on the peninsula. The situation was far from good. . . . Surely, I thought, there must be some Master Plan in Washington to take care of this situation. The American people were not just sitting idly by, accepting this as the inevitable and doing nothing about it.[12]

At home, there was neither "master plan" nor idle acceptance of the inevitable. There was Franklin Roosevelt, a "non-despairing man," as Robert Sherwood called him. The President early in 1938 wrote to Representative Edward Taylor, chairman of the House Appropriations Committee: "World events have caused me growing concern. . . . In the world as a whole, many nations are not only continuing but enlarging their armament programs. . . . Facts are facts and the United States must face them. . . . After the next session of Congress has met, I may send supplementary estimates for commencing construction of a number of ships in addition" to those being requested in the budget for the fiscal year beginning July 1, 1938.

The basic budget plan seemed big enough. It asked $528,263,632 for the Navy, the highest figure since 1920, when Roosevelt was Assistant Secretary of the Navy. In the four years, 1934-1938, naval budgets had totaled $1,860,000,000. More naval construction was under way as the Seventy-fifth Congress began its session than at any time since the Great War. But by comparison with the navies of Great Britain and Japan, the United States fleet was considered deficient in both heavy and light cruisers. Congressional action was relatively quick on the military bills, which included new legislation for speedy mobilization of Army forces. The *Panay* incident had created a somewhat receptive mood on Capitol Hill, although Senator Gerald Nye, who had conducted investigations of profiteering in World War I, registered indignation against "militarists" and "war scares." By January 21, the House passed the record peacetime naval appropriations measure, granting virtually everything that had been requested. On February 7, the President sent up his supplementary request, the so-called Naval Expansion Act, providing for a two-ocean Navy.

The additional military requests triggered a burst of opposition from the growingly vocal "isolationists," who equated military preparedness with interventionism. Charles A. Beard, the historian, described the opposition in words that expressed his own strong feelings: "Even kindergartners in naval affairs knew that battleships such as proposed, with a large cruising radius, were for use in distant waters, rather than for defense in American waters."[13] The opposition to rearmament came from both "Left" and "Right." In March, a delegation of the Left Wing American Youth Congress, after a parade through the Washington streets, was permitted to call upon the President to protest what was described as the Administration's "militarism." The President melodramatically showed them a newspaper headline, "Hitler Invades Austria." The "Right Wing" made much of the statement by Ambassador Joseph P. Kennedy in London, following the *Anschluss,* that the United States would "solve its own problems if it stopped worrying about Europe."

The ambassador's son, John Fitzgerald Kennedy, was a junior at Harvard at the time, majoring in government, with emphasis on international relations. The future President had spent a fascinating summer in 1937 touring Europe. In 1938 he "restlessly" watched developments there. The following year, he won permission from Harvard to spend his second semester abroad. His 1939 trip provided the material for the college thesis that was published afterward under the title *Why England Slept.*[14]

Lyndon Baines Johnson was a fledgling member of the House of Representatives, to which he had been elected in 1937 in a New Deal campaign, supporting even Roosevelt's ill-fated plan to enlarge the Supreme Court. He was a favorite of Roosevelt, through whose intervention he gained a place on the powerful Naval Affairs Committee, an unusual spot for a young Congressman. From the outset, Johnson was a strong advocate of military preparedness. "He was an outstanding member of the committee when we had to push through the Naval Expansion bill," Representative Carl Vinson, chairman of the panel, recalled. "I placed many responsibilities on his shoulders, named him to head various subcommittees and sent him on investigating missions throughout the country. He wrote many reports supporting preparedness."[15]

Less aware of world matters in those days was a bespectacled young student at the Harvard Graduate School of Business Administration. He was Robert Strange McNamara, who would become, a quarter of a century later, a dynamic Secretary of Defense, responsible for the most powerful assemblage of awesome weapons the world had ever devised. Looking back, McNamara said in 1963 he had had "no awareness of impending war." Nor did he think the people around him showed any awareness of it. In fact, even when he traveled to Europe at the age of twenty-three, and visited Berlin among other cities in 1939, he had no notion of possible war. "Maybe other people realized it, but I didn't," Secretary of Defense Mc-Namara afterward commented.

In March, 1938, under Administration prodding, Congress passed the $1,121,546,000 naval authorization bill. On April 9 the Senate walked en masse from its chamber to watch the Army Day parade and then returned to pass the Army appropriations bill, adding $43 million for a total of $460,201,254. By mid-June more than a billion dollars had been appropriated for the armed forces for the fiscal year beginning July 1, 1938—a record total for peacetime. It included a 20 percent increase in the strength of the fleet, authorization and funds for a large naval construction program, the largest peacetime appropriation for Army ordnance; new antiaircraft guns, semiautomatic rifles, and artillery; additional military manpower and extra money for training Reserves forces. The Army also received money to achieve a previously established goal of 2,340 planes by 1939. Before the end of the year, however, that goal was overrun by bigger building plans.

While keeping one eye cocked at the world threat, the Administration used the military appropriations for economic "pump-priming." This included sizable allocations of PWA money for the construction of Army posts. The military, somewhat self-conscious about its sudden riches, went to great lengths to explain that the naval expansion bill would help the economy. The analyst of the *Army and Navy Journal* claimed that 85 percent of the money poured into Navy ship construction would go into "the pockets of wage earners." Nevertheless, the military money bills were recognized everywhere for exactly what they were: a determined United States effort to join in the world armaments race. Hanson Baldwin, writing in *Foreign Affairs,* said that the President's Naval Expansion Message "not merely signalized abandonment of the old [naval] limitations and ratios, but our determination to stay in the race and not be crowded out at the turns. It marked, therefore, the most important change in our national defense policy since the war."

The Navy was delighted with the expansion bill. Secretary of the Navy Claude Swanson said in his annual report, June 30, 1938, "I am happy to report that the efficiency, morale and spirit of the Navy have never been higher." But many persons thought the Navy should be reorganized, that is, "streamlined"—a very popular word. The Navy was a rather diffuse organization of several powerful fleet and shore units. The post of Chief of Naval Operations had not been created until 1915, and more than two decades later the Chief could do little more than collect information for the purpose of advising the Secretary of the Navy. But those who thought the power of the CNO should be increased had the President to contend with. Mr. Roosevelt had opposed a similar move when he was Assistant Secretary of the Navy under Wilson. He said at the time that increasing the CNO's power would be "valueless" and a blow to civilian authority. As President, he continued to oppose the idea.

However, civilian authority in the Navy obviously was handicapped. The most powerful administrative forces in the Navy were the bureaus. Naturally, Rear Admiral Chester W. Nimitz, chief of the Bureau of Navigation, expressed the view of his conservative colleagues when he testified: "The present organization of the Navy Department has been developed through a long process of evolution. During this evolution practically all the difficulties which have existed at one time or another have been overcome, and today the organization functions efficiently, economically, without friction. It is a historical fact that the bureau system successfully fought the Mexican War, the Civil War, the Spanish War and the World War."[16]

Paralleling the air power struggle in the Army was one in the Navy involving the role of the aircraft carrier. Admiral (then Lieutenant) George W. Anderson, who served a term as Chief of Naval Operations in the Kennedy Administration, was a landing signal officer aboard the aircraft carrier *Yorktown* during the agitation between the naval airmen and the battleship admirals who ran the Navy. The newly commissioned *Yorktown* and *Enterprise* conducted intensive night and day operations in the Atlantic. Their commanding officers were trying to prove that naval aircraft could be used as striking forces rather than merely to protect ships against attack. In fact, in 1934, carrier planes carried out a successful sham attack against Pearl Harbor, just to prove their point in a war game. One of the Navy pilots was Lieutenant (j.g.) David B. McDonald, son of a Georgia minister, who succeeded Anderson as Chief of Naval Operations in 1963.

And yet, for all the agitation about possible war, young naval officers like Anderson had plenty of time for recreation in the leisurely pace of those days. The average sea cruise never lasted more than three months. Flying tactics could be practiced on land. One could get to the golf links by 4 P.M. and play nine holes before dinner. There was fun at the officers club, weekends at the beach, flying trips to other naval bases. It was a relatively relaxed era. Like almost every young officer he knew, Lieutenant Anderson, son of an admiral, believed that war was coming. But they did not know whether Washington believed it. "We were isolated from Washington," Admiral Anderson recalled many years later.[17]

In both the Navy and Army there were isolationists, who criticized political leaders for their "reckless adventurism" right up to Pearl Harbor. In addition, Army planners appeared to be uncertain over the identity of possible enemies. For two decades after World War I, the main enterprise of the War Plans Division of the Army was the preparation of the so-called "color" plans. Only two plans called for general mobilization and these were highly improbable—Red, for a war against Britain; or Red and Orange, against a coalition of Britain and Japan. The plans were not revised until 1938.

The lethargic Army leadership gravely disappointed a young Army captain in the fall of 1938. Captain Albert Wedemeyer, fresh from two years' attendance at the German War College in Berlin as a military exchange student, eagerly reported to his superiors in Washington. He had made a few reports on his observations through the United States military attaché in Berlin. Now he was spilling over with enthusiasm to tell his story in person. He had had first-hand lessons in German military tactics and strategy. More important, he had observed the aggressive enthusiasm of the German officers after the success of the Austrian *Anschluss* and the Sudetan takeover. Young Captain Wedemeyer and his German classmates used to ski in the border areas, studying the terrain. The Germans had not sent any exchange students to the American military schools, yet Wedemeyer was never excluded from any courses. Occasionally, he and a young Italian Army officer would be asked to leave a classroom, but these were mere gestures toward security. The American Army captain thus had a unique opportunity for intimate study of the new German officer corps.

"I came back and reported to all the heads of the General Staff," he recalled years later, by then a retired general who had won fame in the war that came, "but they seemed busy with the details of their offices. They didn't seem to grasp what I was trying to bring out. They didn't seem to want to be informed about explosive developments in Europe. General Malin Craig, the Chief of Staff, asked some questions about the social life of people like Göring, the Nazi Air Marshal. My father-in-law, General Stanley D. Emblick, was then Vice Chief of Staff. He had been over to visit me in Germany and he knew what the score was, but he was not an aggressive man. He had no interest in political nuances. He was 'strictly a soldier' in the old-fashioned sense. Sometimes, in my eagerness to stress the advances made by the Germans, I was accused of being 'pro-German,' since I had a German name.

"Not until I talked to the head of the War Plans division did I find anyone interested in what I had experienced and learned in Europe. That was Brigadier General George Catlett Marshall. When I left Germany, I had prepared and submitted to the War Department a hundred-page report on my studies of German troops in training. When I entered General Marshall's office, a copy of the report was on his desk. It had many notations in the margins of the paper. He developed questions on each of these during his conversations with me. He alone among the responsible officers I met in Washington at the time seemed to grasp the fact that the Germans were building up an efficient as well as a large military force."[18]

General Marshall's arrival in Washington in 1938 marked the end of an exile, apparently abetted by General MacArthur. With MacArthur no longer Chief of Staff in Washington, Marshall was brought in to succeed Malin Craig. The earnest, unassuming General Marshall, a graduate of Virginia Military Institute rather than of West Point, was aghast at the state of the Army when he took over as head of the War Plans Division. He found his work in the old Post Office Building in a particularly hot Washington summer both "exacting and depressing."[19] How badly off the Army was could be sensed in the reports of the civilian and military leaders, reports which undoubtedly were influenced by the views of their chief planning officer. In his annual report for 1938, Secretary of War Woodring said:

There remain deficiencies in organization, equipment and personnel which must be corrected before we can be assured of maintenance of a military force adequate to our defense needs. . . . We must recognize that our initial protective force, less than half of which comprise fulltime personnel of the Regular Army scattered throughout the continental U.S. and in our outlying territories, is a very small foundation upon which to erect a *towering wartime edifice.* [Italics mine.]

Woodring was blunt, but Louis Johnson, his Assistant Secretary of War—and rival—was blunter. Johnson wrote in his accompanying report:

World events during the past twelve months have focused the attention of the nations on measures of preparation for conflicts which seem to be pending. In our country the problem of national defense has become more acute than at any time since the Great War. My office is charged by law with the preparation of plans for providing the sinews of war in the event that this country is again forced into hostilities.

If Mr. Johnson was not Secretary of War as he yearned to be, he at least did not hesitate to make the most of his statutory responsibilities as Assistant Secretary and to underscore them. In his report he called attention to his "educational orders" to munitions firms. These orders fell short of outright stockpiling, but were intended to keep the factories in fighting trim for more serious exertions. The "educational orders" constituted a pittance, but they were a significant start in the development of American war industries.

The report of the Army Chief of Staff, Malin Craig, reinforced the civilians' warnings of peril. The National Defense Act had authorized an Army of 280,000 enlisted men. Instead, the Army had fallen to 118,500 before having only recently been authorized to rise to 165,000. "Our Regular Army at this latter strength ranks only 18th among the standing armies of the world," General Craig pointed out. The remarkable part of General Craig's report was his discussion of weaponry, however. Reading it twenty-five years later it is not hard to understand why young Captain Wedemeyer had been so frustrated. General Craig held stubbornly to the military homilies of ground warfare with which he had grown up on the Western plains and which had not been dislodged by the early type aircraft and tanks of World War I. "The current operations in Spain and China," he said,

illustrate from day to day the greatly increasing power of the new defensive weapons. They have restored to the defense the superiority it seemed to lose with the advent of the new offensive arms. It is largely because of the new defensive weapons that we find current operations confirming anew the testimony of history that the infantry is the core and essential substance of the Army. It alone of all the arms approximates a military entity. It alone can win a decision. Each of the other arms is but an auxiliary—its utility measured by the aid it can bring to the infantry.

The *Army and Navy Journal*, commenting on General Craig's report, wrote on November 26, 1938: "What General Craig said of the Army, about the Infantry, applies to the Navy as well. Each of the other arms is but an auxiliary. . . . In the case of Navy, the battleship is the 'infantry' of the Fleet."

General Craig fought valiantly for his ideas, and he was not without some support from General Marshall. Together they stressed "balance" against the new tank and airplane enthusiasts. But General Craig, in his final year as Chief of Staff, was handicapped also by the bitter rivalry between the two leading War Department officials.

One day, after General Marshall was appointed Deputy Chief of Staff, apparently in preparation for the top job, Marshall and his wife went to call on General and Mrs. Craig at Fort Myer, across the Potomac from Washington. General Craig put his arm around Marshall's shoulder with great emotion and said, "Thank God, George, you have come to hold up my trembling hands." Then the two men went to a separate room to talk. Mrs. Craig turned to Mrs. Marshall and said with some passion, "I'll never forgive Washington; they have crucified my husband." At first Mrs. Marshall did not understand what her hostess meant, but she soon found out.

Woodring, Secretary of War, and Johnson, the Assistant Secretary, were completely at odds. Repeated announcements of Woodring's resignation were inspired, many believed, by Johnson. Then Woodring would deny that he had any intention of resigning. In the meantime poor General Craig did not know how to get off the fence. If he followed the Secretary's instructions, he would be in trouble with Assistant Secretary Johnson, and Mr. Johnson had the reputation of wielding great political power. If General Craig followed Johnson's lead, Woodring would call him to account. General Marshall afterward inherited the feud.[20]

The Woodring case was an interesting sidelight on the Roosevelt Administration and provides background for the state of the Army on the eve of the war. Woodring, a former Governor of Kansas, entered the New Deal Administration as Assistant Secretary of War and was appointed Secretary when Harry Dern died in 1936. But he was an unimpressive man. On November 7, 1936, Secretary of the Interior Ickes got the impression from Steve Early, the President's press secretary, that "Woodring does not stand high in the President's regard."[21] A month later, December 24, Mr. Ickes reported in his diary that the President had told him Woodring would go. He quoted the President as saying: "Harry is a nice fellow but—." The President told him, Mr. Ickes went on, that Woodring knew his appointment had been temporary.

Johnson, a West Virginia lawyer and former commander of the American Legion, told almost anyone who would listen that President Roosevelt had promised him the job. And apparently Roosevelt had offered it to Johnson in the first place. But Johnson's American Legion friends asked him not to accept immediately for political reasons. So Johnson took the Assistant Secretaryship with the expectation of subsequent promotion. In his subordinate post, he clearly outshone the Secretary. His frustration at not getting the Cabinet position turned to bitterness when in 1939, instead of succeeding Woodring, he was shunted aside for Henry L. Stimson, a

Republican who had been Secretary of State under Herbert Hoover. Johnson finally became Secretary of Defense in the Truman Administration and was ousted during the Korean War after a stormy reign at the Pentagon. But that's another story.

The troubles in the Army civilian leadership were hardly conducive to orderly planning by the uniformed leaders. For one thing, training objectives were diluted by domestic considerations. Army planners assumed that in the event of war a dictatorial government of the type suddenly fashionable abroad would have to be established because of the "inevitable" totalitarian character of any future war. Plans for the use of Army troops to "keep order" were openly reported. Some idea of what Army leaders had in mind was given in an article by Woodring in *Liberty* magazine in January, 1934. He wrote:

"People who believe that the United States Army is not ready and able to take charge of this nation in an emergency simply do not know the facts. Our Army happens to be the only branch of the Government which is already organized and available not only to defend our territory, but also to cope with the social and economic problems in an emergency. It is our secret insurance against chaos. It is our 'ace in the hole' for peace as well as war." The execution of the Army's plan for mobilization, he went on, would "accomplish in a large measure the purpose of those who have advocated a 'universal draft' of property, money, and civilian labor."

"It is my opinion," he continued, "that the Army should take over immediately some of the new activities which are now being handled by some of the new executive agencies. Whether or not it is true, as many hold, that the C.C.C. camps are the forerunners of the great civilian labor armies of the future, I believe that this activity should be expanded and put under control of the Army. . . . If the Army were so directed, it could organize the veterans of the World War, the C.C.C. men, and through them the administration of the emergency relief, into a system of *economic storm troops* [italics mine] that could support the Government's efforts to smash the depression. If the Army is not so directed, it will, as always, stand by and await orders."

Woodring was rebuked by President Roosevelt for his fascistic statement, but he was appointed to the Cabinet nevertheless. And undoubtedly even the President must have considered desperate measures in the grim, turbulent depression days. We know that some Army leaders fully expected to be called to preserve order in the country. At Fort Bragg, North Carolina, there were repeated spot drills in which troops were ordered out on short notice in training exercises to cope with imagined strike and mob situations.

On the afternoon of September 12, 1938, the President, Harry Hopkins and Howard Hunter were in the President's railroad car at Rochester, Minnesota. Mr. Roosevelt's son, James, was undergoing an operation at the famous Mayo Clinic. Seated in the railroad car, the three men listened to a short-wave set bringing a speech by Hitler at a Nazi rally in Nuremberg. Mr. Roosevelt could understand German. Listening to the *Führer's* hysterical voice spluttering over the radio, Roosevelt "was sure then that we were going to get into war." The President turned to Hopkins and suggested that he go to the West Coast and make a secret survey of the capacity of the factories there to build airplanes.[22]

On October 13, 1938, Ambassador Bullitt, home from Paris for consultation in Washington, kept the President up late with a "dire message of warning." In particular, his description of the mighty German air force and the terror which it inspired made a profound impression on the President. At his news conference the next morning, a reporter opened the question with a jocular observation, referring to the Chief Executive's new suit: "You look snappy this morning." The President replied, "I am not feeling snappy. I sat up late last night hearing the European side of things from Ambassador Bullitt." The President then went on to announce that he had decided to revise his budget plans on the basis of Mr. Bullitt's recital. Asked for specific reasons that had "led to this decision to reorganize the whole national defense picture," the President answered "offhand" that it had been in progress for about a year and it had, in a sense, been forced to a head by events, developments and information received within the past month. One of these reports, it appeared, was a confidential letter from Ambassador Hugh Wilson in Berlin, July 11, 1938.[23]

The President, aware of the need to prepare public opinion, leaked to the press through visitors that he was thinking of a major airplane production program, one that could produce ten thousand planes. In the meantime he gathered his facts, particularly the material he received from Hopkins' secret mission to California. The President also, by this time, had become imbued with the strategy of air power. He had even developed a theory of tactics that might be employed by Britain, France and Russia if Germany started a major war.[24]

On November 14, 1938, President Roosevelt called his leading military aides to an historic but then secret discussion of his plane production plans. This was the beginning of the aircraft portion of the "vast rearmament." Present at the White House meeting were, in addition to the President, Secretary of the Treasury Henry Morgenthau; the ubiquitous Harry Hopkins; Robert H. Jackson, the Solicitor General, who was soon to become Attorney General; Louis Johnson (note the absence of Secretary Woodring); Herman Oliphant, General Counsel of the Treasury; General Malin Craig, Brigadier General George Marshall; Major General Henry (Hap) Arnold, chief of the new Air Corps; Colonel James H. Burns, Mr. Johnson's executive assistant; Colonel E. M. (Pop) Watson, the President's military aide; and Captain Daniel Callahan, the naval aide.[25]

President Roosevelt did most of the talking. It was evident that he had done considerable "homework." He came out fervently for air power. He was dissatisfied with a War Department report on Army needs. "A new regiment of Field Artillery or a new barracks at an Army post in Wyoming or new machine tools in an ordnance arsenal, he said sharply, would not scare Hitler one blankety-blank bit," General Arnold recounted in his postwar book.[26]

The President pointed out that in World War I it had taken a year to get a large Army into France for action and that the country must not be caught napping again—"Such a thing must not be repeated." For it was a "terrible thing" that the Allies had to hold up the United States end of air defenses during that first year of war due to lack of planes. As President Roosevelt spoke eloquently of the great fleets of planes he desired, Mr. Johnson asked how many he had in mind. The President said he thought a good round figure to start with, by way of illustration, would be 2,500 training planes, 3,700 combat planes in the air and 3,750 in reserve. That was more than the Army and Navy together had at the time.

When the President had concluded most of his recitation, "everybody began to talk, counterproposals were put forward." But the President was not to be dissuaded. He said that he wanted a plan drawn up at once to carry out the new goals. Johnson promised to have it before the end of the week. Right after the meeting, Colonel Burns and General Arnold drove General Craig to General Arnold's office and gave the old cavalryman "a get rich quick course" in the elements necessary to make an Air Force. General Arnold recalled generously that the Chief of Staff was a "very apt pupil and from then on until his tour was completed fought for our program." Significantly, however, the Chief of Staff needed the course.

The Army Chiefs, worried by what they considered undue emphasis on air power, set themselves to carry out the military plan but with a "more balanced" approach. Sensing Presidential support for a major military build-up, they included manpower and equipment increases across the board. Their enthusiasm infected the Navy. When the President got wind of what was happening, he summoned his military leaders to the White House to inform them sharply that, contrary to the confidence they were showing, it was extremely doubtful whether they could ask Congress for more than $500 million in new armament money for the next fiscal year. Woodring piped up, "I want $200 million for guns." And Leahy wanted "$125 million for the Navy," and the President fairly shouted, "I started all this to get airplanes. I can't deter the Germans with an Army and warships." He finally said the Army and Navy could share $300 million in the planned supplemental request, but he wanted to keep $200 million for airplanes.

General Craig, under General Arnold's guidance, then submitted a program in which the $200 million was allotted chiefly to training planes. General Arnold was interested more in building an American air force and less in providing planes for the Allies. For this he got into a row with Secretary of the Treasury Morgenthau, who favored aid to the Allies. Colonel Burns told Assistant Secretary Johnson of the latest development and Mr. Johnson told the President and the President called another meeting. The President "laid down the law," demanding combat planes swiftly. And he "laid down the law to General Arnold, too."[27]

The November 14 meeting was notable in two respects. First, it was President Roosevelt's first significant military readiness measure with the prospect of United States involvement in war. The naval program that had begun in 1934 and that was vastly expanded early in 1938 still retained many "pump-priming" economic motivations. Second, the President demonstrated his willingness to accept the expert views of his military aides, but did not surrender to them on matters of basic policy. He was determined to create a powerful air force, backed by a large airplane industry, and he resented proposals for "balance" that would have watered down these aims.

With the President on their side, Air Corps leaders threw themselves into the task of developing doctrine for a new form of warfare—long-range, strategic bombing. A South American "goodwill" mission in 1937 under Major Robert Olds had already demonstrated some capabilities of the four-motored B-17 "Flying Fortresses." In the spring of 1938 Major Olds and his team of aviators flew three B-17s on a mock mission to "intercept" the Italian luxury liner *Rex* crossing the Atlantic. The B-17s swooped over the ship 615 miles out from the Atlantic Coast and dropped a message on its deck. Air Corps leaders gleefully thought they had "proved" something, but the result was a War Department order restricting all Air Corps activities to within one hundred miles from the coast.

One of the men on the Latin-American journey of B-17s was First Lieutenant Curtis Emerson LeMay. In the war to come he would gain fame as a bomber commander. In the post-World War II period of "cold war" he would fashion the Strategic Air Command as an awesome force of nuclear-armed bombers. His name in the Kennedy Administration would be symbolic of the "bomber generals," that modern counterpart of the "battleship admirals" who held fast to the great weapons of a bygone era. But in early 1938 LeMay's chief experience had been with fighter aircraft. He was assigned to Langley Field, Virginia, to help work out long-range bombing plans for thirteen spanking-new B-17 Flying Fortresses.

For men like LeMay, flying still had much of the glamour of its pioneering days. It was hard to adjust to the desk discipline of military strategy and doctrine. At Langley, he "got a sense of urgency" from Colonel Olds (later Major General Olds). The first day LeMay reported to Colonel Olds he was given enough work to do for a week. That was good, he thought. He could now pace himself on his own. Then on the second day Colonel Olds gave him an additional week-long assignment. And on the third day still more work. "I realized then," General LeMay recalled years later when he was Air Force Chief of Staff, "that someone was expecting to use those navigation and bombing doctrines, and they were in a hurry."[28]

But even in the Air Corps, soon to become a virtually autonomous Air Force, high staff officers were not "thinking big." General Arnold wrote scornfully afterward of how he polled his air staff on the number of planes the United States ought to have to meet world obligations. They came up with an estimate of fifteen hundred. Well, he insisted, suppose they were local commanders, in the Philippines, Hawaii, Panama, etc., and they were not trying to take a broad look, but were selfishly estimating their needs. This time the estimated total leaped to 7,500. Eventually, the number of factory acceptances in the period 1940-1945 reached 229,230.

On December 31, 1938, with expanded military programs in the offing, the United States armed forces consisted of 186,488 men in the Army, including 20,200 in the Air Corps, six understrength ground combat divisions and 1,895 combat planes; 119,088 men in the Navy, 353 combat ships, of which 5 were aircraft carriers, and 1,213 combat planes. Compared to the peak wartime force of 12,-345,155 men, 6,843 ships including 99 carriers and more than 150,000 planes of all types, the military establishment of 1938 was still an unimpressive cadre despite the world-wide smell of war.

Summarizing events of the previous year, Francis Brown wrote in the *New York Times*, January 1, 1939:

The bells that last night joyously rang out the old year and rang in the new marked the end of as turbulent a twelve-month as the world has known since the relative calm of the Twenties. It was a year when the twin currents of instability and uncertainty ran fast, washing out frontiers, dissolving treaties, bringing political and economic change. There was also the challenge of war, and around the world nations were beating their pruning hooks into swords.

III

---☆

The Call to Arms

I

"We should be getting the nation prepared."
—Grenville Clark, May, 1940

One man, a private citizen, played a leading role in the Selective Service Act of 1940. This law was of historical as well as practical significance. It was the first military conscription law ever adopted by the United States when not at war. It offended the nation's self-approval as an unmilitaristic oasis. When finally put before Congress, the draft law that year met powerful opposition, but by reason of an effective campaign and the pressure of events overseas was enacted by a large majority in Congress. It was one of the military mobilization measures that had profound effects long after the end of the war. And it came about largely because of a tall, square-jawed New York lawyer, Grenville Clark, who had engaged in a similar campaign for military training in World War I.

In 1915 Clark initiated the "Plattsburg Movement" to train Army officers. The early volunteers were ridiculed as "society swells."

Clark himself was born to wealth and prominence in a Fifth Avenue mansion. He was a graduate of Harvard Law School and knew Franklin Roosevelt when they were both young lawyers. Despite the ridicule, Congress set up the "Plattsburg" training camps in major cities and these produced many of the officers for the American Expeditionary Forces under General Pershing.

One war later, Clark resumed his preachments of military preparedness through military training but found little support. The World War II that broke out with blitzkrieg fury in 1939 settled into stalemate and was labeled "sitzkrieg." But symbolically, on April 7, 1940 there was an eclipse of the sun. On April 9 Hitler invaded Norway and the war was on again in earnest. A month later, on May 8, 1940, several members of the World War I Military Training Camps Association met to make plans for the organization's twenty-fifth anniversary. Clark suggested that the best way to observe the anniversary would be to start a fresh campaign in behalf of military training in the new emergency, every bit as dangerous as the one they were commemorating. "Instead of merely planning a party, we should be getting the nation prepared," Clark said.

The campaign kick-off dinner, on May 22, was attended by nearly a hundred "Plattsburgers," including, in addition to Clark, Henry L. Stimson, then out of government, an active lawyer; Robert P. Patterson, a Federal judge; William J. "Wild Bill" Donovan, also a lawyer, who would later head the Office of Strategic Services; Mr. Clark's law partner, Elihu Root, Jr., son of the great Secretary of War under McKinley; and Julius Ochs Adler, vice president and assistant publisher of the *New York Times*. Adler, an ardent Reserve officer who rose to major general, stayed with Clark to the end in the drive for a draft act.[1]

The campaign got a rousing boost with a front-page story in the *Times*. But the sponsors knew they faced trouble. Congressional leaders had been negative about a draft. According to one estimate, not one in three would vote for it. Secretary of War Harry Woodring, who had turned isolationist, actively opposed the draft and this would finally cost him his job. President Roosevelt privately supported the idea but would not come out for it publicly. He thought the country was not "ready" for such a measure. In addition, he feared that his support of military conscription might affect his pending candidacy for a third term.

On June 4 General Marshall requested a 120,000-man increase in the Regular Army, but did not mention the draft. Marshall advocated instead a so-called "Civilian Volunteer Effort," which would recruit men voluntarily through state agencies, clearly ignoring the report of the Joint Army and Navy Selective Service Committee that had stressed:

The Government must sooner or later use some form of draft, and the longer this measure is delayed, the more confusion is bred in the entire war effort, military and industrial. "The Civilian Volunteer Effort" which has just been described cannot be puffed into an alternative to Selective Service. It is only a makeshift, adopted more in the hope than in the conviction that it will meet the situation for a couple of months until Selective Service can begin producing men at the training station. "The Civilian Volunteer Effort" is a stopgap. Selective Service is the only sound measure yet devised for the United States.

Clark and Adler led a group to Washington to "lobby" for the proposal, but even those legislators who agreed with them felt the government should take the lead. President Roosevelt was reticent, however, telling draft advocates, in effect, "You try it and see how it goes. If it has any prospects I'll back it." General Marshall, the Army Chief of Staff, hesitated to break up the Army's trained units to provide cadres for a flood of recruits. He believed he might need the trained units for possible deployment to Latin America. In addition, he feared that he might jeopardize his budget requests with so controversial a proposal as Selective Service.[2] He told Clark in one interview that the draft bill might hurt his plan for voluntary recruiting.

Grenville Clark pressed on. He worked on a "great idea" to get Henry L. Stimson, who favored the draft, into the Cabinet as Secretary of War. In this cause, because his own relations with President Roosevelt had become tenuous as a result of his opposition to the Supreme Court packing plan, Clark enlisted Supreme Court Justice Felix Frankfurter. Frankfurter was no mere aloof member of the Court. His administrative suggestions in those days were powerful recommendations. By 1940, according to one writer, he had long since become the proprietor of an organization for filling Government positions of every kind from a Cabinet post to a clerkship. . . . No ward heeler ever patrolled the neighborhood saloons as energetically and with as business-like sense of detail as Frankfurter did the nation's salons. He was in fact a kind of alderman-at-large for the better element. As a consummate practitioner of the policies of principle in sponsoring Stimson, Frankfurter not only scored a brilliant political coup but performed a public service as well.[3]

Clark's move to get Stimson into the Cabinet was directed chiefly against Marshall, whose opposition to the draft he regarded as a "roadblock." Having succeeded in that, he still had to get a draft bill passed in Congress. In this he and Adler seemed to be on a treadmill, neither losing nor gaining. It was their plan to get endorsement from six men, three Republicans and three Democrats in each House, to give the bill a nonpartisan and psychologically overwhelming introduction. It became clear to them they would have trouble getting the perquisite two, one in each House, of any political persuasion.

Representative James Wadsworth, the New York Republican, they got early in the game. Wadsworth's great-great-granduncle, Colonel Jeremiah Wadsworth, had introduced the first draft act in American history in 1790. Clark and Adler now needed a Senator. Adler called raspy Senator Kenneth McKellar, of Tennessee, who had been hostile to the idea in earlier approaches. Adler, publisher of the Chattanooga *Times,* knew the Tennessee Senator and on June 19 got him to grant an appointment for ten-thirty the next morning. The draft advocates had not particularly wanted McKellar's imprint on their bill, but they were getting desperate. They feared Congress might adjourn before they could get their bill passed. Clark, meanwhile, got an appointment with another last-minute prospect, young Senator Henry Cabot Lodge, Jr., of Massachusetts, grandson of the renowned foe of the League of Nations. Lodge would have sponsored the bill but lost out narrowly.

The next morning, Clark went to Senator Lodge's office. Lodge was not there. Clark waited half an hour. Fearing to wait longer, and with still another name in mind, Clark wandered over to the office of Senator Edward R. Burke of Nebraska. Burke was a Democrat but not especially friendly to the New Deal. Although he had no appointment, Clark was allowed in to see Senator Burke. When Clark explained his mission and showed a copy of the proposed bill to Burke, the Senator exclaimed, "This is what I've been waiting for."

At this point, Senator Burke telephoned Lodge's office and left word that he would be glad to have the Massachusetts Senator join him in introducing the bill. A little later Clark called Lodge's office. This time the Senator's secretary relayed a message from him, saying that perhaps Clark ought to stick with Burke alone in view of the "change in plans." Lodge apparently was miffed and believed that Clark had deliberately bypassed him. There was no time to argue. With Burke's sponsorship assured, Clark called McKellar's office to notify his associate, Adler. McKellar had just agreed to consider sponsoring the bill, saying he was impressed by Adler's persuasiveness. But instead of thanks, he now heard Adler say, "Senator, I'm sorry I have pushed you so hard. I have this a little on my conscience."

"On the contrary," Senator McKellar said, "I'm just in the mood. I—"

"Oh, no, Senator," Adler insisted to the presumably open-mouthed McKellar. "We simply must not be precipitous."

Adler then beat an embarrassing retreat from the office, somewhat precipitously, it might be said.

The Senate had a short session scheduled that day. With a few penciled changes suggested by Senator Burke, the proposed draft law was rushed to the Senate hopper a few minutes before recess and just as the news came that Henry L. Stimson, Republican, had that morning been nominated to be Secretary of War. The next day Wadsworth introduced the identical measure in the House.[4]

Stimson moved swiftly to win backing for the conscription act of which he already was a public advocate. Not waiting for his nomination to be confirmed, Stimson counseled the President against the Army's plan for a Civilian Volunteer Effort. The plan died forthwith. He rushed to Washington to forestall a War Department report on peacetime conscription that supporters of the Burke-Wadsworth bill feared would hurt the chances of the bill's passage. The Secretary-designate called General Marshall and other leaders to his Washington residence. He "made clear his desire to compose essential differences but to have the Army support the principle of the Burke-Wadsworth bill," whereupon General Marshall, given specific policy direction, responded unhesitatingly.[5]

The Congressional debate that followed was not nearly so difficult as had been feared by the draft advocates. The surrender of Holland and Belgium, the Battle of Dunkirk and the raging Battle of Britain no doubt prompted the surprisingly easy passage in the House, 263-149. The Senate vote was 58-31, with 7 not voting. On September 16, 1940, at 3:08 P.M. in the White House, as the people of London across the Atlantic suffered under German fire bombings, President Roosevelt signed the Selective Service Act. Mark Watson, the Army historian, has pointed out:

One of the most surprising aspects of the case is that this measure, a vital impulse to the upbuilding of American defenses more than a year before Pearl Harbor, was designed and given its initial push, not by the Army or Navy or White House, but by a mere handful of farsighted and energetic civilians. Nor did the White House give active assistance to the measure until Congressional and public support of the draft indicated the bill would pass.[6]

General Marshall, who had counted on the Selective Service Act only as a wartime measure, recalled afterward being denounced by a Senator who charged that the draft was "one of the most stupid and outrageous things that 'the generals' had ever perpetrated on Congress." Clark, on the other hand, felt with apparent good reason that the draft act had been passed "in spite of the Army." Clark retired in 1944. But he did not rest on his laurels. He became active in new efforts to prevent war, co-authored the book *World Peace through World Law* with Louis B. Sohn of Harvard, and put forward respected proposals for coping with population growth problems through disarmament and a world development program.

The Clark story deserves a postscript, told by another man, now President of the United States, who played a key political role in getting the draft act extended a year after its initial passages. The bill squeaked through the House by one vote after Representative Lyndon B. Johnson of Texas displayed the kind of legislative acumen that was to become his hallmark. This is the story:

"I guess that one of the most important and dramatic events of my time in the House—I always served on the Armed Services Committee there—was when we were extending the draft in 1941. I went by Mr. [Sam] Rayburn's home that morning for breakfast, and we tried to get a nose count and it didn't look too good. It was August, before Pearl Harbor. We canvassed a good many members. And I finally suggested to the Speaker, mid-morning, that we should try to get Secretary of State Cordell Hull to write a letter urging Congress to extend the draft. Mr. Rayburn was a very deliberate man and rather cautious and he didn't know about the wisdom of asking the Secretary of State to be sending a letter, interfere with the debate in the House at the last moment. But after some reflection, he agreed to it. And the letter was delivered about ten minutes before the debate closed. Mr. Rayburn went to the well of the House, and with some doubts, I think, about the wisdom of the suggestion I had made, he read the letter from Cordell Hull. As you know, Secretary Hull was a former member of the House and was greatly respected in the Congress. And that brought great applause. And then Rayburn took the gavel and the Speaker's chair, and we were several votes behind as a roll call was needed. And a few members changed their votes. And finally we got one vote ahead and Mr. Rayburn banged the gavel and announced the vote and our Army was not sent home in August—before Pearl Harbor in December."[7]

When Henry L. Stimson joined the Roosevelt war Cabinet, he was seventy-three years old. In fact, when Stimson was first asked to join the cabinet, he mentioned his age, but Roosevelt retorted he knew that. Stimson had, with the exception of the Harding Administration, served in Federal Government in one responsibility or another from the time Theodore Roosevelt appointed him a Federal attorney in New York. Stimson's ardent advocacy of military training was not inconsistent with his own conduct. He had joined the National Guard when war with Spain broke out. He served for nine years in New York's famous Cavalry Squadron A, rising from private to first lieutenant. As a junior member in the law firm of Elihu Root, he followed with interest that war Secretary's reorganization of the military establishment. This "unconsciously" developed his background "for opportunities which many years later came my way in 1911, 1917, 1928, and 1940."[8]

Secretary of War under Taft, from 1911 to 1913, Stimson served as an officer in World War I; was Calvin Coolidge's mediator in Nicaragua in 1927; served as Governor General of the Philippines before the retirement that ended with his appointment to Franklin Roosevelt's war Cabinet. Stimson knew and trusted men in uniform, although he had more reason than most to know their faults as well as their virtues. General Marshall was an officer he had known for more than twenty years. On the basis of their meeting at the Staff College in Langres, France, during World War I, Stimson had tried, albeit unsuccessfully, to bring Marshall with him as an aide in the Philippines. After confirmation as Secretary of War, July 9, 1940, Stimson looked upon the future with considerable confidence despite the magnitude of the task he saw before him. "He was in charge of the United States Army, which for thirty years he had known and loved and trusted. And he had a good Chief of Staff. No man, he later said, could have asked for more of fortune in a time of peril."[9]

Part of the Stimson deal arranged by Clark was that Judge Robert P. Patterson would be Assistant Secretary of War. Patterson, a zealous man, would have preferred to put on again the uniform in which he had served in Europe in 1918. As Assistant Secretary of War he proved to be just as vigorous a fighter as his predecessor in the number two post. Stimson said Patterson "had a fierce hatred of all delay and any compromise; his only test of any measure was whether it would help to win, and for any group or individual who blinked at sacrifice he had only scorn. . . . Patterson was a fighter, and although he was perhaps not always perfect in his choice of a battleground, his instinct in the choice of enemies was unerring."[10] Others on Stimson's team in the War Department were Assistant Secretaries John J. McCloy, who became Military Governor in Germany after the war, and Robert Lovett, who became Secretary of Defense in the Truman Administration.

II

We must "win at any price."

—The American people

At the important November 14, 1938 meeting at the White House President Roosevelt forcefully told his military aides that he wanted a major airplane build-up. As of September 28, the President pointed out, France had less than 600 airplanes, with a productive capacity of approximately 3,600 a year. England had from 1,500 to 2,200 planes, with a productive capacity of 4,800 a year. Germany, on the other hand, had somewhere between 5,000 and 10,000 airplanes available, with a productive capacity of 12,000 a year. Italy was said to have about 2,000 first-line combat airplanes with 1,000 in reserve and a productive capacity of 2,400 a year. The Army at the time had 1,401 airplanes, of which fewer than 900 could be classed as combat-ready and many of these were obsolescent. The Navy had 800 "first-line" planes, including several hundred old airplanes that would have been declared obsolescent if there had been others to replace them. The government should have its own plants, the President explained, "in order to learn the art of making airplanes," as well as to assure reserve production facilities. He had in mind, the President said, seven plants to be constructed by the WPA, most of them to be located on War Department reservations, but only two would be operated immediately. But private industry would provide most of the airplane build-up.

In the planning sessions that followed, the President was forced to make some concessions to "balance." General Marshall, then Deputy to Chief of Staff General Malin Craig, joined with his superior to impress upon Mr. Roosevelt the futility of merely producing combat airplanes without training planes, supply points and trained pilots, although the President kept insisting that he wanted large numbers of aircraft to "impress" Germany. In any event, the rearming of the United States could begin. "At last we had a program," General Arnold observed delightedly.

General Henry H. "Hap" Arnold, a moon-faced man with aluminum-gray hair and a benign look, was a pioneer military pilot. A small scar on his chin testified to a forced landing in the ocean near Plymouth Beach in 1912 when he clung battered and bleeding to the wing of his wrecked plane. A West Point graduate, one of his first assignments in aviation duties was as supply officer of the newly formed aviation school in San Diego, California, in 1912. In the pre-World War II and wartime period he proved to be "a kind of intuitive administrative genius with a double goal; the nation's victory in war and an independent Air Force in postwar."[11] General Arnold quite properly came to be known as the "Father of the Air Force," although his dedication to this mission got him into trouble with the President. While the President was primarily interested in providing planes for Britain and France, the general jealously sought to reserve them for the United States. "Between 'helping to arm our future Allies' and giving everything away, a realistic line had to be drawn or there would never be a United States Air Force except on paper," General Arnold said. His zeal once provoked Roosevelt to threaten Arnold with exile to Guam.

As spectacular as the growth of the aircraft industry in World War II was its reluctance to grow. The foundations of the industry were laid in World War I, but postwar readjustments were severe. Only the strongest companies had enjoyed the boom years of the late twenties. Despite a swift rise in the commercial plane market, the relatively meager government procurement for the Army and Navy had remained the industry's chief support. Indeed, at one point in the thirties, the Army and Navy had used Federal Works Agency funds to buy aircraft.

In 1939 aircraft industry output was valued below $280 million, ranking forty-first among the industries of the United States. The thirteen leading companies had a net worth of about $138 million and a total working capital of about $60 million. Using only 60 to 75 percent of productive capacity, the industry had its best year in 1939, with an output of 5,856 planes. But only 940 were military types. Production of light private planes totaled 3,555 that year. And despite the prospect of increasing orders, including the military, only a few companies undertook limited expansions. These were based on foreign military orders, which accounted for $400 million of the $680 million backlog at the end of 1939. The British and French Government contracts thus played an important part in the actual and potential production of the American aircraft industry at the start of World War II.

The financial arrangements for expanding the aircraft industry proved difficult. Under a 1940 amendment to the Vinson-Tramell Act, profits on government aircraft contracts were limited to 8 percent of cost instead of 12 percent. Aircraft manufacturers refused to sign proffered contracts. In addition to complaining about the profits cut, they demanded the right to amortize new facilities against taxes over a period of five years or as long as the emergency would last, otherwise it would take them sixteen to twenty years to amortize the cost of plants that might be left surplus afterward. So adamant were the manufacturers in these demands that in August, 1940, seven weeks after Congress had appropriated $400 million for the purchase of 4,000 planes, contracts for only 343 combat aircraft had been let in the previous hundred days. "It looked to many people as if the aircraft industry were on strike against the government, placing its profits ahead of patriotism and retarding industrial expansion and production to a dangerous extent."[12] The President and military leaders, anxious to get the planes, supported the manufacturers' demands and persuaded Congress to adopt an excess-profits tax in lieu of fixed limitations on profits. But even after the new legislation was passed in October, some manufacturers, loaded down with lucrative British orders, remained uninclined to take on American contracts. In the end the aircraft manufacturers came round, but not until the government devised a variety of schemes for financing new plants for them.

The government also had to use strong pressure to set up the bases for expanded airplane production in the automobile industry. It had to overcome quite frank indisposition on the part of supplier firms, enjoying monopolies, to permit subcontracting on crucial items such as propellers, landing gear, gun turrets and oleo struts—the latter being the shock absorbers on the landing gear. By December 7, 1941, "not one of the new plants authorized after June 1940 and designed to build combat planes had yet produced a single plane; and none of them was destined to get into full production before 1943."[13] Most of the expansion of existing plants had been completed, however.

The government provided 89 percent of the $3.84 billion invested in aircraft plants between 1940 and 1945. This was almost one-sixth of the $25 billion invested in all American manufacturing facilities, including plants, tools and conversions, in the same period. The largest share of the money spent under Air Force cognizance, about 61 percent, went for machinery and equipment; only 35 percent was allotted to construction and alteration of buildings and 4 percent to land and land improvements. Machine tools were the greatest single item. At the end of 1944, the government owned about 85 percent of the facilities producing Air Force matériel despite the decision not to build government factories.

The automobile industry was no more anxious to get into the aircraft field than the aircraft industry was willing to accept competition. Even after President Roosevelt announced, in May, 1940, his goal of fifty thousand airplanes, the automobile companies stubbornly resisted converting to airplane production. When in May, 1941, the government ordered a 20 percent curtailment in automobile production, the auto firms used the interim period between the order and its effective date to stockpile materials, especially steel, to drive private auto production to new heights. Not until after Pearl Harbor did the conversion of automobile plants to arms production begin in earnest. Once the war was on, however, all doubts and hesitancies were resolved. The automobile industry then converted to armaments more swiftly than its owners previously intimated had been possible. By June, 1942, the major part of the conversion was finished.

But the auto companies were no less supported by wartime government financing than the aircraft companies. Three of the six corporations which received the greatest amount of government funds for expansion in connection with aircraft production between 1940 and 1945 were auto companies. And these three auto companies received more than $922 million, compared with the $828 million received by their aircraft neighbors in the top six. In the process, there was constant hassling between airplane and auto manufacturers. The president of one aircraft company charged in May, 1942, that the auto industry was a "bottleneck" in producing parts.[14]

One element in the development of military industry was the type of contract that was used. When the emergency developed, many procurement officials at first hesitated to put themselves under suspicion of unwise or improper practices. These officials persisted with advertised, sealed-bid procedures to insure low prices. Consequently, an official historian later pointed out: "Each time the Army announced its intention of buying new trucks, scores of manufacturers submitted bids. Nearly every time a different company was the low bidder and got the contract. As a result, the Army continued to add new makes and models to its heterogeneous collection of trucks left over from the World War."[15] However:

The sense of overriding urgency, which increased throughout the defense period and reached its peak early in 1942, dictated the immediate placement of contracts and the launching of production "at any price." The task of converting industry to war production, of obtaining the necessary expansion of plant and equipment, of devising a satisfactory system for distributing scarce materials to war suppliers, all took precedent over refinements of price. The inevitable result was the feverish placement of contracts at prices which later turned out to be far above actual costs of production. Negotiated prices were hurriedly approved on the basis of contractor estimates which included allowances for almost every conceivable contingency. But pricing in contracts placed through competitive bidding fared no better. By the end of 1941, effective competition for many classes of sellers had disappeared and prices in competitive contracts were also based on generous estimates of cost. By the spring of 1942, there was substantial evidence of widespread overpricing in war contracts.[16]

After a while Army officers, eager to "win at any price," a determination that fitted the temperament of the American people once they were at war, did not hesitate much when it came to distributing the coin out of suddenly bottomless barrels of Federal treasure. Commented then Senator Harry S. Truman, during his committee's hearing on a military management bill in 1942: "I will say this for General Somervell, he will get the stuff, but it is going to be hell on the taxpayer. He has a WPA attitude on the expenditure of money."

One of the most controversial forms of contract in military procurement was the so-called cost-plus-a-fixed-fee contract. It was not the same as the cost-plus-a-percentage-of-cost contract that had been a target of investigation and criticism in World War I. The earlier type of contract rewarded producers in direct proportion to the amount of money they spent. The CPFF contract was an attempt to make up to the contractor the costs of producing items for which there was no manufacturing experience. In effect, the costs were regarded as an "expense account." The fixed fee was the presumed reasonable profit margin.

Many military men felt the government got a better break through

CPFF contracts than through fixed prices. Lieutenant General Leslie R. Groves, who headed the Manhattan Project, reviewed the Army's construction experience in World War II with these comments:

There is no question in my mind but what these fixed price jobs were more expensive in many instances than would have been fixed fee work. . . . The principal reason for excessive bids was the fact that in such a bid there was no limit to the losses a contractor might suffer. There was however a definite limit as to the profits he might make. . . . Supposing the job cost him $20,000,000, and his profit was $1,800,000. By re-negotiation this would probably be reduced to $1,200,000, and his net profit after taxes would then be $108,000. . . . On the other hand, if his bid was not high enough he could easily be faced with a loss running as high as $3,000,000. . . . For this reason the average contractor included in his bid items for every possible contingency. These included too hot weather, too cold weather, rainy weather, dry weather, and everything else on a similar basis. It was an impossible situation and resulted in bids for as much as $34,000,000 where fair estimate where the tax situation was not controlling would have been about $25,000,000. I found it impossible however to convince the proponents of lump sum bids as to the facts of life. They insisted on closing their eyes to this phase of the problem with the rather idiotic philosophy that anyone who earned enough to pay a 91 per cent tax ought not to worry about his financial status.[17]

Nevertheless the cost-plus-fixed-fee contract engendered as much suspicion as its predecessor, the CPPC, which was outlawed on recommendation of the Army and Navy Departments. One of the problems that developed, for example, was how to compute costs of stunts intended to "boost morale" at a plant—such as importing a bevy of Hollywood beauties. And if an employer was profligate with wages, bonuses and costly facilities for workers that he would not otherwise have provided in a competitive situation, could a New Deal Administration balk at defraying the related expenses? The Truman Committee found "sufficient evidence of waste and excessive expenditures under CPFF contracts" to seek their abandonment.

But this was more easily said than done. In the four-and-one-half-year period from June, 1940 to the end of 1944, the Air Forces placed nearly $25 billion CPFF supply contracts. These accounted for more than 55 percent of all its individual contracts in excess of $10 million. Although the fees were reduced gradually without protest from the manufacturers from about 7 percent of estimated cost at the beginning of the mobilization effort to about 5 percent in 1942—a further reduction to 4 percent was achieved only after Under Secretary Patterson threatened one company with reprisals—"the great volume of awards during the defense period had converted aircraft contractors almost literally from pygmies into giants, and fees of even 5 percent on unfilled orders provided contractors with profits huge in proportion to their net worth. By early 1944, Boeing, Bell, Lockheed and Republic had multiplied their output over 100 times since 1938 and the net worth of the four companies combined amounted to about 1 percent of their unfilled orders."[18]

Industry's resistance to government demands for converting the CPFF contracts was so great that by 1945 only a handful had been altered. Characteristic was this telephone conversation in March, 1945, between General Kenneth B. Wolfe and K. T. Keller, head of the Chrysler Corporation, in which Keller threatened to quit rather than convert to a fixed price contract the operation of the $175 million Chrysler aircraft motor plant at Chicago:

KELLER: Say, K.B., what's the matter with that contract of ours over there?

WOLFE: We have a directive from Under Secretary Patterson.

KELLER: How would you like a directive from me now?

WOLFE: That's all right. We have lots of bosses.

KELLER: Now, we have the plant going. It will be up to schedule this month. Why don't you turn it over to Wright and combine it with their Lockland operation and make it all one job. I will take Coppert and Neuburgh out of there, and a few of our men and bring them back to Detroit. We've established the thing now. The job is of no interest to us.

WOLFE: I don't agree with you.

KELLER: We don't seem to be able to get along satisfactorily with you fellows. . . . We can't write contracts that go through. We're not going to go through another mess of writing another contract. We have men all over the country. The labor situation is getting tough anyway. . . . There is no interest, no desire, on our part to undertake the job of writing the contract, or to shoulder the many changes that are involved.

WOLFE: What do you suggest that I tell them?

KELLER: Tell them that we're not interested at all in continuing the operation of the Chicago plant under any other contract than what we have, and that we worked hard on that job and we'll have it up to full production this month, and if somebody can be enthused and interested in doing the job, the other way, we will be perfectly willing to step out.[19]

Not until the end of the war did the efforts to convert fixed-fee contracts begin to make any substantial progress. But the principle on which they were based, defense production regardless of cost, remained in force long after the end of the war. In times of crisis the people were willing to pay. As Stimson said, reflecting the national character, "The only important goal of the war was victory and the only proper test of wartime action was whether it would help to win."

The mobilization effort created a military-industry intimacy that had long-term impact. Industrialists like William Knudsen, head of General Motors, who was given the rank of general, were brought into the government to direct mobilization planning. Professional military men were assigned, in turn, to ride herd on the industrialists. James H. Doolittle, for example, then an Air Corps major, was assigned to Detroit in the fall of 1940 to serve as liaison officer with the Automotive Committee for Air Defense and assist in its planning. In like manner Army, Navy and Air Corps officers spread throughout the country, visiting plants, studying operations, becoming so expert themselves that they confidently rendered judgments on management effectiveness.

One Navy officer in 1940 was sent to Orange, Texas, to establish the office of the supervisor of shipbuilding in that town. "I was the sole personnel," he recalled. "My records and reference library were under my hat, and I clutched a copy of Navy regulations in my hands. My job was to build a few shipyards and some ships and to get those ships built as quickly as possible."[20] As the aircraft industry carefully tooled up, new problems presented themselves in the form of matériel shortages, particularly aluminum. With the government instituting controls over resources, the Army Air Force joined in the fight for aluminum and "became the spokesman for the aircraft manufacturers."[21]

The production achievement was mammoth. By December 7, 1941, the United States had become the foremost producer of military aircraft in the world. In 1939 production in figures showed Germany first with 8,295, followed by Britain, 7,940; Japan, 4,467; and the United States, 2,141 planes. In 1944 the United States produced 96,318 aircraft; Germany, 39,807; Japan, 28,180; Britain, 26,263. No official Russian figures are available. Stalin said after the war that his country's plane production had reached a rate of forty thousand per year in 1944. In the course of the war, the United States produced 299,293 planes. Little wonder, then, that despite their grappling during wartime tensions, the military and industrial leaders in this achievement could look back afterward and regard themselves as a successful "team."

A man who profoundly shaped military-industrial relations in war and peace was James Vincent Forrestal, Assistant Secretary of the Navy. He came to Washington from Wall Street in 1940 as a special assistant to the President on defense matters. He remained through the war and became the first Secretary of Defense in 1947. Forrestal gave up a reported $180,000-a-year income to go to prewar Washington as a "businessman trying to do a job." He was a slight, wiry man, with penetrating blue eyes and a brisk manner. A broken nose received in a college boxing match gave him a pugnacious look. Forrestal's father was an Irish Catholic politician in President Roosevelt's home county of Dutchess, New York. Known in youth by his middle name, "Vince," young Forrestal started his career as a newspaper reporter upon graduating from high school. After saving enough money for college, he entered Dartmouth but transferred to Princeton. His chairmanship of the *Daily Princetonian* led to a post-college opportunity as a bond salesman with the firm of William A. Read and Company, subsequently Dillon, Read and Company. Forrestal became president of the firm in 1937 at the age of forty-five. He had already gained some notoriety. He revealed at a Congressional hearing how he legally avoided paying taxes on $864,000 of stock market profits in 1929 by forming two personal holding companies. He was one of the "young bloods" of Wall Street.

Forrestal was a complex man, with a profound respect for intellectual attainment that prompted him sometimes to advertise his own intellectuality by carrying "egghead" books under his arm. This may have been due to his never having graduated from Princeton. He quit in his senior year, apparently because of a feud with a teacher. He never quite succeeded in erasing his identification with "Wall Street" despite many years in public service and he seemed self-conscious about this. He contributed to the financial support of the Left Wing magazine, *The Nation,* with a letter emphasizing his disagreement with most of the articles it carried. Forrestal was obsessed with the Communist conspiracy, at home as well as abroad, and tended to fear Communist influences upon some of his high-ranking colleagues. He was nevertheless a lovable "Mick," as he called himself, and his complete dedication to his responsibilities during the war and afterward contributed greatly to American military power.[22]

With Harry Hopkins' endorsement, Forrestal took a $10,000-a-year job as an administrative assistant to the President, but before long he was named Under Secretary of the Navy under Frank Knox. Knox placed the job of building the two-ocean navy directly in Forrestal's hands. Forrestal's remarkable achievement in this respect fitted in with similar achievements in Army and Air Force production. In 1944, after succeeding the late Frank Knox to the Navy Secretaryship, Forrestal founded the Navy Industrial Association with six hundred of the nation's leading industrialists. It was the forerunner of the postwar National Industrial Security Association, which Forrestal also sponsored. It reflected the feeling, as one Navy officer put it, that "Perhaps one of the most striking lessons learned in this late war is that the man who uses the weapons is dependent upon the man who makes the weapons." It also established a pattern of military-industrial liaison in peacetime that heretofore had been accepted only in war.

IV

---☆

Men at War

"We are in the war, we are all in it—every single man, woman and child is a partner in the most tremendous undertaking of our American history."
—FRANKLIN D. ROOSEVELT, December 9, 1941

The military ran the war "but they ran the war the way the American people and American statesmen wanted it run."
—S. P. HUNTINGTON, in *The Soldier and the State*

Sunday morning, 7:55 A.M., December 7, 1941, Japanese airplanes struck the United States naval base at Pearl Harbor, achieving complete surprise. Within two hours the attackers destroyed or damaged 8 battleships, 3 light cruisers, 4 miscellaneous vessels, 188 airplanes and 4 important shore installations. There were 3,435 casualties; among them, 2,403 dead. Most of the dead were caught in the sinking of a few great warships. The stunned Army and Navy anti-aircraft batteries rallied ineffectually. Thirty American fighter planes managed to take to the air, but the Japanese lost only 29 out of 400 attacking aircraft. The few American planes that sought to pursue the air raiders headed southwest on a false chase. The waiting

Japanese carriers were off to the north, where they smugly reclaimed most of their aircraft and vanished through the fog toward Japan.

The message to Washington from Pearl Harbor, "Air raid on Pearl Harbor. This is not a drill," reached the Navy Department at 1:50 P.M., six hours after the attack. "My God," Secretary Knox exclaimed incredulously. "This can't be true. This must mean the Philippines." He immediately telephoned the White House. There President Roosevelt, wearing an old sweater belonging to one of his sons, was at his desk, chatting with Harry Hopkins. They had just had a light lunch. The President had counted on a lazy day and planned to peruse his neglected stamp collection. The telephone rang and the switchboard operator apologized, saying that the Secretary of the Navy had insisted upon being put through. The President said amiably, "Put him on." The Secretary of the Navy said, "Mr. President, it looks as if the Japanese have attacked Pearl Harbor." The President gave out a startled "No!" For the next eighteen minutes he talked only to Hopkins. What they talked about was indicated later only by Hopkins' observation in his memoirs, "The Japanese had made the decision for him."

At 2:05 P.M. the President called Secretary of State Cordell Hull. Within a few hours he met with his War Council, the Secretaries of State, War and Navy, the Chief of Staff of the Army and the Chief of Naval Operations. There was a Cabinet meeting later in the evening which the President described as the most serious "since Lincoln met with his cabinet at the outbreak of the Civil War." Winston Churchill telephoned the White House and proposed to come to Washington with his military aides. The President agreed at once. The Congressional leaders were called to the White House.

By this time the tension and excitement of the day had mounted to an unbearable degree. The Oval Room was filled with agitated civilians, offering advice, demanding explanations, and equally agitated military men, wounded and resentful over the ignored warnings and ironic lapses in a crisis which had been for the most part foreseen. A visitor with a previously arranged appointment to see the President, not knowing whether to go home, waited anyway and watched the turmoil in the hall outside the Oval Room. One distinguished Senator shouted at an equally distinguished admiral, "You're not fit to command a rowboat!"[1]

Outside on Pennsylvania Avenue a crowd gathered at the iron fence of the White House lawn despite the blustery weather that had developed after days of unseasonable bright skies and warmth. The blinds of the White House were drawn over gleaming windows. The floodlamps on the Capitol dome were out, symbol of lights being extinguished everywhere. The capital city, no stranger to war, was again alive with men in uniform. Troops from Fort Myer were posted in front of the War and Navy buildings on Constitution Avenue; police were everywhere.

Across the nation, people listened anxiously to cryptic radio bulletins that brought no details, only grim allusions to a disaster at Pearl Harbor and the inevitability of war. Fear flashed through the country that enemy bombers might strike continental soil. Army interceptor planes were said to be alert at coastal airports, ready to fly missions against invading bombers. Enemy planes were reported along the California coast, headed for the cluster of shipyards and defense plants in the vicinity of San Francisco. Detachments of soldiers were ordered to the West Coast. Some cities set off air raid sirens, screaming their first signals. The Office of Civil Defense issued emergency air raid instructions, but there was some confusion over blackout regulations. The next day President Roosevelt addressed Congress, officially notifying that body of the grievous events of the day that would "live in infamy" and received a declaration of war in half an hour. On December 11 Congress quickly reciprocated the declarations of war by Germany and Italy.

For the time being political bickering over defense and foreign policies was stilled. Arthur Krock, the *New York Times'* Washington correspondent, wrote that one could hear national unity "click into place." Government agencies issued production control orders. Labor and management promised to avoid strikes. Emergency legislation passed through Congress without discussion. The Army and Navy Departments issued instructions to all subordinate commands putting war plans into effect. After twenty-three years of peace America was again at war.

For the first time in its history, however, the United States was at least partly prepared. On December 7 the United States had more than 1.3 million men in uniform and was expecting to have three million within a few months; had carried out extensive ground maneuvers; had built up a sizable air corps supported by what had become the biggest airplane industry in the world; had procured formidable although still insufficient stocks of vehicles, tanks, guns and ammunition and—more important—had surveyed and geared a substantial portion of American industry for the military effort; had undertaken a huge shipbuilding program that did much to ameliorate the heavy losses sustained at Pearl Harbor; and had completely updated strategic plans and strategic and tactical doctrines on the basis of the hostilities in Europe and Asia.

It was clear at the outset of World War II that the aerial dogfights and trench warfare of the previous Great War would not be repeated, but that this would be a war of fluidity, covering huge expanses in ground and sea; a war with widely separated points linked by radio, cable, airplanes, railroads, steamships and motor transport. As Admiral Ernest King said in the first of his official reports during the war: "The war has been variously termed a war of production and a war of machines. Whatever else it is, so far as the United States is concerned, it is a war of logistics. The ways and means to supply and support our forces in all parts of the world . . . have presented problems nothing short of colossal, and have required the most careful and intricate planning."[2] When finally caught in the war, the United States had by no means solved these problems, but it was ready for them. The editor of the *American Machinist* offered this kudos: "The Army and Navy knew what they wanted when the present emergency began. That, in the opinion of expert military men, is the outstanding difference between 1917 and today. The thousands of plants surveyed are now starting to make the products allocated to them under the plan. . . . Precious time has been saved . . . the efforts quietly exerted by the Army and Navy during the years when war seemed remote have paid dividends."

The readiness of the military, no less than of the nation as a whole, had not come easily. Only slowly had new military weapons received the priorities they deserved. The tank had almost as much trouble gaining full acceptance as the airplane. National pacifism and isolationism had inhibited planners from thinking of dynamic military strategies. As late as May, 1938, the Deputy Chief of Staff of the Army returned an Air Corps proposal for long-range bombers with this sharp reminder: "Our national policy contemplates preparations for defense, not aggression." In the Navy, air power won acceptance only after a difficult struggle with the battleship admirals. Yet when Pearl Harbor came, although the disaster inevitably resulted in some command changes, the military hierarchy remained remarkably stable and lasted without significant alteration throughout the war; the strategic plans that had been overhauled in the years preceding the war could be put into effect immediately.

In his subsequent review Professor Walt Rostow, highly critical of the advance war planning, the state of military technology and the "grossly inadequate" order of battle, was nevertheless able to concede:

Fortunately, the American professional tradition as of 1939 was adequate for the war the United States was about to fight. Its leadership was guided by certain relevant lessons from the experience of coalition in 1917-18; it indoctrinated them in the values of the society as well as in the disciplined requirements of their profession; it managed to select from them those most capable of command in war; it incorporated strategic concepts of operations and a tactical style well suited to the national temper; it developed a respect for logistics and a skill in supply which merged with the capabilities of the society, the tasks of bringing American power to bear, and the needs of celerity in combat.[3]

America was perhaps most blessed in the readiness of its President to assume his Constitutional responsibilities as "commander in chief of the Army and Navy of the United States and of the militia of the several states, when called into actual service of the United States." President Roosevelt became one of the most active wartime commanders in chief in American history. He enjoyed the role and once asked Secretary of State Hull to introduce him to a Cabinet luncheon by the title of Commander in Chief rather than as President. His education and preparation for war leadership began as a young Assistant Secretary of the Navy, proud to follow the footsteps of his cousin, Theodore Roosevelt. He was conscious of the difficulties President Wilson had encountered in World War I, often solely because of a pacifistic aversion to the military. Wilson once threatened to abolish the Army and Navy planning boards when they sought to press their views on him.

Roosevelt was conscious also of the technique of leadership as well as the broad lessons of the First World War. Something Marshal Foch had told him stuck in his mind: "If I concerned myself with details I could not win the war. I can consider only major advances or major requirements. The knowledge of movements of two or three kilometers here or there would confuse me by diverting my attention from the great objective. Only major results and major strategy concern the commander in chief."[4] Roosevelt respected the professionals. During the war he said: "You can't imagine how tired I sometimes get when I am told that something that looks simple is going to take three months—six months to do. Well, that is part of the job of a commander in chief. Sometimes I have to be disappointed, sometimes I have to go along with the estimates of the professionals."[5]

Roosevelt dealt easily with the military. He had met many of them as Assistant Secretary of the Navy. He was not awed by them. Neither was he guilty of the educated civilian's tendency to scorn the "military mind." Admiral William D. Leahy he had known and liked and depended upon in one task or another since the Wilson Administration. In July, 1939, when he pinned the Distinguished Service Medal on the admiral's tunic during the ceremony of Leahy's retirement as Chief of Naval Operations, a few months prior to sending him to Puerto Rico as Governor, Roosevelt said, "Bill, if we have a war, you're going to be right back here helping me run it." In the early days of the New Deal, Roosevelt had placed the National Recovery Administration in the hands of a West Pointer, Major General Hugh S. Johnson, who ran the NRA with a military colleague, George A. Lynch, as executive officer. He named another West Pointer, Francis C. Harrington, Administrator of the Works Progress Administration to succeed Harry Hopkins.

As the war crisis sharpened, Roosevelt tended to draw the military chiefs to himself. As early as 1939 he issued a "military order," transferring the Army and Navy Chiefs of Staff, the Aeronautical Board, the Joint Economy Board and the Army-Navy Joint Munitions Board to his own "direction and supervision." In April, 1941, at the suggestion of Harry Hopkins, Army leaders began a series of briefings of the President at the White House "designed to begin the education of the President as to the true tragic situation."[6] General Marshall conducted the briefings. The President was so impressed by Marshall in this and subsequent dealings that he was later torn between assigning him to glory as a field commander and keeping him in Washington to help direct the war. To General Eisenhower, in North Africa, the President said in 1943: "Ike, you and I know who was the chief of staff during the last years of the Civil War, but practically no one else knows, although the names of the field generals—Grant, of course, Lee, and Jackson, Sherman, Sheridan and others—every schoolboy knows them. I hate to think that fifty years from now practically no one will know who George Marshall was. That is one of the reasons why I want George to have the big command— he is entitled to establish his place in history as a great general."[7] But when the time came to assign command of the Allied forces, the President kept Marshall in Washington with the now famous remark, "I feel I could not sleep at night with you out of the country." As Louis Morton, the Army historian, observed, unlike Lincoln, Roosevelt found his general early.

While the President turned to the military, his Secretary of State faded from the scene. "I have washed my hands of it," Hull said to Stimson when it became clear that negotiations with Japan had reached a dead end, "and it is now in the hands of you and Knox— the Army and the Navy." Hull's memoirs, while confirming his separation from military planning, indicated the abdication was not entirely voluntary, however. He wrote:

Prior to Pearl Harbor I had been a member of the War Council . . . and I took part in its meetings. After Pearl Harbor I did not sit in on meetings concerned with military matters. This was because the President did not invite me to such meetings. I raised the question with him several times. . . . The President did not take me with him to the Casablanca, Cairo or Teheran conferences, nor did I take part in his military discussions with Prime Minister Churchill in Washington, some of which had widespread diplomatic repercussions. . . . I learned from other sources than the President what had occurred at the Casablanca, Cairo and Teheran conferences. . . . I was not told about the atomic bomb. Occasionally someone gave me a veiled hint but I did not press any questions.[8]

When Secretary Hull pointed out that the British Foreign Minister, Anthony Eden, invariably accompanied Prime Minister Churchill to international meetings, President Roosevelt replied that the United States system was different. The military Secretaries had more contact with the President than the Secretary of State, but they too found themselves left out of many of the critical decision-making conferences. President Roosevelt regarded the Joint Chiefs of Staff primarily as his own advisers and the Chiefs considered that as a body they were responsible only to the President. The Secretaries of War and Navy were not included in the regular distribution list of Joint Chiefs of Staff papers, although the Joint Chiefs of Staff continually dealt with matters for which the Secretaries of War and the Navy were largely responsible. When other departments of government wanted action, they adopted the procedure of writing directly to the Joint Chiefs of Staff for their information. The Chiefs responded frequently without reference to the Secretaries of War and Navy. The result was "a situation where civilian agencies of our government were conducting major business involving policy with our military services without participation of the Secretaries of War and Navy."[9]

This situation did not affect Stimson so much as it did Knox. Stimson continued to enjoy a relationship of complete mutual confidence with the President and with Generals Marshall and Arnold. Secretary of the Navy Knox, like Stimson a Republican, did not enjoy a similar close relationship. Knox complained to President Roosevelt several times that he was being cut off and twice he went to the White House to demand who was running the Navy. Each time, as a result, he was briefed, but he was not invited to attend the meetings of the Chiefs. Ernest King, the Chief of Naval Operations, purposely kept Knox ignorant. King, a tough sea dog, did not trust Knox to keep a secret. His fears first were aroused early in June, 1942, when the Secretary of the Navy almost disclosed that the United States could read Japanese codes; another time, after the christening of the battle-ship *Iowa*, Knox exuberantly said things that uniformed Navy men thought should be kept from the public. After Knox died in April, 1944, Forrestal became Secretary of the Navy and he had his troubles with Admiral King, too. The unyielding admiral was determined to run the Navy without interference, except by the Commander in Chief.

King, like Leahy, was a veteran of the Spanish-American War and had been heading for retirement at the age of sixty-four in November, 1942. But in March, undoubtedly with Leahy's support, he was named Chief of Naval Operations. Tall, slim, tough, King enjoyed his reputation as an iron disciplinarian. He let it be known that one of his favorite naval heroes was Admiral Sir John Jarvis, who, after a ship's mutiny, ordered the chief of the mutineers to be hanged by his own shipmates. At the Naval Academy, where he was fourth in his class, the yearbook observed of him: "Temper? Don't fool with nitroglycerin." Of his appointment as Chief of Naval Operations, King remarked: "In time of war, they send for the sonsofbitches." So pronounced was his battle zeal even before the war broke out that it was said afterward, "He was always one speech ahead of the President."

General Marshall, a mild man, proved to be no less prepared for his task than his Commander in Chief. For him, too, experience in World War I had provided vital lessons. In World War I, Pershing in Europe exercised virtually independent command. The War Department in Washington "was simply a mobilization and supply agency in the zone of interior, in a position of authority parallel perhaps with the American Expeditionary Forces but clearly not superior."[10] In World War II, the position of the Chief of Staff and the superiority of the War Department remained unassailable throughout. General Marshall, who inherited an organization that was similar to the one that existed in World War I, shaped it to meet the requirements of global war in a scientific-industrial age; when the existing staffs and agencies of the War Department appeared to be inadequate, Marshall created a new planning unit, the Operations Division, upon which he relied heavily throughout the war.

Much of what Marshall did could be attributed to his individual genius. However, his capacities and his technique, as well as the suddenly unveiled capacities and techniques of other American leaders in World War II, belied the persistent stereotype of unsophisticated military officers who spent most of their careers in sheltered existence away from the "mainstream of life." Certainly, such isolation was true of a majority of officers. In the same sense, a majority of government officials, academicians, lawyers and businessmen lived in their own circle and were sheltered from great events. From early American history, however, Army and Navy officers had conducted negotiations with foreign countries in Europe and North Africa, concluded treaties in the Far East, attended international conferences and carried out foreign military occupations;[11] at home, starting with the Civil War, officers became responsible for and experienced in the new demands of military logistics in the era of the industrial revolution; and in the westward expansion, Army engineers in particular associated with government and private business in the building of the nation; finally, military officers in Washington were no strangers to politics, either as it affected them personally or as it influenced their responsibilities.

Thus the experience of military command in the American armed forces did not exclude familiarity with the problems of national policy and relations with the civil authority to the extent that was implied by the widespread surprise over the way in which military professionals met their expanded responsibilities in war. The period from World War I to the outbreak of World War II saw a pronounced effort on the part of the military to prepare officers for functions that went beyond the training and directing of combat forces. Not everyone would agree that the military planners did a good job, but they seemed to be the best planners available. "The isolationism of the 1920-1940 period had produced a vacuum of political objectives," John J. McCloy observed afterward. "The State Department did not have, indeed it was not encouraged to have, any political aims in the world. More thinking along political lines was being done and being asserted in the Munitions Building—this was before the era of the Pentagon—than in the old State Building."[12] In addition to increased attempts at high-level planning among senior officers in Washington, the military postgraduate schools were devoted to preparing outstanding young officers for problems that transcended the orders of battle.

"The school system was the thing that saved us," General Alfred M. Gruenther recalled many years later. "I went to Leavenworth in 1936. I was a captain. I handled problems on the division level, even the Corps. Now, mind you, at that time, I was wondering whether I would ever get to be a colonel before I reached sixty-four and retirement. I had been a lieutenant for ten years. So the thought that I might ever get to be a general hardly entered my mind. But it was refreshing to take the over-all view of responsibility for running one or more divisions. Then in 1938 I came to the Army War College in Washington. I was still a captain. And at this higher level, we were beginning to blend strategy with politics. We had lectures and lessons on the over-all conduct of a war. By this time, things were beginning to happen in Europe. So it was more than academic. People were beginning to predict war. We were dealing with problems in the stratosphere, on a War Department level, worrying about industrial production, supply, international relations. We were being introduced to a climate of thinking and a method of doing that we could draw upon later.

"In fact, that was the crux of the matter. What we learned in the military postgraduate schools that paid off so well later on was the method of doing: staff work, how to assign responsibilities, how to arrange for training in certain duties, how to undertake new problems. And just the individual capable officer learning how to do these things was not the whole answer. The crucial factor was that a large number of people were all trained to meet such problems in the same way, all speaking the same language. Later on, of course, when we did get higher responsibilities, we would joke and say, 'Nobody told us about this at Leavenworth!' 'Nobody told us this at the War College.' Yet the thing that counted was that our problems were not entirely unfamiliar and we knew each other and we knew our own limitations, too."[13]

General Gruenther recalled helping General Mark Clark set up the headquarters for the Fifth Army in North Africa in 1943. Except for a brief maneuver in the States, most of the officers had never seen an Army headquarters. Gruenther decided to be tough in handing out allocations for the table of organization. Instead of using the formula he had been taught in school, he gave the quartermaster officer ten men instead of 275. Quickly the officer came to him and complained. Gruenther said, "Those were only theoretical tables we had in school; they didn't know about war." So the quartermaster looked his colleague in the eye and demanded, "What the hell do *we* know about war?" Gruenther raised the allocation, but he never did reach the theoretical table.

"It was only because we had had our careful schooling," General Gruenther pointed out, in telling the story, "that we had a standard for making practical changes." The point, coming from Gruenther, was significant. He proved to be one of the best organizers of the war, as deputy chief of staff under Eisenhower and chief of staff under Clark. He returned to the Army War College in 1945, only to be selected by General Eisenhower again to assist in organizing the Atlantic Pact forces in Europe. Reminiscing about his own selections for high responsibility, the "organization man," now head of the American Red Cross, modestly modified his tribute to military methodology with another anecdote.

"There was a lot of luck in the system, too," he said. "Look at my case. At West Point I stood high in everything except drawing. There were 277 in the graduating class and I was 285th in drawing, counting the dropouts. I didn't care then. But twelve years later I was assigned to a big WPA project at Fort Hoyle with thirty-five draftsmen and I was put in charge of the draftsmen. I would have known more about a ballet. The commanding general was very interested in the work of the draftsmen, however, and each day he would call me in and discuss their sketches. I would nod my head. I didn't know what the hell he was talking about, and he knew it. Well, after nine months I finally got another job. But I had to get an efficiency rating. A bad report would ruin me and I kissed off Leavenworth. Six months after that, on my new job, I got a call from the post adjutant. It seemed the general, in the rush of leaving for another assignment, had neglected to make up some efficiency reports, including mine. Would I mind if the time period were incorporated in my new assignment? Would I mind? Well, you can't prove that I might not have gotten to Leavenworth anyway, but I would not have bet much on it.

"Then I had another bit of luck. In 1938 I was a captain, at General Headquarters in Washington. A fellow came up to me and said I could answer yes or no to his next question, without commitment, but would I be interested in going to Third Army headquarters in Texas under General Krueger. Now I had served under Krueger and I had not enjoyed it one bit. He used to ride me mercilessly. So I said, no, I would prefer not to return to Krueger. Next thing I knew General Leslie McNair, head of the General Headquarters, called me in, very annoyed, 'I hear you've turned down an opportunity to go to Third Army headquarters,' he said and I answered, 'No, I didn't turn it down; the question was put to me on an informal yes or no basis without commitment,' and then I hurriedly explained that Krueger used to ride me and didn't like me. McNair said I was mistaken and that Krueger actually thought I was a hot shot and that's why he had asked for me. Then McNair said, 'Do you know Eisenhower?' And I said I had heard of him, and then McNair said, 'Well, he's a comer and you'll be working for him.' So I accepted, because obviously it helped to be in the eyes of a man who was marked as a comer."

General J. Lawton Collins, a combat hero in the Pacific and in Europe, who later became Chief of Staff of the Army and, after retirement, a successful business executive, said: "The important thing was the practice of handing out big responsibilities to young men. Shortly after I was graduated from West Point, in 1917, I found myself commanding a battalion and I was barely twenty-two. That's how we got experience. We took over responsibilities greater than we were supposed to according to our age and common practice. That's why so many officers did well. At one point I was a company commander, battalion adjutant and trial judge advocate all at the same time. I tried thirty-nine cases in thirty days. I worked eighteen hours a day. I guess I did well, because no cases came back to me for retrial. In fact, a friend of mine, a National Guardsman, nearly tempted me into going into the law and once I even wrote to Columbia Law School and got an acceptance. But I decided to stay in the service.

"The extent and excellence of the military school system cannot be exaggerated, no matter how inadequate they seem today in retrospect. And the excellence of individual officers had the same impact as individual professors at a great university. They inspired us, raised our sights. I was an instructor at Benning under General Marshall. He conducted meetings in his own home, once a month, for a dozen or fifteen men, where we discussed books, sociology, economics. We took turns delivering oral reports; then we'd have a round robin discussion. It was like any university, only we were probably much more serious and aware of our responsibilities than students at civilian schools.

"I spent two years at Leavenworth and, as a major, I taught at the Army War College. I had taught chemistry and electricity at West Point, but at the War College we dealt with war plans and theories. We studied problems of occupation and had lectures from leading members of government. We studied the causes of war. The war college course was easily the equivalent of work for a Ph.D. any-where else. It was all part of our training, to give us a reservoir of ideas and techniques that we could apply at some future time. And let me add, when I led troops in combat I relied upon those tech-niques. I went to Guadacanal and the Marines who were there be-fore us told us, 'Throw away the book, this is different,' but I followed the book and I succeeded. There and later in Europe. I fought the way I was taught and it went like clockwork. I did not extemporize during the war except in minor details. I handled artillery as the doctrine prescribed it at Fort Sill. Of course, we all gained a lot of experience and maturity. But I relied heavily on what I was taught in the Army schools."[14]

The new mechanized equipment, the scientific marvels, the huge distances, the great masses of fighting men, the unprecedented quan-tities of weapons and supporting equipment required imaginative planning but also bureaucratic routine and perseverance as to detail. It was a war of staff work, industrial production, logistics, communi-cations and personal relations among top-level executives not much different in their essentials from the problems of Big Business or Big Government, except in the order of magnitude. One observer com-mented that the commanders of World War II did not fight the war so much as they administered it. Or, as Ray Cline, author of *Washington Command Post*, put it, "Some of the greatest generals in World War II, far from striking the classic posture of the man on horseback, issued their military orders from the quiet of their desks and fought their decisive battles at conference tables." That is why in World War II, contrary to the fears of President Roosevelt, General Marshall who stayed in Washington came to be appreciated as much as the battlefield heroes.

It was recognized early and remembered by many that Brigadier General Brehon Somervell, a lanky doctor's son from Little Rock, Arkansas, handled fantastic problems of logistics, including, as General Marshall explained in his first wartime report, "the supply, equipping and movement of troops at home and overseas; food, clothing, equipment, ammunition, medical service, motor, rail and ship transportation . . . harbor improvements with depots and railroad management . . . in the Persian Gulf . . . construction of bases in Australia and through the Pacific, and bases at Karachi and Calcutta."[15] Somervell, a hard-headed engineer officer, gray in his forties, was a professional soldier with a record that would have engendered pride in any civilian. He had served on Pershing's staff in World War I. After the war, he spent six months surveying the Rhine and Danube rivers for the League of Nations. Following that, he handled surveying jobs on United States waterways; and wrote a seven-volume economic survey of Turkey. He was Works Progress Administrator for New York City in 1936. On an Army pay of $6,816 a year he purged the gnats from Flushing Meadow for the New York World's Fair of 1939 and built La Guardia Airport.

There were others. Vice Admiral Samuel Murray Robinson, after serving as head of the Bureau of Ships, took over as head of the Navy's Office of Procurement and Matériel. A raw-boned Texan, Annapolis graduate, Robinson was an engineer by profession with a genius for the management of supplies that made the great naval armadas a possibility.

Colonel, later Major General, James H. Burns, a West Pointer, turned out to be a master planner. Many years later, in his Washington apartment, Burns told this author, "We learned from experience most of what we knew about military mobilization, and once we geared the machinery into production, we overproduced. But there was little to choose between the civilians and the military as to who knew more or gave better advice." Burns had been a major in the Ordnance Corps, when he was assigned to the Office of the Assistant Secretary in 1923. He became a key figure in the early airplane build-up and then ran the Lend-Lease Administration.

Leslie Groves' responsibilities as an Army engineer were so great and challenging that when he was first offered the opportunity to supervise the Manhattan Project that produced the atom bomb he belittled the new assignment. He already was in charge of all Army construction in the United States as well as offshore bases, including the building of camps, airfields, ordnance and chemical manufacturing plants. While the new job, then estimated to involve $100 million, would be bigger than any single job under Groves' jurisdiction, he reasoned, it was much less than his over-all responsibilities. The Corps of Engineers, with almost a million men engaged, was then completing about $600 million worth of work each month.[16]

Of course, there were many more civilians than professionals in uniform during the war. And in combat as well as in headquarters management civilians countless times affirmed the truth of Clausewitz' statement: "The principles of the art of war are in themselves extremely simple and quite within the reach of sound common sense. Extensive knowledge and deep learning are by no means necessary nor are extraordinary intellectual faculties." Even when the key positions inevitably fell to the military professionals, the civilian contribution was enormous, often crucial. So intimate an Army planning unit as the Operations Division included civilians such as Dean Rusk, who became Secretary of State in the Kennedy Administration. Rusk, an associate professor of government and dean of the faculty at Mills College, saw combat duty in Burma and then went to the General Staff in Washington. At the same time, since talent finds its own level, Rusk's military superiors in the policy section, Colonel Charles H. Bonesteel III and Brigadier General George A. Lincoln, were both, like Rusk, former Rhodes Scholars.

The war brought glory to many battle heroes on land, at sea, in the air; special places in history to two giants: Dwight D. Eisenhower, an ordinary man with extraordinary vision, and Douglas MacArthur, an extraordinary man with limited vision. Eisenhower was selected for his role by a perspicacious Chief of Staff, who realized that perhaps above all else the commander in Europe had to be an organizer imbued with a philosophy of compromise and cooperation. Eisenhower, who had graduated in the top third of his class at West Point in 1915, early gained a reputation as a first-class organizer at the tank training center at Colt, Pennsylvania. He did not serve in France during World War I. But he was selected for the Command and General Staff School at Fort Leavenworth, where he finished at the top of his class. He attended the Army War College, then spent three years in the office of the Assistant Secretary of War. In this post, by his own account, he handled problems of mobilization, composition of armies, world-wide military developments, the role of air forces and navies in war, mechanization of equipment and the acute dependence of military forces on industry. He served five years as an assistant to General MacArthur in the Philippines. But the two men who strongly influenced his thinking were Marshall, who delegated authority, and Fox Conner, under whom he served in Panama, who preached that the key to future warfare would be coalition of forces and unity of command. Eisenhower distinguished himself as chief of staff to General Walter Kreuger in the Third Army maneuvers in Louisiana in 1941. Five days after Pearl Harbor General Marshall called General Eisenhower to Washington to become deputy, then chief, of the War Plans Division. For six months he worked night and day, under the perceptive eye of Marshall, on plans for expanding the Army and schemes for battling the Axis.

As a planner Eisenhower contributed to one of the most basic decisions of the war. In January, 1942, he jotted this note:

The struggle to secure the adoption by all concerned of a common concept of strategical objectives is wearing me down. Everybody is too much engaged with small things of his own. We've got to go to Europe and fight—we've got to quit wasting resources all over the world—and still worse—wasting time. If we're to keep Russia in, save the Middle East, India and Burma, we've got to begin slugging with air at West Europe; to be followed by a land attack as soon as possible.[17]

A few weeks later, after the fall of Singapore, General Eisenhower observed, "We've got to go on a harassing defensive west of Hawaii; hold India and Ceylon; build up air and land forces in England, and when we're strong enough, go after Germany's vitals." Three days later: "We've got to keep Russia in the war—and hold India! Then we can get ready to crack Germany through England."[18] These ideas, with their single-minded focus on Germany, supported in the plans of the Operations Division, became Bolero, the strategy for the cross-channel invasion of Europe, which was carried out under Eisenhower's command.

Eisenhower, as Marshall knew he would, brought to his job as supreme commander diplomatic tact and a "minimum ego" that suited coalition warfare. He had a sense of history, too. The day after the North African landings he wrote:

Inconsequential thoughts of a commander during one of the interminable waiting periods. War brings about strange, sometimes ridiculous situations. In my service I've often thought or dreamed of commands of various types that I might one day hold—war commands, peace commands, battle commands, administrative commands, etc. One I now have could never, under any conditions, have entered my mind even fleetingly. I have operational command of Gibraltar! The symbol of the solidity of the British Empire—the hallmark of safety and security at home—the jealously guarded rock that has played a tremendous part in the trade development of the English race! An American is in charge and I am he! Hundreds of feet within the bowels of the Rock itself I have my CP. I simply must have a grandchild or I'll never have the fun of telling this when I'm fishing, grey-bearded, on the banks of a quiet bayou in the deep south. Again—what soldier ever took the trouble to contemplate the possibility of holding an Allied command! And of all things, an Allied command of ground, air and naval forces? Usually we pity the soldier of history that had to work with Allies. But we don't now, and through months of war we've rather successfully integrated the forces and the commands and staffs of British and American contingents—now we have to get together with the North African French. Just how the French angle will develop only the future can tell, but I am proud of this British-U.S. command! The final result I don't know—but I do know that every element of my command—all U.S. and British services are working together beautifully and harmoniously! That's something.[19]

Eisenhower's enormous pride in Allied command reflected the qualities that helped make it successful first in North Africa, later in the Allied sweep across Europe, still later in the creation of the postwar North Atlantic Treaty Organization. His analysis of the task of a modern general indicated why so many successful military leaders found places in the bureaucracies of modern government and big business after the war.

The military methods and machinery for making and waging war have become so extraordinarily complex and intricate that high commanders must have gargantuan staffs for control and direction. . . . It was not a matter of great moment if a Wellington happened to be a crusty, unapproachable individual who found one of his chief delights in penning sarcastic quips to the War Office. He was the single head, who saw the whole battlefield and directed operations through a small administrative staff and a few aides and orderlies. As long as he had the stamina and the courage to make decisions and to stand by them, and as long as his tactical skill met the requirements of his particular time and conditions, he was a great commander. But the teams and staffs through which the modern commander absorbs information and exercises his authority must be a beautifully interlocked, smooth-working mechanism. Ideally, the whole should be practically a single mind.[20]

This "romantic conception," as Professor Walt Rostow termed it, was in fact an expression of military staff methodology in which everything "works like clockwork." It was the expression of a dutiful "team" man as distinguished from a flamboyant, heroic figure like Douglas MacArthur.

General MacArthur was, at the outbreak of the war, America's most famous soldier next to Pershing. His father, Arthur MacArthur, also had been a swashbuckling officer, known as the "boy colonel" of the West for his service in the Union Army, which he had joined at the age of seventeen. The father had even died in style. At the fiftieth annual reunion of his Civil War regiment, General Arthur MacArthur went to the rostrum, announced he would make his last speech, managed a few words, then dropped dead. His adjutant tottered over, draped the body with the flag, then also collapsed. The faithful adjutant died two weeks later.

Douglas MacArthur, born on an Army post in Arkansas, saw his first battle at the age of four, an Indian raid in which he was sheltered by his mother. Douglas MacArthur achieved a spectacular record in World War I as a brigade commander, then division commander of the Rainbow Division; collected two wounds, one gassing and thirteen decorations for gallantry, seven citations for extraordinary valor and twenty-four decorations from foreign governments. At fifty he became the youngest Army Chief of Staff. He was given to the grand gesture, exorbitant oratory and invocations of God and flag that stirred even his detractors, of whom there were many in and out of uniform.

"No one, of course, has ever been neutral on the subject of General MacArthur," wrote Colonel R. Ernest Dupuy. As secretary of the General Staff under General Leonard Wood, MacArthur was not on speaking terms with the rest of the staff. In setting up his World War II headquarters in Australia, unlike Eisenhower, who underscored Allied effort, MacArthur organized a staff of Americans despite urgings from General Marshall and hints from President Roosevelt to include Australian and Dutch officers.[21] MacArthur thought of himself as a commander rather than a member of a team. He would say to his staff, whom he sometimes jokingly referred to as "slaves," "I'll do the thinking, you do the work." He could hand out "do or die" orders such as the one to General Robert Eichelberger: "Bob, I'm putting you in command at Buna. . . . I want you to take Buna or not come back alive."[22] Understandably, he carried on a drumbeat of appeals for prosecuting the war against Japan, even at the expense of the European struggle.

In August, 1944, after the Pacific tide had turned, President Roosevelt notified MacArthur at a conference in Honolulu of the plan to by-pass the Philippines in the final campaign against Japan. MacArthur, an acknowledged warrior, resorted to his equally well-known forensic skills. In "an amazing forty-five-minute oration, speaking from memory alone," he appraised the entire military situation the way he saw it and got Admiral Leahy, Roosevelt's chief of staff, to agree with him. In a second, briefer meeting, he reminded the President of the United States' solemn covenant to the Philippine people and the American prisoners there, climaxing his appeal with a drill field salute, about-face and march to the door. But the President called him back and told him he had been convinced. MacArthur redeemed his promise to "return" to the Philippines, outfought and outmaneuvered the Japanese—even managed a semblance of cooperative effort with Admiral Chester Nimitz' Pacific fleet—and firmly established his reputation as one of the great military captains of his era.[23]

But MacArthur was a unique American soldier in another way. He was openly "political" and identified himself with the Republican party. He was mentioned as a possible Presidential candidate as early as 1929. In 1943 he calmly allowed his name to come up and waited out a formal inquiry in Washington by Senator Arthur Vandenberg as to whether a military commander in wartime was eligible for political candidacy. The War Department solemnly said yes. Throughout World War II, a brilliant, arrogant power unto himself, MacArthur had to be handled with kid gloves. Roosevelt barely managed it. When the war was over, Truman handled MacArthur for a while by letting the general run his own show as occupation commander in the Far East.

The world was still struggling with the aftermath of the great war, when on June 25, 1950, at 4 A.M., North Korean Communist forces invaded South Korea and a new war broke out. In the grim campaign that ensued MacArthur, at the head of mostly American forces under the United Nations flag, sought "victory"; but the Administration sought only an honorable end to the fighting, considering that failure to limit the war could lead only to a war on the Chinese mainland and perhaps a new global struggle—this time with the Moscow-Peking axis and featuring atomic weapons. In this war, MacArthur reinforced his reputation as a warrior with the bold and successful Inchon landing. But he denigrated his reputation by failing to understand the nature and consequences of the Communist Chinese decision to enter the struggle. MacArthur had thought the war about won and told President Truman at a conference at Wake Island that he did not believe the Chinese would enter it. When they did, his demands for lashing back, even at the threat of a great war, which Washington was seeking to avoid, became intolerable to the Administration. Public criticism of the Administration by the Far East Commander provided the last straw. "MacArthur left me no choice—I could no longer tolerate his insubordination," President Truman said.[24] General MacArthur was relieved on the unanimous recommendation of the Joint Chiefs of Staff. General Marshall, who had succeeded Louis Johnson as Secretary of Defense, agreed with Secretary of State Acheson that MacArthur should have been relieved two years earlier.

The Truman-MacArthur episode was cited afterward as an example of military challenge to civilian authority. This was true only in a narrow sense. It really was a challenge of a single military man and not of "the military." The military leadership of the United States was not vested in MacArthur, but in the Secretary of Defense, Marshall, and the Joint Chiefs of Staff, headed by General Omar Bradley. MacArthur represented a theater commander's divergence from headquarters policy. More than that, MacArthur was a voluntary instrument of political challenge to the Democratic Administration by a wing of the Republican party with which he was in correspondence. His military argument with the Joint Chiefs was answered by General Bradley, who testified before Congress: "This [MacArthur] strategy would involve us in the wrong war, at the wrong place, at the wrong time with the wrong enemy." MacArthur's behavior toward President Truman, whose job he coveted, was personal and political.

The Truman-MacArthur episode was widely interpreted as an affirmation of civil over military authority, and to the extent that it thus evoked this principle, the President enjoyed overwhelming and not surprising support from the American people. In its own way the Republican Convention of 1952 afforded a more specific endorsement of the principle when General Douglas MacArthur, the warrior who looked the part, was rejected while Dwight D. Eisenhower, the military "chairman of the board" who looked and sounded like a Rotarian, was nominated. The final perspective on the Truman-MacArthur dispute was provided after General Eisenhower won the Presidency and quickly signed the truce in Korea which MacArthur and his Republican associates had condemned in advance.

In World War II, President Roosevelt's respect for the military professionals was underscored in practice. Once the war was under way, he accepted the advice of his Chiefs on all but two or three occasions. Captain T. B. Kittredge of the historical section of the Joint Chiefs pointed out:

It may be true that the President formally overruled them on very few occasions but this was only because informal discussions of the President with Leahy, Marshall, King and Arnold, usually led them to know in advance the President's views. They, no doubt, frequently recognized the advantage of accepting the President's suggestions with their own interpretations, rather than of risking an overruling by presenting formally proposals they knew could not be accepted.[25]

The military, as Professor Huntington observed, ran the war, "but they ran the war the way the American people and American statesmen wanted it run."

President Truman, whose ambitions to be a West Pointer had been frustrated by poor eyesight, was even readier than his predecessor to rely upon the military. Admiral Leahy continued in the White House as the President's personal chief of staff. General Marshall served at various times as Secretary of State and Secretary of Defense. The Central Intelligence Agency was directed and largely staffed by military men. Major General John H. Hilldring, who had handled personnel and civil affairs for the Army, became Assistant Secretary of State for the Occupied Areas. The occupied areas stayed in military hands long after the Allies turned their similar responsibilities over to civilians. The foreign service was infiltrated with General Water Bedell Smith as Ambassador to Moscow and Admiral Alan Kirk as Ambassador to Belgium. Kirk later served as envoy to the Soviet Union and, before his death, to Nationalist China.

This was only the beginning of a trend that Hanson Baldwin said as early as 1947 bore watching. He warned of "the militarization of our Government and of the American state of mind."[26] In 1947 also a Marine Corps brigadier general resigned because he could no longer countenance "the assumption of power by the military." The general, Merritt A. Edson, said: "I'm a military man and proud of it. But when we reach the point where the military are directing, instead of supporting, our country's policies, we are far along the road to losing what this country has always stood for."[27] Yet it seemed perfectly natural for the best of the generals and admirals, who had proved themselves capable in "administering" the war, to be called upon for the equally difficult and similar postwar problems. The military had come to learn intimately the mechanics of industrial production, scientific effort and civilian labor utilization, as well as those of diplomacy and public opinion. The distinction between civilian and military methodology had faded and " 'the military mind' . . . did not seem, when it reached the highest levels of responsibility and authority, to be markedly different from the diplomatic or legal or business mind."[28]

The military responsibilities of the war proved a training ground both for military professionals and the civilians who were drawn into it. "In my own case," General Lucius Clay explained, "I spent many years as an engineer officer in river and harbor work where my associates were largely civilian and where our activities were closely concerned with the community in which we lived. At the outbreak of World War II, I became General Somervell's deputy for procurement and production for the Army. In this capacity, I was fortunate in being able to assemble a staff which included some very able executives from the business world. Their caliber is indicated by mentioning only a few names: S. E. Skinner, later executive vice president of General Motors; Frank Denton, later chairman of the Mellon National Bank, and George Woods [later head of the International Bank]. The staff also included many able officers from the regular army.

"Thus there was a constant interchange of ideas representing both the military and business aspects of our problems. Later, several of the Army officers in retirement became successful in the business and industrial world. I suspect this interchange which I saw take place in my own areas of responsibility occurred in other places, too. This did develop a mutual respect between the business and military worlds. It is possible that this also developed in World War I. However, our subsequent expenditures for defense were not a significant part of our economy and the relationships resulting from World War I did not endure. Since World War II, our expenditures for defense have been large and thus the relationships established in World War II have endured. Today, defense is perhaps our major business. . . .

"I think that the real factors in the improved standing which the military leader of today enjoys in comparison with the past lie first in the increased association with the business and industrial world resulting from the major role of defense spending in our national economy; and secondly, as a by-product of our emerging concern with international affairs. We have learned that foreign and military policy must go hand in hand and we have found that our military leaders, living much of their lives abroad, do have considerable knowledge of our international problems and their proper role in our international relationships."[29]

General Clay, who was Military Governor in Germany, became head of the Continental Can Corporation and later a senior partner in Lehman Brothers. General Douglas MacArthur went to head the board at Remington Rand. Admiral Ben Moreel went to Jones and Laughlin Steel Corporation. General Somervell became president of Koppers Company. General Omar Bradley headed Bulova Watch Company. The list is endless. The easy transference of military professionals into the top echelons of industry underscored not only their individual caliber, but the similarities between modern military and industrial management.

At the same time military planning and strategy became a more integral part of government policy. As General Clay observed, national devotion to defense did not shrink after World War II, although military expenditures dropped from the wartime peak. The national security functions of government became vital. In 1947 they were institutionalized in the National Security Council with the President as chairman and the Secretaries of State and Treasury members as well as the Secretary of Defense and the Vice President. Despite recurrent outcries against military domination, leaders in all walks of American life continued to rely upon military officers in peace as they had in war. Stimson had said: ". . . the enhanced prestige of the War Department will often operate to draw its officials into activities which even in wartime are no central part of their business, and frequently the men who mutter most about 'military dominance' will be among the first to seek military support when they think they can get it; others, reluctant to accept the responsibility for unpopular decisions, will secure War Department approval for their action and then let it be understood that they have acted under military pressure."[30]

As the military budget grew, its very size evoked alarm. To which General Omar Bradley, chairman of the Joint Chiefs of Staff, responded in 1952:

The budget is not in reality a military budget; it is a civilian budget. Civilians are in charge. In the Defense Department, the budget is controlled and finally approved, not by the Joint Chiefs of Staff, but by four civilian secretaries. In the White House, it is carefully reviewed and inspected, and even changed, by an all-civilian Bureau of the Budget. After it goes to Congress, the budget undergoes careful examination by the appropriations committee of the House and Senate. This would not appear to me to be dangerous "military influence" on our economic life. In our international negotiations, some of our great decisions are influenced by the recommendations of the Joint Chiefs of Staff—our four top military leaders. But this dependence on military counsel is not of the soldier's choosing. All the military men I know believe profoundly in civilian control and look to civilian leadership in national and international affairs. But in international affairs, just as in matters of the defense budget, civilians make the final decision.[31]

V

──────────────────────────────── ☆

Science in the War

I

"I am become death, the shatterer of worlds."
—Bhagavad-Gita, sacred book of the Hindus,
quoted by Dr. Robert Oppenheimer

The making of the first atomic bomb highlighted the scientific effort of World War II. As with military conscription in 1940, the atomic bomb was the product of civilian initiative. The scientists who worked on atomic energy in this country were mostly refugees from war and Hitlerism. At first the refugee scientists thought of nuclear fission solely as a power source. But some of them feared that the Nazis would develop an atomic bomb. In 1939 a group of them, including Albert Einstein, Leo Szilard, Eugene P. Wigner, Edward Teller, V. F. Weisskopf and Enrico Fermi, conveyed their fears to Alexander Sachs, a Russian-born New York economist, who was a friend of President Roosevelt. They decided that Einstein, as the most famous person among them, would write a letter which Sachs would deliver to the President.

In the letter, Einstein said:

Some recent work by E. Fermi and L. Szilard which has been communicated to me in manuscript leads me to expect that the element of uranium may be turned into a new important source of energy in the immediate future. Certain aspects of the situation which has arisen seem to call for watchfulness and, if necessary, quick action on the part of the Administration. . . . In the course of the last four months, it has been made probable through the work of Joliot in France as well as Fermi and Szilard in America—that it may be possible to set up a nuclear chain reaction in a large mass of uranium, by which vast amounts of power and large quantities of new radium-like elements would be generated. Now it appears almost certain that this could be achieved in the immediate future. This new phenomena would also lead to the construction of bombs, and it is conceivable—though much less certain—that extremely powerful bombs of a new type may thus be constructed. A single bomb of this type, carried by boat and exploded in a port, might very well destroy the whole port together with some of the surrounding territory.

Einstein, who said he thought the bomb "might well prove to be too heavy for transportation by air," recommended immediate government liaison with the nuclear scientists and financial investment in their work in order to speed it up. He closed with a warning that the Germans were working on the bomb.[1]

With this letter Sachs induced the President to appoint an Advisory Committee on Uranium, with Dr. Lyman J. Briggs, Director of the National Bureau of Standards, as its chairman. The military services—previously only slightly aware of the scientific developments[2]—now became modestly involved. The Briggs advisory committee held two meetings, in October, 1939, and April, 1940, and received $6,000 from the Army and Navy for the purchase of supplies. As a result of the committee's work the two services approved an allotment of $102,300 for investigating the separation of the uranium isotopes—the first installments in what became a $2 billion enterprise.

At around this time, leading American scientists were becoming concerned over the lack of a comprehensive national scientific effort to cope with the pending crisis. By order of President Roosevelt in June, 1939, the National Advisory Committee for Aeronautics became a consulting and research agency for the Joint Army and Navy Aeronautical Board. Dr. Vannevar Bush, a professor of electrical engineering and vice president of the Massachusetts Institute of Technology, was appointed to the NACA. He was named its chairman shortly after leaving M.I.T. in 1939 to become president of the Carnegie Institution.

Bush was a Cape Cod Yankee whose scientific bent did not obscure his Yankee practicality. Son of a pastor in Everett, Massachusetts, he had often pumped the church organ—wondering why electricity could not be substituted for foot power. By the time he became an assistant professor of engineering, he had patented some fifty inventions or "contraptions" from vacuum tubes to calculating machines. A gaunt, angular man, with a thin face capped by a shock of straight, forward-shooting hair, he was described by a newspaper artist as looking "something like Ichabod Crane."

Bush discussed with Karl T. Compton, president of M.I.T., and other scientists the need of an over-all scientific organization for war. He called on the Chiefs of Staff. General Marshall expressed pleasure at the prospect of turning over to a special committee some problems in current Army research and indicated his willingness to assign some funds for that purpose. Members of the Corps of Engineers and the War Plans Division already had been in touch with Bush on the subject of basic research.[3] Admiral Harold R. Stark of the Navy similarly approved the plan. In General Hap Arnold, Bush found an enthusiastic, research-minded ally.

The Air Corps general's interest in science had been sharpened as early as 1934 when he had been introduced to Dr. Irving Krick, a meteorologist, at the California Institute of Technology. Weather was the essence of air operations and Arnold listened eagerly as Dr. Krick told him he could really predict weather. Dr. Krick showed the general telegrams indicating he had advised a Christmas tree harvester in Nova Scotia on the best time to cut his trees, avoiding frost, a tugboat operator who did not want to chance a storm in Lake Michigan, a gold mine operator in Alaska who wanted to know how long he could work his diggings before winter closed in. Dr. Krick later joined the Air Force and a weather service was set up. "Before that, the way all Hitler's operations moved or stood in marvelous relation to the weather indicated to me that there must be a Herr Doktor Krick in Germany, too," General Arnold observed after the war.[4]

Bush's next step was to seek President Roosevelt's support for his proposed National Defense Research Committee. Like others in Washington, Bush knew that the easiest way to President Roosevelt lay through Harry Hopkins. He had little trouble in interesting Hopkins, for whom he prepared a succinct memorandum. Hopkins then arranged an appointment for Bush to talk with the President. Bush was prepared for all kinds of questions and probable objections, but he found that Roosevelt had already studied the memorandum with Hopkins. After uttering a pleasantry or two, the President wrote, "OK—FDR." Bush was out of the President's office within a few minutes.[5] On June 15, 1940, the day following the fall of Paris, President Roosevelt signed the letter, creating the National Defense Research Committee, with Bush as chairman.

In the meantime, the studies on the uranium atom attracted some public attention. Well-known scientists began predicting that the enormous energy latent in the atom—"secret of the universe," it was called—could be tapped for power, explosive power, perhaps. At its meeting May 23, 1940, the executive committee of the Carnegie Institution voted $20,000 for studies of uranium.

On July 1, Briggs asked Bush for $140,000 to study the "fundamental constants," and contracts were subsequently let to the universities at Columbia, Harvard, Minnesota, Chicago, Iowa State College, Princeton and California. Some officials objected that these appropriations for atomic studies were directed to pure research and would divert scientists from some of the high-priority items that needed solution. To Bush also, it seemed a year later that there was "certainly no clear-cut path to defense results of great importance lying open before us at the present time." But a special committee of physicists, asked "to coldbloodedly evaluate" whether a "radical expansion of our efforts" was needed to pursue "the possible military aspects of atomic fission," came back on May 5, 1941, with an encouraging call for a "strongly intensified effort."[6] In the meantime, news came from Britain of increasing optimism there and President Roosevelt ordered complete interchange with Britain.

All this time the laboratory scientists worked intensively. The scientific leaders arranged to keep their work secret, lest the Germans who were known to be studying the same bomb prospects profit from the Americans' work as much as the Americans had profited from the Germans'. Nevertheless, scientists everywhere could surmise what was going on. In the book, *Applied Nuclear Physics,* by Ernest C. Pollard and William L. Davidson, published in 1942, the authors wrote: "The separation of the uranium isotopes in quantity lots is now being attempted in several places. If the reader wakes some morning to read in his newspaper that half the United States was blown into the sea overnight he can rest assured that someone somewhere succeeded."[7]

So determined—and increasingly confident—were the leaders of the bomb project that they decided in September, 1942, to establish an Army project to construct a bomb, although the physical principles upon which it depended were still unproved. The construction of the first atomic pile, to produce the first man-made chain reaction, did not begin at Stagg Field, Chicago, until November. There, in the squash court beneath the grandstands under the direction of Enrico Fermi, week after week, graphite bricks were machined for the pile. Said one of the scientists: "We found out how coal miners feel. After eight hours of machining graphite we looked as if we were made up for minstrel." As the pile grew to its final shape, Fermi made his calculations so precise that he was soon ready to forecast the exact moment of success. The "exact moment" could have been reached December 1, 1942, but Fermi was not on shift at the time. The next day, climaxing a tense series of manipulations of the control rod in the graphite pile, Fermi "initiated a self-sustaining nuclear reaction—and then stopped it. He . . . realized the energy of the atom and controlled that energy."[8] Arthur Compton went to the long-distance telephone to call James B. Conant of Harvard. "The Italian navigator has landed in the New World," Dr. Compton said. "How were the natives?" Conant asked. "Very friendly" was the reply.

The success at Chicago, however, was only the halfway mark on the way to perfecting an atomic bomb. The technological gap between producing a controlled chain reaction and using it as a large-scale power source or an explosive was comparable "to the gap between the discovery of fire and the manufacture of a steam loco- motive."[9] The engineering and administrative task for the production of the bomb was placed in the hands of Leslie R. Groves, a heavy-set, genial and rather homespun West Pointer. Groves turned out to be another example of how a great performance is evoked by a great task. Son of an Army chaplain, Groves had studied two years at Massachusetts Institute of Technology before getting his appoint- ment to West Point. He was fourth in his class when he was com- missioned in 1918, a twenty-two-year-old second lieutenant of engineers. Then followed a series of routine Army engineering assignments, highlighted by a three-month observation tour in post- World War I Europe. There was a pleasant stint in Hawaii and a 1929 survey of Nicaragua for a proposed interoceanic canal. He had a hand in the construction of the Pentagon before he was appointed, in September, 1942, to be head of the Manhattan District, the code name given to the bomb project.

A site on the Clinch and Tennessee rivers eighteen miles west of Knoxville, Tennessee, already had been selected for the Clinton Engineer Works. Here in three adjoining valleys were built the plutonium pilot plant, the electromagnetic separation plant and the huge gaseous diffusion plant. Steam from the powerhouse of the third plant was used in a thermal diffusion plant for the separation of U-235, in accordance with a technique worked out at the Naval Research Laboratory. The product of the fourth plant was fed into the nearby electromagnetic plant, increasing its production rate. Fear of endangering nearby towns led to the decision in January, 1943, to build the large plutonium plant on the Columbia River, near Hanford, Washington. On the 59,000-acre site in Tennessee the modern city of Oak Ridge grew up, its population of 78,000 ranking it fifth in the state. The large tract of about 670 square miles near Hanford included, in addition to the three large piles of the Hanford Engineer Works and a number of separation plants—each removed from the other by several miles—a construction camp that housed sixty thousand persons. It later became a ghost town. On the other hand, Richland, home of the operating crew, became a thriving town of seventeen thousand.

For combined reasons of health and security, the third part of the project—the construction of the bomb itself—was set up in a new special laboratory at Los Alamos, a mesa twenty miles from Sante Fe, New Mexico. Here in an isolated spot, reachable only through a winding mountain pass, an extraordinary group of scientists collected. From throughout the country—indeed, the world—they came, slipping quietly away from their normal routines, leaving no forwarding address. George B. Kistiakowsky, chief of the Explosives Division of the Office of Scientific Research and Development, arrived to be head of explosives at Los Alamos. From the Radiation Laboratory at Berkeley came I. I. Rabi and Louis Alvarez. Sir James Chadwick, discoverer of the neutron, headed a British group. Niels Bohr, who had escaped to England from Nazi-occupied Denmark in a small boat, also showed up.

Their chief was a forty-one-year-old theoretical physicist from the University of California, a soft-spoken, thin six-footer, with closely cropped hair and a chain-smoking addiction to cigarettes. His name was J. Robert Oppenheimer—"Oppie" they called him— and he was regarded as an authentic genius. Born in New York City, son of a well-to-do textile importer and an artist mother, Oppenheimer was elected to the New York Mineralogical Society at the age of eleven. He completed Harvard College *summa cum laude* in three years. He studied at Cambridge and won his physics doctorate at Göttingen, Germany, finishing his thesis on quantum mechanics three weeks after he enrolled. At twenty-five, he began teaching in California. He was immensely popular on the campus. He was not a scientific recluse, but held wide interests including philosophy, art, music and literature. His erudition delighted his students. He was articulate, speaking and writing with poetic grace. He was well versed in eight languages. But there was something rather old-fashioned about his intellectuality. No radio, no telephone, no newspapers or current magazines intruded on his contacts with students and other scientists. "I was interested in man and his experience," Dr. Oppenheimer said later, "I was deeply interested in my science, but I had no understanding of the relations of man to his society." This recollection was perhaps an overstatement, applying more to political rather than social "understanding." As director of the Los Alamos Laboratory he showed scientific and administrative abilities of a high order. He became known as the "administrator, scientist and diplomat" of the super-secret project. He had enough of a public relations bent to make a symbol of his pork-pie hat in travels between groups of scientists working on the bomb. His hat was hung in laboratories and offices as an indication that he was at hand.

The final assembly of the first bomb—"Fat Man"—began on the night of Friday, July 12, 1945, in an old ranch house on the Los Alamos mesa. A heart-shaking moment developed in the desert when Dr. R. F. Bacher began inserting the vital core. Although the parts were machine-tooled to the finest measurement, it apparently got wedged and would go no farther. But a few minutes later, with Dr. Bacher the only undismayed man in the group, the trouble was corrected and the assembly was completed. The next morning "Fat Man" was placed on top of a hundred-foot steel tower in a remote part of Alamogordo Air Base, about 120 miles southwest of Albuquerque. Bad weather delayed the test to Monday at dawn. The command post, "South 10,000," was a timber and earth shelter dug into the desert sands five miles to the south of the tower. Dr. K. T. Bainbridge of Harvard directed the detonation. Dr. Samuel K. Allison counted into the microphone. Oppenheimer became visibly tense as the minutes turned to seconds before the signal to detonate. He scarcely breathed and held onto a post to steady himself. Dr. Allison "got scared." Fearing that an electrical shock might run through the circuit when the bomb exploded, he let go of the microphone on the table in front of him and shouted into it. As a result some of the witnesses did not hear the last few seconds' countdown. Finally he shouted, "Now!"

"And there came this tremendous burst of light," General Thomas Farrell, Groves' deputy, afterward reported, "followed shortly thereafter by the deep growling roar of the explosion." Dr. Oppenheimer's face relaxed in an expression of tremendous relief. The desert was suddenly illuminated by an awesome light—"a searing light with an intensity many times that of the midday sun," General Farrell said. The fireball, changing in color from white to orange and gradually to purple, billowed up from the sands and formed the strange new mushroom cloud. On Compania Hill, twenty miles northwest of Point Zero, Dr. Ernest O. Lawrence embraced Dr. Charles A. Thomas. They jumped up and down, shouting, "It works." Also on Compania Hill were Dr. Hans Bethe, head of the theoretical division at Los Alamos, and one of his assistants, Dr. Edward Teller. Standing with Oppenheimer was Kistiakowsky, the Russian-born chemist, who had spent the night sleeplessly guarding "Fat Man" in the now vaporized tower. He put his arm on Oppenheimer's shoulder and said, "Oppie, you owe me ten dollars." They had bet on the outcome. The director pulled his wallet out of his pocket, looked in and said quietly, "I haven't any money." General Farrell drove the director back to the base camp in a jeep. He was "a subdued man," Farrell observed.

They joined in the handshaking with General Groves, Dr. Bush, director of OSRD, and Dr. James Bryant Conant, Dr. Bush's assistant. Dr. Bush recalled afterward that as he lay on a tarpaulin on the ground waiting for the test, his thoughts turned to his two sons in the Pacific and the impending invasion of Japan. "I knew that if it worked out right, the war was over." Characteristically, Oppenheimer drew from his vast erudition the words that expressed his feelings that morning, a passage from the Bhagavad-Gita, sacred book of the Hindus: "If the radiance of a thousand suns were to burst into the sky, that would be like the splendor of the mighty one." As the mushroom cloud rose over the desert sands, another line came into Dr. Oppenheimer's mind. "I am become death, the shatterer of worlds."[10]

Having manufactured the atom bomb, the government was suddenly faced with a moral issue regarding its use. A debate developed among the leaders over whether a humane warning should be given the Japanese. Everyone realized that this was not merely a bigger weapon but a cataclysmic one. Some of the scientists were completely overwrought by what they had created. Szilard led a group of scientists who opposed the use of the bomb. They petitioned General Groves and the President either not to use it at all or to do so only after its terrible effects could be demonstrated to the Japanese, thus giving the foe a chance to surrender in advance. President Truman never got the petition, although it is clear from the record that it would not have made any difference.

General Marshall also had reservations about the use of the bomb. At a meeting in Secretary Stimson's office, he suggested that the new weapon be used first against a large naval installation. If this did not have the desired effect, a number of industrial centers would be publicly named as impending targets, with the people being given advance warning to leave. Assistant Secretary of War John McCloy, who wrote a memorandum of the meeting, May 29, 1945, expressed General Marshall's view as follows: "Every effort should be made to keep our record of warning clear. We must offset by such warning methods the opprobrium which might follow from an ill-considered employment of such force."[11] General Eisenhower in his memoirs recalls that when Secretary of War Stimson informed him of the plan to drop an atomic bomb on Japan he voiced "grave misgivings" and warned Mr. Stimson that doing so was militarily unnecessary and might shock world opinion.[12] Thus even the military were awed by this most powerful weapon ever made. But there was never any real question that it would be used. On August 6 the first atomic bomb was dropped on Hiroshima, Japan, devastating the city. This and the atomic bombing of Nagasaki on August 9 precipitated the end of the war. Five days later Japan surrendered unconditionally.

In President Truman's announcement of the Hiroshima bombing, he said that the "greatest marvel" in the bomb was the "achievement of scientific brains in putting together infinitely complex pieces of knowledge held by many men in different fields of science into a workable plan." The cost was estimated at $1,950 million. Scientists, engineers, industrial managers, a work force totaling 600,000 and military agencies—notably the Army Corps of Engineers—had collaborated in an epochal deed. Before the bomb itself was completed and used, the Manhattan District was conducting fundamental research in nuclear physics, general physics, radiation chemistry, nuclear chemistry, product chemistry, general chemistry, metallurgy, engineering, general biology, and on clinical problems dealing with radial pathology and hematology in addition to the direct research and applications for the bomb itself.

Moreover, while Bush and his civilian associates acted as over-seers, the military had done the job. General Groves was at first responsible only for the engineering, construction and operation of the plants to produce bomb materials. Had the work been routine and clearly defined, his responsibility might have ended there. It had soon become evident, however, that the Corps of Engineers—the Manhattan Engineering District in particular—would have to expand its research activities and take over control of all the atomic research projects then under the management of the Office of Scientific Research and Development; thus, in the military tradition, uniting authority with responsibility.

The transfer was carried out without difficulty. Upon expiration of the contracts let by Bush's office, the various universities and other institutions signed new contracts with General Groves' unit. The changeover was done so quietly that some of the people involved did not know they were working directly for the Army. Gradually, Groves took over other unforeseen responsibilities, such as security and counterintelligence. He became responsible for military intel-ligence on atomic developments throughout the world. The fact that he could not operate without becoming deeply involved in future planning soon projected him into high-level policy, including international relations. At one point he went to London, apparently at Winston Churchill's request, to discuss atomic progress with officials there. After a while, as he pointed out in his memoirs, he became responsible for selecting the target cities, preparing the orders and instructions for the bombing operations and arranging for Army and Navy units to provide the necessary support for these operations, subject to the approval of the Chief of Staff and the Secretary of War.[13] In this manner did limited responsibilities burgeon for military officers during the war. In July, 1940, Groves had been an Army major. Within five years he had managed the greatest scientific-industrial project in history. In the words of his citation to the Distinguished Service Medal: "His was the responsi-bility for procuring matériel and personnel, marshaling the forces of government and history, erecting huge plants, blending the scientific efforts of the United States and foreign countries, and maintaining completely secret the search for a key to release atomic energy."

II

The atomic bomb was by no means the only scientific achievement of World War II, although it overshadowed them all. Major accomplishments in science during the war effort were wrought in the development of radar, jet propulsion, the proximity fuse, penicillin, aviation medicine, insecticides and rodenticides, rockets, bombsights, land and sea vehicles, DDT, psychiatry, packaging blood and blood substitutes. In all these developments, the private research and education institutes played a major role.

While science and scientists were fundamental to the war effort, a new and interesting relationship developed that was to persist long afterward. Never before had private research institutions been so heavily subsidized by the government. Until World War II science and technology evolved through the actions of individual specialists and specialized organizations. Natural groupings of scientific leaders and a small number of decision-makers in narrow industrial and educational fields exerted a relatively broad influence in scientific direction. But the individual scientists and inventors—"the solitary inventor, tinkering in his shop," as President Eisenhower put it—could break into the open. Political considerations, industrial practices, the patent and tax laws exerted some influence, of course, but "the government" was a relatively minor factor in scientific advancement.

With World War II, this changed. The direction of scientific effort was determined by vast government expenditures. In war, there was no discernible difference between the immediate aims of the scientists and those of "the government." And since it was the ideas of the scientists that were being supported, there was logic in the welcome that awaited government money in the hallowed halls of independent scientific research. Indeed, from the historic Einstein letter, such money was not only welcomed but solicited.

Expenditures for all United States scientific research by industry and government increased from $140 million in 1930 to $309 million in 1940. Outlays for the colleges and universities increased from $20 million to $31 million, while those for the research institutes declined from $5.2 million to $4.5 million during the same ten-year period. But in the World War II period the Office of Scientific Research and Development handed out more than $500 million worth of contracts. The Massachusetts Institute of Technology alone received seventy-five contracts valued at $116,941,352.05. Second was the California Institute of Technology, with forty-eight contracts valued at $83,451,746.45. The biggest industrial contractor, Western Electric, with ninety-four contracts totaling $17,091,819.00, ranked fifth behind four educational institutions.[14]

Were the scientific leaders at the time concerned with possible restrictions on their freedom of scientific inquiry through such largess? Was there any question of military "domination," or was there any concern over the subtle creation of a link of "self-interestedness" between military applications and the traditions of unfettered inquiry? According to Dr. Bush, the question of military domination never arose in that form. The whole purpose of the OSRD was to provide the military with the scientific support it needed. In addition, the authority of the office resided entirely with the director, Dr. Bush. "No contract could be placed without my approval, and the supervision of the contractual work was handled by my organization," Dr. Bush said in response to an inquiry. "In other words, military domination was a statement that meant nothing whatever under those circumstances."[15]

However, in his great book, *Modern Arms and Free Men*, Dr. Bush did cite certain dangers. He wrote: "With the Federal Government plunging into the support of research on an enormous scale, there is danger of the encouragement of mediocrity and grandiose projects, discouragement of individual genius, and hardening of administrative consciences in the universities."[16]

In the postwar debate over the formation of a National Science Foundation, two bills reflected the conflict between those who believed that government expenditures for scientific research should be primarily directed to national security, and therefore controlled or administered by the military, and those who believed the Foundation should be broad-gauged, permitting any element of society, the military among them, to benefit from its efforts. The fear of military domination was expressed by Dr. Ralph McDonald, executive secretary of the Department of Higher Education of the National Education Association, during the hearings:

"The research program of the United States must not be solely or even primarily directed to military purposes, and under no circumstances should it be under military control. We strongly favor the fullest possible application of scientific knowledge to military methods and plans. We most urgently advocate the most thoroughgoing and most intelligent application in the military field of every scintilla of up-to-the-minute scientific knowledge, with provision for applied research in every branch of science related to the national defense. Research directed primarily to military ends, however, will not produce the most valuable results, even for military purposes. For example, the scientific knowledge upon which radar and the atomic bomb were founded arose not from research directed to military purposes, but from basic research of a wholly nonmilitary nature. Without the primary discoveries from pure science, the military applications would have been impossible."

The National Science Foundation was organized in 1950. It was civilian controlled. But its total expenditures in ten years through 1963 was only $1,175 million, including a record $322.5 million for the fiscal year 1963. By contrast, the Pentagon's research and development expenditures for the fiscal year 1963 alone totaled $7 billion; the National Aeronautics and Space Administration's outlay for the same year was set at $4.2 billion. Thus while the National Science Foundation was civilian controlled, the military continued to wield greater influence in the national research programs.

The formation of the Atomic Energy Commission immediately after the end of the war also was the subject of a fierce debate over whether it should be civilian or military controlled. Ultimately, in a compromise, the Atomic Energy Act of 1946 provided for clear-cut civilian control. But more than half its budget went to military applications. When the National Aeronautics and Space Administration was formed in 1959, the issue of civilian versus military control arose once more. Although the principle was firmly rooted in American practice, many persons believed that space exploration should not be divided between two administrative institutions and that national security came first, particularly since the Russians were carrying out their highly successful space program through their military organization.

But even without the programs allocated to the civilian space agency, the military establishment created scientific research facilities of considerable size. Before World War II the military had maintained a handful of research units, some of them quite well known and quite productive. Among these were the Naval Research Laboratory in Washington, the Army Signal Corps Center at Fort Monmouth, New Jersey, and the Air Force's research and development center at Wright-Patterson Field. The cost of maintaining military research institutions was $1.4 billion a year. In 1963 the Pentagon operated fifty-three major research and development installations of five hundred men or more; and forty-eight smaller installations. The Pentagon spent $2 billion in 1963 to maintain these "in house" facilities, engaged in wonder projects ranging from radio transistors the size of a pin to ten-story ballistic missiles. About 100,000 civilians worked for the research laboratories of the Department of Defense, one-third of them professionals. More than 47,000 military men were assigned, most of them in the test and evaluation of new equipment.

The civilian scientific talent at work in military laboratories was comparable with that available in the civilian institutions from which they were recruited and to which they sent men in a "cross-fertilization" that was not common before the war. Military men, many with doctorates, did substantive work along with the civilian scientists in the Pentagon laboratories. A continuing problem, however, was the rotation system. In order to achieve rank, officers were expected to have experience commanding troops, a ship or some operational installation. Nevertheless, a few outstanding military men exemplified the scientific management skills that existed in military ranks: Admiral Hyman G. Rickover, "father" of the atomic submarine; Admiral Francis "Red" Raborn, the developer of the nuclear-powered submarine; General Bernard Schriever and Major General Charles H. Terhune, developers of the Air Force's ballistic missiles; Rear Admiral Levering Smith, hailed by Admiral Raborn as the "finest scientist in uniform"; Commander Clifford Duncan, expert on inertial guidance; Major General Chester Clark, a research chemist specializing in metals. These men were not merely organizers. They had scientific and engineering training.

Perhaps one of the most important scientific developments that grew out of the war and "cold war" period was the task force system which combined the military and civilian talents. The experience of the Manhattan Engineering District became a precedent for the Special Projects Office in the Navy that produced the Polaris. Similarly, even for large-scale experiments, such as a nuclear explosion, various agencies of government, but particularly the Defense Department and the Atomic Energy Commission, developed a system for pooling scientific and managerial talents under a task force commander. Responsibility for various phases of the operations was divided. Military and civilians from government or on loan from private laboratories worked together.

Finally, most significant development of all was the raised status of scientific endeavor in the governmental structure. Instead of high-ranking scientists assuming temporary responsibility as Bush did during the war, a full-time scientific adviser to the President was installed in the Executive offices. Now the world of science would need no *ex officio* intermediary to dispatch proposals through a friend of the President. A formal channel of communication was established. The President's scientific adviser, in addition to being a scientific "friend in court," also served the President directly as the number of purely scientific policy decisions facing the President increased.

VI

—————————————————————— ☆

America's Military Outposts

I

War's end did not bring real peace. It did create new fundamental power relationships that left the United States with occupation responsibilities and defense frontiers extending across the Atlantic to the Elbe River in Germany, with a special bastion in the conquered German capital of Berlin one hundred miles behind the Soviet occupation line, through the Mediterranean to Turkey and the Middle East; to the west, all the way across the Pacific to a line running from Japan through the Ryuku Islands to the Philippines. American power and influence were thus projected many thousands of miles away from American shores. The sun never set on the American armed forces.

While the State Department ostensibly set the policies for the occupied areas, the real controls and—equally important—the image of authority were purely military. Few Americans challenged the role of the military in what was regarded as the punitive or negative aspect of government in the wake of hostilities—except for occa-

[101]

sional charges that military men were rather "naïve" about how to handle war criminals. But many persons were disturbed by the thought of a protracted occupation in which military men held positive assignments such as developing political parties, restoring social stability and encouraging various cultural activities. At the outset of the war some liberals—"New Deal cherubs" Stimson called them —objected to a military government school they found the Army operating. Their complaint to the President prompted a sharp inquiry. But the President was soon assured of the need for the school to train Army personnel for civil affairs responsibilities.[1] A consensus developed, nevertheless, that civilian high commissions should quickly replace military commands in the occupied areas. The "cold war" frustrated that intention.

In the meantime, in the occupation areas of Germany and the Far East, military leaders exercised virtual one-man authority, much as proconsuls had represented the authority of Rome in the days of the Caesars. The American proconsul in Germany, for the critical period that included the Soviet blockade of Berlin, was Lucius Du Bignon Clay, son of a United States Senator from Georgia and great-grandnephew of Henry Clay. General Clay, a slightly built, dark-eyed man, was, like many professional military men, given to what one correspondent described as a sort of "antique probity." In his battles with Washington he frequently frustrated State Department "realists" with such ancient verities as "Truth will out," "In union there is strength," "Laws must be placed above emotion." When he agreed to the reduction of the life sentence meted out to Ilse Koch, the so-called Bitch of Buchenwald, Clay's action was denounced throughout the world. Some men in Washington wavered. Clay held his ground, insisting the woman had not been found guilty, as charged, of making lampshades out of the skins of inmates in her concentration camp. The United States, Clay said, must not descend to mob justice. At the same time in his compassion for the Jewish displaced persons in the postwar camps, he staved off German police attempts to regain responsibility for law and order in those places. One day at a press conference a German newspaperman bitterly asked when General Clay would allow German police to go in and clean up alleged black-marketing in these camps. The General replied coldly: "Never, probably, and one of the reasons I say that is the way you asked that question."

Clay had not intended to become a soldier. When his father died in 1910, strained family finances prompted him to accept an appointment to West Point offered by his father's successor in the Senate. At West Point he was something of a disciplinary problem. Although twenty-seventh in his class of 1918, he was 111th in conduct in a class of 137. He spent the night before his graduation "walking off" a penalty. He was nevertheless among the members of his class who, because of the wartime need for officers, were commissioned captains rather than second lieutenants on the day of their graduation. One day in 1922 he walked into an officers club. With a sigh that seemed gigantic for his slight frame, he dropped into an overstuffed chair and said to a young second lieutenant nearby, "I've just finished revising the engineers manual." "That was as though he had just claimed rewriting the Bible," said Maxwell D. Taylor, the lieutenant, who recalled the incident. And, of course, it turned out Clay *had* revised the engineers manual.[2]

Clay's feat in November, 1944, in clearing a serious bottleneck in the port at Cherbourg impressed Eisenhower and led to his appointment as Military Governor in Germany. Clay was surprised "because the limited discussion I had heard of that appointment had pointed to the selection of a civilian."[3] Clay, however, had already been endorsed by James F. Byrnes, for whom Clay was working in the Office of War Mobilization, as "the most civilian-minded man in the Army."[4]

It was symptomatic of the relative positions of the State and War Departments that when Clay left for his assignment in Germany, April, 1945, he conferred with many persons in Washington but no State Department officials. "Nor was it suggested that I do so," General Clay afterward recalled. "No one at that time advised me of the role of the State Department in occupation matters or of its relationship to military government, and I am inclined to believe that no one had thought it out."[5] As Military Governor, Clay demanded and received his instructions directly through the War Department. State Department messages conveyed through the political adviser, Robert Murphy, were mere "suggestions."[6] Civilians in the military government accused military officials of not really comprehending the political nature of the occupation task.[7] Some condemned the "inadequate staff work" of the Army.[8] Much of the criticism reflected personal feelings. Civilians in the military government complained they did not get the "services and perquisites which played so important a role in daily life [of occupiers] in Germany."[9]

In fact, American military forces had a large body of experience to draw from, having participated in several occupations following the Mexican, Civil, Spanish-American and Great Wars. The post-World War I occupation of Germany had been especially instructive. Moreover, Clay, by training a soldier, was no political novice. Certainly anyone brought up in the home of a Southern Senator would have had a strong political education. In addition, Clay had served in the Corps of Engineers, whose work in damming floods, building bridges and other major "pork barrel" projects was traditionally subject to political influence. Those who objected to Clay's dominance of American policy in Germany on the grounds that he was "just a soldier" ignored his adroit and subtle mind, tempered in long noncombat but highly political service throughout his military career.

That he was shaping as well as carrying out policy was evident to many of us who were in Germany at the time. He ordered an abrupt halt to the dismantling of reparations plants for the Soviet Union in an effort to make Moscow more cooperative in four-power occupation policies. He speeded local political party formations and elections against the advice of Washington. He publicly committed the United States—and the West—to remaining in Berlin after the Russians broke up the four-power government in Germany—this despite his gnawing doubts whether the Western sectors could be fed. He talked Washington out of withdrawing American dependent women and children from West Berlin, although he had cabled Washington that war was an imminent possibility.

A typical telecommunication conference between Washington and Berlin illustrated his lonely position on the Berlin limb. The teleprinter tape would come ticking into Berlin and the conference would open with the words: "Here, Washington—Bradley, Marshall, Forrestal, Royall, Draper," the names of key officials. From Berlin would tick back the lone words: "Here, Clay."[10] General Clay repeatedly denied that he acted on his own. He repeatedly insisted that his actions coincided with United States policy prepared at home. One day he blurted out, "It's a good thing Washington always backs me."

Military government was scheduled to be supplanted in July, 1948, and Clay was supposed to retire on that date. But the Russian walk-out of the Four Power Control Council and the Berlin blockade extended General Clay's proconsulship. He was finally called home May 15, 1950, as the Berlin blockade ended.

John J. McCloy succeeded General Clay. McCloy had been designated for the job even before the war ended. One day in 1945 as the Allied Armies swept triumphantly into the heartland of Europe, McCloy, then Assistant Secretary of the Army, was summoned to President Roosevelt's office at the White House. A round, bald, unassuming man, McCloy was greeted by the jovial President at his desk with an exaggerated Hitler salute and a loud "Heil, commissar!" The President laughed heartily. McCloy expected what was coming, but gave the President a quizzical look. The President then explained that he and Secretary of War Stimson had decided upon McCloy as American Civilian High Commissioner for Germany. The commissioner-designate had had more to do with civil affairs and politico-military problems than any other person in government, including Stimson. McCloy represented the War Department on the State-War-Navy Coordinating Committee and watched over the Civil Affairs Division of the Army General Staff.

Moreover, as he commented afterward, he seemed destined to have his life shaped by things German. His wife's family was German and, it turned out, related to the family of Chancellor Konrad Adenauer. As a young lawyer in 1916, McCloy headed a team that traced the "Black Tom" munitions explosion in Jersey City to German agents. He served as an artillery captain in the war against the Kaiser. He followed Stimson into government service in World War II. When the "cold war" made it prudent to postpone the transfer of military authority to a civilian commissioner, McCloy was named head of the International Bank for Reconstruction and Development. Finally, in July, 1950, he went to Germany as High

Commissioner in the American Zone. Under his guidance, governmental power was transferred to the new West German regime.

American troops stayed on, despite the Communist propaganda cries of *"Ami* [American], go home!" The troops and their dependent families brought an American way of life replete with shopping centers, big cars and informal social habits and dress. In the heart of Old Europe where palates had been attuned to wine and beer they created a sensation with their unquenchable thirst for cola drinks. One bewildered Briton said the American area of Germany seemed to be supplied by a vast underground network of pipes which could be tapped for "Coke." Hamburger stands dotted the countryside. Restaurants and night clubs serving the Americans bore such romantic and nostalgic names as the Stork Club, Casa Carioca and Manor House—the latter advertised on the American forces radio network as being "only fifteen minutes from downtown Frankfurt, just off the Wiesbaden turnpike."[11]

While the older Americans in and out of uniform brought their wives and raised their families in communities dubbed "Little America," many younger men married European girls and brought them back to the United States. There were other relationships without the benefit of marriage that left countless American-fathered children in Germany's orphanages. Negro troops found a receptiveness that was not characteristic of their own country. These things, as well as the formal directives of military government and occupation, left their stamp on Germany—and to some extent on the rest of Europe, where Americans in uniform were stationed to support the Western defense system.

In the Far East, General Douglas MacArthur conducted a one-man occupation policy. If the State Department seemed ineffectual in Germany, it was virtually shut out in the Far East. Under "the boss," as MacArthur was dubbed, political affairs officers could not even communicate directly with their superiors in Washington. They were "captives" of General MacArthur.[12] The Mikado, who had all authority and no responsibility in Japan before the war, now was virtually an adjutant of the American general. No new regime had to be created, as in Germany. But Japanese Government bureaus quickly learned to confer with United States military officials before doing anything. It became a rule for each Cabinet Minister to obtain advance sanction for any new regulations, before they were made public, lest the Minister be compelled to withdraw his regulations and lose face thereby.

As in Germany, military officials held key responsibilities despite an uneasiness in some American quarters that perhaps they were not the proper postwar tutors for Japan. A correspondent wrote from Tokyo:

There is a basic fallacy in the reasoning behind a national policy which would give an Army the job of democratizing an essentially militarist civilization.

[MacArthur] has found politics [in Japan] an intriguing game. Politics plus power such as no other American ever wielded was, and is, a heavy draught, fascinating, compelling. "The boss" now became a puppeteer with power in his fingertips to make nearly 80,000,000 little figures dance or bow or stand or fall. Where divisions and fleets once did his will, now an entire race, a notable segment of all humankind, obeyed his dicta. Or at least gave that appearance. Not in modern times, if ever, has a white man stood at the crest of history in just such a command post. If there was any self-doubt, any uneasy feeling that perhaps the Army—or The Boss either—was a little out of safe depth, no early manifestation thereof appeared publicly except in some worried dispatches by three or four American newspaper correspondents who found that their stories earned only apathy at home and a resentment at GHQ.[13]

Yet MacArthur, ruling like a benevolent dictator, was credited with many democratic achievements in Japan. At first Washington had thought of handing the occupation responsibility in the Far East to the Navy. The Navy set up draft regulations, military government schools and handbooks, and Japanese language schools to train its occupation officers. It appeared logical to let the Navy run the Far Eastern occupation while the Army conducted the one in Europe. But President Truman turned the task over to General MacArthur with a basic occupation policy document, drafted by the State and War Departments. It was a liberal paper, remarkable for its humane approach. General MacArthur more than carried out its tenets. The Japanese received a new democratic Constitution, effective land reform, a reorganized educational system, labor unions, statutes providing equality of the sexes and admonitions on civil freedom that have been compared in impact with the "brash American principles of 1789," at the very least with the New Deal of Franklin Roosevelt in the thirties.[14]

In all of this, MacArthur held himself, emperor-like, aloof. In contrast with General Clay's constant travel around Germany, meeting with German politicians, reopening synagogues, MacArthur left his headquarters in Tokyo only twice from September, 1945, to June, 1950, when the Korean War broke out. MacArthur's rule in Japan was not so much the rule of the American military as it was of Douglas MacArthur, whose aides insisted he was the greatest man who had ever lived.[15]

II

The United States' image of itself up to World War II was essentially isolationist, George Washington's credo against entangling alliances having been reinforced by the post-World War I decision not to join the League of Nations. But in the wake of World War II, the United States joined the United Nations and signed treaties and agreements that included seventy countries in a system of military alliances and mutual assistance pacts. The United States thus adopted a new peacetime policy of collective security. The Rio Treaty was signed in 1947. It was followed by the Truman Doctrine and the Marshall Plan the same year. And in 1949 the United States was a prime mover in the creation of the North Atlantic Treaty Organization. In the years that followed, the United States promoted the Anzus Treaty in 1951, Seato in 1954, Meto in 1955, Meto's successor, Cento, in 1959, and bilateral treaties with the Philippines, Japan, South Korea and the Republic of China on Taiwan.

At the same time, the United States reconstituted and increased its sprawling wartime network of military bases around the world. Former air bases in Britain were re-established in 1948, this time with nuclear-armed bombers. Airfields at home and overseas were improved to permit jet traffic. Sea bases were modernized and enlarged. The revived base-building program took in Newfoundland, Iceland,

North Africa, the Azores, Spain, Okinawa and Japan. By 1955 the Air Force system of bases extended three-quarters of the way around the earth at an annual direct and indirect cost of $3 billion a year, which proved, in addition to the aid program, a considerable economic boom to many foreign countries.

The air and sea bases around the world facilitated the United States' peace-keeping role. In 1958 United States military forces landed in Lebanon to save the shaky government from a Communist-provoked insurgency. A similar landing in Thailand in 1962 fore-warned Communist forces in Laos against attempting an invasion of that country. These were special, spectacular events. There were also regular, less publicized American military missions. A unique and romantic military patrol was carried on by a small Navy unit, the so-called Middle East Force, "showing the flag" in and around the Persian Gulf. Consisting of a small seaplane tender and two destroyers, this Naval "force," more than 7,500 miles from the United States, plied harbors from Mombassa, Kenya, to the head of the Persian Gulf and eastward to Ceylon. Ship's soccer teams played all comers. Ship's crews occasionally painted a local mission hospital. An Italian missionary school in Eritrea received thirty-three cases of old clothes. Similarly, a small naval operation, dubbed "Soulant Amity" for South Atlantic Amity, covered the West African ports to "demonstrate useful people-to-people association." Commanders and crews of the ships of Soulant Amity were instructed to make "charitable gestures" and to visit schools, make donations of schools, hospital and sports equipment, and provide other souvenirs of American goodwill. In the Congo crisis of 1961 the American ambassador in Léopoldville called upon the ships of Soulant Amity to show up at the mouth of the Congo River. They did and provided a steadying influence. This ever-ready capability illustrated how the United States had succeeded Imperial Britain as sovereign of the seven seas. In 1964 the American Navy underscored its succession as it began sending naval patrols into the Indian Ocean.

The bulwark of the defense system against Soviet power, however, is the North Atlantic Treaty Organization. Since the United States provides most of the combat forces in the Alliance the Supreme Commander in Europe, inevitably, is an American. United

States dominance manifests itself in other ways as well. The supreme military authority in NATO is the Military Committee. This is composed of the Chiefs of Staff of the member countries and meets twice annually. In order for the committee to function throughout the year the representatives of the Chiefs meet "in permanent session" in Washington. The United States, British and French Chiefs, known as the Standing Group, constitute "the superior body responsible for the highest strategic guidance in areas in which Allied NATO forces operate . . . the body to which the NATO commanders are responsible."

When Sir Bernard Montgomery retired as Deputy Commander of SHAPE in 1958, he criticized the location of the Standing Group in Washington as an example of American domination. From time to time, there have been various suggestions for reducing American supremacy. The plan to develop a so-called Multilateral Force, or MLF, in which crews of mixed nationality would operate Polaris missile-bearing surface ships, is an attempt at sharing command control over the NATO nuclear arsenal. But even when suggestions for such sharing are put forward by Americans, no acceptable formula seems possible that would ensure the United States' majority contribution, militarily and economically, to Western forces and yet reasonably take from her the controlling voice in the disposition of these forces. Britain has a small nuclear arsenal but cannot afford to maintain it. France, under de Gaulle, has insisted upon proceeding with the development of strategic nuclear weapons. But this is a prestige gesture. The only significant nuclear power in the West is the United States. The Supreme Allied Commander in Europe continues to be an American. The Standing Group continues to meet in Washington. For all intents and purposes the basic Western military strategy depends upon decisions made in America.

III

The world-wide influence of the Pentagon through military assistance is enormous. An extension of Lend-Lease in many respects, the military aid program was based on the same policy of national self-interest. In World War II the United States extended $48,578,-923,000 in aid to some forty-two countries (and received a total of $7,819,322,000 in reverse Lend-Lease from some ten countries). In the thirteen years of the military assistance program through 1963, an estimated $32 billion has been allocated to take care of the needs of sixty-nine countries. But military assistance appropriations, while easier to obtain from Congress than economic assistance for foreign countries, encounters repeated criticisms. There are many stories of waste, of providing inexperienced countries with weapons they cannot handle, of attempting to bolster dictatorial regimes of Right and Left with military support. Especially controversial was the military assistance program for Yugoslavia, which lasted from 1950 through 1957, when Marshal Tito ended it abruptly, charging that Washington was attaching political strings to it.

The Yugoslav case illustrated, however, an important aspect of the military assistance program. The basic justification for granting military aid to any country is to help that country preserve its independence. But rendering military aid provides the giver with extraordinary influence, which Marshal Tito of course realized when he accepted it. Using another country's military equipment makes the receiver dependent upon the provider for maintaining the forces, getting spare parts, adding new equipment, and training men. When I was a correspondent in Yugoslavia, the military officials of that country frequently complained that every time they needed a spare part for the American-granted jet planes they were dependent upon supplies based in France or North Africa, if not the United States. In addition, the official United States handbook on military assistance training observes:

As a side effect trainees from under-developed countries obtain a better appreciation of Western culture. Mutual understanding and communication are enhanced by English language training. Field reports attest to the strong pro-Western orientation of foreign personnel who have received training under the Military Assistance Program, especially those who have received training in the United States.

In 1953 the Tito regime, harassed by its former friends of the Cominform, joined in the formation of a Balkan Alliance with Greece and Turkey, both of whom were members of the Atlantic

Pact. Thus the military strategy of this Alliance had to be adjusted to the Atlantic Treaty strategy. For a time, as a result of the United States program of military assistance, Tito cooperated with the Atlantic Pact through the Balkan Alliance. After Tito's reconciliation with the Soviet Union in 1955, the Balkan pact withered and Tito discontinued the United States military assistance program. The Yugoslav Communist did, however, continue to seek economic assistance and he continued to purchase military equipment in the United States. He sent his pilots to the United States for training in the use of American equipment, which comprised most of his arsenal. Occasionally, anti-Communists in the United States protested the sale of the equipment and training of Yugoslav fliers. But American military authorities felt it was better to retain this link with the Balkan country than to permit a complete transfer of military ties to the Soviet Union.

American military schools propagate United States influence throughout the world. More than 110,000 foreigners took American military training in the dozen years after 1950. Some came to America for a few weeks. Others took extensive training programs over a period of many months. The average pilot stayed for eighteen months. Many foreign officers attended some of the military postgraduate schools. Many foreigners graduated from the military academies. Keeping in mind the future role of Africa, the Pentagon began in the summer of 1963 six-month leadership training programs for African soldiers selected by their governments. The Pentagon began also a long-range program of five-year courses for Africans, four at a civilian university to be followed by a year of postgraduate military training at one of the military schools. The long-range program, the Pentagon said, "is intended to develop key African military personnel to serve as the nucleus of leadership for the military forces of their respective countries."

"Last month," General Taylor recalled in the spring of 1963, "I stood on a hilltop in Iran and with the military representatives of the CENTO Alliance watched with the Shah a military demonstration presented by the Iranian Army and Air Force. The explanation to the assembled international audience was made in English by Iranian officers in uniforms similar to the United States field uniform and the briefing bore the unmistakable mark of Fort Benning or Fort Sill. One sensed the influence of the American soldier in his role as teacher of the armies of freedom."[16]

The program of military assistance occasionally provides a weapon in diplomatic relations. In July, 1962, when a military junta seized power in Peru, the United States immediately suspended military assistance to that country as a form of pressure. The case of Peru, however, was a good example of how "democratization" through training in the United States did not always work out according to plan. The United States military assistance program to Peru provided the Sherman tank that rammed through the iron gates of the Pizarro Palace when President Prado y Ugarteche was deposed and taken prisoner. The officer who carried out the capture of the palace was trained at the Ranger School at Fort Benning, Georgia. Another officer who spearheaded the Peruvian armed forces' resistance to the Presidential elections which precipitated the coup had just graduated from the United States Naval Academy. Hundreds of Peruvian officers and enlisted men who took part in the coup had attended the specialized training schools maintained by the Pentagon in the Panama Canal Zone. The Peruvian armed forces were considered by the American military officials as a rather model product of the foreign officers training program.

When the United States, aroused by the undemocratic coup against the winner of an election, severed relations with the new regime and withdrew military assistance, the Peruvian officers were dismayed. They did not feel they had done anything wrong. They were convinced of the ineptitude and duplicity of the civilian politicians and regarded their interference as a moral duty.[17] The United States finally relented as the junta restored constitutional rights it had suspended. A year later a civilian regime was installed by election. Then in the summer and fall of 1963 there were similar coups by military juntas in Ecuador, the Dominican Republic and in Honduras. In all of these turnovers, the senior officers had been trained in American military schools.

These incidents disturb many Americans. Some persons may rationalize the American role by noting that the new military men seizing power in these countries intervene only when bumbling efforts at democracy appear to be failing, and not for personal glory and enrichment in the old tradition of the "banana republics." But others insist that the military assistance program serves to nurture authoritarian rule. The Latin-American officers, like the military in the United States, tend to fear political changes in these countries and back the status quo. This policy was said to have kept Syngman Rhee in power in Korea before he was forced to flee; and to have strengthened the hand of Ngo Dinh Diem in South Vietnam until his Mandarin-like regime proved intolerable. Justifying their fear of political change, some Pentagon generals point to the aftermath of the change from Batista to Castro in Cuba. Their attitude was expressed in the observation: "He may have been an S.O.B., but at least he was our S.O.B."

IV

"Armies can not only defend their countries—they can help build them."

—President J. F. Kennedy

The United States military is expanding its world-wide influence in the "military civic action" program. The term "civic action" is, of course, open to various interpretations. Some see it as a military grip on social development. But the idea is based on something more substantial and less nefarious than that. It grew out of the American Army's pride in its own role in American history—building roads, controlling floods, improving rivers and harbors, expanding communications, carrying out health and sanitation projects, as well as fighting Indians. Why could not military organizations in small countries fighting Communism do the same? Instead of limiting aid to combat operations, the United States soldier would work with the government forces on projects useful to the local population. This would provide some worthwhile civic projects under the sponsorship of local military forces and raise the prestige of these forces with their own people. It would also strengthen the resolve of the people to fight Communist insurgents, since quite clearly the United States would not permit its own military forces to be overrun. In carrying out the civic action programs, American officers and men work with local troops in the field, show them how to drive bulldozers as well as jeeps and trucks, string wires, use modern farm tools, operate first-aid stations, provide for sanitation.

Such programs actually began in Korea not long after the shooting stopped. In August, 1953, General Maxwell D. Taylor, then commander of the Eighth Army, wrote the Pentagon, pointing out that $15 million worth of construction material sent to support his forces would not be needed. He suggested that the lumber, cement and other materials could be a boon to the Koreans. President Eisenhower enthusiastically approved the suggestion. Thus was born Armed Forces Assistance to Korea (AFAK). In the ten years that followed 4,537 projects were completed. These included 2,000 new schools, 250 churches, 350 orphanages, 350 public health facilities and 416 civic buildings, as well as many bridges, public utilities, public reclamation work and a vast rehabilitation project for fire-devastated Pusan.

In Guatemala a U.S. Army mobile training unit assisted the Guatemalan Army with irrigation, dispensary services, improving roads and purifying water. In Turkey, in addition to the huge radar scopes and missile and aircraft bases, the United States military brought materials and housing for literacy training centers. In Ethiopia American military advisers prompted an Ethiopian armed forces project that brought from Emperor Haile Selassie this accolade: "Certainly your participation and working with the community in building schools, drilling wells and clearing roads will gain you honor and respect." In Thailand the American-supported Border Patrol Police established 150 schools in remote villages in five years, with 134 Thai Army schoolteachers actually assigned to them.

In South Vietnam the American military's civic action program is as dramatic as the combat operations against the Communist Viet Cong. The Viet Cong, infiltrating the remote areas of the country, seeks to gain adherents with propaganda assaults upon the Saigon Government as a tool of the Occident, with promises of financial rewards for the creation of a variety of "peace" organizations, and with philosophical indoctrination efforts directed to teachers and Buddhist priests. But failing in these attempts, the Viet Cong resorts to violence which also has produced results. For example, villagers who want nothing more than to be left alone are inclined to collaborate when they find their headman assassinated, their villages burned to the ground and the central government too far away and, presumably, too disinterested to be of much help.

To counteract the insurgency, the United States—having decided that as a matter of strategic policy South Vietnam must not fall to the Communists—has undertaken a vast program of military assistance. But along with outright military aid, the American Army has developed a nonmilitary program to bolster outlying villages. The program, nominally led by the South Vietnamese Government but strongly influenced and supported by the American Army, is built around so-called "strategic hamlets." In addition to providing military defenses, it is intended to provide lasting forms of support that will give the villagers a vested interest in the national regime.

In July, 1962, Captain Howard C. Walters, of the United States Military Advisory Group, headed a South Vietnamese military civic action team in a visit to the Tuy Hoa district, an isolated place, virtually devoid of the most limited governmental services and frequently the site of Viet Cong incursions. The eight-man team raised the South Vietnamese colors and set up a public address system carrying radio broadcasts from the nation's capital. Over and over the loudspeakers intoned: "This is a visit from your government. Movies tonight. Free medical treatment in the marketplace. There will be a lottery with door prizes."

"At first we talk only to closed doors," Captain Walters reported.

Not a soul around. Then a few children timidly appear. We are ready for them, with several hundred pieces of sugar candy, to be passed out one by one. Soon a small army of children follows us. We scatter leaflets as we go—putting them on a doorstep, along the paths leading through the village. Slowly, people come out of their homes. We talk to them. Assure them, tell them what we are doing. Few come to the dispensary during the morning. But by late afternoon the place is crowded. We get 300 patients the first day. The next day we get hundreds more, many of them from surrounding hamlets. That night the marketplace is packed solid with people, more than the entire population of the village. We have three hours of movies supplied by the United States Information Agency. . . .

Between reels comes the commercial, a series of five minute talks on what the Vietnamese Government is trying to do in the rural areas. Halfway through the film showings I get a report that the perimeter guards have picked up an eighteen-year-old Viet Cong trying to slip into the village to find out what is going on. Captain Tuy, who is a natural psychologist, goes to work on him—questioning him, scolding him, breaking him down. He really shakes up the kid. Then—and I admit this was risky —we take the kid out and put him before the crowd and tell him to start talking. He does, slowly at first. He describes life in the Viet Cong hideout. He says he was forced to join the Viet Cong. In a few minutes he has worked himself into a lather. He weeps. He curses the communists. The effect on the crowd is electrifying. They begin to stir. They begin to murmur. Then they start getting to their feet. Soon they are shouting, "Down with the Viet Cong! Down with the Viet Cong! Down with the Viet Cong!" Over and over. The waves of the sound of their chant roar out of the marketplace and into the night. I'm astonished. And I think the Viet Cong, out there in the darkness, must be asking themselves what in the hell is going on.[18]

The next day they picked out ten poor families of the village and presented them with a household kit, an aluminum teakettle, cooking pot and meat platter. Next time, they promised to bring rice. Then they held a raffle. Certain of the distributed leaflets had a mark. The winners got kitchen utensils. Captain Tuy organized a children's class in hand-washing and teeth-brushing. He lectured on good health and asked questions. The right answer brought rewards of candy. One of the Army trucks, in turning around, ran into a rice field and crushed a few square feet of rice plants. The owner was called in and compensated on the spot. The crowd seemed amused by this, but afterward the word of it spread farther than any single thing they did in three days' work.

One of the objectives of the operation was to get a Viet Cong reaction. They got it. On the second night the Viet Cong Communists began firing at the loudspeakers. The population thus found the Communist insurgents attacking something of their own, in which they had a vested interest. Captain Walters observed laconically:

"Total cost of the venture: about fifteen American dollars."[19]

The Walters story, obviously an ideal report, does not mean that the South Vietnamese struggle is being won. It is a slow, grim struggle in that Southeast Asian country. It may not end for many years. In December, 1963, 1,000 American "advisers" were pulled out of South Vietnam. That left about 15,000, and it is questionable whether they can be withdrawn by 1965, as was once officially forecast.

In 1964 the United States Army was carrying out military civic action projects in twenty-five countries in the Far East, Middle East and Latin America under a mandate from President Kennedy: "The new generation of military leaders has shown an increasing awareness that armies can not only defend their countries—they can help build them." For the men in the Pentagon, this effort has added a new dimension to their global security responsibilities.

VII

─────────────────────────────────────── ☆

Troop (Indoctrination) Orientation

"Impress upon the mind of every man, from the first to the lowest, the importance of the cause and what it is they are contending for."

—GEORGE WASHINGTON

In the spring of 1961 a news story from Germany directed attention to the programs of indoctrination of American youth in military service. The story reported that an American Army divisional commander was spouting the ideas of the Rightist John Birch Society. This was the beginning of the "Walker Case." In one respect it developed into the personal tragedy of a combat soldier who had served his country with distinction. In a more fundamental respect, it concerned the method, scope and content of military orientation programs designed to imbue troops with a doctrinal cause as well as military proficiency.

Major General Edwin Anderson "Ted" Walker, commander of the 24th Infantry Division in Germany, was a well-known officer; a tall, lean-visaged, Texas bachelor regarded as a great "catch" in the Army social whirl. Staff officers considered him "tough but fair." He had served with commando forces in the Aleutians, Italy and Southern France during World War II. He again led combat troops in the Korean War. As a West Point graduate, class of 1931, and a major general at the age of fifty-two, he seemed to be on the final upswing that carries outstanding career officers to four stars before retirement. But after the Korean War, he revealed signs of restlessness and impatience. There seemed nothing to fight for—or against. When he asked to be relieved of a Pentagon staff assignment within six months, his superiors decided to send him to a "safe" place where he could sort himself out. They chose the Arkansas Military District, where he would handle National Guard and Reserve affairs. Seven weeks after Walker settled into his office in Little Rock, he was responsible for maintaining the peace in President Eisenhower's effort to enforce desegregation at Central High School. The experience was for General Walker—a Southerner with a parochial view—a "last straw." He said afterward he regarded the use of troops in desegregation as a "non-military adventure."[1]

When the Little Rock episode was over, and he was assigned to command the 24th Division in Germany, Walker tendered his resignation from the Army, August 4, 1959. His letter of resignation contained this statement:

It is fair to say that in my opinion the fifth column conspiracy and influence in the United States minimize or nullify the effectiveness of my ideals and principles, military mission and objectives, and the necessary American public spirit to support sons and soldiers. I have no further desire for military service at this time with this conspiracy and influence on the home front.[2]

Secretary of the Army Wilber M. Brucker, former Governor of Michigan, talked Walker out of this resignation attempt. Mr. Brucker recalled afterward that General Walker had come to him in the company of General Lyman L. Lemnitzer, then Army Chief of Staff. "I had quite a talk with General Walker," Mr. Brucker recalled. "I wanted to preserve a courageous military leader with a fine record. He told me he was against Communism and I answered that I sympathized fully with his sentiments, but perhaps he was over-stating the problem and getting too excited. I told him there were others who shared his anti-Communist aims. 'I want to preserve you for the Army,' I told him. 'I urge you in the interest of everything you are talking about to take this command of the 24th Division that you always wanted. The Army can't afford to lose you.'" Mr. Brucker was a lay preacher as well as a lawyer. Walker, who later described the Brucker appeal as "mixed cajolery and opposition," replied with a statement to the effect that if it was believed he could serve usefully, he would stay on. There was no indication that either Secretary Brucker or General Lemnitzer probed what General Walker had meant by a "fifth column conspiracy and influence" that tended to "minimize or nullify" his ideals.

Walker took over the 24th Infantry in Germany in the fall of 1959. Soon afterward, he began voicing his opinions on the patriotic in-adequacies of some prominent Americans, including former President Harry Truman, Ambassador Adlai Stevenson and Mrs. Franklin D. Roosevelt. At first, these opinions did not get outside the "family" of the military forces in Europe, but brought some unofficial re-monstrances from his superiors. In July, 1960, Secretary Brucker inspected the overseas troops and sent the commander he had "saved" for the Army an encouraging letter of praise for the "obviously splendid job being done by the 24th Infantry division personnel."

The stalwart combat commander, however, was dissatisfied with the official troop information programs. He believed that they did not show inspiration, conviction or "commitment to vigorous anti-Communism," and so he undertook his own program. "I led my command in an assault on the most capable and destructive enemy the world has ever known," the fighting man said.[3] He introduced his "pro-Blue" indoctrination program, which he described as fol-lows:

"The pro-Blue program which I set up in the 24th Division in-cluded psychological warfare, as well as troop information and other division activities. Implemented through the chain of com-mand, it was directed to 750 officers, 12,000 soldiers, and the 9,000 dependents of the division, approximately 35,000 people, having passed through the division area during my assignment [November, 1959—April, 1961]. It comprised citizenship in service, religion, discipline, morality, integrity, German-American relations, leadership, Americanism, and other aspects of the soldier's life. The Pro-Blue program set forth: 1. The methods of Communism and how to combat them. 2. The value of the American heritage and how to preserve it. 3. Our duties toward and benefits from, the NATO shield."[4]

This roster of objectives was endorsed at higher headquarters. The Army's Chief of Information at the Pentagon, Major General William W. Quinn, wrote the divisional commander:

DEAR TED:
One of our basic philosophies is that commanders should tailor their troop information programs to their own ideas and needs. Though we preach this on every possible occasion, we haven't, as yet, succeeded in getting the word to everyone. That is why we have followed the progress of your Pro-Blue program with interest and pleasure.[5]

Ironically, Quinn's letter was dated April 6, 1961, a week before the "Walker Case" broke. The editors of the English-language *Overseas Weekly,* published in Germany and popular among troops because of its lurid features, had been having a running battle with General Walker. The general resented many of the stories in the paper because he said they capitalized on the ancient animosities of enlisted men toward "the brass." The general thought that *Overseas Weekly* provoked "mutinous feeling by implying that enlisted men needed protection from their command." At one point General Walker barred an *Overseas Weekly* reporter, Siegfried Naujocks, from his division area.

On April 12, 1961, the *Overseas Weekly* printed a story that was picked up by news agencies and correspondents.[6] The stories reported that General Walker had told two hundred persons at a Parent-Teacher Association meeting that former President Harry Truman, former Secretary of State Dean Acheson and Mrs. Franklin D. Roosevelt were "definitely pink," and that Edward R. Murrow, Walter Lippmann and Eric Sevareid leaned toward Communism. The news reports told how General Walker had established a "special warfare" office to conduct his "pro-Blue" campaign and had opened the campaign with a meeting at which he charged "Communism has infiltrated every institution in the United States in an attempt to overthrow our way of life." Copies of *The Life of John Birch*, a book by the society's chief publicist, Robert Welch, Jr., of Belmont, Massachusetts, were said to have been distributed to the division's day rooms and copies of the society's magazine, *American Opinion*, were put on sale on Army newsstands in the division area. The reports added that the Division's weekly newspaper printed at least one article from the Birchist magazine. The general's headquarters at Augsburg issued a denial that the pro-Blue program was dominated by any organization. The general followed up with an attack upon the *Overseas Weekly*, which he called "immoral, unscrupulous, corrupt and destructive." But when Pentagon officials called him on the telephone from Washington to ask whether he had made the statements attributed to him, Walker's answers appeared to them equivocal. He was ordered relieved of his command to permit an investigation of the reports.[7]

Walker already had been promoted to command the VIII Corps in Austin, Texas. This would have meant an assignment in his home state and a third star. Instead, the promotion was held in abeyance and he was ordered to a colonel's post in Heidelberg. There, it was implied, someone could keep an eye on him. Lieutenant General Frederic Brown, commander of the Fifth Army headquarters in Heidelberg, was ordered to make a formal inspector general's investigation of the charges contained in the news dispatches. The outcome was a confirmation of most of the charges and a formal verbal "admonishment" of General Walker for failing to heed "cautions" from his superiors against participating in "controversial activities which were contrary to long-standing customs of the military service and beyond the prerogatives of a senior military commander."[8]

General Brown also reported that Walker had sought to influence the voting of his troops in the 1960 elections by "recommending the use of voting materials not obtained through military sources." This was the so-called "index" of the Americans for Constitutional Action, a Rightist group, which provided assessments of political candidates. In an editorial in the *Taro Leaf*, the Division newspaper, Walker had urged the troops to telephone a certain number "to have your representative's record determined before your vote is cast." This appeared to be a violation of the Hatch Act prohibiting political activity by military men. Moreover, according to the Brown report, Walker had refused to answer certain questions. This was within Walker's legal prerogative but smacked, ironically, of the military equivalent of "taking the Fifth Amendment," a tactic that fervent anti-Communists invariably denounced.

The "Walker Case" might have ended with the Brown report and the formal admonition. Walker received an assignment in Hawaii to get him out of the spotlight. But the affair coincided with an uproar in Washington over charges that military men were being "muzzled" by the Kennedy Administration. The fate of Walker was lumped in the press with nonrelated examples of the Kennedy Administration's censorship of speeches by high officers. In the inevitable Congressional investigation Walker was called as a witness, even though, in another fit of frustration and despondency, perhaps sparked by a glimmer of political ambition, he finally had resigned from the Army. This time no one was interested in preserving him in uniform and his resignation was quickly accepted. On April 4, 1962, he appeared before the Senate Special Preparedness Subcommittee, headed by Senator John C. Stennis, Democrat of Mississippi.

The hearings were a wide-ranging affair, covering many facets of the role of military leaders in American public affairs. But they also provided an extensive forum for discussion of troop indoctrination, quite aside from the "Walker Case." As for Walker, he lost all sense of caution and proportion. In a paroxysm of charges, he lashed out against what he described as his mortal enemies—undefined but apparently powerful "influences" that played the Communist "game" —and said these were responsible for his fate. At one point he suggested that President Eisenhower had been under Communist influence. Another time he said that Dean Rusk was influential in the "real control apparatus" that frustrated militant, anti-Communist activity. Walker told the committee that his original assignment to the 24th Division in Germany was an "entrapment." He said: "A Moscow dossier was being made on me, no doubt, from the time of my Little Rock assignment and even from my career assignment, I am sure." This, according to Walker, led to his being identified by the Communists as an "ultra." "It comes from the [Russian] revolutionary days," he explained. "It is a noun. It means 'get him.' " From what he read "in the Communist party line," he went on, he believed that Secretary Brucker's appeal to him in 1959 to stay in the Army "could have been a deliberate attempt to keep me from resigning at that time and to censor me further in placing me in command of a U.S. Army division."

Few persons could imagine that this appearance by Walker on Capitol Hill, in the same marble-walled caucus room that had held the McCarthy and Hoffa hearings, was not at last the end of the "Walker Case." During a lunch period, he seemed to have delivered his own *coup de grâce* when he punched a reporter in the eye. He went on to Texas to take part in the gubernatorial primaries as a candidate of the ultra Right and conducted what he called a "crusade for the recovery of the American public." He finished last in the four-candidate race.

There was yet another recrudescence. In September, 1962, the man who had "kept the peace" at Little Rock joined and, in at least one instance, incited the rioters on the University of Mississippi campus at the time of the enrollment of James Meredith, a Negro. The resultant battle of brick, rocks, Molotov cocktails and tear gas left two dead and hundreds injured. The former Army officer was charged with insurrection and seditious conspiracy. The charges afterward were dropped. He was arrested and placed under psychiatric examination, but then released. Perhaps the final irony was the statement by Representative Rousselot, a California Republican and member of the John Birch Society, who suggested that Walker's membership in the Society be revoked. In 1963 Walker joined the Reverend Billy James Hargis, founder of the Right Wing Christian Crusade, in "Operation Midnight Ride," a coast-to-coast speaking tour to "alert the nation to the dangers of Communism." On April 10, 1963, while Walker was sitting in his home in Dallas, a sniper fired into the casement window from a nearby alley and the bullet went just past his head, showering slivers of glass over his forearm. Police said at the time there was no doubt that the sniper intended to kill. In an incredible footnote to history, Dallas police on December 6, 1963, indicated that the wife of Lee Harvey Oswald, accused assassin of President Kennedy, told them her husband had disclosed to her that he was the man who had fired at Walker. The mind must stagger at the obvious thought of what might have been if Oswald had been caught the first time, if in fact he was the man who fired at Walker.

The case of the former major general of the Army focused attention on career military officers. Many persons asked: How does a man like Walker rise to two-star rank in the Army? And what does this mean with respect to the influences such officers have on the young men in their command? From Germany, it had been reported that General Walker was a great leader whose men would follow him unstintingly. But at the Pentagon, where the former officer was disowned emphatically, they said that men like Walker did not rise to high command. The man had changed, they said. For example, General Quinn, who had expressed "interest and pleasure" in Walker's indoctrination program on the basis of reports received at the Pentagon, had this to say of Walker, whom he had known for many years: "He went through a metamorphosis. He is not at all the man he was when he was a combat officer. Rising in the ranks is a tortuous, exacting process. From the time that Army men graduate West Point—the same is true of Navy and Air Force officers—they are under constant review by their fellow officers, superiors and even Congress. In the twenty-five years before a career officer is likely to be considered for brigadier general, he has usually been rated fifty to seventy-five times by as many officers. Nominations for general's rank must be approved at the White House and confirmed by the Congressional Armed Services Committees. Thus career officers are under constant observation. The system invites conformity, but it also works strongly against extremists. If *former* General Walker had expressed himself five years earlier as he did after commanding troops at Little Rock, Arkansas, he would never have risen as high as he did."[9]

And yet the "Walker Case" served to emphasize how narrow was the line between zealousness and zealotry, between patriotism and reaction. Professor Morris Janowitz, in his study of *The Professional Soldier*, had said that military careerists were usually dedicated men—"not too different from the priesthood and ministry in serving a cause."[10]

As for the indoctrination programs that Walker inaugurated, the "Pro-Blue" title was dropped, but the program itself was retained. In Heidelberg, in the spring of 1962, I was advised by Army officials that the responsibility for troop indoctrination was being established at an even lower level of responsibility than division headquarters —at the regimental level. This underscored the old axiom that troop motivation was a "function of command." Did this revive or even aggravate a danger that other Walkers, younger men who had not had to survive his years of being scrutinized, could turn troop indoctrination programs to their own political ends? Perhaps. Yet one of the interesting aspects of the "Walker Case" was that it did not arouse a general outcry against alleged militaristic or Right Wing teachings in the service. Most of the country seemed to accept the notion that Walker was an exception. At no time, according to Pentagon officials, was a question raised in any form that the service-men might be under bad political influences under military officers. The hundreds of letters prompted by the "Walker Case" were devoted chiefly to the adequacy of the official indoctrination program as an anti-Communist medium. This reaction to the case was either an expression of confidence that military service did not subject troops to militarist teachings or an indication of apathy, on the possible grounds that troop indoctrination was not effective one way or another.

According to a United States tradition, "understanding" is the basis of military proficiency. Baron von Steuben, while training American Revolutionary troops, wrote to a Prussian relative: "You say to your soldier 'Do this' and he does it. But I am obliged to say to the American, 'This is why you ought to do this,' and then he does it." American soldiers, it is emphasized, are neither mercenaries nor unthinking hordes. Since their cause is invariably just, then conquer they must, and all true patriots will rally round the flag. Such conceptions do not suffer much from the fact that even soldiers of the Revolution needed to be enticed with grants of land and that draft laws led to rioting in the Civil War. George Washington was quoted as saying: "Impress upon the mind of every man, from the first to the lowest, the importance of the cause and what it is they are contending for." He asked Thomas Paine to write *The Crisis* and other pamphlets to propagate the cause. He ordered the reading of the Declaration of Independence to all troops.

The first organized troop orientation programs, however, began during the Civil War. World War I brought the official newspaper *Stars and Stripes,* which was praised by General Pershing as the outstanding morale booster of the American Expeditionary Forces. In World War II, the "soldier's newspaper" was again published. In addition to this newspaper, World War II brought a concerted official program of indoctrination in print, on radio and with films such as the famous *Why We Fight* series. Government officials did not, of course, like to use the term "indoctrination." And in fact, the so-called Troop Information and Education program was based largely on news information, as opposed to rhetoric and exhortation. Yet straight news often has seemed bland to critics of the programs. The tendency to active indoctrination was strengthened in the wake of the Korean War when the apparent lack of motivation on the part of many soldiers was exaggerated unfairly into a national scandal.

What constitutes proper indoctrination? Is it a knowledge of the Bill of Rights, the Declaration of Independence, the homilies of American history and the threat of world Communism that motivate troops? Or is it the soldier's confidence, according to the old chestnut, that he belongs to the best damn squad in the best damn platoon in the best damn company, etc.? Vice Admiral Robert Pirie discussed the lack of preparedness of lads going into the Marine Corps in 1962 and complained: "Only half of the boys recruited can make a rational explanation of the meaning of the 4th of July."

The best military trainers, however, are not necessarily the best propagators of the democratic faith, even if there is a mystical relationship between combat effectiveness and ideology. Also, for the first time in its history, the United States is maintaining a large standing military force and has been able to do so only through protracted conscription in peacetime. Conscription is not conducive to motivation. The members of the armed forces in the sixties are of an exceptionally high level of education. About 65 percent of enlisted personnel have attended high school, about 55 percent of the officers are college graduates. They need more than slogans to arouse them.

The official view of the problem was well stated by John Broger, a Pentagon official, who said:

"The basic problems at issue here would be then: what concepts of American life, attitudes, motivations and convictions must be refreshed, engendered, or sharpened to a new dimension if we are to keep the morale of the fighting forces prepared 'at the ready' over a protracted period of time to engage in conflict from a small-scale limited war to worldwide conflict? Over this same period United States troops will continue to be stationed in many parts of the world. How are these troops to be trained and educated in the issues of why they are there, who is the enemy, what are the needs of literally day-to-day resistance against enemy propaganda and techniques of subversion? What are the free world values essential to the cementing of our alliances?"[11]

One answer, reflected in the conduct of General Walker and expressed vehemently by several persons during the Stennis subcommittee hearings, holds that Communism is the "gravest problem of our times," and that ruthless, zealous determination to defeat the hated foe is required in all American citizens, but especially in fighters in uniform. The prime mover of the Congressional hearings, Senator Strom Thurmond of South Carolina, a major general in the Army Reserve, and an out-and-out Right Winger, demonstrated time and again his panicky feeling that the enemy was perhaps too skillful and American soldiers too naïve in the great cataclysmic Armageddon with Communism. "No one gets any pleasure out of recalling the successes scored by the Communists in Korea by brainwashing POWs and promoting 'bugouts' by GIs who had not been sufficiently impressed with the nature of the enemy, American ideals, or why it is necessary to fight in that far-off, rough and cold terrain," Senator Thurmond said, perhaps without pleasure, although he rarely missed an opportunity to indulge in this bit of patriotic masochism.

Lieutenant Colonel William E. Mayer, an Army psychiatrist,

aroused some controversy within the Army over his findings that the Korean War showed troop indoctrination to be "more often than not a failure, useless or even negative in its effects." He cited as evidence his interviews with more than a thousand men who were captured in Korea and of whom one-third, Colonel Mayer said, "admitted that they had on occasion, voluntarily and without threats or duress committed acts which they knew were not in the interests of the United States—knowingly collaborated with the enemy in his psychological warfare and propaganda efforts." But surveys such as Colonel Mayer's required a broader perspective. This was provided by General Frederic H. Smith, Jr., the Vice Chief of Staff of the Air Force, when he testified:

"We should examine the good things about our national character as well as the bad. For example, during the Korean War, more than seven thousand Americans were captured. Most of them were captives for about three years. After repatriation, and after all the facts were studied on the cases suspected of collaboration, misbehavior and the like, fourteen were brought to trial and eleven were convicted. These eleven, plus twenty-one who refused at first to return, add up to less than two-tenths of one percent of the total captured. But at the same time more than 87,500 of our servicemen in Korea got awards for exemplary conduct—seventy-nine got the Medal of Honor. Thousands of the captured died as heroes, and thousands of others who never were captured died as heroes. Moreover, thousands of other heroic Americans fought and survived without being captured and are in our armed forces or in civilian life today."[12]

Among the officers at the Stennis subcommittee hearings who presented a rational, confident demeanor in the face of debilitating charges that attributed decadence, stupidity, sabotage, betrayal and weakness to America's leaders and its troops one man especially made a resounding impact in characteristic homespun language. He was General David M. Shoup, Commandant of the Marine Corps, a short, stubby man who looked like a shy, bespectacled bookkeeper but whose fighting credentials were unchallengeable.

General Shoup won the Medal of Honor as commander of the

Second Marines, 2nd Division, on Tarawa, in one of the fiercest
battles of the Pacific during World War II. His citation said in part:

For conspicuous gallantry and intrepidity at the risk of his own life
above and beyond the call of duty . . . Although severely shocked by an
exploding shell soon after landing at the pier, and suffering from a serious,
painful leg wound which had become infected, Colonel Shoup fearlessly
exposed himself . . . rallying his hesitant troops by his own inspiring
heroism. . . . Working without rest under withering enemy fire . . . Brilliant leadership, daring tactics, selfless devotion.

That write-up was prepared by Colonel Shoup's commanding officer.
A great accolade came from his first sergeant, who, in a rare enco-
mium, described his colonel as "the bravest, nerviest, best soldiering
Marine I have ever met." In that great terrible battle against the
Japanese, Shoup demonstrated his ability to say a great deal in a
few words. His situation report concluded with these words: "Casualties many; percentage dead not known; combat efficiency: we are
winning."

General Shoup had more than combat experience to offer the subcommittee, however. Before he became Commandant of the Marine
Corps in 1959, incidentally by-passing nine officers senior to him,
General Shoup had been chief of the Marine Corps recruit depot at
Parris Island, South Carolina—Strom Thurmond's bailiwick—and for
five months in 1956 he had held the post of inspector general for
recruit training. The post was specially created after a public uproar—and revulsion—over harsh Marine training which in one instance led to the death of five recruits. When Shoup appeared before
the Stennis panel, he had already established something of a reputation as a tough commandant, for whom frills meant nothing. He had
banned the traditional officer's swagger stick, on the grounds that it
didn't help weaklings and was not needed by leaders.

Testifying before the committee, General Shoup said the Marine
Corp information program was an integral part of its training. Then
he made this cogent point: "While I believe that a thorough understanding by all Americans of insidious foreign ideologies is a worthy
goal, I am firmly convinced that a Marine properly indoctrinated

will resist these ideologies even in the absence of a complete theoretical understanding of them." In his own public speeches, Shoup said, he did not even bother to use the term "Communism." This seemed to cause Senator Thurmond some consternation. As the interrogation of General Shoup progressed, a duel developed between the Marine Commandant and the Senator. It produced this bit of eloquence from the onetime Indiana farm boy:

"We teach these boys when they come in. We find that they do not have the same love of country, for example, that I had, that I think I had when I was a boy, that I was taught in my school by my teachers, by my history books. We teach them what there is in this country that is worth living for, worth dying for, that is worth giving your life for. I might state right here that inasmuch as there has been some controversy over this, Mr. Chairman, I would like to proceed to tell you again that we do not teach them hate."

"Proceed," said Senator Stennis, and the crowd in the caucus room suddenly fell absolutely silent. The general spoke, softly and slowly:

"Hate I consider is an internal sin and hate is closely associated with fear. I think fear breeds defeatism and that is a disease we cannot afford in this country if we are going to maintain our position in the family of freedom-loving people. I also observe that hate is not what sustained the prisoners in Korea, but it was faith and confidence; faith in their nation and confidence in their way of life in America. That is why some of them did not break, because they had this faith and confidence. It was not because they hated the people that were questioning them. I think this is the thing that we emphasize—ability to tangle with *any* enemy. It so happened that as early as 1912, my brother said to me, 'We are going to have to fight the Japanese some day.' I came into the Marine Corps and many times in our schools we were studying the Japanese, and this was long before 1940, because we thought in our planning and thinking, some day we would have to fight them. We were gathering information. Never once did I hear anyone say to learn to hate them and I think we did a pretty good job against the Japs."[13]

Periodically, Defense Department efforts in troop indoctrination are subjects of complaint, not only from the side of the Radical Right, as in 1962, but also from more representative segments of

American society. In 1956 the Fund for the Advancement of Education, subsidized by the Ford Foundation, published a sharp indictment of the Armed Services Information and Education Program. The principal findings of a two-year study were that the informational programs were educationally substandard, that most of the available materials were held in low esteem by the servicemen, that some of the programs probably were harmful rather than helpful in the way that they dealt with subjects like Communism, that there was overlapping and repetition and waste of time, money and effort, and that the higher military echelons obviously did not care much about the program.

These complaints, essentially, were repeated during the subsequent uproar over troop indoctrination. Yet programs of this nature can never be satisfactory. They are designed to provide information and motivation for military support of the American ideal. They are supposed to represent the American consensus. But what is this consensus? The proper road to freedom and democracy is one about which Americans haggle all the time. In the meantime, in accordance with the platitude that an informed soldier is a good soldier and that a patriotic soldier is an even better soldier, the armed forces spend more than $4 million a year on informational activities. This provides for a massive effort in the distribution of printed materials, news services, newspapers, radio programs, television programs, movies and lectures to the troops and, frequently, their families.

The scope of the program is indicated by some figures. In radio, in 1963, there were 250 Armed Forces Radio Service stations; in television, thirty-four outlets throughout the world. The AFRS sends out news broadcasts that are carefully written to avoid charges of political bias. They are scrupulously handled to avoid giving the servicemen and their families any feeling of propaganda intent, even in international affairs. "The worst thing that could happen to either the Armed Forces radio or Armed Forces television would be to be accused of propaganda and have any part of that accusation stick," Brigadier General William O. Blandford observed.

The Defense Department also publishes 125 different kinds of indoctrination pamphlets, books, magazines and newspapers each year with a total distribution of eight million copies. Some of the publications have been written by Defense employees, some have been purchased, and some are reprints of various pertinent government publications. The printed material includes also a news and feature clip sheet that goes to fourteen hundred service newspapers. In films, twenty-four reels of a screen "magazine" are produced annually which are shown along with contributed commercial films in service movie houses throughout the world. The Defense Department also makes films, usually of half-hour length, for use in special troop information programs. These cover material on the nature, people and customs of foreign countries in which United States troops are stationed; material on democracy and citizenship, Communism and world affairs. The films are often made with the assistance of Hollywood producers.

Typical of the programs presented to the troops through the Defense Department media in recent years were various "Meet the Press" programs, one of which, incidentally, featured Robert Welch, president of the John Birch Society. Another film presentation featured a debate between Associate Justice Arthur Goldberg of the Supreme Court and Senator Barry Goldwater, when Justice Goldberg was Secretary of Labor. Another film presented a discussion of Communism by Dr. Robert Strausz-Hupé, of the University of Pennsylvania's Foreign Policy Research Institute, Attorney General Robert F. Kennedy and Ambassador Henry Cabot Lodge. Election programs also were presented on an "equal time" basis. One film, *Posse for Peace*, was a documentary on "the mutual security program and how it affects our worldwide military and economic situation." Another, *The General Pershing Story*, was the first of a biographical series on great American military leaders. The second in the series dealt with the life of Fleet Admiral Chester W. Nimitz. *The Influence of Woodrow Wilson* summarized that President's efforts to build a lasting peace after World War I. Among the pamphlets, one outlined a forty-year record of Soviet treaty violations; another, *Congress at Work*, discussed the functions and organization of Congress—how a bill becomes a law. There were various "background" issues on such trouble spots as Berlin, Laos and South Vietnam.

Thus has the American soldier been indoctrinated to cope with the problems that face him in the service. Important indoctrination, too. For it is the American soldier abroad who serves as the effective ambassador of his country to the people among whom he lives. As the Bendetsen committee pointed out, "The only face of America which countless foreigners see is a military face; by it they tend to judge our nation." The ability of the average soldier overseas to cope with questions about American life is often as important as his ability to wield a weapon.

The committee under Karl R. Bendetsen, a paper company executive who was Under Secretary of the Army in the Truman Administration, was appointed by Secretary of Defense McNamara to study the "nonmilitary instruction" in the armed forces, as an outgrowth of the Walker case.

"We have found," the committee reported,

that the average serviceman shares the general attitudes and values of the American public of which he is a part. This is true of his devotion to his country and his opposition to communism. There is little evidence to support the view expressed in some quarters that the serviceman lacks an awareness of the communist threat. The fearful, the confused and the pessimistic do not populate our armed forces. These conclusions are in contrast to impressions stemming from distorted and exaggerated views of the conduct of United States servicemen who were prisoners of war during the Korean conflict. We subscribe in this regard to the report of the Defense Advisory Committee on Prisoners of War which found that with notorious exceptions, the prisoner of war performed in a manner which did credit to his Service and his country.[14]

The Bendetsen committee also found faults. The most significant, it felt, was that troop information and education had been considered too often as "an end in itself" and not as a function of command. Its specific recommendations, however, were not nearly so important as one of its observations: "The Armed Forces cannot and should not be expected to correct all the shortcomings there may be in the serviceman's pre-military educational experience." The true indoctrination of American troops thus must take place long before they ever take the oath to "bear true faith and allegiance to the United States of America."

In recent civil rights campaigns, still another troop indoctrination factor has been brought out. Integration of Negroes in the armed forces was carried out fairly effectively after a directive by President Truman in 1947 made desegregation mandatory. But a serious problem has remained in the vicinity of military camps and bases in the Southern part of the United States, where communities practice segregation. A Presidential committee on equal opportunity in the armed forces has cited several discriminatory patterns lingering in the armed services and stressed housing and school discrimination that created pressures "too great to bear" for Negro servicemen and their families.[15] The Defense Secretary's efforts to ameliorate this situation unfortunately have met with some resistance. But he has correctly pointed out: "Military effectiveness is unquestionably reduced as a result of civilian racial discrimination against men in uniform."[16] Clearly, no Negro can be expected to fight Communism with patriotic fervor if he feels deeply the injustices against him in the country he is sworn to defend.

VIII

---⭐

Research and the Federal Government

"The effects of the extraordinary increase in Federal expenditures for research and development, and the increasing reliance on the private sector to perform such work, have been far-reaching."
—Bell Report to President Kennedy, May 1, 1962

"No more significant change has occurred in the world of higher education in recent times."
—Dr. Nathan M. Pusey, President of Harvard University

The most quoted portion of former President Eisenhower's farewell address dealt with the "military-industrial complex." But General Eisenhower, in the same speech, also said: "Akin to and largely responsible for the sweeping changes in our industrial-military posture has been the technological revolution during recent decades. In this revolution research has become central. It also becomes more formalized, complex and costly. A steadily increasing share is con-

[137]

ducted for, by, or at the direction of the Federal Government. Today the solitary inventor, tinkering in his shop, has been overshadowed by task forces of scientists, in laboratories and testing fields. In the same fashion, the free university, historically the fountainhead of free ideas and scientific discovery, has experienced a revolution in the conduct of research. Partly because of the huge costs involved, the Government contract become virtually a substitute for intellectual curiosity. For every old blackboard there are now hundreds of electronic computors. The prospect of domination of the nation's scholars by Federal employment, project allocations and the power of money is ever present and is gravely to be regarded."[1]

At about the time that President Eisenhower was making his farewell address, twenty-six universities and colleges—a national cross-section—undertook a study of the government's impact on their operations. In a report issued July, 1963, they concluded unanimously that Federal aid had been "highly beneficial" to them despite some problems. Yet they expressed awareness of the potential danger to academic freedom from Federal funds spent through and in favor of the universities, much of it for purposes of national defense. The pattern of support had created serious imbalances within departments of universities, between science and nonscience departments, and within the national scientific community. The top one hundred educational institutions of the country, only 5 percent of the total number of such institutions, had received roughly 90 percent of the more than one billion dollars in Federal funds allotted to research fellowships, construction of facilities, education and training. The other nineteen hundred schools had received virtually nothing.

Notre Dame, one of the twenty-six institutions in the survey, received one-sixth of its total operating expenditures for education and general purposes from Federal funds. By categories, it paid from its own pocket virtually the entire cost of research in the Arts and Sciences, Commerce and Law Schools. The Federal Government, on the other hand, paid $2 out of every $3 in engineering and science research. The survey report cited some "points of irritation and at times, areas of great concern." One of these was the refusal of the Administration to pay indirect costs of research projects such as administrative costs and the maintenance of buildings. Some universities complained of being "harassed" by government auditors, as when one auditor questioned expenditures for a few postage stamps. Nevertheless, as though fearing to look a gift horse in the mouth, the report financed by the Carnegie Foundation for the Advancement of Teaching, and published in the *Educational Record* of the American Council on Education, found that the advantages in the availability of funds—at the rate of $1,760 million a year—outweighed the risks. Without the Federal funds, the report said, "the whole character of many universities' research programs (and in consequence, of their instructional programs) would change. Faculties in many instances would shrink. Many research efforts would have to be abandoned completely. Others would be sharply curtailed."[2] In other words, many free academic institutions had become dependent upon the government not only for the additional research activities, but for their "faculties" and "instructional programs."

The academic institutions constituted only a small account in the government's budget of research spending, which had grown from barely $100 million a year before World War II to $1.1 billion in 1950, and $12.4 billion in 1963. The Defense Department alone planned to spend $7 billion on research and development in 1963; the Atomic Energy Commission, $1.4 billion. But for the universities the government outlay represented two-thirds of all the money they had for research. The Massachusetts Institute of Technology was far and away the greatest recipient of defense research money with $74,956,000 in grants and contracts. If included in the 1962 list of 388 private, profit-making, prime contractors in defense research and development, M.I.T. would have been near the top in twenty-first place. And much of the money accepted by M.I.T. from the Pentagon went to the relatively uncreative responsibility of managing government laboratories.

Is it conceivable that institutions such as M.I.T. would be subject to government or Pentagon influence in the honesty of their research effort; would they abandon worthwhile endeavors in order to obtain lucrative contracts? The consensus does not accept such a harsh judgment. Yet there is widespread concern over the rectitude of the smaller colleges and universities which do not have large endowments or profitable real estate holdings. For example, officials in Washington, many of them former administrators at leading universities, have been horrified by some of the practices indulged in by the universities, now that they have seen these from the donor side of the fund-raising relationship.

Some universities, fearing imbalances from heavy investment in science research, are reluctant to accept additional projects. Other institutions employ full-time salesmen, known as "bag men," to solicit grants. An intelligence system has developed among universities similar to that employed by private defense contractors. One day the president of a large Midwestern university telephoned a leading Defense Department official to complain that a research contract was being terminated. The termination action, recommended at lower levels earlier that morning, had not reached the Defense official when the call came through. Several state universities have set up research foundations to receive and dispense grants to their scientists. In this way the funds do not show up in the university budget, where their size might tempt state legislatures to cut appropriations. Some university scientists practice "grantsmanship." They play off various Federal agencies against each other, soliciting the highest bids for their time. Other scientists reportedly promise more than 100 percent of their time to more than one agency, since there is no formal cross-check, and there is no way to control how much research work is actually done. Unlike other professions, science does not lend itself to measurements of time devoted to duty.

Dr. Nathan M. Pusey, president of Harvard, pointed out in his annual report for 1961 that the large sums which the Federal Government spends in universities to promote research do not represent an effort to *help* higher education but represent a "happy coincidence" resulting from the government's pursuit of special objectives. The consequence is lopsided investment.[3] Only the larger institutions are in Harvard's position, able to balance with its own money the sizable Federal sums that go to the Division of Engineering while little or nothing goes to the Arts and Humanities. In 1960 and 1961 Harvard received more income from the Federal Government than from her endowment, although it was among the best-endowed institutions in the country. In 1961 approximately 25 percent of Harvard's income, more than $21 million, came in Federal funds.

In a special report on Harvard and the Federal Government, Dr. Pusey said: "The image of a coercive government dictating what shall and shall not be done in university laboratories and libraries simply does not fit Harvard's experience with Washington." However, he added:

The role of the university cannot be one of withdrawal from the world. But it will serve society well only as it remains true to its essential nature —a university, not an agency of government. It is entitled to demand complete intellectual freedom. To this end it must ask for a measure of detachment from current crises and routine procedures as necessary conditions of fulfilling its fundamental purpose in civilized society.[4]

And then, for all of the Harvard president's assurances in 1961, he was moved to declare in his commencement address at Cambridge a year later: "Certain evidences of an increasing [government] desire to say how things are to be done in laboratories and who may and may not appear in them cannot fail to look like interference from the point of view of a university determined to remain a truly independent, autonomous, open society devoted to intellectual search for the search's sake. I am afraid there will be more and more grounds for conflict of this kind as time goes on."[5]

Dr. Pusey referred specifically to a year of bitter negotiations with the Atomic Energy Commission in connection with the maintenance of a $12 million electron accelerator on Harvard University grounds. The government paid the entire cost of construction. Harvard and the Massachusetts Institute of Technology undertook to operate it for a fee of $5 million a year. The device, a huge, doughnut-shaped affair, 236 feet in diameter and buried beneath tons of earth and concrete, was intended for the study of particles and forces found within the nuclei of atoms. Known as the Cambridge Electron Accelerator, it was one of the major research facilities to be placed on a university campus for "free and unfettered academic research of an unclassified nature."[6]

But the AEC demanded the right to veto the application for employment of any alien, regardless of nationality. It demanded the right to control all visits to the accelerator. It called upon the university to file a lengthy report on any visit, including informal visits, by any scientist from a Communist country. It sought to forbid the release to Soviet bloc nations of any information obtained from the accelerator unless equally valuable information was released by Soviet bloc countries to the United States. In effect, this meant that although the university was presumably working on unclassified research, it would be required to subject its personnel to tight security regulation by the government, foreclose the opportunity of hiring aliens even temporarily if those aliens refused to subject themselves to lengthy clearance processes, undertake an administrative burden of clearance and reporting that was quite remote from academic practices, and introduce security measures for visitors in a manner that was more in keeping with a military installation than a private, free, academic institution.

Harvard finally signed the contract, after winning some concessions. Dr. Franklin B. Ford, dean of the Harvard faculty of Arts and Sciences, called the final contract provisions "irritating" but an improvement over the "intolerable conditions" first proposed.[7] Harvard finally agreed to furnish the AEC with background information on all aliens doing research at the accelerator. The university ceded to the AEC a veto power over Soviet bloc aliens who might be considered for employment. It agreed to notify the AEC in advance of any formal visits by Soviet bloc scientists, although not of "casual" visits. While retaining the right to publish findings from the accelerator, the university agreed to accept requests from Soviet bloc countries for unpublished findings only with counter requests for appropriate exchange information. "There will be little points of friction indefinitely in our relations with the government," Dr. Pusey said. "The only course the university can take is to remain eternally vigilant."[8]

At Chicago University, another type of problem developed in government-university relations based on the national security research effort. There, in June, 1963, the associate director of Chicago University's Laboratories of Applied Sciences resigned because the university had shown reluctance to encourage research related to military matters. The associate director, Lucien Biderman, said: "I think their last involvement in the development of atomic energy and the bomb left a deep scar on the moral fiber of this place from which it has not really recovered. I do not believe that they wish again to get involved in developments which are for the military."

But one of his associates had another opinion. He thought that the reluctance of the university to engage in research projects for the military was due to "pressure on the university from industry." He said that university research into military systems proposed or under evaluation often resulted in negative findings. These "hurt economically" the companies building or proposing to build the systems under study. The director of the Laboratories, Dr. Thorfin R. Hogniss, while suggesting that the resignation was due to other reasons, said nevertheless that the university disliked having work involving national security mixed with its other activities—except in time of war—because it required separate buildings, guards and other special measures.[9] It was clear that at Chicago University, as at Harvard, there were "irritations" because of the growing governmental reliance upon free universities for research in the interests of national security.

Charges of government interference with honest research developed in the dispute that finally led to the dissolution of the Operations Research Office of the Johns Hopkins University. The Operations Research Office was set up in September, 1948, as the Army's equivalent to the Rand Corporation which serviced the Air Force. For more than a decade, and particularly during the Korean War, the Army's relationship with the university unit appeared smooth. ORO, with front-line interviews and scientific analyses of weapons in combat, produced studies on the merits of body armor for infantrymen, the use of big bombers for close support of infantry, obsolescence factors in weapons industries, civil defense requirements and military factors in economic growth. But in May, 1961, the relationship was severed with mutual recriminations over freedom of research, breaches of security and the withholding of funds to exert pressure.

Part of the problem clearly was personal, possibly political. Dr. Ellis O. Johnson, head of ORO, had gained prominence for his work with the Air Force and Navy during World War II before he took on the Army assignment. As a Navy officer, he was responsible for a mine-laying operation around the Japanese home islands whose effectiveness was overshadowed only by the atomic bombings of Hiroshima and Nagasaki. Johnson returned home with graying hair and considerable remorse over his role in the war. His father had left Sweden as a young man rather than face military conscription and Johnson himself had an inner revulsion against military matters. He resigned his commission and went back to geophysics. But he took on the ORO job in 1948 when persuaded that as a scientist he might do more for his country and humanity *before* a war.

The trouble between the Army and ORO never was satisfactorily explained. It became acute toward the end of the Eisenhower Administration. When the break came, Dr. Johnson said that he and Dr. Milton Eisenhower, the President's brother, who was head of Johns Hopkins University, believed that it was "the university's responsibility not to touch on decisions, but to do good research," without regard for the conclusions brought on by scientific inquiry. This implied Army efforts to bend scientific inquiry to its will. Dr. Johnson did not deny that imputation. He added that the Army leaders sought to maintain "strict control in detail," whereas he believed that researchers, once given an assignment, "must do a complete and honest job." The Army, of course, denied the implications of the Johnson statement.

One of the sources of contention, it appeared, was the charge that ORO had "leaked" three of its reports after the Army refused to do anything about them. One report criticized the nation's air defense warning system. Another concluded that Army machine tool stocks were obsolete. A third, comparing United States and Soviet economies, charged that the United States lacked a sense of urgency. Although the break came during the Kennedy Administration, the controversy had developed earlier. The upshot of it all was the dissolution of ORO and its replacement by the Research Analysis Corporation, a subsidized, nonprofit corporation like Rand, not connected with any university.

The "irritation" in academic life—as Dr. Pusey put it—was cited in a study by Brookings Institution:

As these remarks may suggest we are not inclined to dismiss the danger of Federal control as a myth designed simply to serve the interests of local and sectional forces. It is and will remain a continuing danger to the independence of academic institutions and must be guarded against more vigilantly as the role of the Federal Government in higher education grows. A more evident danger which is the more difficult to understand as the expansion of educational institutions and of our society normally takes the same course, is the growth of bureaucracy and its tendency to change universities from academic to impersonal or even business institutions. Often, as new Government programs age, they are run less by men and more by rules, less by personal and more by formal communications, less by the individual examination of individual situations, and more by general regulations. This is control not by dictation but by red tape which can frustrate and devitalize such intellectual effort.

Mobilization of the nation's academic community, albeit in the national interest, could lead to essential nationalization of the campus, the report said.[10]

On the campus, itself, the government invasion with research funds appears to have these effects: teachers are being diverted from the classrooms to the laboratories; university money that would otherwise go to teaching facilities is diverted to research because of contractual provisions requiring that grants be matched; the time of faculty members is often consumed in consultative assignments with the Federal Government.

A corollary to the invasion of the campus by the Federal Government in the interests of national security has been the proliferation of nonprofit institutions to carry out research and analysis. Before 1940, practically all the specialized intellectual work of the government was done "in house" by government laboratories. By 1964, there were some 350 outside nonprofit corporations assisting the government. The Atomic Energy Commission did nearly all of its work outside. The most famous of the "think" organizations is the Rand Corporation, which General Arnold, World War II Air Force Chief, ordered organized and subsidized to "get the best brains and turn them loose on the problems of the future." Rand was established in 1948 with funds supplied by the Ford Foundation and a nucleus staff recruited from the Douglas Aircraft Corporation. The company provided housing, office and laboratory space in Rand's formative years.

Rand's two-story headquarters opposite the City Hall in Santa Monica, California, on a beautiful beach-front site, is more rigorously guarded by security police than the Department of Defense. Unlike the Pentagon, where visitors are free to come and go, all visitors to Rand must have specific appointments. Visitors are tagged with badges which are surrendered upon departure. More meticulously than at the Pentagon, waste baskets are carefully checked and contents burned nightly. Classified papers are locked in safes and security officers constantly remind some of the absent-minded, preoccupied professionals to remember to leave nothing unguarded. Inevitably, one mathematician, who with his head for numbers was the equal of an electronic computor, forgot the combination to a safe. Another scientist had trouble keeping his papers safely locked and he was soon asked to work elsewhere.

Rand, with a liaison office in Washington, operates with a budget of about $13.5 million a year. It maintains a professional staff of 850, of whom about 550 are of top rank in their fields. Unlike most of the other nonprofit "think" organizations, Rand has permitted, even encouraged, its scientists to publish and talk in public, sometimes to the dismay of Pentagon officials. Rand studies, although 90 percent directed to the Air Force, nevertheless are wide-ranging in scope, from subversion and guerrilla warfare tactics to astronautics. Most of the professional staff is young—averaging below forty; and the pay has been around $15,000 a year for the average, above $25,000 for some of the key personnel. "Rand thinkers think twice before leaving," said one observer, citing the good pay and interesting work.

Defense contractors, academic institutions and the Federal Government have sponsored the nonprofit research organizations. The Western Electric Company, otherwise a profit-seeking concern, created the Sandia Corporation, as a nonprofit subsidiary for the manufacture of nuclear bombs. The University of California's Los Alamos and Livermore Laboratories did the original designs of the bombs. Johns Hopkins sponsored the Operations Research Office until the feud in 1961 led to the creation of the independent Research Analysis Corporation. Johns Hopkins established also the Applied Physics Laboratory for the Navy. Johns Hopkins' experience with ORO, incidentally, for all of the institution's indirect allegations of infringements on academic freedom, did not sour its relations with the Pentagon to the point of abstinence. In the 1962 list of 112 government agencies, foreign firms and nonprofit institutions that received research contracts and grants from the Defense Department, Johns Hopkins was third with $43,988,000, behind M.I.T. and the Aerospace Corporation in California. The Massachusetts Institute of Technology set up the Operations Evaluation Group for the Navy, the Lincoln Laboratories as a service to all military departments and the Mitre Corporation (M.I.T. Rand Engineers) for the Air Force.

The Mitre Corporation, originally created in behalf of the Pentagon, and whose technicians were facetiously dubbed M.I.T. RE-jects, worked on complex Air Force electronic systems. It accumulated several buildings in Bedford, Massachusetts, a branch at Colorado Springs near the North American Air Defense headquarters, and several field sites. Among the nonprofit defense research contractors, Mitre ranked fourth in 1962, with $29,481,000 worth of business for the year.

The Navy's OEG, oldest and smallest of the organizations, works in a sealed-off section of the Pentagon. It rarely produces anything for the public. Similar to the OEG is the WSEG, or Weapons Systems Evaluation Group, an amalgam of military officers, civilian officials of the Pentagon and the Atomic Energy Commission and scientists drawn from outside nonprofit institutions. While the work of these panels is officially sponsored, their reports are not always palatable, as we have seen in the ORO case. In another case, according to Edward L. Katzenbach, later a Deputy Assistant Secretary of Defense, an important WSEG study was withheld by the Joint Chiefs from the State Department although it was of the utmost importance.[11]

In 1956 the Defense Department looked with such favor on the service-sponsored nonprofit institutions that it subsidized a new one, the Institute for Defense Analyses. The IDA was set up by a consortium of eight colleges and universities to handle vital studies in disarmament, civil defense and various weapons systems. One of its attractions for the Defense Department was that outside contracting made it possible to hire scientists and technicians at rates of pay that were foreclosed in government service. For example, twenty-three of the eighty-seven professional staff members constituting the top one-third of IDA received salaries larger than the $25,000 a year received by the Secretary of Defense. Sixteen of them received $29,000 a year or more. The nonprofit institutions have attracted scientists who otherwise might hesitate to work directly for the government, although the security regulations are virtually the same. Nonprofit institutions also permit work to be carried on away from the spotlight of the press, which focuses naturally on the government and its key officials. At the same time these institutions have siphoned considerable talent away from university campuses.

The burgeoning of the think organizations has created some uneasiness in Congress. In two successive budget reports for the fiscal years 1962 and 1963, the House Appropriations Committee suggested some effort be made to cut them back. Some people feel it might be worthwhile to revive the old system of government arsenals and laboratories. Others believe it would be better to contract the work out to private competitive unsubsidized firms. "Is it true," Representative George H. Mahon, the chairman of the Defense Appropriations Subcommittee, once asked, "that to some extent the Department of Defense in general and the Air Force in particular are becoming more or less captives of these corporations?" Air Force officials took the position that they had found in these nonprofit corporations a more efficient, less-expensive means of doing research work than had been available in government laboratories or in private, profit-seeking industry.[12]

The Kennedy Administration was barely in office when it too expressed an awareness of the unseemly growth of the practice of contracting out research projects, while the government's own research facilities seemed to be neglected. The result was the so-called Bell report, the product of an interagency study under the direction of David E. Bell, then head of the Budget Bureau and later head of the Administration for International Development. The report reviewed the points of concern—that government was abandoning to outside contractors the management skills and power of decision which it should itself exert, that universities were undertaking research and development programs of a nature that interfered with their educational functions, that cost reimbursement contracts for research and development work on weapons and space systems lent themselves to insufficient controls over costs, that outside contracting was a device to circumvent civil service rules and regulations, particularly with respect to salary limitations; finally, that traditional distinctions between the public and private sectors were being blurred. Was a corporation like the Aerospace Corporation, government created and subsidized, a "public" or "private" agency?

The Bell report found that in recent years "there have been instances—particularly in the Department of Defense—where we have come dangerously close to permitting contract employees to exercise functions which belong to top Government officials"; that the government was having a hard time getting high-caliber scientists and administrators because not only private industry but the universities and nonprofit organizations holding government contracts were paying better; that the cumulative effect of contracting out research and development projects was to "erode the Government's ability to manage its own programs," and that some conflict of interest problems had developed with respect to the role of government advisers or members of controlling boards doing government-subsidized research who were also associated with institutions receiving government procurement contracts. As for the problem of the universities, the government report quite naturally, it seemed, stressed the helpfulness to the government of university research personnel and facilities.[13]

On the basis of the Bell report, the Kennedy Administration took steps to improve the situation in the government laboratories, exercise more control over the nonprofit organizations (although the Bell report stressed, "The principal advantages they have to offer are the detached quality and objectivity of their work") and to regulate situations of possible conflict of interest.

While the problem of the Federal impact on the universities has been hotly discussed on campuses across the country and other techniques of administering research projects also have been discussed within the government, few persons have questioned whether the massive assault on the research front is worthwhile. Commentators have recalled with ridicule the observation by a former Secretary of Defense that he was not interested in the other side of the moon. There appears to be universal faith in the idea expressed by one Pentagon official that "The deliberate application of research and development efforts is virtually certain to lead to the attainment of the objectives sought."[14] Indeed, very few of the defense projects are ever said to have "failed." In the defense field, Congress generally has accepted expenditures for developing new weapons with relatively little debate, on the premise that it is "better to be safe than sorry."

Yet many of the "successes" would have been considered catastrophic failures if undertaken in the private sector, if only because they would have brought financial ruin before final achievement. The history of some privately supported jet transports illustrates the point. It is not surprising therefore that although the Pentagon, for example, has spent some 60 percent of its research funds in the private sector, the "free" enterprises have been so hesitant in investing their own money in research that they have occasionally received scoldings, typified by the remarks of Lieutenant General Arthur G. Trudeau, Chief of Army Research and Development. Addressing the American Management Association, he said:

"Basic research is crucial. But simply to increase government funds is not the answer to the problem. The reverse side of that coin is the need for more and more dynamic and realistic support by private enterprise—industry, educational institutions and scientific foundations. I want to state my belief right here that, in the broad field of basic research, privately funded effort in some areas today is clearly inadequate. In my opinion, certain segments of industry should review their policies with respect to research and cease leaning exclusively on government support in this field. The more they are government-oriented, the more this is true. Historically, in free societies, profit is proportional to risk. Only at his peril can the entrepreneur invert the equation, saying, 'I'll take the profit; you, the government, take the risk,' but some are doing this."[15]

On the other hand, leaders of private enterprise have argued that the government is absorbing so many of the professional scientists and engineers that this is impairing economic growth. Richard Morse, the former civilian head of Army research, appeared before the Senate's Select Committee on Small Business and charged that the government was creating "a scientific WPA" with its federalized research and development projects. He said these did not contribute to commercially practical ideas or to the education and training of management talent in the commercial field.[16] "Industry relies on our universities for both its scientists, engineers and trained management talent," he continued. "Under the impact of more recent Federal funding, many of our larger universities may have been unduly influenced by their desire for growth at the expense of teaching, and, in fact, are operating business activities which could far more appropriately be undertaken by industry. While we should enhance our basic research activities consistent with the limited availability of scientific talent capable of doing basic research, our universities should not become involved with large development programs which more appropriately should be performed by industry."[17]

Speaking for the Chamber of Commerce, Helge Holst, corporate counsel of Arthur D. Little, Inc., an industrial research firm headed by Major General James M. Gavin, a former Army research chief, made a similar point in an appearance before the Congressional Joint Economic Committee. Research and Development usually creates new products and thus contributes to full employment and a rising standard of living, he said. "Unfortunately," he went on, "the evidence is overwhelming that the nation's limited R & D resources have been increasingly diverted from civilian industrial purposes to government programs, primarily military and space developments. Without denying the necessity for strong military defense, and admitting the prestige value of space accomplishments, it is nevertheless desirable to recognize the extent of the diversion of R and D from efforts contributory to the goals of full employment and a rising standard of living."[18]

While President Lyndon B. Johnson has claimed that "our national space program already has produced more than 3,000 new products and processes of private commercial potential,"[19] others have questioned the cheerful assumption that the massive investment in space-military research would inevitably "spin off" a rewarding array of civilian by-products. In fact, President Kennedy observed in his economic message to Congress in 1963 that the defense, space and atomic energy programs were absorbing two-thirds of the trained people available for scientific and technical research. "In the course of meeting specific challenges so brilliantly, we have paid a price by sharply limiting the scarce scientific and engineering resources available to the civilian sectors of the economy," the President said.

Contrary to President Johnson's assurance, the space-military developments appear to grow more and more remote from civilian needs. "Despite the popular impression, industry at large has been relatively slow to introduce new products arising from the atomic energy, missile or space technologies," the National Academy of Sciences' National Research Council has concluded. "The reasons are many and vary from firm to firm and among different industries. Economists and businessmen cite as the major inhibiting factors the uncertainty of the profitable return required to attract risk capital and the need for a return on investment within a relatively short time span."[20] Dr. Jerome B. Wiesner, President Kennedy's science adviser, observed before a Congressional committee, "There is not nearly as direct an application of an Atlas booster to the civilian economy as there was of the B-52 to the 707 [transport plane]."

The increase in the supply of scientists and engineers for Research and Development was expected to be 27,000 in 1963, Dr. J. Herbert Holloman, Assistant Secretary of Commerce for Science and Technology, has observed, adding, however, that the increase in space Research and Development alone would require 25,000 additional scientists and engineers. "From now on forward," Dr. Holloman warned, "in terms of all our national goals, it appears we will have to rob Peter to pay Paul. Some goals are going to be achieved at the expense of other equally vital ones. This may be unavoidable— but the important point is that we recognize that it is happening and that we face up to the urgent necessity to do something now that will enable us to meet all our national commitments."[21]

Dr. Holloman thus struck a note that appears to reflect the consensus, whether on the campus, in institutional nonprofit research organizations or in private industry: let us recognize what is happening! "No more significant change has occurred in the world of higher education in recent times," Dr. Pusey said at Harvard. The Bell report echoed: "The effects of the extraordinary increase in Federal expenditures for research and development, and the increasing reliance on the private sector to perform such work, have been very far reaching."

IX

————————————————————————————☆

Free Enterprise and National Defense

"In the new warfare, the engineering factory is a unit of the Army, and the worker may be in uniform without being aware of it."
—HAROLD LASKI

How free is free enterprise?

About 25,000 privately owned industrial facilities across the nation operate under security regulations devised by the Pentagon and carefully checked by visiting military teams.[1] More than four million industrial employees have been required to obtain security clearances over a ten-year period.[2] In 1963 the Pentagon issued a manual "for the purpose of establishing uniform security practices within industrial plants or educational institutes and all organizations and facilities used by prime and subcontractors having classified information of the military departments or certain foreign governments in their custody." The manual has seventy-seven pages of detailed regulations on how to handle classified materials, check employees, supervise visitors and other admonitions normally associated with military installations. Big corporations have found the "industrial security officer," who previously worried mainly about pilferage, vandalism, embezzlement, sabotage and fire, an increasingly important member of management. As in wartime employees wear lapel badges, sign in and out of certain areas of their plants and perform their tasks under constant surveillance. The situation recalls the prediction by Harold Laski that "In the new warfare, the engineering factory is a unit of the Army, and the worker may be in uniform without being aware of it."[3]

The problem of security has become so vast that in the fall of 1962 the American Society for Industrial Security had 2,490 members with chapters in forty-eight states.[4] What troubles many of these security men, it appears, is that they now have multiple responsibilities—to their superiors in management, to their fellow employees and to the government. "The security officer has to exercise company loyalty and still think like a government security officer," one of them commented. "If you don't think like a government supervisor, you jeopardize your company's defense contracts." A spokesman for one firm said that his company could lose 60 percent of its business overnight if a military agency should become dissatisfied with its security program and withdraw clearance of its facilities. In the summer of 1962 all pending new military contracts for Westinghouse Electric Company's Baltimore plant were held up when "discrepancies" were uncovered in a routine Navy inspection of the plant.[5] According to an article in *Business Week*, management is not happy when a key employee is required to act on so marked an outside loyalty. "But this is part of the price of doing business with the government," sighed one business executive. As a consequence, security officers, operating under guidance from military authorities and often to the displeasure of company officers, have taken over substantial portions of the functions of personnel divisions. In theory, they are not supposed to hire and fire. In practice, their word often is law. "If security frowns at a prospective employee, we won't touch him even if he is a Nobel Prize winner," said one company executive.

Fear of being chided or even punished for failing to meet the Pentagon's security requirements has compelled some firms to enforce military-type security regulations throughout the entire company, instead of limiting these only to the defense areas. As a consequence, production, marketing and promotion chiefs bristle when they find good men for important jobs being kept in "deep freeze" for weeks and even months while references are being cleared in the same way that clearance is required for government work itself, that is, with elaborate checks into the backgrounds of the prospective employees.

The resultant picture of a large portion of American industry being policed by the government conflicts with the image of independence nurtured in the folklore of American free enterprise. If the need to protect national security is unanswerable, however, defense industrialists have found other irritations that put them at the mercy of Washington defense policies and changing military technologies. The arms industry of America has become permanent, but permanent only, it appears, in over-all spending. Each individual military manufacturer may find himself blessed with sudden riches or on the brink of disaster as weapons objectives shift. The impact on the community where the manufacturer's plant is located is almost immediate and dramatic. At Denver, Colorado, onetime Rocky Mountain trading post and cattle town, the annual stock show still opens with a cowboy parade. But the barren-looking plain east of the city is the site of a Titan missile complex of underground silos, and the Martin Company's production line has brought more jobs and money than Denver ever contemplated. A television program produced these interviews:

Representative Peter Dominick, a Republican: "Well, the whole Denver area has an enormous amount of defense installations which have come in—I think—within the last fifteen years. The added salaries and income which they bring in have, of course, contributed to the general welfare of that community, and I think it's had some impact in avoiding some of the rather bad effects of recessions which have gone on over the past six years."

A real estate entrepreneur: "We're building houses in Cherry Wood Village, some 750, and they're a semi-custom-type home ranging in price from $17,000 to $25,000. In our first filing we sold to approximately 50 percent Martin personnel, so, as you can see, they've had a very decisive effect upon our company."

A banker: "We've run several estimates of numbers of depositors that are direct Martin employees and feel that from our information probably 25 to 30 percent of our total deposit numbers are Martin employees."

An economist: "I think the Martin Company installation here in Denver has had several effects. First of all, of course, the direct impact total is something in excess of twelve thousand employees. In the manufacturing industry in Denver that is considerable. It's now by far the largest single manufacturing enterprise in the metropolitan area. Secondly, there have been other effects from the standpoint of requirements the Martin Company has had in supporting industry, such as job shop welders, heat-treating, machine shops. These have introduced new technology on the part of the service industries in metropolitan Denver—both manufacturing and warehousing—which gives Denver a base from which it can supply other nondefense, as well as other defense industries, which five years ago it did not have."

A subcontractor: "We are subcontractor to the Martin K. Eby Company here and the Martin K. Eby Company is a subcontractor to the Martin Company. The Martin Company is considered prime contractor to the Air Force—so you have a long chain of command."

Martin Miller, County District Attorney: "Before the Martin Company came into the Denver area we were a two-or-three-industry establishment town. Wages were not low, but they weren't high either. The Martin Company brings in a great demand for specialists, plumbers, mechanics and electric people—not just simply college-trained, but the production people. This has had a tremendous impact on the community. The Martin Company has created new shops, a demand for new stores, new housing; new schools are going up and the entire feeling is that the Martin Company is— well, it's just like having a direct Federal subsidy, that's what it is."[6]

But at another Martin Company plant, in Baltimore, the reverse impact was evident. There the TV interviewers found unhappy men and women at a plant that was built to produce aircraft, but now the Martin Company, after fifty years of pioneering with planes, has given up producing aircraft to devote itself entirely to missiles. The facility in Baltimore was not designed for missiles. The total work force was reduced by seven thousand within a period of four years. In a single month, fifteen hundred workers were laid off. The TV interviews were as follows:

A worker, seated with his wife: "I've been working at Martin's for ten years and then two years before that. And all at once, the thing drops out. Nothing."

The wife: "I don't know. I just know that the bottom can fall out of government work and that's it. I mean, one day it's here and next day it's gone. We came here in 1948. Why, everything was going! And we've seen this place build up. One time here there was one schoolhouse; now there's three elementaries and three junior high. We've seen it come up like that, and then one time this Middle River Church was in another building—they have a big church now. And then all at once it's all gone, and we don't know where the people are going to."

Not only big businesses but small businesses throughout the country rise and fall in accordance with the garrison economy. For example, a modest-sized machinery fabricator in Birmingham, Alabama, won a $335,000 contract in mid-1961 to build steel containers for the Army's Little John missile. The order, along with other military business, more than doubled the total production volume of the firm. The owners, believing their break into the big time had occurred, erected a $77,000 plant addition to their factory. They soon regretted that they had ever won the first contract. A year afterward, when they sought to continue their container work, they found themselves underbid by 30 percent by a Virginia firm which got the contract. In thirty subsequent bids, the Birmingham firm was unsuccessful. In April, 1963, their plant addition was silent and the owners of the firm were saddled with $690 monthly payments on a loan they took out to finance the initial construction.[7]

Nevertheless, like moths around a flame the small businesses continue to seek the brilliance of defense industry stoking furnaces, fed annually by more than $25 million in procurement contracts. The Pentagon in the sixties buys more than two million items a year, ranging from shoelaces to submarines. The Defense Department's seven million separate contractual transactions a year are multiplied several times in subcontracts that spread the military business throughout the country. Under a special plan, dubbed "Operation Booster," Army, Navy and Air Force officials are admonished to disperse small business awards wherever possible. The law specifically forbids "the payment of a price differential on contracts . . . for the purpose of relieving economic dislocations." Thus the government has found it hard to control the clustering of defense business with certain big firms and in certain geographical areas.

But it is possible under the law to create some spread in these contracts through the so-called "set-asides" for small business, by definition a business with five hundred or fewer employees. By 1965, it is expected that the spread of defense business, as a result of special provisions, will provide small businesses with $10 billion out of the total defense procurement.

Small American businessmen, no less than their big counterparts, complain about the difficulty of doing business with Uncle Sam— the red tape, the costly delays, changing designs and complicated specifications that are difficult to interpret and difficult to satisfy. "Military subcontracting is a wild, brutal battle," said the president of a firm in Orlando, Florida, near the huge Martin-Marietta plant. "Bidding is so close, work becomes a matter of survival instead of profit." Yet there is no lack of defense contractors. The successful counterpart to the unsuccessful Birmingham defense contractor was a onetime awning manufacturer in Miami. He made silicon-coated Dacron radome covers and halved his overhead from 35 percent of sales volume to 13 percent. "This helps us get more business," the company head enthusiastically told a *Wall Street Journal* reporter. "Where we once needed a 40 percent markup to make a profit, we now get the same profit with a 25 percent markup and can quote lower prices."[8]

A few outstanding examples of contemporaries who have waxed big and powerful in defense business have provided sufficient incentive for small businesses despite the teeter-totter fortunes of many of them. The Winfield, Alabama, Manufacturing Company, producers of cotton trousers and jackets, started out as a new business in 1960 and by 1963 had three hundred employees; Brown Engineering Company, in Huntsville, Alabama, jumped from three employees in 1954 to 2,700 in 1963; Northwestern Motors Company,

Eau Claire, Wisconsin, doubled its dollar volume of business from $1.5 million to $3 million in eighteen months.[9]

Virtually every community in America is supported in part by the economic radiation of the defense program. In words that were reminiscent of, but not intended to reinforce, General Eisenhower's observations about the "military-industrial complex," Secretary of Defense McNamara told Congress: "We are aware that the award of new defense contracts and the establishment of new defense facilities in a particular area can make the difference between prosperity and depression."[10] The Secretary did not at that time mention the unashamed struggle for defense contracts, particularly in the aerospace industry, that was exemplified in the titanic competition for a potential $7 billion contract for a new Air Force-Navy biservice jet fighter plane, the F-111. This was the controversial TFX (tactical fighter, experimental) airplane contract which precipitated a lengthy Congressional hearing. Along with the TFX hearings (which will be discussed later), another airplane contract came under fire and was subjected to a Congressional investigation. This was for the V/STOL (vertical or short take-off and landing) aircraft, known as the X-22. The discussion of the merits of the awards was drowned in partisan debate. But the cases forced attention to the procedures of defense contracting and what is known as "source selection." These have developed against a background of conflicting impulses. One factor has been the nation's historic concern over "war profiteering." The other has been its readiness, proved repeatedly, to throw out the rule book in the interests of national defense.

The simplest form of contract calls for a fixed price for a specific quantity of specifically described goods. But when the government operates in an atmosphere of emergency, it may choose to attract producers with CPFF (cost plus fixed fee) contracts, guaranteeing the bidder a profit above costs. In wartime, the device was used to finance the construction of new plants and to cover expensive shifts in requirements. In peacetime, however, the public has resented the fixed fee guarantee, regarding it as a built-in profit. And the Kennedy Administration particularly sought to replace the CPFF with incentive contracts. The form of any contract inevitably is complicated and many of the details must be negotiated. In fact, officials have learned from experience that due to changes imposed by technology as well as exaggerations by eager designers even the costs that are estimated in tough negotiations must be modified in the light of experience. Thus when the competitors for the V/STOL development contract estimated their initial costs for two models around $14 million, the Navy immediately estimated it would come to more than $20 million. And the first contract was concluded at $22 million.

Related to the type of contract to be let is the degree of competition considered feasible in selecting a contractor. Sometimes there is only a single logical source for a weapon. In such a case it is considered cheaper and more efficient to negotiate a contract than to open it to competitive bidding. But even in negotiated contracts there are many competitive elements. The terms "competitive" and "negotiated" are defined in regulations. Thus firms may compete bitterly for the opportunity to be considered for a contract, but the contract itself is technically regarded as negotiated if the detailed terms are negotiated following the initial competition. A Defense official explained the procurement process in this way: "If a new gun is desired, the Pentagon calls a meeting of potential bidders, explains its ideas and invites proposals. Responses, let us say, come from eleven bidders. The Pentagon then selects three of them and asks them to produce a weapons prototype. The samples then are tested and the final choice made. If the actual price is negotiated after the selection, the contract is considered to be negotiated."[11]

In huge or complex weapons systems such as a bomber, missile, submarine or even the controversial TFX airplane, the possible number of original bidders is obviously small. A decision must be made fairly early in the contracting process whether the manufacturers are expected to produce and compete with an actual plane —as was the case with the highly successful Navy F-4B jet plane— or produce only a set of estimates—as in the competition to get missiles contracts. The presentation of estimates, sometimes assailed as "brochuremanship," has been relied upon increasingly as military costs have risen. In the TFX case, the Defense officials were so concerned with the possibilities of unanticipated costs they introduced a new form of competition which they labeled "program definition." In this competition, after all but two firms were scratched, officials and experts of the Pentagon were assigned as teams to work with the two selected competitors and to cooperate with each of them as if they had already been assigned the contract. Thus the competition was carried out on paper in an effort to avoid the cost of producing two planes for competition in the air. The rival firms were each paid a fee during the paper competition, but this was much smaller than the fees that would have been paid each rival to produce competing flight models.

Aside from the political charges that developed in the TFX case, it illustrated the intimacy between the military services and the defense contractors. The Pentagon's Director of Research and Engineering once pointed out: "In the civilian economy the product is produced first and the customer decides to buy the product or not. . . . Survival of the United States depends upon the high quality of the military weapons which are produced and in what numbers. This is not the case for vacuum cleaners or washing machines. It is thus clear that a much closer partnership between the government, particularly the defense contractors—almost a symbiotic relationship—is needed, a relationship very different from that which can prevail between the producers and consumers of automobiles."[12]

Claude Witze, an authoritative writer on Air Force affairs, expressed pride that weapons systems defending the free world were based on concepts that originated on the drawing boards of private corporations. Not surprisingly, the writer said, General Eisenhower had described military-industrial relations as a "complex." To some it was a wonder that the military-industrial relationship was not even closer. "There have been serious discussions," he went on,

some of them on paper, of the plausibility of having the contractor go a step beyond the design, development and production of weapons systems. His support already is essential to maintenance—he has technical representatives at every major air base and missile launching site, including those under the sea—and the only phase of the life of a system where he has no mission is the actual destructive use of the weapons.[13]

Witze added that the "extreme" would be to have a contract between the government and a private consortium providing for expert operation of the weapon system under the direction of a military command. This, he said, "is so remote as to be ridiculous." Yet, he added, in a tenor that suggested he did not consider it so ridiculous after all, the defense contractor is knowledgeable "across the whole spectrum of military operations." He added: "The designer and builder of a modern system must be familiar with enemy capabilities, he must know what future wars will be like, and how to fight them."[14]

The foregoing is a perfect example of how the proper boundary between public and private spheres of interest and responsibility has become blurred in the permanent mobilization of the post-World War II era. The Bell report to the President on government contracting for Research and Development, previously cited, observed: ". . . the developments of recent years have inevitably blurred the traditional dividing lines between the public and private sectors of our nation. A number of profound questions affecting the structure of our society are raised by our inability to apply the classical distinctions between what is public and what is private."

Defense contractors themselves are aware of and concerned over this phenomenon. The most conspicuous group of contractors, the Aerospace Industries Association of America, Inc., asked the Stanford Research Institute, Menlo Park, California, to study the industry-government relationship in the aerospace field. One of its reports observed that the line between "public" and "private" was being breached from both sides, due largely to three interrelated but separate patterns of action. First: the "growth in power and influence of many private organizations that is occurring as a natural outgrowth of our maturing technical-economic system. As a result these organizations achieve a greater capacity to affect the public welfare." Private firms become "vested with public interest," become subject to increasing regulation and control, but also are assisted by the government in their capacity to grow. Second: "the delegation of public authority to private agencies," particularly when a single firm or group of firms is made responsible for an entire weapons system. Third: "the efforts of private organizations to identify themselves with the public good and demonstrate their public responsibility." This "reflects their search for a new legitimacy for their endeavors to replace the one that was once provided by the 'rights' of ownership."

"The elaborate arguments advanced to 'prove' that private corporations are truly responsible to the public are so familiar that they hardly need repetition," the Stanford report commented with remarkable candor for a study prepared for such corporations.

Through skillful public relations programs, the corporation is cast in an image of public concern and its actions justified in terms of some view of the "public interest." Stockholders are described as "public" owners; boards of directors as "public" representatives; corporate charters as acknowledgments of the "public" nature of the organization's purposes. The "public good" is advanced as the legitimate corporate aim.[15]

The mantle of public service may be assumed in order to forestall government intervention. But it often has the opposite effect. When private corporations are identified as operating in the public good, it is logical to demand special demonstrations of public responsibility. The consequence is often regulation.

In reaction, the private corporations supporting defense production have sought to evidence their good faith through "more frequent and vigorous efforts to influence government decisions," the report continued.

This has run the gamut from old-fashioned legislative lobbying to more sophisticated attempts to guide the bureaucracy, often from the inside. It has included attempts to effect the selection of key officials and the announcement of corporate stands on controversial public issues. The corporation has brought itself into politics in significant and often dramatic ways. The unfortunate thing is that whether public-spirited or self-serving, open or covert, such actions tend to obscure further the distinction between public and private institutions and to provide additional justification for the regulation of private corporate power.[16]

With all the antiprofiteering and security controls, both workers and managers in the defense industries must find it little different from working directly in the government. Yet the old-fashioned arsenal system has been considered inadequate in the post-World War II period; private companies are said to be more efficient than government arsenals, due to competition and the profit incentive.

This is the "American way." Some have argued that the United States has avoided large-scale peacetime armaments in the past so there really is no precedent. But the trend away from the arsenal system continues. Early in the Kennedy Administration, Dr. Harold Brown, the Defense Research and Engineering Chief, said the free enterprise system would be used "maximally" to permit the government's exercise of the best possible options. Yet private financing of weapons system development is considered impossible. Development costs can run into billions of dollars. A low rate of profit for speculative investment, risks of obsolescence and changes in government policy discourage private investment in defense.

Discussing this point, Witze, one of the most competent writers in his field, observed: "What they [the Administration] should say, and what Congress should acknowledge—possibly by revising the procurement legislation—is that characteristics of the customer and the product and the requirement for infallible technical capability narrows the source selection to a point where open competitive bidding is neither realistic nor practical."[17] Thus competition is found by its chief exponents to be an anachronism. The renegotiation law—which permits the government to reclaim any excessive profits accruing to the defense contractors—also disturbs the defense business community because, as Witze pointed out, it is really an out-of-date precaution against venality. The statutory profit limits and renegotiation laws grew out of abuses that existed when defense merchandise was primarily munitions and long before the auditing forces of the military had moved into the production plants.

But if profits have been low, where is the harm in renegotiation? And why the apparent fierce striving for defense dollars? At the time of the TFX airplane contract controversy General Dynamics had a backlog of government contracts of $2,065 million; Grumman, its partner in the contract, $315 million and contracts in process which would bring the total to more than $700 million; and Boeing, the loser in the competition, had a total backlog of $1,620 million of which $744 million was from nongovernment sources. "I feel that these companies have had tremendous government business and none has any special claim for any special favor from the government," observed Congressman Mahon, the chairman of the Defense

Appropriations Subcommittee, during a budget hearing. "Amen," echoed Representative Daniel Flood of Pennsylvania.[18] A hybrid arms industry, financed by the government, controlled by the government, but labeled free enterprise, is one of the characteristics of the military-industrial complex.

If the premises for a private military aerospace industry have seemed troublesome if not confusing, the naval industry is a perhaps more complicated problem. In 1962 Congress passed a law requiring that at least 35 percent of naval ship overhaul, repair and conversion work go into the private shipbuilding yards. The reasons given were that private builders were more efficient and, second, they needed the work. The Congressional action caused a furious debate on the merits of private versus government shipyards. Depending upon the advocate, including many members of Congress who came before the House Appropriations Subcommittee to argue in behalf of the yards in their districts, government ownership of shipyards was "socialistic" or private ownership was greedy. Said Edwin M. Hood, vice president of the shipbuilders council: "Oddly enough, this complex exists half free and half nationalized, in contradiction to the free, competitive, economic system we cherish and strive to nourish. Oddly enough, we have the anomaly of nationalized industrial activity competing with private industry. If seminationalization is good for naval purposes, why, then, aren't all other industries furnishing weapons, aircraft, and other military matériel similarly nationalized?"

To which Representative Robert A. Leggett, of California, whose district included the Mare Island Naval Shipyard in Vallejo, retorted: "It sticks a little bit in the craw of myself and many of my fellow Vallejoans to now hear a few Johnny-come-lately alleged private shipbuilding companies claiming that the socialistic Democratic Administration should get out of the shipbuilding business and leave this area to good old private enterprise. The government's getting out of the shipbuilding business is like effecting postal service by competitive contracts, or farming out our Army and Navy on a soldier of fortune basis. . . . It just did not happen that our naval shipyard complex has thrived for better than a hundred years. Private enterprise has fouled the ball for decades."

When President Johnson took office, the naval shipyards found themselves again in the path of an economy drive. Repeated studies had shown that private yards can build and repair ships for less money than it costs to maintain naval yards. The private yards need no special facilities for Navy personnel and are not bound by Civil Service regulations regarding layoffs in slack times. In the past the naval yards have been maintained with arguments that they constitute a mobilization base for national emergency. John F. Griner, president of the American Federation of Government Employees, used it when he said: "The naval shipyards are too important an arm of our national defense to be judged wholly on standards which properly apply only to a profit-making enterprise."[19] That argument, reinforced by local political and economic influences, has been demolished by "cost-efficiency" standards. On the other hand shipbuilding costs in the private yards are so high in comparison with foreign countries that the government must subsidize merchant ship construction. Will it be found that when the government inevitably closes the naval yards such subsidies will have to be increased to permit the maintenance of the fleet? Once again, to what extent is a private enterprise a free enterprise when its existence depends on military contracting?

Both the relatively new aerospace industry and the shipbuilding industry that originated in colonial days exemplify the complicated, deep-rooted grip of the defense economy. From the time of Eli Whitney down to the end of the First World War, as Walter Millis has pointed out, the armaments industries in the United States were never more than an auxiliary to industry's main business of supplying civilian markets. Steel, shipbuilding and other industries might seek government contracts in slack time; holders of armaments patents might compete for contracts; but mostly the government rather than the industries pressed for military production. Out of the Second World War emerged a new phenomenon, multibillion-dollar private armaments industries, almost wholly dependent on government orders.[20]

As the Kennedy Administration military budgets rose spectacularly to $52.4 billion in the fiscal year ending June 30, 1964, the claim by a Columbia professor, Seymour Melmen, that it could be cut to $34 billion received some notice, although few endorsements. One aspect of Melman's study seems to deserve more serious attention than it has received. This deals with certain consequences of the military preoccupation of large sectors of the economy. The following points were made: that the American shipbuilding industry is becoming increasingly less competitive in the world market; that Belgian and French sources are increasingly supplying iron and steel for Midwestern industries; that the American heavy electrical machinery manufacturers are competing with Europeans only through drastic price-cutting; that the American machine tool industry, once a world leader, has dropped to fourth or fifth place in the volume of its output; that the United States typewriter industry, which in 1948 supplied virtually all United States requirements, now supplies only 60 percent, while the remainder are imported from Europe; that with the notable exception of earth-moving equipment, the machinery-producing industries of America are growing obsolescent; that the American machine tool industry, in particular, is obsolescent.

The differences in industrial growth between countries of the European Common Market and the United States were indicated in part by these estimates: that in 1960 United States military expenditures amounted to 9.2 percent of the Gross National Product, while the average among Common Market members was 4.2 percent; that the expenditures in the United States on machinery and equipment was 5.4 percent of the Gross National Product, while the expenditures for this purpose among members of the Common Market totaled 10.2 percent.[21]

An impressive observation in the foregoing analysis of the consequences of military orientation of a large part of American industry is this: One of the characteristics of military products is that they are end products. Once they are made, there is little use for them except in war. The fact that more than half of all research and development is paid for by the United States Government has caused considerable concern among educational and scientific leaders. Its consequences for American business also has drawn attention. In a report to the Senate Small Business Committee, in August, 1962, Assistant Democratic Majority Leader Hubert Humphrey said:

In Germany, 85 per cent—85 cents out of every research dollar—is private, and less than five cents of that goes into the civilian economy, so that today the German plant competition for world markets of civilian goods is being automated, modernized, equipped in the latest and best fashion, and new products are developing, while we are developing new wrappings. . . . What is happening to our civilian economy as we plow more and more of our scientific personnel, our brains, into atomic energy for military purposes? Where are we going to end up in this trade competition with these Belgians and these Dutch, who are clever, who are spending more money for civilian aspects and will develop products cheaper, better and more serviceable?

Senator Humphrey's question seems to be answered by Professor Melman's study.

The Military and Politics

I

"The necessary and wise subordination of the military to civil power will be best sustained when life-long professional soldiers abstain from seeking high political office."
—General Dwight David Eisenhower,
January 22, 1948

One of the stereotypes of the military role in American life is that it is divorced from politics. High military officers admit or even boast that they have not voted in elections throughout most of their careers. Frequently they have refused to identify themselves with any political party. Many who formally entered political life expressed indifference to party labels. George Washington was never a party candidate and never acknowledged any party, although he was identified with the Federalists. Grant admitted that the only vote he ever cast was for a Democrat (Buchanan), but he accepted the Republican nomination in 1868. After his election, Grant said,

"I am not the representative of a political party, though a party voted for me."

In more recent times, General Eisenhower refused several times to say whether he was a Democrat or a Republican. In 1948 there was a short-lived move to give both the Democratic and Republican nominations to Eisenhower. Eisenhower, with apparent sincerity, would have loved to get both nominations as an endorsement of his nonpolitical nature. When the political bug finally bit him, he proved adequately partisan, however. As a matter of fact, Representative Joe Martin, Republican of Massachusetts, knew that Eisenhower was a Republican. Martin was present when the general was introduced to an audience as Eisenhower of Denison, Texas, and the general corrected it to Eisenhower of Abilene, Kansas. "I knew then that Eisenhower was a Republican," Martin said.[1]

In the course of American history, certain arguments have been made to reinforce the premise that there is no room for partisan political activity by the military. James Buchanan, in losing the Democratic nomination in 1852, attacked the Whig candidacy of General Scott with these words: "What fatal effects would it not have on the discipline and efficiency of the Army to have aspirants for the Presidency among its principal officers? How many military cliques would be formed? . . . . In times of war and danger what fatal consequences might result to the country from the fact that the President and the Commanding general of the Army are rival and hostile candidates for the Presidency."[2]

The concern expressed by Buchanan was not entirely academic. During the Mexican War President Polk, a Democrat, sought to counter the popularity of General Taylor by proposing to supersede him with a Democratic Senator, although the latter was without military experience. Abraham Lincoln was accused several times during the Civil War of discriminating against General McClellan for political reasons. When President Wilson passed over General Wood in assigning command of the American Expeditionary Forces in World War I, he was said to fear that Wood would cover himself with glory and attain the Presidency. Wilson was similarly criticized when he refused to give Theodore Roosevelt a command. In World

War II, Governor Dewey joined those who charged that President Roosevelt had withheld men and supplies from MacArthur to weaken a possible Presidential boom for the General.[3]

Despite the American predilection for sending men with military reputations to the White House, the "martial talent," as Sidney Hyman has described it, has been inconclusive in Presidential politics. Many military commanders failed as candidates of major parties. Some of them, however, lost to other military men. General Winfield Scott, hero of the Mexican War, was the highest-ranking officer in the Army when he lost to Pierce. Grover Cleveland, who dodged military service by hiring a substitute in the Civil War, a common practice, lost to General Benjamin Harrison in 1888 but beat the general four years later. Admiral George W. Dewey, the hero of Manila Bay, had a promising boom going for him in 1900, but his bid turned futile when he said: "If the American people want me for this high office, I shall be only too willing to serve them. . . . Since studying this subject I am convinced that the office of President is not such a very difficult one to fill. All you have to do . . . is take orders from Congress."[4]

For nearly twenty years after the Civil War the White House was occupied by men who had been generals in the Union Army. Theodore Roosevelt, famous in the Spanish-American War, was followed by six Presidents without military experience. General Leonard Wood, a hero of World War I, received substantial big business backing but failed in his drive for the Republican nomination in 1920. Paralleling the Dewey effort was a mild boom for General John J. "Black Jack" Pershing. But if Pershing had any temptations in this direction, they must have withered after Heywood Broun, the newspaper columnist, wrote: "It would seem rather foolish to me for any party that hopes to win an election to nominate a man who would go to the polls with the votes of four million veterans solidly against him.[5]

While high-ranking military men as a rule have proclaimed themselves "above politics," only one ever flatly and permanently rejected the opportunity to enter the White House. William Tecumseh Sherman, Civil War general, in a remark that has become a classic formula, said in a wire to the Republican convention of 1884: "If nominated, I will not accept; if elected, I will not serve." Earlier, during the Civil War, he said in a letter to H. W. Halleck: "If forced to choose between the penitentiary and the White House for four years, I would say, 'the penitentiary, thank you.' "[6] General George Marshall quietly squelched an effort to start a Presidential boom in his favor during World War II, when there was still some speculation regarding President Roosevelt's fourth-term candidacy. In 1947 Marshall said: "I will never become involved in political matters . . . I never could be drafted." General Douglas MacArthur, on the other hand, courted the Presidency several times.

It is apparent that General Eisenhower's instinctive reaction to talk of his candidacy was incredulity. In his Presidential memoirs, Eisenhower recalls that the "earliest serious suggestion" made to him to become a Presidential candidate came from Virgil Pinkley, then a United Press news correspondent in North Africa, in 1943. "Virgil," Eisenhower retorted, "you've been staying out in the sun too long."[7] Later on during the North African campaign Eisenhower received a newspaper clipping from his friend George Allen which reported that an American Legion post had passed a resolution endorsing him for President. "Baloney!" Eisenhower scrawled on the clipping, asking it be returned to the sender. "Why can't a simple soldier be left alone to carry out his orders? And I furiously object to the word 'candidate'—I ain't and I won't." In June, 1945, Eisenhower told reporters he had "no political ambitions at all" and "I'd like to go further than Sherman in expressing myself on this subject." A couple of years later he said: "I wouldn't have the effrontery to say I wouldn't be President. No one has asked me."

In one of his calls on President Truman as Chief of Staff, General Eisenhower discussed politics and heroes. President Truman, having made up his mind to run in 1948, asked Eisenhower what the general's intentions were. Eisenhower cited a letter he had written to a friend which had previously been released. Eisenhower wrote: "The necessary and wise subordination of the military to civil power will be best sustained . . . when life-long professional soldiers, in the absence of some obvious and overriding reasons, abstain from seeking high political office."[8] But later on his lofty disclaimers slid downhill.

General Eisenhower was the only President besides Grant who was graduated from a military academy. He was the only President besides Taylor who spent most of his adult career in uniform. He was the only complete military professional to take residence in the White House who had been trained and reared to command by the General Staff. Inevitably, in 1950 the question developed as to Eisenhower's fitness on the basis of an entire career in military service. He had spent twenty-seven years as an obscure Army officer, eight years as a military figure of international renown. Early in his career, in a near-parallel with Grant, who actually left the service, Eisenhower thought of resigning his commission and going into private business or newspaper work. When he finally made his name in the Allied victory, there were many critics of his military prowess. But he was acclaimed for his political genius, his ability to handle the rival generals and the rival nations that made up the Western Allied forces. Instead of a nickname like "Blood and Guts" or "Old Fuss and Feathers" or "Old Hickory" or "Black Jack," his nickname was an unmilitary diminutive, "Ike." His personality was described by Richard Rovere as "standard American." He thus fitted neatly a popular American conception of a President as a man of the people and was elected on that basis.

II

"My dear Secretary, I write to suggest that you request and advise all officers of the service, whether active or retired, to refrain from public comment of any kind upon the military or political situation on the other side of the water. . . . It seems to me highly unwise and improper."
                    —President Woodrow Wilson, letter to Secretary
                        of War Lindley M. Garrison, August, 1914

"It is inappropriate for any members of the Defense Department to speak on the subject of foreign policy."
                    —Secretary of Defense Robert S. McNamara

Political activity by military men has not been limited to Presidential candidacies. "The average career officer learns of his dependence upon 'politics' from the moment he solicits his first application blank for a service academy," observed that master politician, former President Harry Truman.[9] As military men rise in rank and responsibility, they come in contact with state and Federal governments. They meet politicians and their supporters; inevitably they learn the refinements of political tactics and public persuasion. General Marshall, for example, the prototype of nonpartisan military men, owed his good relations with Congress to the influential Democratic politicians he met when he served as commander of the Illinois National Guard in 1933.[10] Forrest C. Pogue, in his authoritative biography of General Marshall, tells of the General's efforts to repress some of the influential men in Washington who were backing him for appointment as Army Chief of Staff: "Johnson wanted me for Chief of Staff, but I didn't want Woodring to know he was for me. Craig was for me but I wanted it kept from the President. Woodring was for me, but I didn't want the others to know. Someone mentioned me to Senator Guffey and asked about 'your fellow Pennsylvanian.' He didn't know me. Then he found he was a friend of my sister's. (He lived near her.) Said he wanted to come over; I said, 'I prefer to come to you.' I went up there. He was all excited. I had the damnedest time to keep him from seeing the President. I said you will destroy me. Let things take their course and perhaps I will get it."[11] As Alfred Vagts has written, "Group interests and personal interests force every Army to be 'in politics' in the larger sense." Professor Janowitz wrote: "The targets of [military] persuasion are no longer merely the leaders of opposing nations in wartime. The targets have become total populations, not only of unfriendly states, but of Allies, neutrals and *of one's own nation as well.*" In Washington the military services have lobbied no less strenuously than other elements of American society who were dependent upon Congress. Both Eisenhower and MacArthur had this lobbying experience.

Politicians know that what military men say, couched in professional jargon, can and does affect public attitudes. And the generals and admirals know it, too. When the Kennedy Administration took office, many of its new officials were disturbed by the active public roles of military leaders. The tone of many speeches by military men was hardly different from that of political partisans. American military officers, inhibited by tradition from open political activity, have developed a speechmaking technique that is politically effective. Whether a "tough" attitude should be displayed toward the Soviet Union, whether encouragement should be given to the Nationalist Chinese for attempted recovery of the mainland, whether Castro in Cuba should be squeezed or annihilated, whether Communism is merely an external threat or an internal danger as well, whether military forces are adequate for a particular kind of strategy, whether one can "do business" with some particular kind of Communist leader are subjects highly charged with domestic politics. When these subjects were discussed by military men, beneath a veneer of broad patriotic or "professional" platitudes, so that public exception to them became difficult, it troubled the new combination of politicians and intellectuals who took office in 1961. In addition, many of the officials of the liberally oriented Administration were highly suspicious of the basic conservatism of the military leaders they found in the Pentagon. General Eisenhower, it has been noted, replaced all the members of the Joint Chiefs of Staff for openly political reasons. While President Kennedy did not "clean house," he and Secretary of Defense McNamara undertook to reduce some of the political potential at the Pentagon.

"It is inappropriate for any members of the Defense Department to speak on the subject of foreign policy," Secretary McNamara said soon after he assumed his post. "That's a field that should be reserved to the President, the Secretary of State and other officials of the State Department. A military officer speaking on a matter of foreign policy is speaking about a field that lies outside his responsibility and yet as a representative of this government—an official representative—his words are taken as the policy of the government. That is inappropriate."

The Secretary soon discovered it was not easy to enforce what he called his "management philosophy." One of the working conditions at the Pentagon, he found, was that virtually all of its high officers were engaged in a remarkably active program of speechmaking. Pentagon records showed that Defense Department officials in the first eight months of the Kennedy Administration had made 1,050 speeches, of which 831 or 79.1 percent were by the military (of general and flag officer rank) and 219 or 20.9 percent by civilians. The summary did not include ninety-five speeches alone on Armed Forces Day. Compared with this torrent, "principal officers" of the State Department had given some 540 speeches during the same period.

There were, of course, 782 officials of various rank at the Pentagon compared with 254 at the State Department. But there was another explanation. The Pentagon's responsibilities cut across virtually every activity in the American social and economic spectrum. Its officials are intimately related with problems of military service for youth, contracts for industrial firms, education programs in colleges, scientific endeavors, engineering works and community relations in and around military bases, not to speak of the broader fundamental problems of war and peace. Representatives of the Pentagon, particularly the uniformed military heroes, are in greater demand as speakers before private patriotic societies, chambers of commerce, business conventions and similar gatherings than the relatively obscure "striped pants" professionals of the State Department, not to mention the even more obscure members of the other government departments.

Military regulations acknowledge that the American people have a "right to maximum information" concerning the armed services. In the Army, for example, regulations provide explicitly that "the impetus for release of information should come from the Army as part of a comprehensive effort to achieve information objectives." These objectives are to "gain public understanding and support of the Army's role in a sound national military program; inspire public confidence in the Army's ability to accomplish its mission now and in the future; develop public esteem and respect for the Army and Army personnel."

Inevitably, therefore, speakers for the Army—and the Air Force and the Navy—have seized every opportunity to "sell" the objectives of their particular service. The result in the fifties was a series of military "great debates" on public platforms. In some well-known debates, Navy spokesmen opposed the Air Force on the merits of aircraft carriers, Army spokesmen fought the Air Force on limited-war preparedness, spokesmen for each of the services engaged in a three-way competition for space weapons and missions. Service spokesmen did not openly attack rival service programs. They merely advocated their own. In the same way, they have not challenged incumbent Administrations when government policies hamper their individual service objectives. The military simply has related the objective "facts" in a way designed to advance the arguments of military leaders.

In interpreting foreign affairs in support of specific military programs, military speakers often have run afoul of their superiors in the government. The situation was not new in the Kennedy Administration. When resistance to the alleged "muzzling" of the military developed in 1962, a Pentagon historian dug out of the files General Order No. 60 of the War Department, published August 4, 1914, that contained the following text of a letter addressed to then Secretary of War Lindley M. Garrison:

MY DEAR SECRETARY:

I write to suggest that you request and advise all officers of the service, whether active or retired, to refrain from public comment of any kind upon the military or political situation on the other side of the water. I would be obliged if you would let them know that the request and advice comes from me. It seems to me highly unwise and improper that officers of the Army and Navy of the United States should make any public utterances to which any color of political or military criticism can be given where other nations are involved.

Cordially and faithfully yours,
WOODROW WILSON

The "military and political" situation to which President Wilson referred was World War I, which had broken out in Europe; and his "request and advice" applied to retired as well as active officers— most particularly to the celebrated naval philosopher, Rear Admiral Alfred Thayer Mahan. The silencing of Mahan was a *cause célèbre* in those days.

General MacArthur's publicly disputing the Administration's policies in the Korean War led to a tough memorandum from President Truman even in advance of the general's eventual dismissal. "In the light of the present critical international situation, and until further notice from me," President Truman advised his leading officials,

I wish that each one of you would take immediate steps to reduce the number of public speeches pertaining to foreign or military policy made by officials of the Departments and agencies of the executive branch. This applies to officials in the field as well as those in Washington. No speech, press release or other public statements concerning foreign policy should be released until it has received clearance from the Department of State. No speech, press release, or other statement concerning military policy should be released until it has received clearance from the Department of Defense. In addition to the copies submitted to the Departments of State or Defense for clearance, advance copies of speeches and press releases concerning foreign policy or military policy should be submitted to the White House for information.[12]

It was this eleven-year-old order, and not any new one, that Kennedy Administration officials claimed to be implementing in the "muzzling" furor of 1962. "The United States military," President Kennedy said at the time, "due to one of the wisest actions of our Constitutional founders, have been kept out of politics, and they continue their responsibilities, regardless of the changes of Administration. . . . There is no desire to restrain or prevent any military man from speaking. What we are concerned about, however, always is that they not be exploited for any partisan purpose. And I think, basically, it is for their own protection as well as the protection of the country."[13]

Shortly after President Kennedy's inauguration, it became known that a proposed speech by Admiral Arleigh A. Burke, Chief of Naval Operations, had been censored. This writer was somewhat involved in that story. I had heard from a member of the Air Force that a speech by General Thomas D. White, Chief of Staff of the Air Force, had been censored. I checked that report with Air Force spokesmen, who denied knowing anything about it. One of them said he had heard it was not White but Admiral Burke who had been censored. Checking the Navy, I could get nothing from the usual Navy sources. I finally located someone in a position to know and he told me that he would respond to my questions only on condition that I would not use the material if I could not get confirmation elsewhere; that is, he was prepared to confirm that the admiral's speech had been censored, but he exacted from me the promise, which I gave, that I would not write about it unless I received the information from an authorized source as well. Thus armed with knowledge of the accuracy of the report but still not free to use it, I went to Assistant Secretary of Defense Arthur Sylvester.

Sylvester unhesitatingly confirmed that action had been taken against speeches by both Admiral Burke and General White. Two passages in the White speech had been questioned but finally allowed to pass. Admiral Burke's speech, Mr. Sylvester explained, incurred official displeasure for the following reason: "because it dealt with matters of foreign policy in sensitive areas at a time of transition from one Administration to another and concerned policies on which the President and Secretary of State should be spokesmen."[14]

Burke's speech, described as "characteristically Burke," implied strongly that the Russians could not be trusted. Reacting to Soviet charges that United States planes were "buzzing" Soviet ships, Admiral Burke had questioned Soviet conduct in shooting down United States aircraft. He cited the RB-47 fliers, downed in the Barents Sea in July, 1960. However, it was precisely at the time the admiral proposed to make these remarks that the new Kennedy Administration was awaiting the successfully negotiated return from Moscow of two imprisoned RB-47 fliers. In fact, the fliers did return on the day I learned of the censorship.

I was told that the question of speeches by military leaders had already, in the brief tenure of the President, been under serious study "from the President down" and that Burke's speech in particular had "appalled" the White House. Yet the speech was little different from others the admiral and other military men had made before. Admiral Burke, in fact, had painstakingly gone to extra trouble to get his speech cleared by the new Administration. He had prepared it long before the scheduled speaking date, January 27. He had refrained from getting approval of the speech by the outgoing Eisenhower Administration because he hoped that with the new Administration's sanction he would be one of the first to make a major policy pronouncement. What the admiral did not realize was that the new Administration was not about to let a military man speak for it.

When my story of the censored Burke speech appeared on the front page of the *New York Times,* January 28, 1961, it provoked immediate political reaction. The late Senator Styles Bridges, chairman of the Senate Republican Policy Committee, assailed the "muzzling" and demanded: "Does this mean we are entering an era of appeasement with Communist Russia?" This was the opening cue for the furor, climaxed by Senatorial hearings, that resulted from the Administration's tightened control over statements emanating from the Pentagon. In April there was another incident. Rear Admiral Samuel B. Frankel, Deputy Director of Naval Intelligence, was ordered to revise a speech he had prepared for delivery before a group in Texas. Again Sylvester confirmed the censorship action, stressing that parts of the speech had questioned the usefulness of negotiations with Russians. He said that Admiral Frankel's speech had implied criticism of both former President Eisenhower and President Kennedy because of their readiness to negotiate with the Soviets.[15]

The Administration action was based publicly on the unchallengeable premise that uniformed personnel were not to be the spokesmen for Administration policies. In addition, however, the Kennedy officials recognized beneath the veneer of discussions of principles strong political implications. For, in the release of the RB-47 fliers, the agreements on Cuba that left Soviet soldiers on the island, and even the nuclear test-ban treaty of 1963, the Kennedy Administration's chief political opposition in foreign policy came in the argument that it was "soft" on Communism. To the extent that this argument could be reinforced with statements by men in uniform the Kennedy Administration saw political danger as well as obstacles to good management in government.

A campaign of military speechmaking was based ostensibly on a reported policy decision of the National Security Council, during the Eisenhower Administration, that military leaders ought to help "educate" the public in the implications of the "cold war." President Eisenhower and his aides appeared to have been impressed by the fanaticism of Communists as compared with apathy on the part of the American public. Eisenhower felt that military men could help to galvanize American public opinion.[16] President Eisenhower afterward denied the existence of any specific National Security Council directive on the subject. Nevertheless the "cold war" and "national strategy" seminars on and near military posts were widespread and caused alarm to the new civilian team in the Pentagon.

Typical of the seminars that disturbed the Administration was one at the Naval Air Station, Wold-Chamberlain Field, Minneapolis, on April 28 and 29, 1961. The commanding officer was listed as co-sponsor of the program with a committee of the Minneapolis–St. Paul Chamber of Commerce. The seminar was labeled "Project Action" and the official announcement said:

The purpose of Project Action is to inspire the citizens of this area to take an active part in the war against the danger that threatens our freedom and American way of life. The program of talks and presentations by nationally known leaders for the cause of democracy will bring to light the facts and figures concerning the rising crime rate, juvenile delinquency, drug addiction, the general degradation of morals, the complacent attitude toward patriotism and the *tremendous gains the Communist conspiracy is making in this country.*

Among the many letters that reached the Pentagon in the following days was one from a newspaper editor that said in part: "Perhaps someone can clear up for us our lack of understanding as to just how co-sponsorship of such activities fits in with the Navy mission, or the overall mission for that matter. It must be admitted that the local Project Action is politically partisan in a very real sense although the partisanship is not of the party label type."

Another example of activities that bothered the new Administration was that of Captain Kenneth Sanger, the commanding officer of the Sands Point Naval Air Station, Seattle, Washington. Captain Sanger with a "team" of aides toured his area, making speeches and showing films. One of the films was the controversial *Operation Abolition,* produced by the House Un-American Activities Committee, which depicted student riots in San Francisco. The message of the film was that Communist influences had infiltrated school life across the nation. Another film presented by the Navy team from Sands Point was *Communism on the Map,* indicating that the United States was engulfed in a world either socialist or Communist. Among those the film narrator held responsible for this condition were President Roosevelt for having recognized the Soviet Union and General George Marshall for having "made possible" the Communist conquest of China. The Navy commander's own speech apparently contained no political material. The impact of the total presentation, however, was clearly political.

Still another politically sensitive seminar was the Fourth Dimensional Warfare Seminar, in Pittsburgh, in April, 1961, which included in its list of supporters Lieutenant General Ridgeley Gaither, commander of the Second Army, and Major General Ralph Cooper. The seminar was sponsored and conducted by the Chamber of Commerce. Agencies of the Department of the Army provided "limited administrative support," such as assisting in the procurement of training material and authorizing training credit for Reserve officers who attended.[17] As in other seminars, a mixture of views was expressed during the program. Thus the Army, like the Navy, could justify its participation on the wholly American concept of hearing various opinions. One of the opinions the Pittsburgh seminar heard was that of retired Rear Admiral Chester A. Ward, who was reported in the local newspapers to have said that "some of the advisers now surrounding the President" have philosophies regarding foreign affairs "that would chill the average American." He mentioned by name in this connection Adlai E. Stevenson, the United States Ambassador to the United Nations, and George F. Kennan, then United States Ambassador to Yugoslavia.

Senator J. William Fulbright, chairman of the Senate Foreign Relations Committee, placed before the public the formal issue that developed from the spate of military speechmaking. A memorandum he wrote in August, 1962, at the suggestion of Secretary McNamara and his subsequent speech at the opening session of the National War College and Industrial College of the Armed Forces constituted a basic summary of the Administration's attitude toward the role of the military in public affairs.

The participation of military men in the various "alerts," "seminars," "freedom forums" and "fourth dimensional warfare seminars" served to identify men in uniform with "the fact of the program and at least to some extent, its content," Senator Fulbright said. Running through these programs, although the content varied, was a central theme that "the primary, if not the exclusive danger to this country, is internal communist infiltration." Past and current international difficulties, Fulbright went on, had been attributed to Comumnist subversion or "softness," "sellouts," "appeasements," etc. "Radical Right Wing speakers" had dominated the programs. The theses of these seminars, Fulbright continued, often was developed by equating social legislation with socialism and socialism with Communism. Much of the Administration's domestic legislative program, including continuation of the graduated income tax, expansion of Social Security, particularly medical care under Social Security and Federal aid to education, would, under the equating technique, be characterized as steps toward Communism. Such a view of the Communist menace pictured foreign aid and cultural exchanges as extremely wasteful if not actually subversive.

"There are many indications that the philosophy of the programs is representative of a substantial element of military thought, and has great appeal to the military mind," Senator Fulbright continued. "A strong case can be made logically that this type of activity is the inevitable consequence of such a [NSC] directive. There is little in the education, training or experience of most military officers to equip them with the balance of judgment necessary to put their own ultimate solutions—those with which their education, training and experience are concerned—into proper perspective in the President's total 'strategy for the nuclear age.' The propaganda activities may well become important obstacles to public acceptance of the President's program and leadership if they are not already."

Calling attention to the growing intensity of the "cold war," and President Kennedy's appraisal that the country faced "the burden of a long twilight struggle," which may not be solved "in our lifetime on this planet," Senator Fulbright continued: "The radicalism of the right can be expected to have great mass appeal during such periods. It offers the simple solution, easily understood: scourging of the devils within the body politic, or, in the extreme, lashing out at the enemy. If the military is infected with this virus of right wing radicalism, the danger is worthy of attention. If it believes the public is, the danger is enhanced. If by the process of the military 'educating' the public, the fevers of both groups are raised, the danger is great indeed. Perhaps it is farfetched to call forth the revolt of the French generals as an example of the ultimate danger. Nevertheless military officers, French or American, have some common characteristics arising from their profession and there are numerous 'fingers on the trigger' throughout the world. While this danger may appear very remote, contrary to American tradition, and even American military tradition, so also is the 'long twilight struggle' and so also is the very existence of an American military program for educating the public."

The Senator thus set the stage for that part of the Senate Preparedness Subcommittee hearings the following January that dealt with the role and responsibility of military officers in the domestic aspects of the "cold war."

The fundamental issue raised by the Fulbright memorandum, however, was not clearly defined or settled in the hearings. Most of the testimony, including that by General Eisenhower, fully endorsed the old platitudes: that the military must be subordinate to civil authority; that the military, however, were all fine, upstanding, highly qualified persons by and large; that military men might be useful in educating the public in "cold war" problems although the military should not engage in "politics." Some military men, like General Eisenhower, resented the "recent spate of attacks upon the competence and loyalty of the military," who, he charged, were the object of efforts to "thrust them, so to speak, behind an American Iron Curtain, ordered to stand mutely by as hostile forces tirelessly strive to undermine every aspect of American life." Since Eisenhower's Administration had been no less active in "muzzling" the military, his statement on this score from a position where he no longer held responsibility was clearly political, and unworthy of him.

Military men were also nettled by Senator Fulbright's suggestion that there was nothing in their education and training that equipped them with a requisite "balance of judgment" in a total strategy for the nuclear age. This appeared to ignore the contributions military men had been making to national strategy for many years. Yet the key question is not whether ranking military men are equipped by education and training to discuss public affairs, but whether by so doing they are engaging in partisan politics.

The Senate hearings centered at one point on the examples of official censorship of approximately 170 speeches by government officials, mostly military men. There were many instances of ordered changes in texts which, as the committee later judged in its report, defied "logical explanation." "There is evidence," the committee added, "of inconsistency, caprice, personal judgment, and even irresponsibility." By and large, expressions about Communism and the Soviet and Communist regimes that appeared to be "harsh and vigorous" were deleted by official censors from proposed speeches. Why? Study of the deletions justifies the conclusion that in addition to being "harsh and vigorous," many of the deleted phrases represented an aggressive approach to foreign affairs and a defeatist fear of Communist envelopment in domestic affairs that is characteristic of the extreme conservative wing of American political life. In this respect, Senator Strom Thurmond was close to being right in implying that many of the deletions were "political"; they *were* political to the same extent that the statements offered by the proposed speakers were political, even if, as a newspaperman had already noted, the partisanship was not "of the party label type."

An irony in the Kennedy Administration's campaign against politically potent speaking activities by military men was the fact that the Democratic party had profited from such activities during the Eisenhower Administration. In the great debates over national defense in the late fifties, military men repeatedly took to the public forum the arguments they had lost in the confines of the Pentagon. General Maxwell Taylor, as Army Chief of Staff, argued his case for limited-war preparedness in many speeches and articles, one of which was completely censored. So effective were the military's public arguments over policy during the Eisenhower Administration that the general in the White House lashed out one day against these "parochial generals." He might just as easily have said "political" generals.

It was obvious to the high officers who joined in the debates, carefully nurtured by the Democratic political opposition in Congress, that they were playing a political role. One day during one of the "missile gap" hearings I observed to a renowned officer that his latest statement had probably helped the Democrats more than several speeches by one of their candidates for the nomination. He grinned and said, "You get the idea, don't you?" The long-standing formal inhibitions placed on the American military, insofar as political predilections are concerned, have created a new form of military politics, peculiar to the American system. As Finer has pointed out, the American system "forces the military not only to speak but to establish relations with political forces."[18]

How significant is this? Finer observed that the pressure of the American system which compels the military to shout for its objectives "gives an impression of a vast military influence in government, whereas it is evidence of only a vast amount of necessitated noise." Much of the high-decibel rate can be attributed to the conflicting claims for attention by the separate services. Janowitz has commented: "The military profession is not a monolithic power group. A deep split pervades its ranks in respect to its doctrine and viewpoints on foreign affairs, a split which mirrors civilian disagreement."[19] Thus the service rivalries have been described as a safety valve insofar as any unified military assault on American public opinion and institutions might be concerned. To these observations, those who are concerned over the military involvement in politics can cite two points: one, changing technologies and increased Administration pressures are surely reducing the service distinctions and, inevitably, the service rivalries; two, American military men do appear to have some common political philosophies. In Janowitz' polls of military officers assigned to the Pentagon, most of them regarded themselves as "conservative."

If one accepts the notion that retired officers, who are freer to speak their opinions, reflect to any extent the political leanings of active military men, then Janowitz himself has made an interesting additional point:

. . . . the taboo against the regular officer entering partisan politics upon retirement remains powerful and essentially effective. Yet, since the end of World War II, there have been important exceptions. For the most part, these officers have been advocates of the absolutist doctrine, and have affiliated themselves with the extreme Right Wing of the Republican party. They give voice to the underlying sentiments which can become manifest during periods of extreme political frustration.[20]

The true criterion of partisanship cannot logically be limited to the existence of party labels. Yet any effort to silence the military would require a major alteration in the practice wherein military men are called upon to render public judgments. It is all part of the American way. The public has a "right to know" and military officers "a duty to tell." Commenting on the substantial public literature of military and civilian members of the Defense Department, Robert A. Lovett, a former Deputy Secretary of Defense, said: "I cannot escape the feeling that, as a government, we tend to talk too much. To be sure, we are an open society but we give the impression of being unbuttoned."[21] In an unbuttoned society, the military's involvement in partisan politics is demonstrable.

XI

The Military Lobbies

"The way to a man's 'aye' is through his stomach."
—SAM WARD, King of the Lobbyists

"I don't care how obstreperous a Congressman is toward a certain piece of legislation. If I once get him on a junket, I figure the odds have begun to shift in our favor. Our lobbying effectiveness is at its height, not here on Capitol Hill, but in the field where we get the Congressmen to 'see for themselves.' "
—Military legislative officer

The term "lobbyist" sprang etymologically from the medieval Latin word *lobbium,* a monastic walk or cloister; politically from the halls and corridors of the British House of Commons, where it applied without discrimination to job seekers, gossips and newsmen who congregated there; finally, its United States origins were traced by H. L. Mencken to 1829 when it appeared as "lobby agent" to denote seekers after special privilege at the New York State Capitol in Albany. There Thurlow Weed and others gave the title a rousing bad name. It was soon adapted for Washington use.

The all-time "King of the Lobbyists," who relished the title, was Samuel Ward, brother of Julia Ward Howe, the reformist lady who wrote "The Battle Hymn of the Republic" and cousin of Ward Mc-Allister, originator of Society's Four Hundred. Bald, bold and brazen, Sam Ward operated flamboyantly during the Civil War. He would say: "The way to a man's 'Aye' is through his stomach." Ward earned the sobriquet of "old wicked Sam Ward" from Henry Adams, who did some lobbying of his own. Sam, ever-smiling, was a Wall Street broker, but he was equally at home with philosophers and financiers. He came to Washington as a Copperhead determined to promote peace between North and South. He stayed on in the capital to promote war instead of peace at the behest of Hugh McCullough, the Indiana banker who was to become Lincoln's Secretary of the Treasury. McCullough paid Sam Ward $12,000 a year "plus dinner expenses" to "court, woo, and charm Congressmen, especially Democrats prone to oppose the war."[1]

Sam lobbied for fees, although he was not averse to picking up commissions for getting war contracts. One of his successes was a law to tax lotteries, not because he opposed lotteries but because his client, the so-called "boss" of the lotteries, believed it would drive rivals out of business. Sam boldly patrolled the halls of Congress where his sweeping mustache and diamonds glistening in his shirt front were a familiar sight. Once he presented the retiring Speaker of the House with a silver cup inscribed from "Rex Vistiari" (King of the Lobby). Sam always insisted, however, that while he would do almost anything to sway a vote, he never knowingly helped in a swindle. When Sam died in 1884, his nephew remarked that he had "died as he had lived, with a vagueness concerning all points of morality, which would have been terrible in a man less actively good than he was."

Another great lobby personality of a century ago, preceding Sam by a decade, was the handsome and florid Alexander Hay. Hay was in charge of lobbying operations for Samuel Colt, the revolver manufacturer. A Congressional committee disclosed that Colt had paid a "contingent fee" of $10,000 to a Congressman for withdrawing his opposition to a revolver patent extension bill. Hay presided over gay parties in various Washington hotels to which he invited leading members of Congress. He distributed specially made-up Colt revolvers as gifts. He also offered more attractive enticements—three charming female "spiritualists," who were said in the Congressional committee report to have been "moving with the members" of Congress. There were also other ladies, less delicately described as "chicks." The report did not indicate whether they also moved with the members.[2]

Such flamboyant lobbying tactics are gone from the Washington scene, probably forever, although they persisted long after Sam Ward and Alexander Hay. There were gay parties, replete with Broadway show girls, during a World War II effort to lobby a bill to validate defaulted Philippine railway bonds. The resultant scandal led to the 1946 act requiring registration of lobbyists. The registration act, however, designated as lobbyists only those who sought to influence legislation. Yet for all practical purposes lobbyists represent special interests in all areas of government, including the Executive Department and its special agencies.

The law requiring the registration of lobbyists confirmed the legal right of the people, including special interest groups, to exert influence on government. Lobbying thus is technically respectable, although its practitioners seek to avoid the title. Since their efforts are designed to *sway* government, lobbying is usually conducted in the name of the national interest. This is particularly true of the various military-oriented special interest groups that operate in Washington. Some of these groups are economic, like the National Security Industrial Association, which developed from an organization of Navy suppliers during World War II. Another economic grouping is the Aerospace Industries Association. Unlike the NSIA, the Aerospace Industries Association has registered lobbyists representing it on Capitol Hill. This candor by the association which represents most of the leading defense contractors has served nevertheless to reinforce much of the suspicion traditionally directed in America against so-called "merchants of death."

Eisenhower, long before he made his resounding speech to the nation on the military-industrial complex, revived many qualms over the defense manufacturers' supposed influence on national defense policies. At the height of a particularly aggravating public dispute over the respective merits of the Army's Nike-Hercules anti-aircraft missile and the Air Force's Bomarc, Eisenhower was asked about a conversation at the White House with a group of Senators. Had he expressed concern over the influence of the "munitions lobby"? The President, annoyed that someone had made "those remarks public property," said he did not recall using the term "munitions makers," but "obviously political and financial considerations" rather than "strictly military needs" were influencing the debate over military weapons. No flaming radical could have done more to encourage national suspicion of the military-industrial complex than the President with his reference to "obviously political and financial considerations."[3]

The special interest groups that best epitomize the military-industrial complex are the organizations of military service supporters, such as the Association of the United States Army, the Air Force Association and the Navy League. The Navy League, the oldest, and generally credited with being the most sophisticated and competent in representing the interests of members, is also the smallest in membership, with about 25,000. The Army Association has 55,000; the Air Force Association, 58,000. The members are active, reserve and retired members of the armed forces, defense contractors, community leaders and other supporters. The organizations are financed by membership fees and sums from contractors who pay for exhibits at conventions, subscribe to various dinner meetings and rallies, and place advertisements in the official publications. These organizations of service supporters unabashedly fight the battles of the military. The Navy League calls itself the "civilian arm of the Navy."

The organizations' activities in behalf of the services come in statements supporting the services' policies. The Army Association has repeatedly advocated a large standing Army and supports Army weapons projects and expansion of the capability for fighting ground warfare. The Navy League was an early and consistent supporter of the Polaris and is a champion of continued reliance upon aircraft carriers. It also has fought bravely in support of the Navy's traditional resistance to service unification. The Air Force Association has backed investments in bombers as well as missiles and has championed Air Force policies in favor of military unification and counterforce strategies.

The effectiveness of the big military associations is hard to gauge. Like the services, the backers' organizations often fight each other. Significantly, the first time they ever issued a joint statement in favor of a single program was in 1963 to back increased pay scales for military personnel. Yet there is no question that together their activities tend to stress all possible dangers to national security. Together they press for large military budgets in order to cope with such dangers. Since their chief financial backers are the defense contractors, these associations clearly constitute military-industrial pressure groups.

An important military-oriented lobbying group consists of veterans organizations. Most of the veterans organizations tend to support the gamut of national security programs. At the same time, the veterans groups concentrate on programs of direct benefit to their members in the form of cash payments, tax benefits and the like. Such organizations include the American Legion, AMVETS, Veterans of Foreign Wars, Disabled American Veterans, Disabled Officers Association and Retired Officers. The biggest spenders among the lobbies are not normally military-oriented, but in 1960 the Veterans of World War I of the U.S.A., or "Wonnies," as they were known, headed the list of lobby registrants. The "Wonnies" represented 930,000 persons. They spent $200,623 that year in a fruitless effort to obtain a law that would set up a separate pension system for the veterans of the 1917-1918 conflict. The "Wonnies" told a reporter for the *Congressional Quarterly* that they had no paid lobbyist in Washington. Instead, they preferred to bring veterans from throughout the country to visit their respective Senators and Representatives. For this "home-town" approach veterans were paid $20 a day plus transportation costs. This boosted the World War I group to a lobbyist spending record. But it was a one-shot effort.

The American Legion, one of the most durable organizations, spends about $100,000 a year to push various types of veterans legislation. It also takes stands on other issues. There was a time when the American Legion was regarded as the most powerful lobby in

Washington. John Thomas Taylor, a Washington lawyer, once boasted informally that he "personally had written between 1,500 and 2,000 bills" during his first ten years as head of the American Legion lobby. Many of these bills became law, as Taylor perfected a technique that was soon adopted by other lobbyists. The leadership of the Legion would decide upon a particular bill. They would designate a local post of the Legion to introduce it as a resolution. Thus it had "grass roots" blessing. Then the bill was endorsed, amidst publicity, at a Legion departmental convention and finally at the Legion's national convention. By this time it had attracted attention. Delegates were assigned to push the bill through the resolutions committee and presented to the membership for endorsement and acclaim.

At this point the Legion lobbyists were able to assert that the bill they had devised in the first place was inspired by widespread demands of the membership and they called upon a friendly member of Congress to introduce it. The proposed text was handed to the Congressman, along with explanatory material. Roger Burlingame, in an article in the *Atlantic Monthly*, in 1933, described Taylor walking through the halls of Congress "like a commander." Any Congressman who turned down his suggestions would be flooded with letters from Legionnaires in his home town within twenty-four hours. When President Harding vetoed a veterans bonus bill, the Legion lobby prevailed and Congress passed it over the veto. When President Coolidge similarly vetoed a bonus bill, the Legion lobby again prevailed—despite a counterattack by a well-financed anti-bonus lobby organized by Wall Street bankers. The Legion is still active, but it no longer can get its way so easily.

Among the most powerful special-interest groups with a military orientation are the Reserve organizations, particularly the National Guard Association. Most of the Pentagon chiefs regard the Reserve organizations as more of a nuisance than an ally. But the Reserve organizations, many of whose members are also members of Congress, command strong support in Congress and in the state governments as well. The political strength of the National Guard is based on its origins and its status as a state militia. National Guard leaders trace the Guard to the colonial militias. The principle of citizen-soldier militias was written into the Constitution, and reserved to the states "the appointment of the officers and the authority of training the militia according to discipline prescribed by Congress."

Each state governor is commander in chief of the Guard in his own state and the Guard units are organized and administered as state organizations. Only when a National Guard unit is brought into Federal service under specific regulations does it come under command of the President.

Most National Guard outfits also are closely linked with their communities and enjoy status that goes far beyond military functions. Senior leaders of the Guard organizations are active in the social and government life of their states. They include mayors, governors, state officials, members of Congress, Senators, town clerks, businessmen, schoolteachers and the like. National Guard leaders work hard to maintain these close contacts. Guard units organize various social and cultural programs, charity drives, sports programs. They build playgrounds and other facilities. One Guard unit built a landing strip for its town. Another turned out a regiment to collect for the March of Dimes. The efforts of the Guard leadership to maintain stability and retain members as career reservists also pays off in strong political support against Federal intervention, although the military side of the organization is financed largely with Federal funds.

Guard officials do not hesitate to underscore their political power. President Major General Ellard A. Walsh pointed out in 1963: "True it is that the Guard has been and still is compelled to appeal to the Congress from time to time for the enactment of legislation which it considers to be beneficial and essential, or in opposition to legislation which it regards as detrimental either to the Guard *or to national security*. This course of action has been dictated because of periodic attempts to eliminate the National Guard from the defense structure. This matter of politics in the Guard has been summed up by General Palmer in his book, *Statesmanship or War*, published in 1927, and far better than I could possibly do. I quote: 'Critics of the National Guard should remember that it has won its position against strong and persistent opposition. For many years it has been *forced into politics* in order to maintain the traditions of a national citizens army. This conflict has had a necessary influence on the quality and character of some of its leaders. During the many years while the struggle lasted, the citizens army required leaders who could employ political means for overcoming the persistent resistance of the War Department. Now that the fight has been won, the Guard is prepared to accept military efficiency as the sole basis for leadership.' "⁴

But, General Walsh continued, the fight waged by the Guard "was anything but won; rather, it had just begun." Thus the Guard leadership was still in politics. "This then is the primary reason why the Army and Air National Guard is compelled to maintain a highly organized, compact, disciplined, and effective National Guard Association of the United States."

In carrying out its lobbying activities the Guard maintains a headquarters at the handsome National Guard Memorial Building near the Capitol with competent, alert legislative and public relations experts. Because so many of the National Guard members serve frequent periods of active duty they are in close touch with developments in the armed forces. Their link with the Pentagon's National Guard Bureau is intimate. They are quickly apprised of any moves to reduce their role and they have proved to be effective in thwarting most such moves.

Similar to the National Guard Association is the Reserve Officers Association, which also carries on extensive lobbying activities and has close links with members of Congress, many of whom are active in Reserve affairs.

The military services make use of special-interest groups in many ways. For example, a high-ranking Air Force general, addressing a panel at the Air Force Association Convention in 1962, spoke with warm praise of the work of Reservists assigned to various Air Force units. He mentioned this example: "An ex-SAC jet pilot, Captain Barry Trader, is now working in aerospace defense. Captain Trader is in the news department of a major Denver radio-TV station, and he pulls his Reserve duty with the Command Office of Information. Not only does he contribute materially to the information function of ADC when he is in the Air Force uniform, but he *advocates the Air Force message* as an announcer and news writer in his civilian radio-TV capacity."[5] Undoubtedly the Air Force, the Air Force Reserve and presumably the commercial supporters of air power benefited by this newsman's advantageous position in public relations, according to the candid appraisal of the Air Force general. Whether the station got an entirely unbiased presentation of news insofar as air power was concerned was of course another matter.

Similarly, a ceremony at Denver, Colorado, September 20, 1962, appeared to symbolize the military-industrial complex. In the ceremony, held in connection with the annual meeting of the National Guard Association, the Air Force and the State of Maryland cited the Martin Company for its outstanding contribution to the Air National Guard program. Two units of the Guard were based on the company's private airport at Baltimore, Maryland, in what the company announcement described as a "unique arrangement." It was said to be the only private airfield in the service of the Guard. The citation from the Secretary of the Air Force said:

Five years ago the State of Maryland faced the prospective transfer of its Air National Guard jet fighter squadron due to lack of an airfield to support its operation. In an outstanding display of citizenship, the Martin Company helped to prevent this loss by offering use of its company-owned Middle River Airport. This action permitted continued flying training for Maryland's citizen airmen. It also gained for the Martin Company the distinction of having the nation's only private airfield from which Air National Guard jets carry out their vital defense mission.

The Secretary of the Air Force then added his "personal congratulations" to the Martin Company management for "its most unusual and valued contribution to the deterrent capability of the United States," finding nothing ludicrous in the apparent dependence of the "vital defense mission" and the "deterrent capability of the United States" on a private airfield maintained by one of the leading defense contractors.[6] But perhaps it would have been ludicrous only if the Martin Company had not made the airport available, since the company's entire business is with the government— its only customer.

The military services' own lobbying and pressure tactics are not insignificant. The services carry on extensive public relations campaigns and maintain powerful direct contacts with Congress through legislative liaison officers. It is a standard joke in Washington that on the eve of any Congressional session there will be a flurry of reports about enemy weapons capabilities. The Navy sights enemy submarines, Air Force intelligence sources unveil new enemy aircraft of a design not yet attained by the United States, and the Army describes the complete re-equipment of enemy ground forces with modern weapons. These reports, emanating from United States military sources, presumably are intended to earn backing for the military services' own weapons requests.

Just as there probably will never be another lobbying era to match the halcyon days of Sam Ward, some believe there probably will never be another military service struggle for Congressional support as marked the Navy's fight for an aircraft carrier in 1949. It precipitated the so-called "revolt of the admirals" and served as a prototype for subsequent military funding campaigns directed to the public and Congress. The mastermind of that pressure operation was Arleigh A. Burke, whose name later was stricken from a promotion list by an angry President Truman. President Eisenhower, who had never met Burke, raised him over the heads of ninety-two senior admirals to be Chief of Naval Operations. Burke was retained for an unprecedented series of three two-year terms, despite a remarkable record of dissents against civilian high policy in both Democratic and Republican Administrations. When he retired Burke said: "As I look back over my career the biggest mistakes I have made occurred when I have conformed to what I believed to be something somebody else wanted without really having fought the fight. The reason I conformed, usually, was because I did not know that they were not right. They could have been right. If I were living my life again I would, I think, be more outspoken."[7] This from one of the most outspoken men who ever wore the uniform of his country!

A burly two-hundred-pounder, Burke was a Boulder, Colorado, farm boy of Swedish ancestry who entered the Naval Academy in 1919. The family name of Bjorkegren was changed by his grandfather. During World War II Burke made a reputation for his exploits with destroyers. He earned the nickname "Thirty-one Knot" Burke when he sent a message to higher headquarters in the Pacific that he was proceeding to a rendezvous at thirty-one knots, although this was one knot faster than the top speed generally expected of destroyers. Upon receiving additional orders from Admiral "Bull" Halsey's headquarters, Burke again cockily radioed back he was maintaining his thirty-one-knot speed. Whereupon he received another message, sarcastically addressed to "Thirty-one Knot Burke" to get athwart the Buka-Rabaul neck of the Solomon Sea. Burke did so, one and one-half hours earlier than ordered; earlier, too, than enemy ships expected. Burke sank three Japanese destroyers and chased two more off the scene in what has since become a Navy battle classic. Burke later served with carriers and in the postwar period handled studies for the Navy on the diplomatic implications of its forces.

With that background he appeared to be a suitable choice to run "Op-23" in the Pentagon when the Navy was faced with one of its major postwar crises. This happened when Defense Secretary Louis Johnson, in one of the United States' recurrent military cost-cutting moods, canceled the plan for the Navy's big new carrier. The cancellation coincided with an Air Force move to take over the Navy's air missions and declare all carriers surplus. In the period before the Congressional hearings, the Navy proceeded to prepare its ammunition to justify its own demands and to fight the claims of its sister service.

At the hearings, including a special series on air power, the admirals paraded past the committees with lengthy, well-researched statements in defense of the Navy's aviation requirements and against growing Administration disposition to side with the Air Force. A newspaper writer dubbed it the "revolt of the admirals" and this was picked up by others. Informed observers realized that Captain Burke, of "Op-" or "Operation-23," a Navy research unit, was supplying all the facts and figures being used by the Navy witnesses. But when newspapermen tried to get some of the material for their own stories, the Navy forbade Captain Burke to see them. This added some mystery to the operation. Burke had an associate, the late Captain Walter Karig, a Navy historian. While Captain Burke was not supposed to see newsmen, Captain Karig held regular briefings for them. Karig was, as one reporter put it, a "brainwasher" who sent newsmen away feeling the salt spray on their lips.

Captain Karig blamed "a few overzealous young naval officers" for passing out "confidential" propaganda material intended to counter Air Force claims.[8] Blaming "overzealous young officers" is characteristic of military officials, who do not hesitate to brief these young officers on just what ought to be made available. In the Navy–Air Force battle over the relative merits of the carriers and the B-36 bombers, both services occasionally handed out allegedly "confidential" papers to excite newspaper interest with the purpose of getting favorable headlines.

The late Anthony Leviero, who covered the Defense Department for the *New York Times*, stepped away from his table while lunching at a restaurant and found, upon his return, that a set of papers and photographs had been left on his seat. The photographs showed the results of a secret Air Force simulated "bombing raid" on a Navy carrier. This ploy by an Air Force supporter was balanced by similar dropped papers coming from Navy supporters. Since so much of the Navy material appeared to come from Admiral Burke's office, Defense Secretary Johnson and Secretary of the Navy Francis P. Matthews ordered the Inspector General to raid the office. The investigator impounded the captain's files and placed his staff under technical arrest. No secret papers or incriminating data were found. The comic opera aspects of the episode were not equaled until 1963, when the Air Force Inspector General suggested that the Deputy Defense Secretary and the Navy and Air Force Secretaries state their readiness to take lie detector tests in connection with the leak of a document the Secretary of Defense thought he had locked in his safe. (In the lie detector affair, an embarrassing Air Force memorandum was leaked to the press. The Air Force Inspector General, asked to investigate, blandly started at the top. He asked each person with knowledge of the memorandum to sign a sworn statement and indicate willingness to take a lie detector test to prove he had not given it out. The top officials agreed, but at least one Assistant Secretary refused on grounds that his word should be good enough. When the story of the lie detectors appeared in the press, President Kennedy immediately ordered a halt to this investigative technique.[9])

In any event, as a consequence of the "revolt of the admirals" the Navy did get its carrier. Moreover, the technique of leaking papers and thorough preparation of potential witnesses before Congress has been followed ever since.

Each of the military departments at the Pentagon, as well as the Office of the Secretary of Defense, has its own staff of legislative liaison representatives and its own public relations organization. An official count in May, 1963, broke it down as follows: Public relations: Office of Secretary of Defense, 149; Army, 119; Navy, 99; Marine Corps, 24; and Air Force, 116, for a total of 507. Legislative liaison: Office of Secretary of Defense, 13; Army, 23; Navy and Marine Corps, 20; and Air Force, 40.

The public relations officers have been quite successful in maintaining contacts with newsmen. Just as private lobbyists stress national interests, the military spokesmen stress the public's "right to know." An Air Force officer observed:

As an information officer I do care how many friends I have, how many reporters, commentators, journalists and publishers I know on a first-name basis. But if promoting the Air Force or handling press inquiries were the sole measure of my activities or those of my office, I would consider myself a failure. . . . I simply want to acknowledge the fact that in the American scheme of things, a government of, by, and for a people governed by their own consent, the right to know is with the public.[10]

In the name of this unarguable mission, the military services carry out vast public affairs programs. They issue press releases, pamphlets, documentary films; send speakers throughout the country and arrange for orientation tours by representatives of press, industry, education, etc. The size of the program and the rivalries by the military services for exposure in the press prompted the Government Accounting Office of the Congress to initiate a study in 1963 to determine whether all the public relations expenditures were justified, and whether there was not considerable overlapping in their operation.

The military's relations with Congress are based on something more explicit than the public's "right to know." Congress has the Constitutional responsibility for raising and supporting the armed forces. A single bill such as the defense appropriations bill fully occupies several dozen members of Congress and several committee staffs for the better part of six months. Not only the armed services and appropriations committees are concerned with military affairs. The government operations committees keeps an eye on the administrative efficiency of the services, the aeronautical and space science committees monitor the space programs, the judiciary committees watch the policies and practices of the military in the field of individual rights; the foreign relations committees study military power as an essential element of foreign policy; the Post Office and Civil Service committees observe the practices affecting civilian employees; and the Joint Atomic Energy and Joint Defense Procurement committees exercise self-evident interests in the defense programs.

The military services are thus directly concerned with legislation on the budget, broad military policies, pay, promotion, retirement, housing, medical care and many other matters. The services maintain offices in the Capital to keep the members of Congress informed, to solicit their interest in particular problems—in general, to "lobby." With defense problems growing more complicated over the years, this is an important and often worthwhile practice. The Executive Department has found it irritating, however, since it offers the services an important means of fighting Administration policies by generating campaigns among sympathizers in Congress. Each of the services has its own sympathizers. Many of the members of Congress are active Reservists; many come from areas that are dependent upon weapons-manufacturing programs and the maintenance of military installations.

The legislative liaison officers handle hundreds of inquiries a week from Congressmen, ranging from interest in specific members of the Armed Forces to studies of basic strategies. They also provide military transportation and other facilities for members of Congress on what are presumed to be official tours. They take the members of Congress on orientation junkets to show off the latest equipment and training programs. As one legislative officer put it privately: "I don't care how obstreperous a Congressman is toward a certain piece of legislation. If I once get him on a junket, I figure the odds have begun to shift in our favor. Our lobbying effectiveness is at its height, not here on Capitol Hill, but in the field where we get the Congressmen to 'see for themselves.'"

The high point of the military lobby activities comes when the Chiefs and their aides appear before the committees to answer questions. Some of these questions are carefully planted in advance with favorite and cooperative Congressmen. Others are anticipated. The answers are given as "personal opinions" to avoid the suggestion of insubordination if they are in conflict with Administration policy. But they are candidly intended to influence legislation. Thus the Air Force carries on its campaigns for bombers, and the Navy fights for its carriers and the Army for modern equipment, despite powerful efforts by succeeding Administrations to keep expenditures down. Much of the military testimony is public and is carefully phrased to advance service viewpoints.

The military services' own public relations and lobbying apparatus has disturbed some observers. The question has been posed whether the total effect of the military pleadings is contrary to the national interest. One writer has charged:

The path to these heights of power and influence is cleared for the military and its industrial allies by a public relations establishment that has no equal in American public or private life. The establishment uses the press, television, movies, comic strips, civic organizations, veterans groups, schools and troops to sell the military point of view to the American public. No other point of view, save that of the President alone, can reach the public from so many sides at once.[11]

Professor Janowitz suggested that "the new public relations of the military services" (in which he included its lobbying activities) "has the potentiality for threatening the political balance." He continued: "An organ of Government lobbying in its own behalf—especially one which deals with such a vital function—is difficult to contain."[12] But the professor cited this as a long-term danger. For the present, he said, "The conflicting interests among the military profession are perpetuated in associational life. Each faction as it bids for public and political support can best be described as exercising a veto." This view is similar to what John K. Galbraith termed, in a discussion of American capitalism, "the concept of Countervailing Power." According to this view, the competing demands of the special interest groups tend to cancel each other out. A Congressman, for example, might be an Army Reservist with a strong tendency toward its doctrine of national strategy, but he would vote for an Air Force appropriation if it meant a factory for his home city, for a Navy appropriation if he were rallied by his political leaders on Capitol Hill, and for an across-the-board economy cut if he belonged to the party of the President demanding such measures. Not nearly so important as the technique of lobbying are the aims of the lobbyists. And these aims must be judged separately.

XII

Questions of Probity

"Probity cannot be legislated."
>   —Report of Senate Subcommittee on
>   National Policy Machinery

On November 24, 1947, a major general who had been Deputy Procurement Chief for the Air Force during the war was stripped of his decorations, dismissed from military service and denounced as a "crook" by the Secretary of the Air Force. The general was subsequently sentenced to Federal prison for perjury and income tax evasion. He had been the secret head of an airplane company which, as a procurement official, he provided with lucrative Air Force contracts.[1] The case aroused considerable public commotion during Congressional hearings. Many military officers handle huge sums which in private business would be entrusted only to highly paid executives, but in most instances of influence bartering that have come to public attention military codes of honor have stood up well.

In 1959 hearings by a House Armed Services Subcommittee cast light on what appeared to be a blatant if presumably innocent mass acceptance of favors from a defense contractor by military officers who were in a position to be useful to that contractor. At least twenty-seven high officers, including the then chairman of the Joint Chiefs of Staff, were entertained over a period of three years by the Martin Company at the company-owned Lotton Bay Club on Eleuthera Island in the Bahamas. When the story was published, none of the officers deigned to justify himself in public. For the committee, the generals and admirals involved in the publicity completed a questionnaire. The consensus of their responses: they did not participate directly in contractual negotiations; they had no direct business relationship with the Martin Company; as guests, they did not discuss contractual negotiations.[2] George Bunker, president of the Martin Company, said the same thing in a somewhat different way, however. He told the House panel during an angry session: "A man could neither operate nor compete effectively unless he had a close personal relationship." He also said: "I cannot conceive that anyone could possibly believe men of their character and responsibilities could be influenced by playing golf with me on Eleuthera." The golfing interludes, the contractor then explained, were designed to get the military and the contractor better acquainted and to help negotiations proceed in a friendly atmosphere for working out the most effective weapons systems in the interests of national defense.[3]

At just about this time a curious incident occurred. Invitations went out to a "small off-the-record party" to discuss the work and plans of the Air Research and Development Command under newly promoted Lieutenant General Bernard A. Schriever. Ten members of Congress, all but two of whom were members of the Armed Services or Appropriations committees of the House and Senate, received the invitations issued by three defense contractors: Bunker; Frank Pace, former Secretary of the Army who was then head of General Dynamics; and Dan A. Kimball, former Secretary of the Navy and head of Aerojet-General. Pace said the party was planned as "means of advancing the interests of the United States of America." It was called off because of "publicity."

Officers are barred by conflict-of-interest laws from taking most jobs in Federal Government, a circumstance that has resulted in considerable loss of talent to the government. Many officers eventually get lucrative positions with big firms that hold government contracts, however. The Hebert subcommittee, in a now famous survey, disclosed that more than fourteen hundred retired officers in the rank of major or above, including 261 of general or flag rank, were employed by the leading one hundred defense contractors. General Dynamics, headed by the former Army Secretary, Frank Pace, led with 187, including 27 retired generals and admirals. It is only natural that military men should find jobs in military industries. As technicians and managers familiar with weapons and the requirements of the Defense Department, they serve both their new employers and the United States. But never as "salesmen," they insist. Officers are prohibited by law from engaging in salesmanship for a specific period following retirement from active duty.

The care with which salesmanship is "avoided" was indicated by Retired Admiral William M. Fechteler, a former Chief of Naval Operations. He was a consultant to the Atomic Products Division of the General Electric Company. He explained to the Hebert subcommittee how he had arranged some appointments for one of the vice presidents of the company: "I took him to see Mr. Gates, the Secretary of the Navy [later Secretary of Defense]. I took him in to see Admiral Burke. He had not met Admiral Burke before. And then I made appointments for him with the Chief of the Bureau of Ships. But I did not accompany him there, because those are material bureaus which make contracts, and I studiously avoid even being in the room when anybody talks about contracts."[4] If this was not "salesmanship," was it influence peddling?

What disturbs many people is that military men who have held important positions at the Pentagon up to the time of retirement go into private industry as their own counterparts. For example, Lieutenant General Donald Putt, the Air Force Deputy Chief of Staff for Development, retired in March, 1958. Shortly afterward he became the first employee and president of the United Technology Corporation, set up as a subsidiary by the United Aircraft Corporation, one of the nation's leading contractors. The subsidiary was formed in an effort by United Aircraft to get into the rocket field, the potentialities of which the Air Force general knew quite well. A month after becoming president of the corporation, the retired general was named a member of the Air Force's Scientific Advisory Board. The award of a $2 million contract to the retired general's new firm in 1961 aroused the attention of a *New York Times* reporter, John W. Finney, who made inquiries about it at the Pentagon. The Air Force responded as follows:

We do not believe that General Putt's membership on the Board creates *per se* a conflict between his public trust as a chairman and his private interests as president of the United Technology Corporation. To begin with General Putt, as chairman, exercises only broad supervision over the board's activities. With rare exception, the general has not participated in any of the panel meetings where the board's recommendations are actually hammered out; in those very instances where he did attend, the subject matter discussed was of no interest to the United Technology Corporation. Moreover, General Putt and the other board members are conversant with the various directives which set forth governmental policy as regards conflicts of interest. In addition, the Scientific Advisory Board, as its name suggests, carries out what is in fact a purely advisory function, and is accountable directly to the Chief of Staff. Of particular significance in this respect is that the board, in an overall sense, provides basic recommendations on how modern science and technology can best be applied to the successful accomplishment of the Air Force mission—the board and its panels cannot and do not handle any matters dealing with the selection of contractors. Under these circumstances, it has been unnecessary for General Putt to disqualify himself from any of the Board's discussions.[5]

The question that remained in Mr. Finney's mind, however—and in this he appeared to speak for many persons—was "whether such a clear distinction can be drawn between policy recommendations and contract decisions."[6] In fact, it is precisely because of the presumed relationship between policy and procurement that high-ranking civilian officials have been forced to divest themselves of their stock holdings in defense firms. General Putt resigned as chairman of the advisory board in accordance with a wish he had expressed in advance of the publicity given to his dual responsibilities. Then the Pentagon revised its regulations to preclude any new Putt cases. Throughout, the attitude of the military was that it was above reproach; General Putt, asked about the situation, said he saw no conflict of interest—"If I had, I would have resigned."

The same attitude was exemplified in the testimony of officers before the Hebert subcommittee. None, while in office, ever experienced any "pressure" from retired former colleagues, they testified. "I would throw them out on their ear [if they had tried it]," Retired Lieutenant General Clarence S. Irvine told the subcommittee. He had retired as Air Force Deputy Chief of Staff for Matériel in May, 1959, and joined the Avco Corporation a month later as vice president and director for planning. But Vice Admiral Hyman G. Rickover observed to the subcommittee that after high-ranking officers left the service their former jobs were filled by "their dear friends, or even by people whom they have been influential in appointing, and naturally they will be listened to."

An earlier case publicized in a subcommittee hearing in 1956, also conducted under Representative Hebert, involved Air Force General Joseph T. McNarney and Stuart Symington, who had previously been Secretary of the Air Force but held no public office at the time. On the day of his retirement, January 31, 1952, General McNarney said, he received a "cryptic" telephone tip from Mr. Symington that led to his employment by the Consolidated Vultee Aircraft Corporation two months later. Consolidated Vultee subsequently became the Convair division of General Dynamics Corporation, which had manufactured the B-36. As Secretary of the Air Force Senator Symington had been a key figure in the fight for the B-36 bomber. General McNarney had fought for the bomber also as a member of the senior officers board in the Defense Department.

General McNarney testified that on the last day of his retirement Mr. Symington, later Senator from Missouri, telephoned from St. Louis to ask whether he had "signed up" with anyone for private employment. The general replied he had not. Mr. Symington then gave him a telephone number to call in Indio, California. The general said Mr. Symington did not say whose number it was. The general added, however, that he knew that Floyd B. Odlum, then board chairman of Consolidated Vultee, had a ranch at Indio. He said he called the number and started the negotiations that led to a five-year, $75,000-a-year contract.[7] Senator Symington, advised of the general's testimony, issued a statement recalling that "the management of Convair asked me in early 1952 if I knew anybody who could run that company. I told them that I considered General Joseph McNarney, who had just retired, the finest administrator I had met during my service in the Pentagon. Mr. Floyd Odlum asked me if I would put McNarney in touch with him or his organizations and I said I would be glad to. This I did."

If high-ranking military officers, as a group, did not have extraordinarily good reputations, the circumstances of their job hunting —and getting—would arouse more suspicion. But the occasional investigations into the transfer of officers from responsible service positions to highly paid positions in defense industries that cater to the services rarely arouse more than a murmur. No evidence of venality or misconduct was produced during the 1959 hearings even when "appearances" were clouded. Hebert said: "The question of defense industry hiring of former military men is a delicate one. The cases are not all black and they are not all white. That's why we have to be careful."[8]

On the civilian side of Pentagon officialdom three cases stand out. Harold E. Talbott, a businessman in the airplane field from its pioneering days, was named by newly elected President Eisenhower to be his first Secretary of the Air Force in 1953. At the Senate hearings on his confirmation, Talbott anounced that he had divested himself of all connections with four of his companies. He said, however, that he had retained a "special partnership" in Paul B. Mulligan & Company, a New York engineering firm specializing in industrial management efficiency.

In July, 1955, the Senate Permanent Investigating Subcommittee, headed by Senator John L. McClellan, ordered hearings on evidence that the Secretary of the Air Force had continued to profit from the Mulligan firm in business with defense contractors. The spadework on the evidence was handled by Robert F. Kennedy, then the twenty-nine-year-old counsel for the subcommittee and four years out of University of Virginia Law School. A few days before the hearings opened William H. Lawrence, a reporter for the *New York Times*, obtained and published letters written by Talbott on his stationery as Secretary of the Air Force. The letters made clear that Talbott was actively promoting his firm. The hearings showed that the Secretary of the Air Force in one instance had persisted in his efforts to obtain a contract with the Radio Corporation of America after R.C.A. had expressed doubts about the contract's legality and propriety.[9]

Talbott, accustomed to considerably greater earnings, was getting $18,000 a year as Secretary of the Air Force. He earned more than $130,000 from his partnership with the Mulligan Company during his two years at the Pentagon. And also, it turned out, he had not sold all of his stock holdings, as indicated at the time of his confirmation, but had given some stocks to his children. All of this came out in major headlines in the press. Within six weeks, Talbott resigned to spare the President further embarrassment. In an official report, six months later, the subcommittee said simply that Talbott had "acted indiscreetly."

Another case in 1957 involved a lesser official at the Pentagon, a former Republican representative, Robert Tripp Ross, whose wife's firm manufactured trousers for the Army. Ross had been an official of the firm up to the time of his appointment in 1954 as Deputy Assistant Secretary of Defense for Legislative and Public Affairs. He became Assistant Secretary a year later. The hearings brought out that Ross' wife's firm, located in Tennessee, continued to list the Pentagon official as an officer of the firm a year after he went into government service. This, the official said, was an "auditor's error." Then, it turned out during the hearings that the firm was involved in so-called "double bidding" in which two firms under the same ownership were competing for government contracts. Ross claimed he took "no action whatsoever" to influence government procurement agents to give clothing contracts to his wife's firm. But his brother-in-law testified that on one occasion Ross did set up an interview for him with Marine Corps procurement officers. "They frankly kicked me out after about twenty minutes," the brother-in-law said.[10]

The upshot of the Ross case, as in the Talbott case, was a finding that the official himself had done nothing legally wrong. The House Government Operations Subcommittee in the Ross case added, however:

His fault lay not so much in what he did but in his failure to realize that the very nature of his position in the Department of Defense made it awkward and unwise and incompatible with the highest standards of public conduct to maintain that position while his immediate family had business dealings with the department. The fact that he occupied a high and influential post in the Department of Defense would not be lost upon military procurement officers.[11]

In the case of the Marines, however, apparently Ross' high position was lost upon them.

The third case involved Fred Korth, one of the Secretaries of the Navy in the Kennedy Administration, an exuberant six-foot-two-inch Texas rancher and banker, who had said when he took his Washington assignment in January, 1962, that he did not plan to stay very long. "I am not making government a career," he told a reporter in his home city of Fort Worth. "I am going to come back to Fort Worth, Azleway [his twelve-hundred-acre ranch] and the Continental National Bank." But not even Korth suspected that his retreat from Washington would occur as abruptly as it did with his resignation in October, 1963.

In behavior that strongly resembled that of Harold Talbott, it developed that Korth had kept a close watch on the affairs of the bank of which he had been president. On Navy stationery, he advised an official at the bank to bring "extra good customers" to Washington for a cruise aboard the Navy yacht *Sequoia*. He arranged an appointment with Navy procurement officers for a Houston company that wanted to sell its products to the Navy. He wrote to Edward Marcus of the Neiman-Marcus department store in Dallas, expressing the hope that the store would reinstate its bank account with Continental National. He intervened with the Owens-Corning Fiberglas Corporation in behalf of a Waxahachie, Texas, bank that was soliciting the Owens-Corning bank account. He forwarded to Continental National Bank a $50,000 savings account deposit from a press agent who had been his guest on a *Sequoia* cruise. Korth freely made known these contacts, insisted that he had not been asked to resign, and said he deeply resented "any insinuations that these few trivial incidents and communications raise a question concerning my character or that they furnish or could have furnished a valid basis for my reluctant decision to resign to attend to my long neglected personal and family affairs."[12]

The Korth resignation might not have developed in the way that it did had it not been for his involvement in the TFX controversy. This was a classic embodiment of virtually all the influences in the military-industrial complex. It concerned a potential $7 billion contract for a new type jet fighter to be used by both the Navy and Air Force which was awarded to the General Dynamics Corporation. The award came under investigation when military sources disclosed that the Air Force and Navy military chiefs had recommended Boeing. While Boeing planned to place the work in its Wichita, Kansas, plant, General Dynamics intended to develop and build the plane at its Convair division in Fort Worth. Not only was Vice President Johnson from Texas, but the first Secretary of the Navy in the Kennedy Administration, John B. Connally, was Governor of Texas, and Korth was one of the most prominent citizens of Fort Worth.

The Senate Permanent Investigating Subcommittee, which had handled the Talbott case, brought out that the bank of which Korth had been president held the General Dynamics Corporation checking account in Fort Worth. The bank had also been one of the nineteen participants in a loan to the General Dynamics Corporation. The loan was for a total of $200 million and Continental's share was relatively small, however—for not more than $400,000. Korth reacted violently when one of the investigating Senators, Karl Mundt, Republican of South Dakota, called him "Mr. Fort Worth" and asserted that Korth's position would have "staggered a Solomon." Korth angrily replied that he considered himself an American first and a citizen of Fort Worth second. If found to have committed a wrong, he would resign, Mr. Korth said during one of the hearings—a rather tame promise, it seemed at the time. As events turned out, his resignation coincided with the disclosure that he had been—as President Kennedy later observed—"busier than he should have been" on private business affairs. Yet the President defended Korth against charges of impropriety in the TFX case.

Meanwhile, the interest of individual members of Congress in the outcome of the TFX award was also brought to public light. During his testimony, Air Force Secretary Eugene Zuckert listed twelve members of Congress who had been in touch with him during the contract negotiations. Senator Mike Monroney of Oklahoma, whose name was on the published list, issued a statement that he had visited Zuckert's office to "remind him of the vast Government-owned [aircraft manufacturing] plant in Tulsa, Oklahoma, which the Douglas Aircraft Company operates and its large unused machinery and manpower capabilities." Senator Symington, another on the list, and a former Secretary of the Air Force, said he had visited the incumbent Secretary to discuss the possibility of Missouri companies obtaining subcontracts from whichever manufacturers got the TFX contract. Senator Warren Magnuson, of Washington, issued a statement that he had inquired about the status of the competition. "When they put a company from your area into such extended competition, especially one with the fine reputation of Boeing, you naturally want to know when the contract is going to be awarded," Senator Magnuson's spokesman said. Senator Henry M. Jackson, also of Washington and a member of the committee investigating the contract, already had said he insisted upon the investigation when Boeing did not win. Senators Frank Carlson and James B. Pearson and Representative Garner E. Shriver, all of Kansas, where Boeing had an idle plant at Wichita, said they had visited Zuckert as a group and had told the Air Force Secretary that Boeing could do the job better than its competitor. As members of Congress from a state where the planes would be built, Senator Carlson said, "We not only were justified [in making the visit]; we should do it."[13]

Such justifications are not available to members of the Executive Branch, however. In a case parallel to the TFX, Korth showed that he was not completely insensitive to appearances. He voluntarily withdrew from any role in the award of a contract for a new type V/STOL (vertical or short take-off and landing) airplane. He had been director of Bell Aircraft Company, one of the concerns competing for the contract and its ultimate winner. But Korth found it difficult to withdraw completely, it was indicated in hearings conducted by the Senate Preparedness Subcommittee. As in the TFX case, the recommendations of the military were overruled in the V/STOL decision. The Navy officers had favored Douglas Aircraft

Company. Deputy Defense Secretary Roswell L. Gilpatric, who made the final decision, said he had based it on the management capability and record of Bell, although Douglas had produced a better technical paper during the competition. Gilpatric then testified that in reaching his decision he had telephoned Korth to ask him, as a former Bell director, his opinion of the company's qualifications. Korth's opinion presumably was not derogatory since Bell got the contract.[14]

Gilpatric himself became involved in conflict-of-interest publicity in the TFX hearings. Gilpatric had been an attorney in the law firm that handled the account of the winning General Dynamics Corporation. When this became an issue, he called attention to other prominent lawyers whose firms had handled defense business, and who nevertheless had assumed positions of responsibility in the military departments—Elihu Root, Henry Stimson, John McCloy, to name a few. But by then the TFX hearings, dragging over most of 1963, had become so complicated with minor sensations that nothing any of its central figures had to say seemed to carry any weight. Senator John L. McClellan, chairman of the investigating panel, seemed determined to "catch" someone, although he kept insisting that he was interested only in establishing whether the Pentagon was procuring the better airplane. The Pentagon officials retaliated with inspired stories attacking the Senator for daring to challenge their wisdom.

Gilpatric, like Korth, was cleared officially by the Department of Justice of any conflict of interest. But legal clearance is no solution for officials in high government office, once they have been the targets of suspicion. Many persons felt that Gilpatric should have withdrawn from any role in the TFX decision. Gilpatric and others countered that the top-ranking officers could not withdraw from such responsibilities; that withdrawal would be an admission of possible bias, rendering every other decision questionable. The Gilpatric situation bore out the observation of the Senate subcommittee on National Policy Machinery that lawyers were particular victims of the "disjointed, overlapping, ambiguous and improperly focused" conflict-of-interest laws.[15] The subcommittee, conceding that "probity can not be legislated," nevertheless made an urgent appeal for a complete revision of these century-old laws, but Congress consistently has refused to act.

The conflict-of-interest laws date from corruption-ridden wartime Washington in 1863, when a freshman Senator from Michigan named Jacob Merritt Howard managed to win passage of an amendment to an omnibus bill on government spending. The amendment was intended to curb petty officials who might try to steer commissary purchases to their own farms or textile purchases to their own mills. The statutes, clearly reflecting the petty crimes they were intended to forestall, call for a criminal penalty up to $2,000 in fines and two years in prison for anyone who "is employed or acts as an officer or agent of the United States for the transaction of [a] business entity" in which that person is "directly or indirectly interested in the pecuniary profits."

Under the interpretation of Congressional committees, the statutes have developed into a preventive device against wrongdoing in high places by persons least likely to want or need the money but most likely to draw political charges no matter how they behave. As a consequence, many persons, especially of the business community, have proved unwilling to accept positions in government, even when they could afford to accept the substantial cuts in income. The extreme demands made upon businessmen brought into the government was exemplified by the cases of two Secretaries of Defense, which in turn provided a contrast with the relaxed attitude the law displays toward members of Congress.

When the late Charles E. Wilson came to Washington as Secretary of Defense in the Eisenhower Administration, he was forced to sell $2.5 million worth of stock of the General Motors Corporation of which he had been president. Some persons claimed that the law was not intended to demand stock divestment, that it was intended solely to prevent officials from acting in transactions involving any firm in which they had a financial interest. In answer, the Senate Armed Services Committee said that although the Secretary of Defense or some other official might not be directly involved in procurement, their policy decisions affected the procurement. Yet they could not disqualify themselves from doing their jobs as policy-makers. Thus, to avoid subsequent embarrassment or suspicion, it was best for officials, especially the Secretary of Defense, not to own any shares of stocks of firms doing business with the Pentagon.

The Senate panel which demanded that Wilson dispose of the stocks did not bother to ask what he did with the money. When Robert S. McNamara, the Ford Company president, came to Washington as Secretary of Defense in the Kennedy Administration, he was called upon to dispose of $1.5 million worth of Ford stock. But he found himself also restricted in what he could do with proceeds of the sale. McNamara offered to place his money in a trust over which he would have no control. The trust would be operated by financial managers who would make such investments as they saw fit, reporting to him from time to time to tell him of the over-all financial standing of the trust. The Senate Armed Services Committee objected to the scheme and insisted that the trust be prohibited from making any purchases or sales of defense stocks, regardless of whether the Secretary of Defense was aware of these transactions. Whereupon McNamara suggested the trust be barred only from doing business in outright defense companies such as those producing missiles, airplanes and ships, but that it be permitted to make investments in firms that were only incidentally in the defense field. The committee insisted it would be impossible to draw the line. Nor was the committee persuaded by McNamara's observation that if he bought government bonds, he would probably be in a position to exert greater self-interest through any contribution he made on regulations regarding Federal interest rates or decisions on the Federal budget than through any profits he might earn in the scheme he proposed. Nobody seemed to take notice of the implied irony directed at the widely applauded decision of President Kennedy to place his money in government bonds.

While tightening the moral requirements for confirmation of high Defense officials, Congress in recent years has tended to ignore possible questionable conduct of its own members, following efforts at stringency that were instituted in disgust with the situation on Capitol Hill in the mid-1800s. In one of the notorious cases, Senator Simmons of Rhode Island was promised a $10,000 commission in return for introducing a manufacturer to the Secretary of War. A commission investigating ordnance stores attributed the affair to a "vicious system of Administration" and concluded that neither the Senator nor the manufacturer had violated the law.[16] An issue debated at the time was whether members of Congress should be free to represent clients at courts-martial. One member, who opposed the remunerative practice, told of a Congressman who appeared as a counsel and said to a member of the court: "You expect soon to be promoted and I give you to understand that your confirmation will not get through the Senate without some difficulty."[17] As a result a law was passed to forbid members of Congress from receiving "any money or thing of value" for helping in the procurement of government contracts.

The question, of course, has remained whether members of Congress who, as a matter of course, strive to obtain defense contracts for their communities are not coming close to ignoring the admonition against assisting in defense procurement for "personal" gain. The question is pertinent, not because it was the intention of Congress to preclude the activities of members of Congress in behalf of their communities. Indeed, this was not the case. But the question arises because the statute did not demand a Congressman's divestment of personal interest, for example, divestment of stock shares. Yet it did demand that a member of the Executive Branch divest himself of financial interest in firms doing business with their departments. It thus seems logical to ask whether some action should not be taken to restrict members of Congress seeking defense business in behalf of their home towns. Often such a defense interest involves only a single contractor in whose enterprise a Congressman might very well have stock interests.

The dual standard once prompted the late Senator Richard L. Neuberger of Oregon to say: "I fear that it has a corroding effect on government generally when a member of the President's Cabinet can be ordered to jettison his corporate portfolio by Senators who themselves may be dabbling in oil, cotton futures, television, hotel chains or uranium."[18]

Congressmen, however, were expected to fight for contracts for their communities. In 1959 Representative John R. Foley of Maryland proposed an amendment to the defense bill that would have added $10 million for the Air Force to buy ten F-27 transport planes from the Fairchild Company of Hagerstown, located in his district. The House turned him down, but the Senate voted $11 million. When the proposal met with resistance, Senator J. Glenn Beall of Maryland beseeched the Senate to insist upon the appropriation in the House-Senate conference. Of the $4 billion allocated for aircraft, he said, "all we ask for Fairchild is $11 million."

Military procurement contracts totaling more than $25 billion have overshadowed the old "pork barrel" military construction upon which favored members of Congress have long depended. Still, the allocation of military installations and bases throughout the country has retained its economic appeal. Thus Representative Ken Hechler of West Virginia once told the House: "I am firmly against the kind of logrolling which would subject our defense program to narrowly sectional or selfish pulling and hauling. But I am getting pretty hot under the collar about the way my state of West Virginia is short-changed in Army, Navy and Air Force installations. . . . I am going to stand up on my hind legs and roar until West Virginia gets the fair treatment she deserves."[19] Early in 1963, another West Virginian, Representative Harley O. Staggers, roared for his colleague when the House passed a $1,633 million military construction bill and, as he put it, "not one penny in it" was for West Virginia.[20]

The fight for military contracts has figured in elections throughout the country. Martin Miller, the county district attorney in Denver, home of the Martin plant, said: "The principal issue in the last Congressional campaign for our district turned on the question of whether or not the United States Government should spend more money for military appropriations and defense, or less. Congressman Johnson, the incumbent, was against increased military spending. He felt that he had to be convinced that it was necessary before he would vote for it. In fact, in the previous Congress, he voted against it. His opponent was for increased military spending in the interest of national defense. Johnson's position was known to the community. It was public. It was everywhere discussed. His opponent, I think, campaigned on this issue in our community: at coffees, at teas, at meetings and so forth, where he would indicate, not directly saying that if I don't vote for increased spending you will lose your job, but without any doubt leaving this implication very clear that increased military expenses were tied directly to the economic security of the area. The folks understood. They got the message certainly. It was passed down, I think, properly, by Martin Company people to their employees and as a block I think they voted for the increased spending for military defense."[21]

Miller's version of the contest was confirmed by Representative Peter Dominick: "Yes, one of the main issues in my campaign for the Second District was the issue of whether or not defense expenditures should be continued at the level that they were then at, or even increased. My opponent for the district, the man who held it during the preceding two years, had voted against the national defense appropriations bill in two years, both in 1959 and in 1960. He was one, I think, of three or four who did this, and interestingly enough every one of these people was defeated."[22]

Senator Edward M. (Ted) Kennedy's campaign for the Senate in 1962 was pegged to the slogan, "He can do more for Massachusetts." The slogan, which aroused ire and scorn even from some who were well disposed toward his candidacy, was directed to the candidate's relationship to the President, his brother, as a means of securing government contracts. Young Kennedy won handily. And he immediately proceeded to push for contracts, not always with success apparently. President Kennedy, at a news conference, observed that his brother had gone to the Pentagon in an attempt to sway the tough Secretary of Defense and had failed. While the President was underscoring the tough integrity of his Secretary of Defense he was also, as a former Senator from Massachusetts, calling attention to his brother's efforts in behalf of the state. Not long afterward young Senator Kennedy did "do more"—he got a $50 million National Aeronautics and Space Administration center for the Boston vicinity.

President Kennedy himself did "something" for Boston, New York and San Francisco early in his Administration. Assuming the unusual role of "tipster," the President touched off a protest against a plan at the Pentagon to close the Philadelphia, Boston and San Francisco Navy Yards. The Boston Navy Yard employed about 8,300 civilians, the Philadelphia yard about 9,600 and the San

Francisco yard about 7,600. The tip occurred when Representative John F. Shelley of San Francisco, a friend of the President, was taking his children on a tour of the White House. They met the President. After joking with the children, the President turned to the Congressman and said, "Jack, I want to speak to you about something," and proceeded to tell him about the Pentagon plan to close the yards. "They can't do that," protested Shelley, "not with this defense build-up." The President grinned and said, "I don't think so either."

At this point the White House and Shelley versions of the encounter differ only slightly. Shelley quoted the President as saying, "Now you know about it, go to work." Pierre Salinger, the White House press secretary, who confirmed the story, said that the San Francisco Congressman volunteered to generate protests. In any event, Shelley returned to his office on the basis of the President's tip and immediately called people in Boston and Philadelphia. By chance, some representatives of the San Francisco Navy Yard Employees Association came to see him at his office. "They nearly had heart failure when I told them," Shelley reported. In December, 1963, on the eve of the publication of a list of outmoded military installations to be closed, Washington echoed with the protests of members of Congress whose communities were affected. Secretary McNamara conceded, when he announced the list, that his telephone had been kept ringing. There was special interest in the fate of the Boston, Philadelphia and San Francisco Navy Yards since several Congressmen were told that these yards were on the list and House Speaker John McCormack personally protested at the White House in behalf of the Massachusetts delegation. When the list appeared, however, these yards were not named. Secretary McNamara observed, nevertheless, that the existing eleven Navy shipyards were surplus to the country's needs and ordered a new survey. He made clear that one or more of the yards would inevitably be closed. It was also clear that this would not happen before the 1964 election campaign.

The gamut of self-interest thus runs from outright criminality to questions of good taste and party politics all bundled under laws and official admonitions against "conflicts of interest." Early in his

Administration President Kennedy sought to bring some coherence into the "conflict-of-interest" regulations "to provide a guide on ethical standards to Government officials." In an executive order, he introduced officially the notion that it was insufficient merely to behave within the law. Government officials were ordered also not "to create the appearance of" using public office for private gain, giving preferential treatment, causing an adverse effect on confidence of the public in the government, etc.[23] But recurrently, incidents of self-serving behavior testified to the great power of what President Kennedy once described as the "temptation of opportunity."

XIII

Fantastic Weapons

"True, the world has always been a dangerous place whether in the jungle or in the paths of Genghis Khan, the Goths, or Hitler's forces. But we had to achieve a high degree of civilization before we could make the danger to the world potentially complete."
—EUGENE M. ZUCKERT, Secretary of the Air Force

A few months after the Soviet sputnik astonished the world and panicked many of its inhabitants in late 1957, an Air Force general outlined his idea of using the moon as a missile base. From such a base, he pointed out, the United States could retaliate against the Soviet Union should Moscow use its newly demonstrated prowess to attack this country. The moon, he pointed out, with the matter-of-factness of a lecturer at a military college, "represents the age-old military advantage of 'high ground.' "[1]

"Utter nonsense," retorted a distinguished scientist. Why transport a hydrogen warhead, together with all men and equipment, 240,000 miles to the moon, just to shoot it 240,000 miles back to earth when the target is only 5,000 miles away in the first place? If you did launch a bomb from the moon to a target on earth, the warhead would take five days to reach earth. The war might be over by then. Can we use the great new technologies of space travel for peaceful and scientific purposes? Or are we going to be led into wild programs of Buck Rogers stunts and insane pseudo-military expeditions?[2]

The Eisenhower Administration heeded the advice of those scientists who sought to de-emphasize the military role of the moon —or anywhere in space for that matter. Eisenhower sponsored the creation of a new government agency, the National Aeronautics and Space Administration, to conduct most of the nation's space programs. The President explained that he had decided upon a civilian-directed rather than a military agency "because space exploration holds promise of adding importantly to our knowledge of the earth, the solar system and the universe, and because it is of great importance to have the fullest cooperation of the scientific community at home and abroad in moving forward in the fields of space science and technology. Moreover a civilian setting for the administration of space function will emphasize the concern of our nation that outer space be devoted to peaceful and scientific purposes."[3]

Yet even the President's peace-oriented program recognized the military possibilities in space. Among the four factors for urgency cited by his Science Advisory Council was "the need to assure that full advantage is taken of the military potential of space." And among the seven civilian space agency objectives the President cited was "the making available of discoveries of military value to agencies directly concerned with national security."

The new agency, NASA, came into being on July 30, 1958. It got its start with the facilities of the National Committee for Aeronautics, which it incorporated; and with certain installations of the military services, notably the Army's Redstone Arsenal at Huntsville, Alabama. At Huntsville were 2,100 scientists and engineers, including the "team" of German scientists formed around Dr. Wernher von Braun. The "team" was a tight little group composed of German missile technicians who, like von Braun, had worked on the German V-1 and V-2 rockets at the development center at Peenemünde. These men had made possible the launching of the first American satellite, Explorer I. For this achievement, von Braun, the curly-haired, effervescent space enthusiast, who had been decorated by Hitler with the Knight's Cross, received from Eisenhower's hands the President's Award for Distinguished Civil Service. Von Braun and his colleagues were soon put to work fashioning the heavy-thrust Saturn rocket upon which the United States is depending for Apollo, the planned lunar landing.

The Saturn rocket has been designed with one and a half million pounds of thrust—eventually seven million pounds—twice as powerful as the rocket that the Soviets were estimated to be using in their space launches. The United States basic rocket booster, the Atlas, has only 360,000 pounds of thrust—less than half the power of the Soviet boosters. That the United States has not developed more powerful rockets is part of the explanation of the Soviet Union's lead in certain space spectaculars. Ironically, it is explained also by the United States' own lead in nuclear weapons. Officials point out that when the hydrogen bomb was devised, it was hailed largely because it could be perfected into a warhead smaller than an atom bomb. This made it unnecessary to develop heavy-thrust rockets. The Russians, on the other hand, developed their powerful boosters to handle atomic warheads since they did not achieve the lighter hydrogen warhead until much later.

NASA took over most of the spectacular space projects contemplated by the military services, but the problems and prospects of space travel—and warfare—continue to intrigue the professional military men. Despite official demurrers, the military continues to eye the moon. The Army has even produced a military map of the moon. The value of the moon as a military base is said to be: first, that it presents another target or targets, dispersed and difficult to hit in a first strike; second, that targets on earth would be easier to hit from the moon than originally contemplated; third, that with the use of inertial flywheels and similar devices enough energy can be stored or obtained on the moon to permit the establishment of a manned base. "The moon is not nearly so barren as it seems," observed an Air Force physicist in early support of the idea of a lunar military base.[4]

The idea of a base on the moon is only one of the fantastic projects that has come to the minds of military men, despite their comic strip antecedents. Most space vehicles are less outrageous to contemplate today than the ordinary airplanes and submarines of the past, military men say. If Jules Verne's dream of a submarine could be realized, why not his trip to the moon? Why not his space gun, which would be more practical on the moon than on the earth since it would not be handicapped by the atmosphere that surrounds earth? Indeed, are not the second and third rocket stages of booster vehicles, in effect, space guns? And why not even Buck Rogers' ray gun?

Ray gun? That too is being developed. The amplification of light by stimulating the emission of radiation—a technique known as laser —is being studied in dozens of laboratories around the world. The principle, like all successful accomplishments once they are accomplishments, is simple. Ordinary light waves coming from a single source are dispersed, as the electrons of the color spectrum emit light of different frequencies and intensities. An ordinary light strong enough to project as far as the moon would form a focus at best of 25,000 miles. With amplified laser, the waves of light remain "coherent." The electrons of the spectrum are made to emit light at exactly the same energy and frequency. They then achieve tremendous intensity. They also travel enormous distances without bending or spreading.

In a major test, a team of research scientists at the Massachusetts Institute of Technology touched off a flash of intense red laser light from a six-inch ruby rod no thicker than a lead pencil and successfully directed it to the moon. Three seconds later, it burst on the lunar surface southeast of the crater Albategnius and reflected back to M.I.T., where it was caught on sensitive photomultipliers of a telescopic receiver.[5] Man had built a light strong enough to illuminate a celestial body. Light waves, it has been shown, can be amplified just as radio waves have been amplified. It foreshadows an era when light beams may be used to guide space vehicles, communicate between planets and destroy hostile missiles and space vehicles in flight!

General Curtis E. LeMay, Chief of Staff of the Air Force, discussed these potentialities in early 1962 when he told a college audience:

"Our national security in the future may depend on armaments far different from any we know today, and believe me they won't be ultimate weapons either. Perhaps they will be weapons that enable us to neutralize earth-based ICBMs. Perhaps they will be weapons that strike with the speed of light. That kind of speed makes the fifteen-hundred-mile-an-hour ICBM a relatively slow-moving target." The Air Force Chief said such weapons, employing light rays traveling at 186,000 miles an hour in the near-vacuum of space, would bring the world into a new mode of warfare. Nor could he resist the temptation that existed with most American military leaders responsible for the nation's safety. "We've looked into the phenomena associated with this kind of weapon," he said. "We have evidence from scientific papers they have published that the Soviets are also interested."[6]

As a matter of fact, the Russians are interested, as Khrushchev himself confirmed. The Soviet Premier received an American visitor at the height of the Cuba crisis and discussed, among other things, some recent scientific developments. The visitor afterward reported: "He picked up a steel ruler about six inches long and a half inch wide which was also on the table. He said this was another present from his scientists and that if I would hold it up to the light I would see scores of exceedingly fine holes through the metal. He said these were made by laser light. He said he knew our scientists were working on laser developments but that he was convinced that Soviet scientists were ahead of those in the United States."[7]

Within a few years after flashing on the scientific horizon, laser has been hailed as a wondrous contribution to medical science. It has been used in delicate eye and brain operations. It has been used in industry, for welding and cutting metals. Scientists have sought it for computers that would operate, literally, with the speed of light. Inevitably they have worked on laser radar for battlefield use and laser tracking systems for monitoring the flight of missiles. Even those who doubt that laser can be developed to deflect or knock out a missile in flight, as General LeMay implied, acknowledge that a laser beam can be destructive at relatively short range. A single pulse under certain conditions can set wood, paper and other easily inflammable materials ablaze at a distance of two miles. So even if those who work with lasers have not yet assured its use against enemy missiles and satellites, it already is capable of use as a death ray—long a dream of military planners as well as comic strip artists.

The United States possesses an array of military missiles in operation or under development, and a variety of satellites, several of them under secret development, whose potentiality for sheer destructiveness is as awesome as they are ingenious. Among them, the chief instrument of death is the long-range ballistic missile, remarkable progeny of the ancient ballista. In ancient times rocks and fireballs were hurled by placing them on the exposed end of long poles stuck in the ground and bent back so that they could spring forward. The forward, catapulting action of the weapons, known as ballista, sent the "payloads" over the walls of fortresses. In the modern era, the United States boasts a ten-story Atlas intercontinental ballistic missile weighing 269,000 pounds that can be launched at a speed of sixteen thousand miles per hour to a target nine thousand miles away. The Titan, a sister missile, has similar flight capabilities. The Minuteman is a so-called "second-generation" ICBM, and uses solid fuel instead of the more troublesome liquid fuels. The Minuteman, much smaller than its predecessors, weighs 69,000 pounds at launch time and is only fifty-four feet long. It is the chief long-range missile weapon of the sixties, capable of being hurled from underground silos over intercontinental distances. It is a sign of the times that earlier types of ballistic missiles, such as the Thor and Jupiter, which had a range of fifteen hundred miles, and the first Atlas missiles were declared obsolescent in 1963 and 1964 after an operational tenure of only five years.

The Air Force is responsible for the intercontinental "deterrent" weapons, so called because they are intended to deter enemy action by the threat of their retaliatory power. Each of the services, however, has a family of airborne, ship-borne and ground-based missiles that can be used against enemy land targets, attacking aircraft or ships at sea. The Army has 75-mile range Corporals and Sergeants, the 175-mile Redstone and 400-mile Pershing missiles. These have provided new dimensions for the artilleryman's ancient art—this time with nuclear warheads. So refined has the weapons art become that nuclear-armed bazookas, dubbed Davy Crocketts, can be carried and operated by two or three men in front-line combat positions. Another of the outstanding weapons is the Sidewinder, a homing guided missile carried beneath the wings of Air Force and Navy fighter planes. It has a conventional warhead, equipped with an infrared heat-seeking device. When released in the air against an enemy plane, the Sidewinder seeks out the hot exhaust of the enemy jet funnel and explodes.

One of the most remarkable of all weapons systems is the Polaris-armed submarine, product of the "marriage" of the nuclear-powered submarine and the ballistic missile. It combines the "unstoppability" of the missile and the mobility, evasiveness, stealth and endurance of nuclear-powered submarines that can patrol undisclosed hiding places beneath the seas. Each of the submarines, about the size of a destroyer, carries amidships a bay of sixteen bottle-shaped missiles, each twenty-eight feet long and weighing three thousand pounds. These can be popped out of the water with compressed air launchers at the rate of one per minute. As the missile reaches a point just above the surface, powerful rocket engines, fueled by a rubber-like polyeurathane compound, ignite and send the nuclear warhead to its target. Early Polaris missiles had a range of a little over a thousand miles. The latest version is designed for 2,500 miles.

The development of the Polaris-armed submarine represents a revolution in sea power and has demonstrated that the military services are capable of scientific achievements in peacetime every bit as dramatic as those that took place in war. Two Annapolis graduates played prominent roles. One was a Russian-born Jewish boy whose parents migrated before World War I to Chicago, Illinois, where his father was a tailor. The boy became a vice admiral of the United States Navy and world-acclaimed as the "father" of the nuclear submarine. He is Hyman George Rickover, Annapolis '22, a small, spare man, gray hair parted in the middle as in an old tintype —"rather tired-looking most of the time," said a good observer. As a captain during World War II, Rickover headed a four-man Navy delegation to the Manhattan Project. He was a graduate of the submarine school at New London, Connecticut, and served three peacetime years as a submarine officer. It was not surprising, therefore, that he proposed in 1946 a scheme for a submarine with nuclear power. The Navy previously had studied the possibility of nuclear-propelled submarines. A proposal by Dr. Ross Gunn and Dr. Philip Abelson, of the Naval Research Laboratory, had even been approved by the Bureau of Ships. But Rickover finally succeeded where others were thwarted and it is his story that is remembered. His first memorandum on the subject, in which he promised he could build a nuclear-propulsion plant in three years, got nowhere. A year later he wrote a bitter attack on the newly formed Atomic Energy Commission, successor to Manhattan Project, because it was interested chiefly in nuclear power for explosives instead of for engineering. He denounced the big electric companies for failing to invest sufficiently in nuclear power as a source of future electrical energy. For his pains he was brought back to Washington to be an assistant to the Chief of the Bureau of Ships. His small office was a converted ladies' room.

Rickover continued his campaign. Despite resistance in the echelons between him and the top, he found a sympathetic ear in Admiral of the Fleet Chester W. Nimitz, Chief of Naval Operations, also an old submariner. Nimitz appointed Rickover chief of a new nuclear power division in the Navy. But Rickover's struggle had only begun. The little captain met resistance on several counts. He was Jewish. He was arrogant. He was querulous. He was egotistical. He was brilliant but abrasive. He was sincerely trying to improve the Navy, but he had no respect for its cherished "ways." All the charges were true. Rickover's counterweapons were his "enormous ego, his tyrannical methods, his unrelenting pursuit of perfection, his undentable and unbendable belief in his essential idea, his inhuman energy—and his determination to use this entire array against anyone who blocked his way."[8] In 1948 Rickover managed a coup that put him in a remarkable position to carry the project forward. He was placed in charge of the Atomic Energy Commission's nuclear reactors branch. He had two hats—one at the Navy and one at the Atomic Energy Commission and could, and did, write letters to himself, answer them immediately and get an "agreement," for the official record.[9]

Then came a major blow. In July, 1951, Rickover was passed over for promotion to flag rank by a Navy selection board. The reasons, by tradition, were secret. The explanations offered under cover of anonymity were that Rickover's experience was too specialized; that he was not a "nice" person, that is, mannerly and officer-like in the proud traditions of military service. The first turndown for promotion, while distressing to Rickover, was not critical. He worked on. On June 14, 1951, the keel was laid on the *Nautilus,* the first atomic submarine. President Harry Truman said: "The day that the propellers of this new submarine first bite into the water will be the most momentous day in atomic science since that first flash in the desert seven years ago." Rickover was there in civilian clothes, standing at the rear of the crowd. He got his Legion of Merit for the occasion a month later along with a citation hailing "the most important piece of development work in the history of the Navy."

But the day after the keel-laying, a second Rickover selection board rejected recommendations from the Navy Secretary, the officers of the Bureau of Ships and the Atomic Energy Commission and withheld promotion. Rickover was headed for statutory retirement when Representative Sidney Yates of Chicago publicly denounced the "convoy mentality" of the selection board and challenged its motives as well as its methods. Clay Blair, Jr. of *Time* Magazine wrote a lengthy story, which he afterward turned into a book, depicting in considerable detail the upstream battle Rickover had fought and the Navy's shabby treatment of him. A national uproar developed over the Rickover case. Congress threatened to put the entire Navy selection board under examination and held up the confirmations of thirty-nine captains promoted to admiral until a specially instructed selection board finally promoted Rickover.

On January 17, 1955, six years after the first formal operational requirement for the nuclear-powered submarine was written, the *Nautilus* cast off her lines at Groton, Connecticut, and cruised down the Thames River through Block Island Sound to the waters of Long Island Sound. "Under way on nuclear power," came the message from the skipper, Commander Eugene Wilkinson. The horn sounded twice. The officer of the deck called "Dive, dive," and the new *Nautilus,* poking her nose gently downward, slid beneath the surface. Rickover was hailed everywhere except in the Navy. Only Congressional support kept him on the job and assured his promotion to vice admiral in 1958. When in 1963 it appeared that he finally would have to retire, arrangements were made to keep him at his task as a civilian.[10]

The *Nautilus* was not a year old before a new stage was set in the development of modern sea power. On December 4, 1955, Rear Admiral William F. Raborn, Assistant Chief of Staff for Operations, Atlantic Fleet, in Norfolk, was ordered to report to Washington to become head of a new special projects division. Raborn, Texas born, schooled in Oklahoma, had never seen the sea before he got to the Naval Academy in 1924. When he finally did get there, he ran down to the sea wall and looked out on Chesapeake Bay. "I saw a lighthouse out there and thought it was a ship," the farm boy said. His early training was as an aviator. That a flier should have been called to take charge of the development of a new kind of submarine, capable of firing missiles like an underwater artillery piece, might have seemed incongruous. But one look at the burly, barrel-chested redhead was reassuring. Although he had no "fluff on his cheekbones," he appeared to at least one Englishman, member of a seagoing race, "physically and temperamentally the kind of sea dog who might have been a match for Hornblower off the Windward Islands in the old days."

Admiral Burke, Chief of Naval Operations, explained why Raborn was chosen. He had to be an aviator to assure cooperation from the Air Force; available from other duties and yet not a discard—"but mostly he had to be a nice person, who got along with people when the going got tough." One Rickover, apparently, was enough. Unlike Rickover, Raborn was given a "hunting license" in the form of a Burke memorandum which read: "If Admiral Raborn runs into any difficulty with which I can help I will want to know about it at once, along with his recommended course of action. If he needs people, those people will be ordered in."

Raborn traveled constantly, delivering pep talks to scientists, engineers and work crews at government installations and private contractors. These talks became famous as the "Raborn Rededication Treatment," described by one listener as "part locker-room pep talk, part Navy enlistment appeal, part Arthur Godfrey commercial." Everywhere he went the genial redhead won cooperation and unstinting effort. "One of the reasons why so many people want this program to succeed so much is that they want to prove that a guy can run one and not be a —————" was one comment. This was an undisguised thrust at Rickover, whom the Navy would never forgive for forcing it to develop the nuclear submarine. Yet, ironically, Admiral Rickover played a key role in helping Raborn meet his completion date. As a "subcontractor" to the Polaris project, Rickover was responsible for the nuclear reactor. He helped work out a scheme to bisect the *Scorpion,* a nuclear submarine under construction. This permitted installation of a missile bay, although the welders reluctantly tackled the job. It was an affront to their aesthetic sense.[11] The effect was not unlike cutting a cigar in half and putting a match-box in between the two halves. That was how the *George Washington—*the *Scorpion* renamed—was "designed."

After a critical testing period in 1958 and early 1959, in which missiles kept blowing up, a Polaris was launched from a stationary pad in April, 1959. Finally, on July 20, 1960, the pioneering crew of the *George Washington* successfully hurled its first and second missiles out of the blue-green waters off the Florida coast. "Polaris —from out of the deep to target—perfect," wired the jubilant Commander James B. Osborne. Raborn described the event as the most significant in weaponry since the airplane first flew. It was he who had named the missile Polaris, the sailor's friend and guide.

While delighted with this remarkable instrument of war, most Americans now look to technological developments in space to express the national power. When President Kennedy ordered the manned landings on the moon in the decade of the sixties, despite the cost and over powerful opposition, he said: "Our leadership in science and industry, our hopes for peace and security, our obligations to ourselves as well as others, all require us to make this [space] effort, to solve these [space] mysteries . . . for the good of all men, and to become the world's leading space-faring nation."

President Lyndon Johnson, who as a Senator waged a powerful political and legislative campaign for an increased American effort in space, once said, when asked to justify the Kennedy Administration's huge space budget, "I do not see our survival as a free and first-rate nation unless we lead in space." And then he went on:

Visualize, if you will, high-level officials of the world's nations as seated about a negotiating table on matters affecting the peace of the world. The nation with the greatest proven competence in space science and engineering would have a huge negotiating advantage over those nations, which did not have such strength. If the nation so endowed were one to use its space strength to support freedom, the world would gain. If, on the other hand, such nation were one given to blackmail, coercion and domination, freedom would be the loser.[12]

But there is considerable difference of opinion in Washington whether control of space spells control of the world. The question was put to Dr. Harold Brown, the Pentagon's Director of Defense Research and Engineering, during closed Senate hearings, and even the censored transcript of his dialogue with one of the Senators is enlightening.

"What part do you envision that space is going to play in the wars of the future and what are we doing to meet that requirement?" Senator Strom Thurmond asked Dr. Brown.

The answer was: "I believe that it is conceivable but not likely that space may become an area in which armed combat takes place directly from space. . . . [But] I believe that is not very likely because you can probably do it better from the ground, and we have a program that will allow us to do it from the ground. I think that it is possible that in the future we will want to put men up in our military space vehicles so as to make equipment work better, and if that is the case we have to have a larger payload capacity than we have now, we have to be able to support men in space over long periods of time, and so on. I am not at all convinced, by the way, that this will actually prove to be necessary."

"Do you feel, as someone expressed it, that the nation that controls space will control the world? Do you feel that strongly?" Senator Thurmond asked.

"I would not subscribe to that statement partly because I am not quite sure what control of space means," Dr. Brown replied. "I do not see that it is really feasible to control space because a country will always have an advantage in space over its own territory because it can easily operate from the ground up into space. I do not see a way, for example, in which space can be controlled to the extent that one can prevent ballistic missiles from being fired here, going through space and coming down there. If a country could do that, it would indeed be in a fair way to control the world, and we continue to work on ideas that might have that effect. But I think in the end it is not going to be feasible. . . . I do not quite see the purpose of shooting weapons from a platform down onto the earth, not because it cannot be done, but because I think it can be done better from earth to earth."

Military men, particularly in the Air Force, which had the "space mission," resented such conservatism as displayed by Dr. Brown. In another hearing, he expressed the opinion that science had come to a pause in its spectacular revolution. "The future, I think, holds some surprises and some advances, but the number of revolutionary changes we can foresee is not likely to be large," he said. "Do you foresee anything as dramatic in the next eighteen years as we have had in the last eighteen years in the field of weaponry?" he was asked. "Probably not" was the reply.[13]

This young man, who was predicting "no dogfights in space," was not even born when some of his high-ranking military subordinates were earning their first medals. He was the prototype of the "Whiz Kids" or bright young men who held positions of enormous power in the Pentagon during the Kennedy Administration. Born in New York City on September 19, 1927, he showed signs of genius from early childhood. His mother recalled how at the age of four he removed a refrigerator door panel to watch the motor. He was graduated from the Bronx High School of Science in 1943 at fifteen and a half. He had a 99.52 average, won the Phi Beta Kappa award, and prizes in French, English, mathematics, social studies and the physical sciences. As a candidate for a New York State scholarship, he placed first among several thousand secondary school students. At Columbia University he started in engineering, switched to physics, but got his B.A. in two years anyway, graduating at the age of seventeen and a half with honors in physics and mathematics.

When Brown was appointed Director of Research and Engineering at the Pentagon, a job considered third highest among civilians of the Defense Department, he had already served in several major research programs, including Project Plowshare, the plan to adapt nuclear explosions for peaceful purposes such as creating harbors and recovering oil deposits, and as an adviser in the early nuclear test-ban discussions with the Soviet Union in Geneva. He came to the Pentagon from the Livermore Laboratory in California, where he had succeeded Dr. Edward Teller, father of the H-bomb, as director. Six feet tall, two hundred pounds, Brown, who never became a "grind" in school, enjoyed baseball, tennis and swimming. He took up flying in morning sessions before going to his Pentagon office at around 8 A.M.

Unlike the conservative young Dr. Brown, military men forecast major unforeseeable changes and recommend preparations for unknown contingencies. One of the protagonists in the debate, which, in contrast with those during the Eisenhower Administration, rarely comes out in public, is Lieutenant General Bernard Adolf Schriever. Schriever became prominent for his management of the development of intercontinental ballistic missiles. By any standard, except in comparison with Dr. Brown, whose senior he is by seventeen years, General Schriever is one of the young men among the nation's defenders.

Schriever was born in Bremen, Germany, and was seven years old when he was brought to the United States in 1917. His father died when Ben was eight years old and the family lived in various Texas communities. Ben was a brilliant mathematics student and won national honors in math when he was graduated from San Antonio High School in 1927. Upon graduation from the Agriculture and Mechanical College of Texas, in 1931, with an engineering degree, he planned to become an architect. But his college ROTC experience led him into flight training at Kelly Field and a commission in the Air Corps Reserve. After that, except for a brief period when he worked as a co-pilot for Northwest Airlines and helped run a CCC camp in New Mexico, he made his career in military service.

Schriever flew sixty-three combat missions in World War II, mostly with B-17 bombers, the old Flying Fortresses. After the war he became "insane" on the subject of missiles. By the time he was brigadier general at the age of forty-three, he was named assistant for Air Force development and planning. This came at a critical juncture in

American military strategy. In 1953 the Air Force established the so-called "teapot" committee on strategic missiles evaluation. The chairman was the late Professor John von Neumann, then of the Princeton Institute for Advanced Study.[14] The committee's recommendation for an urgent revamping of the missiles program was adopted, and in 1954 Schriever was given a special assignment as commander of the newly created Western Development Division at Inglewood, California. In this job, supervising a force of more than seventy thousand, he guided the development of the Air Force's missile arsenal—Atlas, Titan, Minuteman. He became a four-star general and head of the Air Force's Systems Command, in charge of all development work.

Six feet two inches tall, slender, good-looking, soft-spoken, Schriever looks like a college basketball player. At first, he was outspoken in his demands for heavy investments in military technology in space. As the Kennedy Administration frowned on public outspokenness, Schriever fenced carefully with his Pentagon superiors, including Dr. Brown, on the question of military assignments in space. His eloquent speech to the Air Force Association in the fall of 1961 constitutes a basic policy document on the military's space ambitions. The United States must "rethink" its "traditional approach" to the use of technology, Schriever said and added: "Historically we have tended to overestimate what we could do on a short time basis, and to grossly underestimate what we could do on a long-term basis. As a result, the United States has been notably slow to recognize the military applications of new inventions. Two of the most significant technical achievements of this century—the airplane and the liquid-fueled rocket—are American inventions. Yet in each case their first application was made by other nations."

Schriever went on: "After the first airplane flew at Kitty Hawk, North Carolina, more than three years passed before the United States Army decided to buy one. Even then the military potential of the airplane went unrecognized. When World War I broke out, and when American pilots flew into action, they flew foreign aircraft exclusively. No American-designed plane saw combat during World War I. The work of Robert Goddard, inventor of the liquid-fueled rocket, was neglected in the United States but studied overseas, notably by Germany and the Soviet Union. By 1929, three years after Goddard's first successful rocket flight, Germany had started a rocket program. The Soviet Union started three years later and had substantial accomplishments by 1935.

"By 1939 Germany was spending one-third of her aerodynamic research budget at Peenemünde, the tiny peninsula on the North Sea where Wernher von Braun and other German rocket specialists came to prominence. Germany had twelve thousand workers at Peenemünde and at least one thousand qualified researchers in rocketry elsewhere in the country. In the same year Goddard had five technicians. In the whole of the United States at that time there were probably not more than twenty-five people working with liquid rockets. American scientists began to learn of Goddard's work through captured German documents. Early indications that the Soviet Union might be producing intercontinental ballistic missiles were largely ignored.

"I have cited these examples to indicate the danger that lies in inadequate military planning for the future. Now we may find ourselves in a similar position in regard to space. We should recognize that there is no inherent difference between basic military and non-military space technology. What really matters is not the technology but the intent."[15]

That was the last major speech by a man in uniform calling without inhibition for a military-oriented space program. After that it was made clear officers were not to dispute defense policies in public. General Schriever, as a good soldier, possibly being considered for Air Force Chief of Staff, dutifully kept his peace in public.

Challenged by defense officials to demonstrate their missiles and space requirements, military men have come up with proposals for a remarkable arsenal. Air Force Secretary Zuckert looks "beyond the development of a military orbital space station" to the aerospace plane, "designed to take off from existing runways, without use of a missile-type booster . . . go into orbit, maneuver into a parking orbit, de-orbit, maneuver while entering the earth's atmosphere, and then land conventionally at an air base."[16] To enhance the invulnerability of missiles, thought is being given to a long-endurance aircraft as a launching platform—not necessarily nuclear-powered, but employing turboprop propulsion and incorporating the latest aerodynamic designs. An Air Force officer told the American Institute of Aeronautics and Astronautics in May, 1963, that a hovering aircraft, capable of remaining aloft forty-eight hours, already is feasible.[17]

In the meantime the Pentagon is pushing ahead with a variety of military satellites, mostly for communication, surveillance and warning. The Navy is working on Project Anna, a geodetic satellite system to achieve more accurate mapping and knowledge of the earth's gravitational field. The Navy is developing a satellite navigation system, known as Transit. It calls for the use of satellites in near-earth orbit to provide "fixes" for ships and planes throughout the world in the same way that these are provided by the stars. The Army and Navy are cooperating in developing a communications satellite system. This includes a hovering satellite, launched into a position over the Equator and remaining in that position constantly. Samos, a reconnaissance satellite, is being developed to take pictures of terrain and pick up various types of radio, radar and electronic signals. Under cover of military secrecy several Samos satellites have been launched, unannounced, and the results are said to be far more effective than those obtained with U-2 planes. The Samos is similar to the Tiros satellites, which have successfully taken pictures of cloud formations as an aid to weather forecasting. In fact, the military significance of knowing the weather makes Tiros an obvious military satellite and it is interesting that the Soviets never have complained about Samos or Tiros, although they have whirled over Soviet territory.

Midas, which was undertaken with tremendous publicity, has been officially described as a partial failure. It was intended as an early-warning satellite, capable of detecting ballistic missile launchings with its equipment of infrared sensors. There is some suspicion that the Administration has "reoriented" the program to get it out of the public domain and pursue it secretly. Another secret satellite under development is Saint (the nickname was dropped before the curtain of secrecy was drawn over it, for fear that church groups would object to the name, which came from the term "Satellite Inspector"). Saint was conceived as a satellite to be launched in the vicinity of an unknown satellite in order to inspect its nature and report to earth. Some proposals called for equipping the Saint with a weapon that could "neutralize" enemy satellites.

Also of military interest are proposals for a variety of satellites with men aboard—"military patrols," said one officer—which would improve detection of hostile enemy space activities. In other words, this would be a Saint satellite with a crew. Military men have expressed interest in a military orbital space station, or MODS. Such a station is a "natural focus" for the military portion of the national space program, an officer said.[18] A simple type of manned orbital laboratory, or MOL, contemplates attaching a 25-foot canister, the size of a house trailer, to the Gemini satellite that is being planned by the civilian space agency. Gemini, first step to a lunar landing, is being designed for two men. The Pentagon's MOL similarly would have room for two men. The joined MOL and Gemini would be sent into orbit. The men would walk from the Gemini into the MOL, without space suits. They would conduct experiments, then return. Eventually the MOL might be detached and permitted to fly in space alone, with or without men in it, while the Gemini capsule returned to earth. Then another Gemini would be launched to a rendezvous with the MOL, retrieve any men left behind or permit new experiments with a new crew. The experiments will be carried out to determine what kind of military operations are possible in space.

To overcome opposition to space weapons, some military men have suggested that space warfare could be a form of "limited warfare" rather than the cataclysm most persons regard it. According to this view, two powerful antagonists—say the United States and Soviet Union—might well prefer to fight it out on the moon, or select gladiatorial space ships for a battle, rather than fight with land-based nuclear weapons that could wipe out civilization on the earth. The very thought that such space duels might be possible confirms the real and awesome magnitude of the dangers of the space age. As Air Force Secretary Zuckert remarked: "True, the world has always been a dangerous place whether in the jungle or in the paths of Genghis Khan, the Goths, or Hitler's forces. But we had to achieve a high degree of civilization before we could make the danger to the world potentially complete."[19]

XIV

★

Choosing a National Strategy

"The victory which we seek will see no ticker tape parade down Broadway."

—W. W. Rostow, Chief, Policy Planning,
Department of State

Since World War II certain theories of national strategy have captured wide attention. These theories have catch names—containment, massive retaliation, deterrence, finite deterrence, limited war strategy, counterforce, flexible response. Some of the theories have been endorsed officially and adopted as policies. Others have been put forward in a nationwide discussion that has involved academicians, scientists, lawyers, historians and journalists, all concerned and intrigued with the growing magnitude and complexity of nuclear diplomacy. As conditions in the "cold war" change with new weapons and new power positions, popular support shifts from one strategy to another. At the Pentagon, too, there are fashions.

The national security strategy is not decided at the Pentagon, however. The President alone, surrounded though he may be by clamoring public and private advocates of various national security theses, makes the ultimate decision. The President is the Chief Executive who determines foreign and domestic priorities affecting the national defense, the Commander in Chief who alone can mobilize the country and order the use of nuclear weapons. President Kennedy was fond of quoting the lines of Domingo Ortega:

> Bull fight critics ranked in rows
> Crowd the enormous plaza full;
> But only one man is there who knows,
> And he's the man who fights the bull.*

The President may draw his advice from within or outside the Administration. The Cabinet, having become too big and its members' interests too diverse, is no longer the vehicle for this purpose insofar as national security is concerned. The statutory body is the National Security Council, which was established in 1947 along with the new unified Defense Department. The NSC, a descendant of the wartime State-War-Navy Coordinating Committee, includes in addition to the President who is chairman, the Vice President, the Secretaries of State and Defense, and the Director of the White House Office of Emergency Planning. Associate officials of the Council are the President's special assistant and deputy assistant for National Security Affairs and an executive secretary. It is notable that the Chairman of the Joint Chiefs of Staff is not a member of the National Security Council although he, like the Director of the Central Intelligence Agency, frequently is invited to attend its meetings.

Under the original act and throughout the Eisenhower Administration an Operations Coordinating Board, composed of Cabinet deputies and other high officials, was supposed to follow through on the Council's decisions. But President Kennedy, who regarded the NSC apparatus as too cumbersome anyway, abandoned the Coordinating Board. He did not like to be bound, even psychologically, to the NSC consensus and he preferred small meetings of security advisers who themselves would take responsibility for follow-through. Significantly, in the Cuba crisis of 1962, the President found

* As translated from the Spanish by Robert Graves in *Encounter*, December, 1951.

he needed an expanded consultative group and created the executive committee of the National Security Council. The "Excom," as it was known, included, in addition to its statutory members, the Secretary of the Treasury, the Attorney General (chiefly because he was the President's brother and confidant), the Chairman of the Joint Chiefs of Staff, the Under Secretary of State, Deputy Secretary of Defense, the Director of the CIA, the Special Adviser on Soviet Affairs, the President's special assistant for security affairs and his special counsel.

Under Eisenhower, the National Security Council prepared all-embracing, controlling definitions of policy. The "New Look" defense program, for example, was not merely an intellectual premise for government decision-making, but a formal program, debated and approved by the Council. Other policies similarly were approved and documented after heavily attended meetings of its members and their battalions of experts. In the crisis atmosphere of the fifties, military requirements were a priority item meeting after meeting. The military's long-range objectives became a controlling factor, recorded in position papers that could hardly be altered after all the exhausting work and hard-fought compromises that went into them. Once the premise of military crisis was established anyway, the influence of the military experts was substantial. As a result, long after certain international or technological developments rendered meaningless the slogans attached to national strategic policy, the Administration found itself stuck with them although it did not follow them to the letter.

In the Kennedy and Johnson Administrations there has been more of a "mix" of strategic postulates. An unprecedented rate of military investments in the period 1960-1964 has permitted the adoption, from a position of strength, of a policy of "flexible response"; that is, a strategic policy that permits coping with a wide range of threats to American security, from outright general attack on the American homeland to subversion of the government of an American ally. On this platform, for the first time since World War II, the United States has permitted itself the luxury of a "peace offensive."

The first substantive formulation of postwar American strategy was written by George Frost Kennan, a State Department career official whose uncle had been an expert on Czarist Russia. Kennan was one of the half-dozen young men chosen by the State Department in the late 1920s to be prepared as experts in Soviet affairs. Others were Charles E. Bohlen and Llewellyn Thompson, both of whom, like Kennan, became ambassadors to the Soviet Union. A scholarly, introspective man, Kennan came by his interest in foreign affairs from his father as well as his uncle. His father, Kossuth Kennan, was a lawyer in Milwaukee where George was born in 1904. Each year for twenty years Kossuth Kennan made an annual trip to Europe to recruit immigrants to work on farms served by the Western Railroads. Kennan was educated at St. John's Military Academy in Delafield, Wisconsin. He was graduated from Princeton in 1925, and it seemed perfectly natural for him to return to Princeton's Institute for Advanced Studies in those periods when, following his natural bent, he devoted himself to teaching, lecturing and studying. In 1946 he was appointed head of the newly created policy planning staff under Secretary of State George Marshall. He had just served two years as Minister Counselor in Moscow, under Ambassadors Averell Harriman and General Walter Bedell Smith. Now, at the instigation of James Forrestal, he set forth the famous containment policy in an article in *Foreign Affairs*, signing it "Mr. X."

Kennan had become convinced from his studies and experience that Soviet leaders were driven, not by a series of short-term objectives, each move inspiring the next, but by long-term aims at Communist world hegemony. The United States thus could not afford to wait passively, as in the past, until it became "involved" in a defensive war. It could not afford to see the Soviet Union envelop one state after another in Eastern Europe and strengthen the Communist parties of other countries to the point where these parties would attain power and exercise it under instructions from the Kremlin. The United States had to meet and *contain* Soviet expansionism, even if it meant dangerous collision, although most likely the Soviets would not choose an open struggle.

The policies set forth by Kennan were exemplified in the Truman Doctrine, which successfully bolstered Turkey against threats from Moscow and rescued Greece from Communist insurgency. Other expressions of the policy of containment were the Marshall Plan,

United States support for the Brussels Pact, strong support for the ruling governments against the Communist parties in Italy and France, the continuation of United States forces in Europe, the North Atlantic Treaty Organization, the unyielding resistance to the Soviet blockade of Berlin and the speedy intervention against the Communists in Korea.

The policy of containment, backed by American atomic-armed air power, forced a halt to Soviet expansionism. But it offered no visible "victories" and was hard to defend in domestic politics. In the campaign of 1952, in which General Eisenhower defeated Adlai Stevenson for the Presidency, John Foster Dulles was the Republican party's foreign policy spokesman. Dulles assailed the containment policy as "static." He urged a so-called rollback or "liberation" policy. When Eisenhower became President and Dulles his Secretary of State, no effort was made to roll back anyone. In the anti-Communist revolution in Hungary in 1956, the United States did not intervene and permitted the Soviet forces, which had evacuated the country, to return and quash the revolution.

More significant than Dulles' liberation policy, however, was the doctrine of massive retaliation, enunciated in 1954 in the wake of the Korean War with an eye to further Communist threats to the peace in the Far East. In a speech to the Council on Foreign Relations, Dulles announced that the Eisenhower Administration had adopted a new national policy. He said:

"If an enemy could pick his time and place and method of warfare—and if our policy was to remain the traditional one of meeting aggression by direct and local opposition—then we needed to be ready to fight in the Arctic and in the Tropics; in Asia, the Near East and in Europe; by sea, by land, and by air; with old weapons and with new weapons. . . . This could not be continued for long without grave budgetary, economic and social consequences. But before military planning could be changed, the President and his advisers, as represented by the National Security Council, had to make some basic policy decisions. This has been done. The basic decision was to depend primarily upon a great capacity to retaliate, instantly, by means and at places of our own choosing. . . . That permits of a selection of military means instead of multiplication of means. As a result, it is now possible to get, and share, more basic security at less cost."[1]

The glib Eisenhower Secretary of Defense, Charles E. Wilson, underscored the final point, saying the new policy, or "New Look," as it was called, would provide "a bigger bang for a buck." Essentially, the new strategy was intended to cope with the apparent Soviet technique of not engaging the United States directly but expanding at peripheral points through local aggression. The Eisenhower Administration feared that the United States' power to "contain" would be overloaded, that American resources would be strained through dispersal and consequent attrition. "We can't afford to fight limited wars," Wilson told General Gavin. "We can only afford to fight a big war, and if there is one, that is the kind it will be."

The massive retaliation doctrine was an attempt to awe the Soviet Union. It brandished atomic arms with the threat of using them even for relatively small infractions of the peace. There were to be no more Koreas. The man who phrased that doctrine, which has since been bitterly condemned but never quite discarded, was in fact reflecting the temper of the American people, which "approved of bold statements of defiance to the communist world, yet like the President and the Administration he represented, wanted peace above everything except honor."[2]

John Foster Dulles' name is linked in history with the policy of presenting the Communists with grim alternatives—"brinkmanship," he once called it—but he carefully avoided action that would risk war. In fact, he even amended the policy of "massive retaliation" in response to criticism of it. The manufacture of small atomic arms made possible the idea of small-scale retaliation against aggression, he conceded. One of his fundamental beliefs actually coincided with the policy of containment that he criticized. He was convinced that if the West could only keep the Communists within bounds and at the same time avoid a major war, the Communist societies in Russia and China would eventually break down because of—to use a pet Communist phrase about the capitalists—their "inner contradictions." This was the import of the Kennan doctrine, although Mr. Kennan foresaw change rather than collapse in Moscow. In a speech in 1957 Dulles even conceded the need for a "limited-war" capability. He said, referring to the possibility of localized Communist aggressions: "We and our allies should, between us have the capacity to deal with these without our actions provoking a general nuclear war."[3] This turned out to be the basic premise of the system of alliances Dulles put together. For if weak countries could be strengthened to meet aggression, the United States would be spared the need to retaliate massively.

Dulles performed an important function for America in that he persuaded the conservative elements of the Republican party to accept internationalist policies. Instead of a shift to isolationism with the Eisenhower victory in 1952, there was a pronounced American participation in world affairs. Dulles spoke with the precision of a lawyer, the moral sanctimony of some ministers, and from a wealth of experience that began at the age of four. That is when, according to the oft-told anecdote about him, he decided he would be Secretary of State. The son of a Presbyterian minister, he was the grandson of the forty-fourth Secretary of State, John W. Foster, who served under Benjamin Harrison, and the nephew of the fifty-seventh, Robert Lansing, who held office under Woodrow Wilson. When he died in 1959 at the age of seventy-five, a victim of cancer, he was buried with military honors in Arlington National Cemetery.

Dulles' legacy, however, disturbed many thoughtful Americans. The policy of massive retaliation proved no more satisfying than containment. Its implied threat that any war was bound to be nuclear was hardly reassuring. Actually, in the very year, 1954, that Dulles enunciated his "massive retaliation" policy before the Council of Foreign Relations, the Council undertook a major study project to seek a better answer to the problems posed by growing Soviet influence. The members of the Council predicted accurately, in the light of what happened in Hungary two years later, that the United States would be reluctant to stand up to the Soviet Union on any but the most compelling issues. The Soviets, meanwhile, were carrying out a variety of actions short of military provocation of the United States. The Council organized three subcommittees to cope with the varying aspects of what were believed to be inadequate United States initiatives in the face of the Soviet threat.

The staff director for the subcommittees was Henry Kissinger, a young instructor of government at Harvard who was associate director of the Harvard Center of International Studies. Kissinger, born in Fürth, Germany, in 1923, was brought to the United States by his parents in 1938. He graduated from high school in New York City in 1941 and served with the infantry and with a counterintelligence corps unit in World War II. Following military service, this chubby, brown-haired, bespectacled young man, a naturalized citizen, went to Harvard, where he was graduated *summa cum laude* in 1952 and won his Ph.D. in 1954.

After eighteen months of study, the Council decided that it would not attempt to draft a program that all of its members could agree upon. Instead, Kissinger was asked to write an analysis, aware of the many facts and views that had been presented but free to express them in his own way. The result was the book, *Nuclear Weapons and Foreign Policy*, published in 1957, a landmark achievement. It was "one of the genuinely creative and far reaching works of our time," said August Heckscher, director of the Twentieth Century Fund. It "contradicted statements which in the last years have been so often repeated that they appear to most of us not only true, but axiomatic," said Edward Teller, "father" of the H-bomb. The book provided the intellectual basis for a major shift in United States strategic thinking. It was by no means the only nor even the best-written book of its kind. But the wide publicity it received should make it a familiar point of reference for the average reader. Later in this chapter I will cite less publicized works to illustrate other schools of strategic thought, not because they are the most profound available or because they have been influential, but because they seem to be adequate, simple formulations of the ideas they represent.

Dr. Kissinger's cardinal points were: that the United States must retain its ability to retaliate with an all-out nuclear attack if sufficiently provoked, but that it must also be prepared to retaliate in more limited fashion against provocations that are limited. Thus it must be ready to wage "limited wars," with conventional forces or, if necessary, with small nuclear weapons. In the widespread discussion that followed publication of the book, Kissinger's advocacy of limited-war preparations was emphasized in contrast with the massive retaliation policy of the Eisenhower Administration. It was often forgotten that Kissinger had not suggested abandonment of the large nuclear force. He had actually added a dimension to nuclear weapons policy by suggesting the use of small nuclear arms for limited wars. Nevertheless, his views were assailed as unrealistic. It was suggested that he ignored the "reality" that governments losing limited wars would seek to turn the tide with surprise use of nuclear weapons. Air Force General Nathan F. Twining, who was chairman of the Joint Chiefs of Staff for a while during the Eisenhower Administration, said that readiness for all-out nuclear war included *per se* readiness for limited war and that no special preparations were needed.

In the Taiwan crisis of 1958, however, the newly appointed commander in the Pacific, Admiral Harry Felt, discovered that his forces had only a limited supply of conventional explosives. As a consequence, he stressed in messages to the Pentagon, he would have to use nuclear weapons at an early stage if war broke out. In response to Felt's complaint, additional supplies of conventional ammunition were sent to the American forces in the Pacific. The Pentagon denied at the time a dispatch by this writer that said Admiral Felt had questioned the premises on which the United States policy in the Pacific was then based. But in confirming that it had sent more conventional munitions to his forces at the admiral's request, the military headquarters confirmed the shortage, especially since no fighting had consumed the available stocks.

Another report at the time was that in the early stage of the crisis in Lebanon in 1958 the Pentagon had to rush conventional ammunition to the Sixth Fleet in response to an urgent bid by its commander, Vice Admiral Charles (Cat) Brown. General Maxwell Taylor subsequently revealed that during the Lebanon landing the United States had an Honest John rocket afloat off Beirut, but was not allowed to land it because it could fire an atomic warhead as well as a conventional one. In this instance, the general pointed out, political leaders felt it was not in the national interest to suggest by the presence of the weapon the possibility of using atomic weapons in Lebanon, although the threat of such use was consistent with the proclaimed policy.[4] The Lebanon and Taiwan incidents disproved the Twining thesis that readiness for all-out war obviated the need for special limited-war preparedness.

The Kissinger book achieved a circulation far outside the professional and academic community. It also triggered an outburst of other books and papers with variations on the same theme. The fear of all-out nuclear war created public receptivity to a discussion of less cataclysmic conflict. Kissinger had, in fact, advocated the use of nuclear weapons at the very outset of small hostilities to accomplish either a deterrent effect or, failing that, swift crushing of an incipient all-out war. Subsequently, Kissinger shifted his conclusion. In another book, *The Necessity for Choice*, he made the point that failure to achieve a coherent, acceptable definition of the nature of limited war mitigated against being able, in fact, to limit war.

For example, suppose the Soviet Union attacked Germany and swiftly destroyed it, then agreed to withdraw to the original starting point. The doctrine of limited war would call for acceptance of such a situation, yet any program for defense would immediately collapse, under threat of Soviet blackmail, unless retaliation were attempted for the original attack. Retaliation would inevitably bring all-out war, for from the point of view of the West there would be little sense in retaliating against Moscow by wiping out Rumania. Kissinger thus reappraised his nuclear weapons strategy for limited war. He conceded that a strategy dependent upon these weapons would be difficult to carry out because we would not be psychologically ready to use them except under the most extreme provocation, when limited war would probably be out of the question anyway; and the potential aggressor might be tempted to attack because the threat of the use of nuclear weapons would not be credible.

Therefore, Kissinger now said, the West must build its conventional forces—in Europe especially—and attempt to demonstrate that any mass attack on the ground would be met with superior, if not more numerous conventional forces. The onus of the first use of nuclear weapons should therefore be placed on the aggressor. At the same time, the West should be ready to use nuclear weapons if attacked with nuclear weapons. Kissinger thus did not abandon his advocacy of nuclear weapons readiness for limited-war situations, but he called for a strategy in which the Western forces would be so organized as not to make the use of nuclear weapons mandatory at the outset. This became one of the key military policies of the Kennedy Administration.

As the American Administration changed hands, from Eisenhower to Kennedy, a new book on military strategy created enormous excitement. The book was *On Thermonuclear War*, published in December, 1960. The author, Herman Kahn, an operations analyst, had conducted a study on civil defense at Rand, the research corporation. In so doing, he developed some ideas which he set forth in a series of lectures. Then he put the lectures in book form. His study of civil defense had led Kahn into considering something most of his predecessors in public discussion had failed to do. Instead of merely discussing the threat of nuclear war, Kahn measured the destruction itself. How powerful *were* nuclear bombs? How many people *would be killed* in a given area with a bomb of given size?

"It is necessary to be quantitative," Herman Kahn wrote. "For example, in describing the aftermath of a war it is not particularly illuminating to use such words as 'intolerable,' 'catastrophic,' 'total destruction,' 'annihilating retaliation,' and so on. Such words would be useful, only if it were really true that in a modern war all possible targets would be *overkilled* by factors of five or ten, as so many persons assumed." But the facts, he said, do not lead in this direction. He proceeded, with a barrage of charts, mathematical formulae, imaginary conversations, anecdotes, weapons analyses, political and historical reviews and quantitative analyses, to make his basic argument that nuclear war would not be the end of the world. Regardless of the extent of devastation, there would be some who successfully resisted direct pulverization and even radiation. Advocating a shelter program, he said: "If we have a posture which might result in 40,000,000 dead in a general war, and as a result of poor planning, apathy, or other causes, our posture deteriorates and a war occurs with 80,000,000 dead, we have suffered an additional disaster, an unnecessary additional disaster." Will the survivors envy the dead?[5] Herman Kahn asked rhetorically. And he answered: "Despite a widespread belief to the contrary, objective studies indicate that even though the amount of human tragedy would be greatly increased in the postwar world, the increase would not preclude normal and happy lives for the majority of survivors and their descendants."

"Is there a Herman Kahn?" demanded a reviewer in the *Scientific American*.[6] It was more than a question. It was an exclamation of dismay. Could there be such a person who looked the Gorgons of nuclear war in the face without becoming petrified with fear? "No one could write like this; no one could think like this," said James R. Newman, the writer on mathematics, questioning Kahn's existence. Kahn's was an "evil and tenebrous book, with its loose-lipped pieties and its hayfoot-strawfoot logic . . . its bloodthirsty irrationality." The Kahn book nevertheless became "must" reading for amateur and professional strategists. Jerome Spingarn, arms control expert of the National Planning Association and later of the United States Disarmament and Control Agency, described it as a "landmark in the literature of military strategy and power-oriented diplomacy." Thomas Schelling called Kahn "the most exciting military strategist in this country." But for many it was an unholy work, as though Mars had just published his own *Mein Kampf*.

Kahn himself was an un-Martian figure. He was a jolly, fat, bespectacled physicist. He was born in Bayonne, New Jersey, in 1922 and spent his early childhood in the Bronx. His family moved to Los Angeles, where Army service interrupted his education for about two years. After World War II, he got his B.A. at the University of California. He worked as a mathematician for the Douglas Aircraft Company and as a laboratory analyst for Rand. At Rand he became a specialist in systems analysis and games theories applied to strategic warfare. Following publication of *On Thermonuclear War*, he started the Hudson Institute and, retorting to those who complained about his first book, he wrote another. In it he insisted, we must do some *Thinking About the Unthinkable* and not act like "those ancient kings who punished messengers who brought them bad news."

The Kahn book's philosophic thesis, that war must be faced squarely, has proved to be its most defensible point. But its objective of contributing to a strategy of "counterforce" that includes a shelter program has been sustained only partially in policies adopted by the Kennedy Administration. Counterforce! This is an ubiquitous term in the growing public literature on national strategy, although there does not seem to be general agreement on its meaning. I once asked Kahn to help me define the word, and over luncheon we came up with this: Counterforce is a strategic military policy that calls for enough weapons to permit not only retaliation, in the event of attack, but victory. Counterforce theorists do not accept the notion that there can be no victory in nuclear warfare, although they do not underestimate the magnitude of the suffering. A counterforce system presupposes, however, that the enemy will not necessarily be deterred by the prospect of nuclear war. Advocates of counterforce call for a continually expanding military arsenal to keep pace with the continually expanding military targets. As such targets are identified, the size of the American arsenal must be increased. American military power must never be allowed to become static since the enemy is presumed to be increasing *his* military power. The American weapons must "cover" the enemy weapons or "force." At the same time, to bolster its counterforce posture, the United States must disperse its own military targets and provide shelters for its people.

In contrast with the counterforce advocates, there are strategists who argue for a policy of finite or limited deterrence. These strategists say that if the United States has a sufficient number of weapons to cause "unacceptable" damage to the enemy, regardless of whether these include purely military targets or cities, then that should be enough. More weapons than a specific number, carefully estimated, would provide "overkill" and would be unnecessarily expensive. The United States' strategic aim should be simply to deter. If deterrence fails, little would be gained from unleashing more weapons on an enemy than are needed to take out the most important targets.

Books such as Kissinger's and Kahn's are only the most publicized of a deluge of books by civilians on national military strategy. A vast, colorful literature has developed, discussing in minutest detail the problems of war deterrence, operations, arms control and disarmament. At one end of the spectrum of the strategic bibliography, writers like Kahn have refused to accept the premise that nuclear war is "unthinkable." At the other end men like young Arthur

Waskow, a member of the staff of the Peace Research Institute, argue that no military strategy can preclude war and that therefore a policy of "disarmament plus" must be adopted. Waskow's book, *The Limits of Defense*,[7] is interesting chiefly because it represents what might be called the "peacemonger's irrational." Like Carrie Nation, the peacemongers invade the saloons of the warmakers and seek to smash their intoxicating plans to bits. New weapons "have made even preparations for defensive war intensely deadly and highly threatening in themselves," Mr. Waskow wrote. Thus military strategies are not merely theories for deterrence or armed defense, but provocations. The only workable deterrent, according to Waskow, is what he calls "disarmament-plus"—disarmament alone not being enough.

In Waskow's world of disarmament plus, all nations subscribe to a law against the making, possession or use by an individual of any weapon above the level of small arms. Disarmament-plus is to be achieved with the assistance of a corps of inspectors, trained in an international school of civil service. The corps would be the cadre for a continuing police force and could be built into an international "world army" in case of emergency. If some rascally leader retains a secret armed force and commits aggression, the world army is to "punish" him. "Disarmament-plus, by mobilizing law enforcement, non-violent alternatives, and ultimately, the threat of armed resistance would deter even the least rational of men and Governments from making the tools of war," Waskow wrote. But he was not very illuminating on how to get the nations of the world to sign the treaty that has eluded them since the sixth century B.C. with the collapse of the hundred-year-old disarmament agreement of the Yellow River states of China.

One of the books on strategy was written by a newspaper reporter who pointed out: "The ideas in this book are not mine. They are derived from interviews and from correspondence with numerous specialists on strategy." The reporter, Richard Fryklund, included government specialists in his consensus and the result was a preview of the so-called "no cities" nuclear strategy announced by the Administration in the spring of 1962. Fryklund's book, *One Hundred Million Lives*, was grounded in Khanian "realism," and constituted an explicit outline in public of United States policy. "Some critics of military writers believe it is wrong to try to make war less deadly, because in doing so we only make war palatable and more likely," Fryklund wrote. "In my opinion, wars cannot be made 'palatable' to civilized people. The whole business of war is repellent. I can only say that in the face of possible nuclear war there is a chance we can save 100 million lives in America."

One hundred million lives can be saved, Frylund wrote, because populations away from target areas will survive the carefully paced thermonuclear exchanges in which millions of others may be sacrificed. According to this view, the Soviet Union and the United States would do well to remove their populations from strategic areas or their strategic targets from populations so that, in the event of war, a tacit agreement to avoid hitting population centers could be carried out. "Will Russia play the game?" the author asked rhetorically. "We can make it profitable for them to forego the destruction of cities," he assured his reader, if the United States publicly adopted a weapon-for-weapon policy.[8]

In the spring of 1962 at Ann Arbor, Michigan, Secretary of Defense McNamara publicly announced a second-strike counterforce capability; that is, a "no cities" doctrine. He said: "The United States has come to the conclusion that to the extent feasible, basic military strategy in a possible general nuclear war should be approached in much the same way that more conventional military operations have been regarded in the past. That is to say, principal military objectives, in the event of a nuclear war stemming from major attack on the Alliance, should be the destruction of the enemy's military forces, not his civilian population. The very strength and nature of the Alliance forces make it possible for us to retain reserve striking power to destroy an enemy society if driven to it. In other words, we are giving a possible opponent the strongest imaginable incentive to refrain from striking our own cities."

The McNamara announcement, bearing out reporter Fryklund's studies of Pentagon thinking, appeared to call for Marquis of Queensbury rules for nuclear war. Ironically, it asked the Russians—and/ or the Communist Chinese—with whom disarmament treaties remained elusive, to agree on how to carry on a nuclear war. But the Secretary spoke from a position of strength. He elaborated on his thesis in subsequent testimony to Congress, when he described the program for a second-strike force which could be aimed at Soviet bomber bases, missile sites and other military installations—"and then, if necessary, strike back at the Soviet urban and industrial complex in a controlled and deliberate way." Secretary McNamara told Congress: "Now the foregoing is not to say that we can forecast the nature of a nuclear attack upon the United States. In talking about global nuclear war, the Soviet leaders always say that they would strike at the entire complex of our military power including government and production centers, meaning our cities. If they were to do so, we would, of course, have no alternative but to retaliate in kind. But we have no way of knowing they would actually do so. It would certainly be in their interest as well as ours to try to limit the terrible consequences of a nuclear exchange. By building into our forces a flexible capability we at least eliminate the prospect that we could strike back in only one way, namely, against the entire Soviet target system including their cities. Such a prospect would give no incentive to withhold attack against our cities in a first strike. We want to give them a better alternative. Whether they would accept it in the crisis of a nuclear war, no one can say. Considering what is at stake, we believe it is worth the additional effort on our part to have this option."[9]

By the end of 1963 the Defense Secretary was so confident of United States strategic superiority that he observed: "The most wishful of Soviet planners would have to calculate as a certainty that the most effective surprise attack they could launch would still leave us with the capability to destroy the attacker's *society*. . . . I would not trade our strategic posture for that of the Soviets at any point during the coming decade."[10]

This statement contrasted with the fears of the late 1950's over a "missile gap," a story worth noting here. The Eisenhower Administration had refused to invest heavily in early-type ICBMs, asserting they were too expensive and technologically inadequate. The then Secretary of Defense, Neil H. McElroy, conceded publicly that if the Russians chose to produce that type of missile they probably would achieve a three-to-one edge in ICBMs by 1963. Critics, particularly those in Congress, accused the Administration of wilfully planning a "missile gap," and compared the difference between the number of missiles the Administration intended to produce and the number the Soviets could produce. The Russians, it was said, might rush a missile force into position, outgun the West and terrorize it into submission.

The dispute engaged generals and admirals as well as politicians, scientists and defense industrialists. The Senate preparedness sub-committee, headed by Democratic Majority Leader, Lyndon B. Johnson, provided the forum for a great debate, featuring intelligence estimates, all in the glare of publicity, according to the American tradition. While insisting that United States bomber forces could cope with the possible threat, McElroy's successor, Thomas S. Gates, Jr., sought to reduce criticism by testifying that the latest intelligence estimates indicated the Soviets did not intend to carry out a "crash" program for ICBMs. Whereupon a dispute arose over the wisdom of counting on an enemy's "intentions" rather than his "capabilities." Johnson said the change in the premise for intelligence estimates was "incredibly dangerous" and added: "The missile gap cannot be eliminated by the stroke of a pen."[11] At that time the Administration was getting important intelligence with high-flying U-2 reconnaissance planes, but this did not become public knowledge until the downing of pilot Francis Gary Powers, May 1, 1960. After the U-2 affair it became known that such planes had been traversing Soviet skies for three or four years.

When President Kennedy's Administration took over in 1961, it was conceded that no missile gap had developed. Samos reconnaissance satellites confirmed the indications received from the abandoned U-2 flights, that it was the Russians who suffered from a missile gap. In the Soviet–United States confrontation over Cuba in 1962, the Administration's confidence in its military superiority permitted an unhurried, measured reaction. Once the United States demanded that the Soviets withdraw the threatening missiles, the possibility of escalation of threats to actual hostilities became apparent. In the crisis, the United States intended each move to be a "message" to Soviet Premier Khrushchev that a next step of military force was in the offing. "But each move was also intended to convince him that he could withdraw without armed conflict, if he would withdraw."[12] The Soviets withdrew their missiles.

If the victory of Cuba has been blurred somewhat by the continued existence of that Communist state in the Western Hemisphere, there is reason nevertheless to consider it a suitable and satisfying test case in the United States' new strategy of flexible response. In the "cold war," after all, there can be no complete victories. That, too, is not new in history. The War of 1812 ended in something less than a victory for the United States, but it served to deter foreign intervention in United States affairs for many decades. The Korean War ended bitterly, without victory, yet it served to reduce the scale of hostilities which an aggressor could dare to commit against the United States.

The Cuba confrontation has other lessons for the guardians of American security. As Secretary McNamara pointed out, the Soviet ability to place threatening missiles in Cuba demonstrated how the "expanding arsenals of nuclear weapons on both sides of the Iron Curtain have created an extremely dangerous situation not only for their possessors but for the entire world."[13] The Soviet Union no less than the United States is "hardening" and dispersing its ICBMs and building a fleet of nuclear-powered ballistic missile submarines. There are no anti-ICBM defenses, and the kind of shelter program realistically feasible, even if adopted, would not prevent casualties in the tens of millions. Thus, while claiming the ability to withstand attack and yet destroy Soviet society in retaliation, officials concede that even if the United States were to initiate a nuclear strike against the Soviet Union it would not preclude major damage upon this country. Insofar as strategic nuclear forces are concerned, a stalemate of terror is apparent. It could be broken only by a threat to national existence, or a move interpreted as such a threat—aggression in Western Europe, for example.

Moreover, there is evidence in the Defense budget for the fiscal year 1965 that the Kennedy-Johnson Administration recognizes that further expansion of strategic nuclear forces would indeed create an "overkill" capability. Even before the budget was presented in January, 1964, Secretary McNamara pointed out that the funding for the main United States strategic forces had been largely completed, while the Soviet Union, having acquired respectable strategic forces, showed no inclination to further challenge the mutual deterrent posture. McNamara said: "Larger budgets for U.S. strategic forces would not change that fact. They could have only a decreasing incremental effect in limiting somewhat the damage that the U.S. and its allies could suffer in general nuclear war. In short, we cannot buy the capability to make a strategic bombing campaign once again a unilateral prospect."[14] Short of a technological breakthrough, a calculated general nuclear war seems out of the question so long as each side maintains existing strategic forces as insurance.

This by no means disposes of the problem of national security. The ignominy of failure in the United States–supported rebel invasion of Cuba in 1961 was a major political and diplomatic shock on many counts. In terms of United States military effectiveness it dramatized the nation's apparent inability to carry out any but a large-scale war. "We intend to re-examine and to profit from this [Cuba] lesson," President Kennedy said. "We intend to re-examine and reorient our forces of all kinds, our tactics and our other institutions here in this community. We intend to intensify our efforts for a struggle in many ways more difficult than war."[15] The President recalled General Maxwell D. Taylor, who had left the Army in 1959 frustrated over the Eisenhower Administration's refusal to adopt his views on limited war requirements. General Taylor, in his book, *The Uncertain Trumpet,* had denounced as a "great fallacy" the idea that the United States threat of "massive retaliation" would deter wars.

President Kennedy adopted the thesis that General Taylor unsuccessfully preached throughout the Eisenhower Administration, that small wars were more likely than big wars. The situation facing Kennedy when he took office bore out the assertion. There were four major crises, in Cuba, the Congo, Laos and Vietnam. Each represented the successful breaching of truce lines that had been stabilized between the West and Communism in the aftermath of World War II. President Kennedy reacted with "stunned amazement" when he learned a few weeks after entering the White House that if he sent 10,000 men to Southeast Asia there would be practically no strategic Army reserve left for other contingencies.[16] The President, an activist military thinker in the tradition of Roosevelt, pushed hard for an increase in the number of army divisions and personally sponsored and propagandized for an increase in the guerrilla-fighting Special Forces. He was, like Winston Churchill, concerned with military details and flooded the Pentagon with memoranda. He re-established the Green Beret as a mark of distinction for the Special Forces.[17] He let it be known that he had read the works of Che Guevera and Mao Tse-tung on guerrilla warfare. These then became "must" reading at the Pentagon.

Premier Khrushchev's promise to support so-called "wars of national liberation" disturbed President Kennedy, who saw it presaging wide-ranging Communist strangulation of that part of the free world that was weak and unstable. Kennedy saw the need of a national strategy which not only provided security against all-out nuclear attack but permitted coping with subtler threats of insurgency against free people remote from our shores and requiring perhaps decades of resistance. This was his strategic legacy to the Johnson Administration, and it is worth keeping in mind in these days of weakened resolve to maintain foreign assistance programs. The "creeping socialism" we may really have to worry about is not a welfare program in this country but a slow but steady Communist encroachment on other countries. Despite possibilities of a thaw in East-West relations that were publicized in early 1964, the United States cannot afford to abandon the war against Communist insurgency any more than it can abandon its defenses against simpler forms of Communist danger. We can be sure that if we leave the Communist powers alone to exercise their aims at aggression they will in the end not leave us alone to exercise our right to peace. As Walt Rostow put it:

"The victory we seek will see no ticker tape parades down Broadway—no climactic battles, no great American celebrations of victory. It is a victory which will take many years and decades of hard work and dedication—by many peoples—to bring about. This will not be the victory of the United States over the Soviet Union. It will not be a victory of capitalism over socialism. . . . What this victory involves—in the end—is the assertion by nations of their right to independence and by men and women of their right to freedom as they understand it. And we deeply believe this victory will come."[18]

XV

---☆

Disarmament

> "A specter is haunting the chancelleries and general staffs. . . .
> it is the specter of Peace."
>
> —KENNETH BOULDING

In 1921 a League of Nations Commission, appointed to inquire into
the private manufacture of arms, came to the following conclusions:
that armament firms had been active in fomenting war scares and
in persuading their own countries to adopt warlike policies and to
increase armaments; that armament firms had attempted to bribe
government officials; that armament firms had disseminated false
reports concerning the military and naval programs of various countries in order to stimulate armament expenditure; that armament
firms had sought to influence public opinion through control of
newspapers in their own and foreign countries; that armament firms
had organized international rings, accentuating the armaments race
by playing off one country against another; that armament firms had
organized international armaments trusts which had increased the
price of armaments to governments.

The attribution of wars to the merchants of arms was dramatized in the post-World War I period in such books as George Seldes' *Iron, Blood and Profits.* He wrote: "No reason for war remains except sudden profits for the fifty men who run the ammunitions rackets." H. C. Engelbrecht and F. C. Hanighen argued that war was due to nationalism and chauvinism, to economic rivalry and economic capitalism, to political and territorial disputes, to race hatred and population pressures. But the title of their book, *Merchants of Death,* provided a slogan for those who took a more personalized view of the problem.

One of the most notorious arms merchants was Sir Basil Zaharoff. He was the so-called "mystery man of Europe" because of the aura of secrecy that surrounded his international financing and munitions manufacturing operations. Zaharoff, Turkish born, of Greek origin, was educated in England and amassed a great fortune with the British arms manufacturers, Vickers-Armstrong. He was knighted by King George V and decorated by the French Government for his services in World War I. Known as the greatest munitions salesman the world had ever known, he was said to play a vital if unofficial role in international affairs. It was Zaharoff, as the subject of a book titled *Zarahoff, High Priest of War* (Guiles Davenport, 1934), who personified the baneful traffickers in arms who brought about wars.

In 1934 President Roosevelt, pledging his cooperation in the pending Senate investigation of the munitions industry, said: "The peoples of many countries are being taxed to the point of poverty and starvation in order to enable governments to engage in a mad race in armament which, if permitted to continue, may well result in war. This grave menace to the peace of the world is due in no small measure to the uncontrolled activities of the manufacturers and merchants of engines of destruction, and it must be met by the concerted action of the peoples of all nations."

A Congressional investigation in 1929-1930 had brought out stories that shocked the nation. One, particularly, concerned William B. Shearer, an "observer" for the Bethlehem Shipbuilding Corporation, the Newport News Shipbuilding and Drydock Company and the Brown Boveri Electric Corporation and his efforts to wreck the 1927 Geneva Naval Reduction Conference. The scheme came to public notice when Shearer brought a suit in 1929, claiming $255,655 he said was due him for his work. The case prompted President Hoover to observe:

Every American has the right to express his opinion and engage in open propaganda if he wishes, but it is obviously against public interest for those who have financial interests in, or may be engaged in, contracts for the construction of naval vessels, to attempt secretly to influence public opinion or public officials in favor of larger armaments or to attempt to defeat the efforts of governments in world limitation of such armaments or to employ persons for such purposes.[1]

The Senate investigations under Gerald P. Nye showed that great profits were made by firms in munitions or defense industries. The United States Steel Corporation, for example, earned $633 million from 1916 through 1918, more than three times as much as in the previous three years. The Hercules Powder Company increased its dividends from 8 percent in 1914 to 95 percent in 1916 and declared a stock dividend of 100 percent in 1922. Profits ranging up to 36 percent were cited in World War I contracts, although there was no proof of collusion.

Equally as spectacular as the profits stories was the revelation during the Nye investigations that the United States Ambassador in London had suggested proper timing for United States entry in the war. The American Ambassador, Walter Hines Page, wrote from his post in London to President Wilson on March 5, 1917, a month before the United States declared war, that economic conditions made it imperative for the United States to enter the war at that time. "[The] international situation . . . is most alarming to the financial and industrial outlook of the United States," he wrote.

[England] cannot continue her present extensive purchases in the United States without shipping gold as payment for them, and there are two reasons why she cannot make large shipments of gold. . . . There is, therefore, a pressing danger that the Franco-American and Anglo-American exchange will be greatly disturbed . . . and that trans-Atlantic trade will practically come to an end. The result of such a stoppage will be a panic in the United States. . . . If the United States declares war against

Germany, the greatest help we could give Great Britain and its Allies would be such a credit. . . . A great advantage would be that all the money would be kept in the United States. We could keep on with our trade and increase it, till the war ends, and after the war Europe would purchase food and an enormous supply of materials with which to re-equip her peace industries. We should thus reap the profit of an uninterrupted and perhaps an enlarging trade over a number of years and we should hold their securities in payment. . . . It is not improbable that the only way of maintaining our preemient trade position and averting a panic is by declaring war on Germany.[2]

This was only one of many revelations about the pre-World War I period that contributed to the American isolationism of the thirties. The public adopted the view that but for the business "interests" they might have stayed out of that war. This view led to the adoption of neutrality legislation and arms embargoes that hampered virtually all readiness measures right up to the Nazi invasion of Poland and, in certain respects, up to Pearl Harbor. The public was aggrieved by arms traffic to Latin America and there was disquietude over arms shipments to Japan. The use of American arms against American Marines in Nicaragua prompted Senator Nye to warn in a radio speech in 1934 that "if we should by some unbelievable chance find ourselves at war with Japan, it is safe to wager that our soldiers and sailors will find their enemy armed with, and mowed down by, instruments produced by American manufacturers —at a profit, of course."

When war broke out in Europe in 1939, the late Raymond Clapper cited American fears of "creeping involvement" due to economic "interests." "We do not trust ourselves," he wrote.[3] To recapitulate those days and fears seems somehow like reviving old-fashioned nightmares. The fears that have abounded over the military industrial complex are not personified in a single Zaharoff. Instead of a single man or a single firm or a group of munitions racketeers, all of American society in the fifties and sixties appears to have been given a vested interest in the arms business even as it protests the economic "burdens" of the arms race. Nobody wants war. But almost everyone in the country wants the prosperity that comes from defense expenditures.

Would disarmament hurt us? Some fear that disarmament would cause a sudden and severe decline in economic activity—a depression. Second, while some persons discount a sudden economic drop, like a falling stock market, they predict that a slow-paced but sustained reduction of defense expenditures might hamper the widely proclaimed effort to "get the country moving again." Third, there is talk of a "serious structural readjustment" that would be demanded of certain companies, industries, workers and communities heavily involved in defense activities. Fourth, it is said that shifting people and resources to new uses would not only take time, but would create "considerable hardships" for the parts of the economy that had to make the shifts.[4]

The reasons for concern are based on the influential role of the defense program in the American economy. Defense absorbs nearly a tenth of the total United States production of goods and services. It employs, directly or indirectly, a similar percentage of the labor force, including the men in uniform. In some industries employment dependence on defense is extremely high—95 percent in aircraft and missiles, 60 percent in shipbuilding, 40 percent in radio and communications. In some basic industries job dependence upon defense is low—6 percent in transportation, 2 percent in construction and less than 1.5 percent in trade and services. But certain cities and even states are largely dependent on defense expenditures. Their manufacturing facilities have become so specialized that the possibilities for conversion to civilian production is limited.

A special committee, under Professor Emil Benoit of Columbia University, conducted studies for the United States Disarmament and Control Agency. Its work on the possible impact of real disarmament has shed considerable light on the question of disarmament economics. The committee assumed that defense expenditures might rise to $60 billion at the time a disarmament treaty goes into effect. This high figure was purposely used in order to reduce the possibility of underestimating the impact of a decline, although military spending in the fiscal year 1964 was estimated at $52 billion and the Administration predicted a leveling-off, perhaps even a slight reduction, in 1965. The Benoit committee projected a reduction in defense expenditures of $17 billion in the first three years of disarmament, a further cut of $12 billion in the second three-year stage, partly offset by a $3.5 billion contribution to disarmament inspection costs, and continued slashes until it achieved a reduction in spending of $38.5 billion over a twelve-year period. Instead of $52 billion for defense the United States would be spending $13.5 billion. The cutbacks would be partly offset by extra spending in programs related to defense—such as atomic energy and space, and including the plan to land men on the moon.

The chief popular economic fear of disarmament—sudden severe depression—was said by the Benoit committee to be "a rather improbable contingency." The committee observed, however:

Perhaps the chief danger of a precipitant decline would be psychological. We would be facing an extended series of future defense cuts over more than a decade ahead. We have never had a situation exactly parallel to this in our history, and we cannot be sure just how this would affect business and consumer anticipations and expenditure plans. Pessimism might be heightened by a major break in stock market prices, which . . . would be likely to occur at such a time. A great deal might depend on whether the government could provide sufficient reassurance by demonstrating that a definite program of offsets had been readied and would be promptly implemented. In this connection, people's expectations would be considerably affected by their experience in the years prior to disarmament. If public policy had succeeded in reducing excessive unemployment and restoring a rapid rate of growth, the economy could more readily absorb deflationary impacts without serious hurt, and confidence in the Government's power to protect prosperity would be higher.[5]

Dealing effectively with long-term, year-by-year declines in defense spending would pose a problem more difficult than forestalling a psychological break. Men would be leaving the military services and entering the employment pool. At the same time, others would be leaving defense industries, also looking for new jobs. Meanwhile the population would be increasing; improvements in industrial productivity would, initially at least, be reducing employment requirements. On top of that, similar events in other countries would heighten the competition. In this aspect of its report the Benoit committee had the most difficulty in arriving at an encouraging conclusion. It warned: "The major problem of policy planning would be to choose a policy which, first, is sufficient to prevent serious unemployment and excess capacity and second, will guide the labor and resources freed by disarmament to where the needs are determined to be greatest."

Here the committee did not have too many original ideas. The committee urged expanded and improved progress in education and research, transportation, urban renewal, public health, etc. It cautiously suggested it would be possible to "take up the slack" with shorter working hours, increased length of vacations, reduction in the retirement age, a rise in the average age at which young people start looking for jobs and a reduction in the number of women seeking jobs. It admitted, "It is not clear to what extent Government policy can readily influence some of these choices." And it hesitated to endorse such measures even if possible.

Some of the most stubborn problems connected with disarmament would be "structural," the committee indicated. It defined these as the problems arising out of the concentration of persons and productive resources in particular industries, areas or vocational groups. The committee stressed the advantage of bringing industries to depressed areas, rather than trying to shift labor forces. Its recommendations, in the event of disarmament, were similar to those being advanced anyway to cope with technological changes, population shifts and previous changes in the composition of the defense program.

The committee felt, however, that there would be plenty to do even without defense business. It devoted a special section in its report to research and development. It recommended developing teaching machines and related communications equipment, solar engines, water purification and other techniques for overcoming aridity and restoring desert areas, new methods of providing cheap power to remote areas, work on the elimination of tropical and other endemic diseases, population control, economic assistance programs to underdeveloped areas, new techniques that would make effective use of unskilled labor for the mass production of road-making materials and machinery, simple housing and office buildings, power systems and even simple machine tools and standard types of industrial plants.

The committee concluded:

a) Disarmament of the type anticipated in existing proposals and negotiations "should create small danger of provoking immediate depression in our economy."

b) A steady decline in defense spending "may prove a significant drag on the economy," but the problems "can be mastered by the application of appropriate policies, the chief obstacles to which would be political resistance rather than deficiencies in our economic knowledge."

c) "Structural problems in particular industries are unavoidable and could be serious for the individuals, companies and communities prominently affected," but these "would only accentuate" structural problems which already exist in the economy and must be solved anyhow.

d) "Advance planning by Government at all levels and by business firms, labor unions and other private organizations is required if the economy is to adjust smoothly to significant changes in the level of defense spending, particularly such as would result from general and complete disarmament."

In an extension of the Benoit committee effort, the Senate Foreign Relations Subcommittee on Disarmament conducted a confidential study into the economic implications of disarmament. The study was confidential in order to obtain frank answers from the participants. A questionnaire was sent to 439 companies engaged in defense business in various degrees. Each company was asked to divulge figures on total sales, defense sales, unfilled orders, labor force, payrolls, materials and supplies for its entire establishment and for each division or plant, identifying the locations. The year 1959 was used, in order to permit complete assessment of paid bills, profits after renegotiation and other statistical considerations. Senator Hubert Humphrey, chairman of the subcommittee, pointed out that although businessmen dislike to fill out government questionnaires, 370 companies with 1,193 employees had cooperated.

Senator Humphrey, in a speech on the Senate floor, observed: "The companies represented in the subcommittee's study accounted for some 85 percent of the total amount of procurement and research and development purchased by the government from private industry for defense purposes. Not one, I repeat, not one of these companies even hinted it opposed a disarmament agreement on grounds that it would cause them economic difficulty. Many, in fact, thanked the subcommittee for making its study."[6]

Senator Humphrey quoted one company as reporting to the committee:

There is no doubt that a sudden withdrawal of defense business would create severe problems for our company and its employees. At the same time we do not believe that such problems of transition should constitute a barrier to a workable and effective arms reduction program. If that can be achieved on a basis that will not reduce the security of the United States, the problem of economic dislocation incident thereto should not be allowed to be an obstacle. The ingenuity of industry and government should be equal to the challenge of such a problem.

The Humphrey subcommittee found that the bulk of defense work was done by a relatively few concerns. Twenty-four companies accounted for 70 percent of the entire defense expenditures included in the Senate study. While Senator Humphrey noted that the concentration of economic power represented by this phenomenon "should worry us," it also "provided a ready handle" in terms of preparing for disarmament. It would be possible to look to these companies first in working out plans for future shifts in production and research. Most of the defense contractors polled by the subcommittee believed they could make their own adjustments without any large-scale assistance from the government, Senator Humphrey said. Many companies thought they would need considerable help, however, and "only a few" had conducted similar studies of their own.

At the same time, some observers warn that any foreseeable disarmament or arms control agreement would not necessarily mean savings in security expenditures. After all, it is the expansionist tendencies of the Soviet Union and China that have forced the West to build up arms, and without the abandonment of these Communist pressures there can be little prospect for extensive security precautions—whether with armies and armaments or some other devices in the continuing "cold war." Thus the Communist expansionists might well agree to nuclear test bans, arms reductions and even reductions of regular military forces while carrying on policies that would require greater Western defense expenditures in the economic and counterinsurgency fields.[7]

Disarmament prospects were believed to be improving in the Soviet–United States *détente* following the Cuba missile crisis. One sign was the agreement to establish a "hot line" between Washington and Moscow over which, in a dire emergency, the Soviet and United States leaders could communicate speedily, directly if necessary. The proposal was made by the United States in the light of the Cuba experience, during which, at times, the President and his aides were uncertain whether the Soviet leaders fully understood the import of steps that could lead to nuclear war. It was feared that in another situation either side, hampered by relatively slow diplomatic communications, might take a step that would be misinterpreted by the other and lead to conflict that might have been avoided through speedy, candid exchanges. The "hot line," as agreed upon during negotiations in Geneva, was set up in September, 1963.

Another sign of hope for a disarmament agreement was the United States–British–Soviet treaty to refrain from nuclear tests in the atmosphere, in space and under water. It was a limited treaty in that the powers that signed it with considerable fanfare August 6, 1963, in Moscow, were free to continue nuclear tests underground. It prohibited only those tests which could be detected if carried out in violation of the treaty. It did not require the signatories to trust each other. The treaty nevertheless was hailed as a good omen, as an expression of the ability of the Big Powers to agree on something, with perhaps the added possibility that other countries would refrain from testing and thus reduce the feared proliferation of nuclear arms.

These evidences of cooperation—but not trust—between the leading Communist and non-Communist nuclear powers are hardly conclusive as steps toward disarmament. The "hot line" is a practical attempt to foreclose accidental war; the limited test-ban treaty is largely a gesture of goodwill, of which there have been many starting with the Geneva Conference of 1954. There is as yet no ban on the manufacture of arms in prospect and there has been only talk of nonaggression pacts and arms reductions. In fact, as President Kennedy asked the Senate to give its advice and consent to the treaty, he emphasized: "This treaty is not a substitute for, and does not diminish the need for, continued Western and American military strength to meet all contingencies. It will not prevent us from building all the strength that we need; and it is not a justification for unilaterally cutting our defensive strength at this time. Our choice is not between a limited treaty and effective strategic strength —we need and can have both." Thus disarmament is still a long way off, although new undertakings toward arms reductions were publicized in early 1964.

Not all measures for reducing the possibility of war are negotiated. For example, the United States has taken unilateral steps to forestall accidental war. First, there is the purely administrative decision that only the President can authorize the use of atomic or hydrogen warheads; there is the two-man rule that requires at least two responsible persons to be present at every level of operation in the handling of nuclear weapons; the fail-safe procedure, distorted in the novel, which precludes nuclear-armed airplanes from proceeding to a target without an explicit "go" order; physical restraints such as an arming switch that can be operated only in a complicated procedure too much for one man to handle. "It would take an octopus, one with a twenty-foot reach, to ready a one-man fighter bomber for armed take-off," John T. McNaughton, Pentagon legal counsel, said. "As for missiles," he went on, "the critical power supply for the 'button' may be provided—in this age of automation—by a man in a distant corner turning a hand crank not unlike that used on an ice cream freezer."[8]

In the modern era, the quality and disposition of the armed forces themselves constitute a form of arms control closely related to disarmament. For example, in the age of rocket warfare, the fear of surprise attack and the importance of retaliation make speed of reaction a crucial factor. But fear of surprise attack can be "reflected back and forth like images in a room of mirrors." Thus it is important that at least one side make a special effort to create conditions permitting time for thought. This the United States has done with its dispersal of land-based nuclear forces and its fleet of Polaris submarines. These do not have to be activated on the mere threat of war in order to avoid being caught in an attack. United States forces are deployed in an effort to make it possible to evaluate a situation that may appear to be an attack; to make it possible also for the enemy not to fear the fears of the United States, and the United States not to fear that the enemy fears its fears. For in the Pearl Harbor psychology of the United States, such fears might well trigger instant retaliation that would afterward be regretted.

These precautionary measures of dispersal are a form of unilateral disarmament. According to the Pentagon experts, it would be considerably cheaper to merely expand the missile forces than to achieve "survivability" through expensive methods of controlled response. While the unilateral measures fall short of an agreed disarmament or arms control treaty, they demonstrate the Pentagon's concern with the dynamics of arms control, hoping that the Soviet Union evinces similar concern.

At the Pentagon, in recent years, military professionals as well as civilians have devoted themselves to questions of disarmament with greater intensity than was required of them in the past. Early in the Kennedy Administration Deputy Defense Secretary Gilpatric admonished a group of uniformed officers: "We must be asking ourselves not merely 'What can we stand in the way of disarmament and arms control without weakening our security' but 'What can we suggest that will add to our security?' " It is easy, he continued, to think in terms of a stronger defense, but he suggested that the Pentagon produce arms control proposals that might add to the security of all nations without jeopardizing the legitimate interests of any nation. Thus, he made clear, the officers at the Pentagon were to work out arms control proposals which from their expert knowledge they knew would give the Soviets an incentive to accept, proposals for example that would protect even an enemy against surprise attack.

Asking military men to think creatively about disarmament seemed a rather incongruous idea at first. One officer said it was "like asking a priest to work out campaigns for spreading atheism." Military men are more receptive to the term "arms control" than to disarmament. This term accepts the military professional's premise that true disarmament is not possible and not necessarily desirable, but that controls over arms build-ups, mutually agreed upon, can satisfy national security requirements. Secretary of the Navy Paul H. Nitze, when he was Assistant Secretary of Defense for International Security Affairs, said, "Military preparedness and arms control are two sides of the same coin."

One of the handicaps to military contributions to disarmament and arms control thinking, however, is not so much philosophic attitude as a matter of career incentive. Only a handful of officers are engaged in disarmament staff work. Young officers have little reason to devote themselves to it as a means of advancement. Promotion comes with troop commands and combat training. The older officers find themselves in a "negative position" most of the time. One of them observed, "We are asked to contribute arms control schemes, but in fact the problem is not military, except from a negative position."

Problems of nuclear weaponry, he pointed out, are the scientist's province; the strategy of targeting nuclear forces are the political economist's province as much as that of the military, and the question of withdrawing conventional forces from advanced positions is as much a political as it is a military tactical question.

"The application of force is another matter altogether," he went on. "We know a great deal about moving men and machines and directing them most economically in the effort to gain an objective. But thinking about disarmament is an exercise in walking backward for most officers. You can be *fairly* confident you won't fall, of course, because after all you're going back along the same path, but not *absolutely* confident, because as you recede along that path you become less certain of just what dangers face you in the growing distance."[9]

The Joint Chiefs have worked hard at disarmament and arms control nevertheless. During the nuclear test-ban negotiations in the summer of 1963, hardly a week went by that they did not hear a briefing on the subject. The Chiefs of Staff endorsed the nuclear test-ban treaty with admonitions of caution and apparent disappointment that they would not get a chance to test warheads for some of their weapons. At the same time, the military leaders were careful not to present an image of obstinate recalcitrance to steps toward disarmament. Their responsibilities required them to be cautious, to maintain a balance if not superiority of military power. Any steps toward disarmament can upset that balance in the same way that increments of power affect it. Simultaneous reductions in nuclear arms would not necessarily leave the powers in military balance, since so much depends on the size of the stockpiles in the first place and the size and disposition of conventional forces. Even the sudden, world-wide disappearance of all military forces, if imaginable, might leave serious imbalances in populations and economic power that would require some form of police controls. These controls might escalate into armed forces. Any disarmament agreement can be affected by petty deceits, real or imagined, which might create new suspicions and frictions.

Military forces, after all, are a symptom and not a cause of world tensions. "Nations are armed because they differ—they do not differ because they are armed," an officer wrote, attacking "the disarmament myth."[10] Military men have balked at the idea that certain types of weapons are more provocative than others, a favorite assumption by some writers on the subject. It has been contended, for example, that supposedly invulnerable Polaris missiles or land-based Minutemen underground are less of a provocation than airplanes or large ground forces because they are not subject to surprise attack and therefore do not have to be released quickly in the event of a dispute. Major General Dale O. Smith, a specialist on arms control in the staff of the Joint Chiefs of Staff, wrote:

A weakness in this rationale is that it implicitly assumes that the provocative effect of armaments can be considered in a political vacuum. Many arguments have been waged whether armaments caused tensions or tensions caused armaments. More likely there is a little of each. So it is an over-simplification to assume that the political effects of armaments can be judged in isolation from the existing political environment.[11]

Smith is an example of the kind of men that have been drawn into the Pentagon's small but intense and growing concentration on questions of disarmament or arms control. A West Pointer, he had his first plane ride in an old A-3 pursuit ship at Kelly Field in the early thirties. He was so cramped in the cockpit of the plane that he couldn't handle the rudder and the result was a continuous taxiing circle on the ground. Smith was transferred to bombers and later became one of the group that developed the technique of bombing with the Norden bombsight. His catholicity of interests was evident upon graduation from the Military Academy when he spent his graduation summer on a midshipman's cruise aboard a battleship. He received degrees as Master of Arts and Doctor of Education from Stanford University and wrote a book on military doctrine as well as many articles. Men like Smith—and there are others in the high councils of the Pentagon—do not fit the stereotype of trigger-happy Pentagon militarists that so often pops into disarmament discussions.

In the old days, military men could afford a heroic approach to war. Many of them were fond of quoting John Stuart Mill: "War is an ugly thing, but not the ugliest of things; the decayed and degraded state of moral and patriotic feeling which thinks nothing is worth a war is worse. . . . A man who has nothing which he cares about more than his personal safety is a miserable creature who had no chance of being free, unless made and kept so by the exertions of better men than himself." In the new days, military men do not retreat from the concept that the United States must be ready to go to war, if necessary, to maintain its vital interests. But they tend to evince more understanding that Hiroshima has changed the world considerably. Secretary of State Dean Rusk testified before a Senate panel, "I was on the General Staff in uniform at the time Hiroshima occurred. I remember vividly a comment a fellow officer made that morning. 'War has turned upon itself and devoured itself, for no human purpose can be achieved by war under these conditions.'"

In 1961 a young Marine Corps officer wrote of a "new philosophy" as follows:

The new military philosophy recognizes that military force is a means, an instrument, a tool for obtaining objectives—not an objective in and of itself. There is nothing inherently good in military force or in military operations, quite the contrary in fact. These are good only to the extent that they contribute to the objectives of the society they serve. Moreover military force is but one of many means available to a society to seek its objectives. Diplomacy, economic aid and economic warfare, and psychological strategy provide other means of varying effectiveness. . . . The new military philosophy recognizes the necessity for coordinating many functions that were previously not well coordinated. Thus we have witnessed a need for closer coordinations of military strategy, logistics and finance; of Army, Navy and Air Force operations; of political, economic and military considerations; and finally and perhaps most challenging of all, we have witnessed a need for integrating all of the above on an international basis. We have been forced to project to the more difficult international level problems which have by no means been solved on the national level. . . . The new military philosophy recognizes that there are costs, dangers, limitations and disadvantages inherent in the application of military force. Wars have proven the scourge of mankind since time immemorial and have caused the downfall of many past civilizations. War constitutes an economic waste that no nation can afford in this age of rapidly increasing populations, widespread desires for greater public and private consumption, and demands for economic investment to make this consumption possible. Also war seldom develops in the way anticipated by the participants, and it leaves many surprises in its wake. Victory in war may produce a less satisfactory world for a nation than that existing before the victory.[12]

The premises of the "new philosophy"—that war is but a means to an end, that war is a scourge, that war is affected by many nonmilitary factors—are little different from the premises of the old philosophy. But enunciated in the new way, they clearly provide room for the growing notion at the Pentagon, among military and civilians alike, that disarmament and arms control are seriously to be regarded as national security measures, no less significant than superiority in arms and policy threats to use them.

XVI

★

The "McNamara Monarchy"

"The Navy, the Air Force and Army must work as a unit. If I had my way they would all be in the same uniform."
—GENERAL DWIGHT D. EISENHOWER

"I do not believe that the head of the proposed Governmental colossus . . . will ever have more than the most superficial knowledge of the Department."
—JAMES V. FORRESTAL

The first Secretary of Defense, James Forrestal, used to say that he was not so much interested in an organization chart as in the names of the men in the little boxes. It was a good point. Organizations are made of men. There is no substitute for their quality. Nevertheless, Paul Hammond correctly pointed out: "Men in Government—at least in the American Government—do not last. The things that last are the institutional arrangements which impart continuity to policy and meaning (however valid) to process, and the modes of thought which made both significant."[1] Thus, regardless of who runs the building, the Pentagon's organization is itself an influential factor in its performance.

The unification of the armed forces in 1947 has been described as the most extensive reorganization of the military establishment since George Washington assumed command of the Continental Army. It separated the Air Force from the Army and established three military departments—Army, Navy and Air Force, all within a single military establishment. The name Department of Defense came two years later. The Secretary of Defense was at first regarded merely as a coordinator with rather ill-defined powers of "general authority, direction and control" over the military departments. On the military side, the chairman of the Joint Chiefs of Staff did not command any troops, nor was he the "superior" of any of his colleagues. He was responsible mainly for the agenda of their deliberations. The JCS staff was specifically limited to one hundred officers as a protection against undue military power accruing to the chairman, whose title was intended to underscore his managerial rather than command function.

Nevertheless even this relatively mild centralization was strongly opposed, particularly by the Navy and its supporters. Secretary of the Navy Forrestal, warning that such a mammoth military element might be dangerous, once testified: "I do not believe that the head of the proposed Governmental colossus . . . will ever have more than the most superficial knowledge of the Department." As much to mollify the Navy as to assure others who worried about the new element of military authority in the Government, President Truman appointed Forrestal the first Secretary of Defense. Moving into the Pentagon, Forrestal remarked: "This office will probably be the biggest cemetery for dead cats in history." Before the year was out he sought more powers. In 1949, on his recommendation, amendments to the National Security Act removed the term "general" from the phrase "general authority, direction and control" to be exercised by the Secretary of Defense, and relieved the service Secretaries of their Cabinet status. The Joint staff was raised from 10 to a maximum of 210. Forrestal did not live to see the Defense Department functioning under the more centralized setup. The years of government service, unceasing administrative struggles with the great problems of the postwar period, wore him down and finally broke his mind. The official Pentagon statement said his condition was "directly the result of excessive work during the war and postwar years." He took his own life May 22, 1949.

The mood of the office of the Secretary of Defense has varied according to the men who have held it. Forrestal's worried tenseness about the fate of the world communicated itself to the men around him, who worshiped him. His successor, Louis Johnson, a wily politician, held his cards closer to his chest. General Marshall was already an elder statesman when he took over; most of the job was done by Robert Lovett, his deputy, who also became his successor. Lovett generated an atmosphere of quiet wisdom. Charles E. Wilson exuded "big business." Thomas S. Gates worked quietly, effectively, unobtrusively.

Yet regardless of their individual personalities the sudden growth of American responsibilities around the world and the inevitable untidiness of the technological explosion in weaponry gave the impression that no man, just as Forrestal feared, could really get on top of the Pentagon job, as though confusion, waste and stubborn resistance to change were part of the price of maintaining the world's most powerful military-industrial complex. Somehow the hallmark of the Pentagon became indecisiveness and inaction, qualities that invite disaster on the battlefield. The grim decisions that lead to war or peace appeared to be tangled in a miasma of interservice rivalries for roles, missions and spending money. Personal feuds were dressed in the obfuscating language of high policy and military tradition.

When President Kennedy took office in 1961, he was handed a report by one of his preinauguration task forces on government that called for another sweeping reorganization of the Department of Defense—the fourth since it was created in 1947. The report said:

Throughout all proposals, past and present, to make more effective the Defense Department organization, has run one central theme—the clarification and strengthening of the authority of the Secretary of Defense over the entire United States Military Establishment. There are some who believed even prior to the 1958 amendment of the National Security Act that existing legislation provided ample basis for the Secretary's authority.

Others took a contrary view. It is the conclusion of this committee that the doctrine of civilian control will be compromised as long as doubt exists on this point.[2]

Robert Strange McNamara, the new Secretary of Defense, lost no time in erasing the doubt. Within a couple of years, he was under sharp attack for exercising too much control at the Pentagon. He was accused—accurately—of forcing the armed services to "speak with one voice"; of establishing super-agencies to take over certain functions that had been handled separately by the individual military services; of downgrading, ignoring and by-passing the military chiefs; of submerging the service Secretaries as well as the uniformed chiefs beneath a hierarchy of Assistant Secretaries under his direct supervision; of overriding the voice of professional experience and "substituting a military party line"; of establishing what Hanson Baldwin described as "the McNamara Monarchy."[3]

Historically, the country has been alert to the dangers of military domination. But under McNamara, in the Kennedy Administration, there were widespread complaints—against a background of praise by those who favored it—of what Mark Watson, another military commentator, described as "the Pentagon's trend toward constant further depreciation of the military as essential advisors—not on political issues, but on strictly military issues." In a colorful and pertinent observation, still another military writer, Jerry Greene, described McNamara as a "civilian on horseback," who had mounted the horse from the offside while the Congress had been concerned with preventing the rise to the saddle of a General on Horseback.

Thus there developed considerable discussion whether one-man civilian rule over the military establishment was not just as dangerous to American democratic precepts as rule excerised by a man in uniform. As Baldwin put it:

The "unification" of the armed services sponsored by Secretary of Defense Robert S. McNamara poses some subtle and insidious dangers—creeping dangers that are political, military and administrative. And they could present, in their ultimate form, almost as great a threat to a secure and free nation as the attempted military coup, envisaged in the recent novel, "Seven Days in May." For the kind of "unification" being practiced and preached today has ominous overtones. It is dangerous to the nation's political system of checks and balances, dangerous to the continued development of sound military advice, dangerous to managerial and administrative efficiency.

On the other hand, others said McNamara had merely righted a military-biased tilt in what was supposed to be a civilian-controlled enterprise. Over the years, according to this view, the military chiefs had turned most of the Secretaries of Defense into "patsies." Until McNamara came along, one of his admirers said, "civilians could be briefed, flattered, outwitted and finally absorbed by generals and admirals who systematically study all leadership patterns among men from Red Square to Wall Street. By the end of the Eisenhower Administration, control of American strategy lay not in the hands of civilian leadership, but in the hands of the uniformed chiefs of staff."[4]

This attribution of overwhelming shrewdness to generals and admirals when dealing with civilians is ludicrous. It resembles the attitude that Right Wing extremists adopt when they picture Communists outwitting supposedly naïve Americans. Moreover, it flies in the face of the titanic struggles that have ensued in the Pentagon and have forced the departure of many high officers. But as a stereotype of the military, consistent with the conspiracy theory of war, it has had wide acceptance. Anyway, when McNamara took office, there was a feeling that he had come along in the nick of time to knock the rival generals' and admirals' heads together and "keep them in line."

McNamara, the man who came along, did not meet the criteria for the job laid down by the experts—although neither did most of his predecessors. Ideally, the Secretary of Defense is supposed to be policy- and strategy-minded, one who commands the admiration of the public, a man of experience, possibly having moved up from other posts in the Department of Defense or some equivalent branch of government; a man who, according to Samuel P. Huntington, probably should be concluding his career and thus not be in a position to use it as a steppingstone.[5] McNamara had virtually no experience either in the military or in government. Far from being ready to conclude his career, he had just risen, at forty-five, to the presidency of the Ford Motor Company. When he was named for the post of Secretary of Defense, it took the country by surprise. Most people in Washington had never heard of him.

McNamara was born just outside of San Francisco in an almost country-like community in the bay area. High school friends almost without exception recall his excruciating neatness. He was the boy in the class who wore jackets, ties and white shirts while the other kids dressed in sweaters and jeans. He was a good student and became president of the yearbook, president of the French club, a member of the glee club and a member of the board of student control. He was popular despite his odd addiction to tidiness. He went to the University of California, where he made Phi Beta Kappa in his junior year. He shipped out on merchant vessels in the summers. He went to Harvard Business School on a partial scholarship, worked with an accounting firm for a year, married his University of California sweetheart and returned to Harvard as an instructor.

McNamara's specialty was statistical control. At the outbreak of World War II, he taught specially selected Army Air Force officers the techniques of calculating the thousands, millions and billions of people and things that went into military logistics. He joined the Air Force as a captain and rose to lieutenant colonel. He reportedly was so serious about the official order to save scarce paper that he did his calculations on the cardboard backs of writing pads. When the war was over, he and nine other "stat control" officers sold themselves as a management team to the Ford Motor Company. They were so successful that they became known as "Whiz Kids," and McNamara himself was named president of the company on November 9, 1960, one day following the election that named John F. Kennedy President of the United States.

McNamara did not fit the image of a millionaire industrialist. He was an aloof "egghead" at Ford, preferring to live in a comfortable, old house in the college community at Ann Arbor rather than in the wealthy Grosse Point suburb peopled with auto executives. He was regarded as a Republican but had been known to support Democrats, including John F. Kennedy, for public office. He was an elder in the Presbyterian Church. When he arrived in Washington, he immediately sent two of his three children to a Quaker school in the District. With his slicked-down, thinning black hair and rimless gold spectacles he gave the impression of a brash college professor.

His relations with the Joint Chiefs of Staff started abrasively as he ignored them on certain issues, sidestepped their recommendations on others and demanded speedy, deadline responses to some fundamental old military quandaries. In an official memorandum, within two months after the new Secretary took over, General Lyman L. Lemnitzer, then chairman of the Joint Chiefs, complained that the Chiefs had not been given a "full opportunity to study carefully" space weapons assignments, "which have far-reaching military implications."[6]

McNamara ordered four major studies in military policy and strategy. These were not assigned to the military, as in the past, but to the new civilian aides at the Pentagon. The basic study on nuclear war strategy, for example, was assigned to Charles J. Hitch, the Pentagon controller, a former official at Rand. The Defense Secretary delved into all details of operations, instead of abiding by the military practice of giving out assignments, demanding results and leaving details to others. He seemed determined to disprove Forrestal's warning that one man could not do the job.

Lemnitzer, an experienced hand in Washington affairs, did not frontally counterattack the civilian assault on what had been regarded in the past as the military area of responsibility. A good soldier, he remained discreetly silent. But shortly before he was transferred from the Pentagon in the fall of 1962 to command the Allied forces in Europe, he expressed his feelings in a speech that received little notice in the press but must have been carefully read in the Secretary's office. Lemnitzer's subject was leadership and his audience the graduating class of the Command and General Staff College.

"We all recognize in the abstract," he said, "that it is simply a physical impossibility for the leader of a higher organization to provide personal leadership at all places where it is simultaneously required. This is why such concepts as the chain of command and span of control have been devised. It is the foundation stone of our whole organizational system. This does not mean that you cannot impose your personality on your unit. Indeed, unless you do so—unless you make yourself the recognized symbol of command—your leadership will be ineffective. But to employ the chain of command concept and to make the organizational system work most effectively, an implicit requirement upon the higher commander is to delegate authority to his subordinates. This obvious requirement—with which everyone promptly agrees—is extremely difficult to achieve in practice. A battle group commander who occupies himself with the internal details of the operation of his companies may be showing how much he knows about being a company commander. But he is also showing how little he knows about commanding a battle group. He is doing an injustice to the ability and conscientiousness of his captains. He is failing to take advantage of the great asset they represent for carrying out the mission of the organization as a whole. Finally, he is displaying his own lack of confidence in his own ability to do his assigned job."

When McNamara assumed control of the Pentagon, much of the wartime glory of the military had receded. Whatever prestige the military incumbents of the Pentagon high command had left was dealt a devastating blow in the Cuban invasion fiasco of 1961. In the immediate aftermath of the Bay of Pigs affair civilians of the Kennedy Administration sneeringly cast the blame for failure on the Chiefs. Newsmen were called into the White House and told that the Chiefs of Staff had selected the beaches for the invasion. A story, apparently inspired at the White House, appeared in the Washington *Post* hammering home the charge that the Chiefs were responsible for the failure in Cuba. On May 19, 1961, Senator Albert Gore, Democrat of Tennessee, called for the removal of all the members of the Joint Chiefs of Staff after hearing secret testimony as a member of the Senate Foreign Relations Committee. The Senator called for "new, wiser and abler men."

Neither the President nor Secretary McNamara spoke out for a week. The President, in fact, told a group of newsmen privately that he could have managed the military responsibilities of the Bay of Pigs affair better than his military experts. McNamara, when asked about the Senator's attack on the Chiefs, shrugged his shoulders and said he had decided against making a public comment, following consultation with General Lemnitzer. However, he telephoned some people on Capitol Hill to assure them of his confidence in the Chiefs. General Lemnitzer, as usual, kept his public silence. To a private visitor he said angrily that he had been on a tour in Southeast Asia when the seemingly high-placed insinuations of incompetence were being launched against him and his colleagues, "and I can assure you they did not help the United States very much."

Even when, at a news conference ten days afterward, McNamara ended the Administration's silence on the Chiefs, he did not deny the allegations against them. He finessed a question on the subject with a reply that he, as Secretary of Defense, was responsible for "the actions of all personnel in the department, both military and civilian" and that he accepted that responsibility. If any errors were committed, he said, they were his errors, and he looked forward to a "long and pleasant association" with the Chiefs.[7]

The chiefs at that time were Lemnitzer, General George H. Decker, of the Army; General Thomas D. White, of the Air Force; Admiral Arleigh A. Burke, Chief of Naval Operations; and General David M. Shoup, Commandant of the Marine Corps. Within a year, all but Shoup were gone. General Maxwell D. Taylor, who was brought out of retirement and given an office at the White House to review United States intelligence, paramilitary and guerrilla warfare activities, as military representative of the President, eventually was named chairman of the Joint Chiefs of Staff. Lemnitzer was transferred to succeed General Lauris Norstad as commander of Allied forces in Europe. Admiral Burke, who had served an unprecedented series of three two-year terms, retired and was succeeded by Admiral George W. Anderson. General White retired and was succeeded by General Curtis E. LeMay. General Decker retired and was succeeded by General Earle G. Wheeler. General Shoup, appointed to a four-year term, retired January 1, 1964.

Admiral Anderson lasted two years, and his experience in the Cuban crisis of 1962 was perhaps the outstanding illustration of the low regard in which the Service Chiefs were held. First there was an incident on October 6. The Defense officials decided they wanted to send a squadron of Navy fighters from Oceana, Virginia, to Key West, Florida, and to put the squadron temporarily under Air Force control. Deputy Defense Secretary Gilpatric, without going through channels, ignored the Chief of Naval Operations, and called directly to Admiral Robert L. Dennison, the Commander in Chief, Atlantic, at Norfolk, Virginia, to give him the order. Admiral Anderson's bruised feelings, shared by many officers in the Pentagon, soon became well known.

As the crisis grew worse, the United States undertook a naval quarantine of Cuba. Secretary McNamara began spending time in the Navy's Flag Plot, or operations center. This room, under Marine Guard, contains visual materials locating the position of every ship. It also has communications links with ship commanders. McNamara insisted upon making decisions on the spot. He wanted to call ship commanders directly on the voice-scrambling, single-side-band radios. Admiral Anderson tried to dissuade the civilian official. The Navy uses formal, stylized voice communications with coded names going through the chain of command. McNamara was inclined to ignore or belittle these techniques. He pointed to a symbol for one ship at sea and demanded of Admiral Anderson, "What's that ship doing there?" The Chief of Naval Operations replied, "I don't know, but I have faith in my officers."

Admiral Anderson, like General Lemnitzer, expressed his feelings on the subject of the exercise of authority when he spoke to the Navy League, May 3, 1963, at San Juan, Puerto Rico. "Without respect flowing both ways between juniors and seniors we have little hope of doing the jobs we will be called upon to do," he said. Three days later the White House announced that Admiral Anderson, who had testified against McNamara in the TFX dispute, had been dropped as Chief of Naval Operations, to be succeeded by Admiral David B. McDonald, a relative unknown. Anderson was named Ambassador to Portugal, apparently as a sop. After he left the Pentagon, Anderson made another speech, to the National Press Club, decrying the lack of "confidence and trust between the civilian and military echelons," but his post-mortem caused hardly a ripple.

During World War II and for many years after it, the Service Chiefs were well-known, heroic figures. They even participated in a variety of political and administrative roles. The chairmen of the Joint Chiefs of Staff in the postwar era, General Omar N. Bradley and Admiral Arthur S. Radford, operated in the continued glow of victory in war, but were impressive in their own right as well. Huntington described them as true "samurai," military statesmen rather than military experts. Their successors, General Nathan F. Twining, an Air Force officer who had risen from sergeant in the National Guard, and General Lemnitzer, who was caught in an administrative changing of the guard, had good war records but were bland, passive men in Washington. In the meantime, civilians came to the fore, especially during the Kennedy Administration. These civilians spread the notion that they had studied the military posture of the country and had found it wanting. "General," one young new Frontiersman was quoted as saying at Strategic Air Command headquarters, "you don't have a war plan. All you have is a sort of horrible spasm."[8] McNamara himself made the charge, consistently denied during the Eisenhower Administration, that there were no unified strategic military plans at the Pentagon before he came along.[9]

As military heroes have receded from the public view, civilians have flourished. Theodore White, author of the classic *Making of the President,* noticed something about the Kennedy team at the Pentagon. They were, with few exceptions, an Ivy League team designed to be a direct descendant of the wartime Ivy League team of Lovett, McCloy, Patterson and Forrestal. "All through the Kennedy Administration runs the most intense, if unrecognized, desire to attach itself to the older traditions of American Government," White observed.[10]

McNamara's first Deputy Defense Secretary, Roswell L. Gilpatric, was a familiar headliner in the press. He had been an Under Secretary of the Air Force in the Truman Administration. Tall, nattily dressed, urbane, a New Yorker, he was considered a suave, tempering balance wheel for McNamara's reputed impolitic way with Congressmen as well as generals and admirals. But, like so many other high civilian officials, he "could not afford" to stay in government and returned to private life in January, 1964. Gilpatric's membership in a famous law firm, education at a good prep school—Hotchkiss—and scholastic honors at Yale made him a member of "The Establishment," that roster of distinguished public men to whom all Administrations turn for helpings of prestige.

Other Ivy Leaguers at the Pentagon are Cyrus R. Vance, of Kent School and Yale, Gilpatric's successor as Deputy Defense Secretary; Eugene M. Zuckert of Salisbury Prep and Yale, Secretary of the Air Force; Paul H. Nitze, of Hotchkiss and Princeton, Secretary of the Navy; Stephen Ailes, of Scarborough and Princeton, Secretary of the Army; and William P. Bundy, of Groton and Harvard, Assistant Secretary for International Security Affairs.

Despite the Ivy League coloration, the Pentagon is marked more by the "technipol" touch of another set of civilians, however, in which McNamara—although he had attended and taught at Harvard Business School—is a star figure. These are the "Whiz Kids," named after the McNamara outfit that gained fame at Ford; sneered at and resented by some of the military as downy-faced lads who seek pretentiously to ladle the fog of war with mathematically precise measuring cups. One star among the Pentagon "Whiz Kids," however, Charles J. Hitch, is by no means a kid, but a quiet-spoken former professor of economics, one of the few on the new team over fifty. He is the Pentagon controller. Others are Henry S. Rowen, a Deputy to Bundy; and Alain Enthoven, a tall, stringy, Seattle-born economist whose specialty is cost-efficiency techniques in strategic weapons systems. Hitch, Rowen and Enthoven were colleagues at Rand.

High-ranking in the technipol hierarchy is Dr. Harold Brown, the Director of Research and Engineering. Another formidable civilian is Adam Yarmolinsky, whose father was a famous scholar in Russian literature, his mother a famous poet, and whose own bent appears to be political trouble-shooting. Yarmolinsky was one of the Kennedy talent scouts who put McNamara's name in the postelection hopper of government office holders. At the Pentagon he serves as McNamara's special assistant, and many believe that he is the "political man" in the building.

What irritates many of the military men at the Pentagon under McNamara is the implication that computer calculations, operational analysis and abstract theories somehow have greater weight in the decision-making process than the voices of experience and the recorded lessons of history. The picture of young smart-alecks invading the precincts of military responsibility was drawn by Retired Air Force Chief of Staff General Thomas D. White when he said that, *"in common with other military men* I am profoundly apprehensive of the pipe-smoking, trees-full-of-owls type of so-called defense intellectuals who have been brought into this nation's capital."[11] Military men in the Pentagon argue, like General White, that civilian aides are making decisions without responsibility. That is, they safely and arrogantly propound various theories of strategy without having the responsibility of command.

And some of the high-ranking civilian officials, no less than the military brass, find McNamara a difficult boss. Many of the civilian officials, including but not limited to the career civil service, criticize the Secretary for delving into the details of management and making many minor decisions himself. In preparing the 1965 budget, he is said to have made more than 500 decisions.

Elvis J. Stahr, who was Secretary of the Army for a little over a year under McNamara, said after quitting to become president of the University of Indiana: "McNamara is certainly the ablest man I have ever been closely associated with. But he has a tendency to overreach in exercising control and intrude in small details of administration. The Defense Department is too big to be run by one man and there are just not enough McNamaras. The machinery of administration ought to be flexible. I, personally, favored most of the administration unification measures undertaken by the Defense Secretary, but I'm afraid there is a tendency to neglect the accumulated wisdom and responsible toughness of the career officers."[12]

President Kennedy was most emphatic in his support of McNamara, however. During one particularly virulent battle between the Secretary of Defense and the military, President Kennedy said: "We have a very good, effective Secretary of Defense, with a great deal of courage who is willing to make hard decisions and who doesn't mind when they are made that a good many people don't like it."[13] And President Johnson's endorsement has been no less emphatic. After his assumption of the Presidency placed him in a new, more intimate and more difficult relationship with the Defense Secretary, Johnson let it be known that he had found the "myth" of McNamara's excellence to be not a myth but "the truth."[14]

The resistance to "McNamara and his band" has been ineffectual. Even General Curtis E. LeMay, an early antagonist, faded into silence although he was reappointed Air Force Chief of Staff in 1963 for a single year instead of the customary two. LeMay had created the all-powerful Strategic Air Command, but the new strategic forces of computer-minded missiles had no place for a crushed-hat bomber pilot. LeMay's retirement in 1964 was inevitable.

One high officer has remained of the age of combat heroes. He is Maxwell Davenport Taylor, the vindicated author of *The Uncertain Trumpet,* whose strategic arguments—all rejected by the Eisenhower Administration—were adopted by Kennedy. Taylor is something special in American military history—a fighting hero, an acknowledged intellectual and a keenly political person with no apparent personal political ambitions. He runs counter to the prevailing image of professional soldiers as inarticulate men of narrow interests, men who are technicians and traditionalists with conceptions of patriotism drawn from textbooks. According to this image, they are fighting champions on the battlefield but helpless without plans of action off it. They are given to bellicose "habit of command" and unchallenging obedience to superior rank except when, like Billy Mitchell, they fight for a "cause" against higher authority.

J. P. Marquand once wrote that "Many generals appear to civilians like deceptively simple men. Most of them possess, from a civilian point of view, an unworldly character. . . . Debate, when protracted, makes [the professional officer] impatient." But General Taylor, who won his high school debating championship, does not fit this image. The son of a Keyesville, Missouri, railroad lawyer, he finished high school at sixteen. He was fourth in his class at West Point in 1922. The class yearbook called him the "most learned" of the graduates. The pre-World War II years brought him to China and Japan as a military attaché and to various European and Latin-American capitals on similar semidiplomatic assignments. As a paratroop commander in World War II and leader of the Eighth Army during the Korean War, he covered his tunic with combat laurels.

Fluent in several languages, he also received eight honorary engineering and law degrees from leading universities. Instead of the tough-talking bellicosity of the military stereotype, Taylor has been impressive for his soft-spoken suavity. During the Eisenhower Administration he did not immediately do battle for his "cause." Indeed, many Army officers felt that he had not pushed his ideas vigorously enough as Chief of Staff. When he finally did speak out, his retirement followed swiftly. Like General Matthew B. Ridgway before him, he could not persuade Eisenhower, a former Army Chief of Staff, that strategic air power, even with nuclear warheads, was a false god.

The return of Maxwell Taylor to the Pentagon is no mere personal drama, however. It has been significant also in terms of his administrative role. "A Secretary of Defense needs a strong chairman to direct the work of the chiefs, to keep their noses to the grindstone, and to extract from them timely advice and recommendations— preferably of a kind which can be accepted and approved without embarrassment," General Taylor wrote in his book criticizing the Eisenhower Administration.

Advice can be unpalatable and unwelcome, particularly if it runs afoul of political or economic considerations which the Administration holds in great store. A Secretary will look to the chairman to prevent this kind of advice and to bring forth harmonious views on appropriate subjects which can then be used in support of the Department's programs. If the chairman is to perform this function, obviously the Secretary must back him on the split issues. . . . Thus the chairman has come to be a sort of party whip, charged with conveying the official line to the Chiefs in the hope and expectation that they will be guided thereby in their actions. . . . It is not an overstatement to say that the Chairman of the Joint Chiefs of Staff has come to assume much of the power of the dreaded single Chief of Staff who has been the bugbear of the Congress and of some elements of the public in past discussions of defense organization. This power is not bad in itself, but it is concealed power unaccompanied by public responsibility—which is bad.[15]

General Taylor wrote that as an Army Chief of Staff he had found himself repeatedly outweighed by Chairman Admiral Radford. To prevent continuance of this situation, he urged a drastic reorganization of the Joint Chiefs' setup. But when he returned as chairman, he did not press for reorganization. He silently proceeded to exercise the powers of the chairman that he recognized so clearly, as "a sort of party whip, charged with conveying the official line to the chiefs."

Taylor, true to his conception of his role, has proved a valuable adjutant to McNamara, although they differ on some fundamental issues. Together, without the legislation that was so often recommended, they have centralized the authority over the armed forces in the offices of the chairman of the Joint Chiefs and the Secretary of Defense, although many of their measures actually were proposed by predecessors. The transfer of authority over the unified and specified commands from the military departments to the Joint Chiefs of Staff was accomplished in the reorganization during the Eisenhower Administration. The creation of the new Strike Command, combining much of the Air Force's tactical aircraft with Army assault troops, was initiated in the Eisenhower Administration. Secretary of Defense Gates began the practice of sitting with the members of the Joint Chiefs to nip disputes in the bud. Gates ordered the formation of a single Defense Intelligence Agency in order to reduce conflicts in intelligence estimates. McNamara's predecessor also ordered the creation of a single defense communications to unify the long-distance networks that were operated separately by the services. Most important, perhaps, of all, Gates forced the services to adopt a single strategic targeting system. Each of these actions, however, although debated vigorously within the Pentagon, became sources of public friction when carried out in McNamara's uncompromising manner.

Much of the unification of the services—and thus centralization of authority—has been made inevitable by the technical changes in weaponry and the consequent changes in force structure. Indeed, General Eisenhower told West Point cadets in 1945 that if he had his way the Army, Navy and Air Force would "all be in the same uniform." That power has been centralized in the hands of a civilian Secretary rather than in a single "Prussian-style" Chief of Staff is due largely to the historical and legal barriers against military dominance that exist in the United States. But does that make one-man rule over so vast an establishment any less dangerous? The question has been asked repeatedly as McNamara realigns the administrative channels into a rather monolithic instrument of government. Critics of the centralization of authority fear that it silences the possible voices of dissent and reduces the arguments that must be offered and heard. In 1947 the defense establishment was created with a single Secretary of Defense who was regarded primarily as a coordinator, aided by three specialist assistants. Now, the civilian hierarchy directly under the Secretary of Defense includes a Deputy Secretary of Defense, a powerful Director of Research, seven Assistant Secretaries, a General Counsel, a Deputy General Counsel, two special Assistants and five Deputy Assistant Secretaries. The acknowledged excellence of a McNamara should not divert us from traditional precautions against centralized military authority outside the White House, whether exercised by a man in uniform or in civilian clothes. It is not the character of the man but the power he wields that should concern us.

XVII

☆

Billions for Defense

"There is something about preparing for destruction that causes men to be more careless in spending money than they would be if they were building for constructive purposes."
— SENATOR RICHARD RUSSELL

"Oh . . . that mine adversary had written a book."
— Job 31:335, quoted by CHARLES J. HITCH, author of *The Economics of Defense in the Nuclear Age* and Controller of the Department of Defense

In the early thirties the United States spent 1 percent of its Gross National Product for defense. In the early sixties it has been spending 10 percent. In the thirties Congress closed its purse to the military. In the post-Korean "cold war" atmosphere Congress has turned its purse inside out for the military. When President Eisenhower left office, the budget had risen to $42 billion a year, and he expressed fears that America was in danger of becoming a garrison state. Within three years after the Kennedy Administration took over the budget reached a new spending plateau of more than $52 billion

—more than a billion dollars a week. Every second penny of Federal expenditures totaling $100 billion goes to the Armed Forces. Yet even this rise does not include money for projects that military people say are essential.

"There is something about preparing for destruction that causes men to be more careless in spending money than they would be if they were building for constructive purposes," observed Richard Russell, head of the Senate Armed Services Committee. "Why that is, I do not know; but I have observed, over a period of almost thirty years in the Senate that there is something about buying arms with which to kill, to destroy, to wipe out cities, and to obliterate great transportation systems which causes men *not* to reckon the dollar cost as closely as they do when they think about proper housing and the care of the health of human beings."[1]

How to cope with the cost of the armed forces, so vital in war and parasitical in peace, has always been a major problem in government. Secretary of Defense McNamara used to say that he was instructed by the President to (1) develop the forces necessary for national security without regard to arbitrary budget ceilings and (2) achieve that force at the lowest possible cost. The first part of the admonition is political. It recalls charges that the Eisenhower Administration had forced military requirements into a budget strait jacket. The second part of the statement is the operative part; "cost efficiency" is the hallmark of McNamara management. It also has propelled him into a running battle with the military and with Congress, frequently in alliance.

The alliance of the brass and the solons is a traditional feature of government in Washington. When the generals and admirals are rebuffed by their civilian superiors, they turn to Congress which has statutory responsibility for raising and maintaining the armed forces. Congress has the right and duty to probe defense affairs with access to subordinate as well as senior officials of the Department of Defense. In addition Congressional power of the purse often determines the posture of the sword. When Congress withholds money, it influences the size and disposition of the armed forces. But when, on occasion, it has sought to shape these forces by voting more funds than the Administration requests, it has found that the

Administration simply refuses to spend the money. Over the years it has become evident, however, that Congress sometimes abdicates its influence over the miliary forces by overappropriating. This has baffled and angered some of the Congressional leaders. They like being known as the "backstage bosses of the Pentagon" and they have not given up without a struggle.

In early 1962 an episode occurred that demonstrated how firmly the new civilian managers had wrested the sword from both the star-studded officers of the Pentagon and the legislators on Capitol Hill. The titan among these Congressmen was Representative Carl Vinson, chairman of the House Armed Services Committee. According to a famous story, President Truman once wanted Vinson for Secretary of Defense and sent an emissary to the Capitol. Vinson said, "Aw, shucks, I'd rather run the Pentagon from here." Vinson came to Congress in 1914 at the age of thirty, a tobacco-chewing, cigar-smoking lawyer from Milledgeville, Georgia, who had attended the Georgia Military College and risen to county judge. He got into military committees almost immediately and became chairman of the Naval Affairs Committee in 1931. When unification came in 1947, he was made chairman of the House Armed Services Committee. Bulbous-nosed, peering over his spectacles, his autocratic behavior at committee hearings became legendary as he snapped orders to some of the most illustrious brass in American history. He carried the fight for the two-ocean Navy for Franklin Roosevelt, battled for funds to buy planes and train pilots before Pearl Harbor, and overrode Harry Truman's effort after the war to reduce military spending—especially for a bigger Air Force than the Administration wanted to acquire.

Vinson could take credit for navigating some of the most important military legislation through Congress, but he felt his reputed power waning. He decided in March, 1962, to make a Constitutional issue of whether Congress did not have the right to shape the armed forces in a positive sense, not merely by withholding money. Backed unanimously by his committee, Vinson sought to push through a clause in the weapons authorization bill "directing" the Administration to spend a half-billion dollars on the controversial RS-70 reconnaissance bomber. McNamara already had said he did not want the extra money. The Defense Secretary thought the RS-70, for which the Air Force had fought so hard, was not only a poor plane, but that it would be useless. The committee—meaning Vinson—had another judgment. It thought that the plane was worthwhile. Moreover, it thought that the Administration was wrong to be abandoning manned bombers. Finally, it was enraged because its judgment on weapons was being repeatedly ignored. Angrily, the committee called attention to some earlier Executive Department refusals to spend money. The Truman Administration impounded $615 million for bombers in 1949. It canceled a supercarrier in 1950. The Eisenhower Administration rejected $46.5 million for an increase in the Marine Corps in 1956 and more than $380 million for a variety of items in 1959, including $140 million for strategic airlift and $90 million for the Minuteman missile. Both the Eisenhower and Kennedy Administrations refused to spend more than $137 million appropriated for the Nike-Zeus antimissile missile, in 1960 and 1961.

Article I, section 8, of the Constitution, relating to the powers of Congress, granted the legislative branch authority "to raise and support Armies . . . to provide and maintain a Navy" the committee pointed out in its report. Citing Constitutional analyses and commentaries, British history and a United States Supreme Court decision, the committee went on:

Does the enactment of laws by the Congress which provide direction to the course of our defense restrict it to the passive role of supine acquiescence in programs handed to it by the Department of Defense? If this is so, then let it be known that this is the true role and function of the Congress. But if the Constitution means that Congress is to be an active participant in the determination of the direction of our defense policy, then let this be rendered similarly clear. The committee finds it hard to believe that its extended and infinitely detailed hearings are designed only as an exercise in self-improvement in the area of *knowledge*. For knowledge is something to be used, not merely to be possessed. Congress is not a bank which can grant or refuse a loan. The committee submits that it can also make its own investments.

Lamenting the growing loss of Congressional powers, the House panel continued:

To any student of Government, it is eminently clear that the role of the Congress in determining national policy, defense or otherwise, has deteriorated over the years. More and more the role of the Congress has come to be that of a sometimes querulous but essentially kind uncle who complains while furiously puffing on his pipe but who finally, as everyone expects, gives in and hands over the allowance, grants the permission, or raises his hand in blessing, and then returns to his rocking chair for another year of somnolence broken only by an occasional anxious glance down the avenue and a muttered doubt as to whether he had done the right thing.

The picture, drawn in sarcasm and protest, turned out to be accurate. The committee's report insisted: "Perhaps this is the time, and the RS-70 the occasion, to reverse this trend"; and it asked: "Is the function of the Congress solely a negative one in that it can withhold authority or funds and prevent something from being done? Or can it exercise a positive authority and by affording the means require something to be done?"[2]

The answer was all too clear. In a famous meeting in the Rose Garden of the White House, the President persuaded "the Swamp Fox of Georgia," as Vinson was known, to withdraw his "mandatory" spending measure. While technically there was no showdown, the moral of the incident was not lost on anyone: the Administration does not have to spend any money it does not want to spend. Insofar as defense stipends are concerned, Congress is indeed a "querulous but essentially kind uncle who complains while furiously puffing his pipe but who finally, as everyone expects, gives in and hands over the allowance."

Significantly, Vinson's other nickname is "Uncle." As the years have gone by, he has had to yell it often. Times have changed for the crusty backwoods Georgian. Unlike some other members of Congress, he has never indulged in the free junketing, lavish entertainment and other personal pleasures available to Congressional leaders. He has been interested only in legislative power and he has exercised it to the hilt. In an unusual effusion he once called Secretary McNamara a "genius" and never withdrew it publicly, although he has made clear that he resents and fears the accretion of power to a single man over military policy and forces. On July

16, 1963, Vinson was hailed for having served forty-six years, eight months and thirteen days in the House of Representatives, longer than any other man. They held a Marine parade in his honor. Then he went home, alone as usual, a widower, many years past his last drink, a remarkably erect old man carrying a cane which he uses, not for support, but as a swagger stick. Later that year Vinson announced he would not seek re-election in 1964. He thus prepared to retire at the age of eighty-one after a half century of service in the House.

There are others like Vinson who play key defense roles in Congress. Vinson's fellow Georgian in the Senate, Richard Russell, is both chairman of the Senate Armed Services Committee and the Senate Appropriations Defense Subcommittee;—and between the two of them they have managed to locate so many military installations in Georgia that it is said, one more base and the state would sink! Another Southerner, Representative George H. Mahon of Texas, perennial chairman of the House Appropriations Defense Subcommittee, presides over the initial money bill hearings and plays an influential role in the appropriations bill that goes before Congress each year. These men are all Democrats. Others who exert influence on military affairs are Democratic Representatives L. Mendel Rivers of South Carolina, slated to succeed Vinson; Daniel J. Flood of Pennsylvania, F. Edward Hebert of Louisiana; Republican Representatives Leslie C. Arends of Illinois, William H. Bates of Massachusetts, Gerald R. Ford, Jr., of Michigan; Democratic Senators John C. Stennis of Mississippi, Stuart L. Symington of Missouri, Henry M. Jackson of Washington; and Republican Senators Leverett J. Saltonstall of Massachusetts, Margaret Chase Smith of Maine and Barry J. Goldwater of Arizona.

As the Vinson committee correctly pointed out, it is Congress' responsibility to raise and support the Armies. In the course of this process Defense officials appear before its committees to explain their money requests and general policies. These long, detailed hearings are conducted in closed session, but the transcripts are then made available to the press with relatively little censored. The hearings provide the members of Congress a means of developing judgments on which to base legislation; and they offer, in one form or another, an accounting to the American people of the policies and programs that guide the nation's armed forces. But can they—Congressmen and populace—absorb it all? Can the average Congressman, who is not a member of one of the key committees, learn enough about the billions of dollars of expenditures to cast an intelligent vote? He cannot. The average Congressman who is not a member of one of the important committees is no better off than the average citizen confronted with the astronomical arms bills and the complicated arguments over weapons systems. And these grow more astronomical and more complicated with the years.

It is this apparent incomprehensibility of the defense budget, with money outlays that stagger the imagination, weapons systems whose designs tax nuclear physicists, troop dispositions that faze international lawyers, and various other activities touching every man, woman, child, every business, every community in the country that provide the civilian managers with the key to their mastery of the Pentagon. A member of Congress once cried out in anger against Robert "I've got all the answers" McNamara, but time and again the Defense Secretary has indicated that if he does not have all the answers, he has more answers at his fingertips than most members of Congress.

Just as McNamara bested the military in the Department of Defense by reducing virtually every issue to names and numbers, he demonstrated in 1963 that he could take on one of the most politically sensitive Congressional pets and make it respond to his demands. This was the Army National Guard and Reserve forces. Year after year, despite appeals from succeeding Administrations, Congress refused to reduce the size of the Reserves. President Eisenhower complained in his final Budget Message to Congress in 1961: "The excess strength [in Reserve forces] which have been provided by the Congress above my recommendations in the last several years are unnecessarily costing the American people over $80,000,000 annually and have been too long based on other than strictly military needs."

McNamara, backed by President Kennedy and displaying his usual thoroughness, ordered a unit-by-unit analysis of the Reserves;

next ordered a reorganization—eliminating eight divisions, dropping seventeen hundred small units, creating a thousand new small ones —and then deluged Congress with details. At first, McNamara's proposal to "realign" four of the National Guard's twenty-seven divisions and four of the Reserve's ten divisions and to reduce their totals respectively from 400,000 to 367,000 and 300,000 to 275,000 met with vehement opposition in State Houses throughout the country as well as in Congress. Confidently, the Governors and the members of Congress advised McNamara to forget it.

The Defense Secretary countered with an announcement of stricter standards for the Reserve forces. First, he said, the Pentagon would not tolerate a lower level of mental or physical qualification for the Army Reserve and Guard than was accepted in the Army; second, 90 percent of the men recruited for a particular unit would have to be qualified in their military occupation specialty; third, Guard and Reserve units would be limited in the number of extra men they could recruit and retain on assignment in order to make up for those that were understrength; finally, men who did not have good attendance records would be dropped from the Reserve units and tossed into the draft pool for potential service as draftees. Congress could not combat these recommendations. McNamara then pointed out something he and his aides had carefully studied and estimated, that the most effective recruiting campaigns were not likely to achieve a total Reserve strength greater than 642,000 anyway. The Reserve episode, in which the new Secretary of Defense made some concessions in order to achieve his main objective, was a major illustration of how successfully he applied his "cost-effectiveness" techniques to the most political elements in the force structure.

On Dec. 3, 1963, John G. Norris of the Washington *Post*, himself a Reserve officer, reported that the controversial McNamara program was "the best thing that ever happened to the reserve forces" in the opinion of National Guard and other Reserve leaders.

Nevertheless, in the larger picture of defense budgeting these developments are peripheral. The budget is a remarkable fiscal machine, like the engine of a great ship. To understand its power and its course, it is useful to study its navigation systems and its fuel pumps. How is defense money managed and allocated? What is happening to communities throughout the country as a consequence?

Some idea of this vital phenomenon in a military-oriented economy is indicated in the budgeting techniques. In 1961, Secretary McNamara suddenly adopted a system of functional budgeting for defense that virtually ignored the Army, Navy, Air Force and Marines in fiscal terms, but provided for support of these forces on the basis of their missions. The concept was not new, President Eisenhower, no less than General Taylor, stressed the fallacy of looking at the armed forces in terms of separate ground, sea and air forces. And in fact, Wilfred J. McNeil, who held the Pentagon controllership uninterruptedly for ten years until 1959, introduced many devices in functional budgeting.

The new regime at the Pentagon, in any case, tackled the question of defense economics with a budgeting technique that had these objectives: to provide policy-makers with a means of looking at total cost in money and man-hours for any given weapons program; to provide a "cost-efficiency" ratio for these programs so that policy-makers can decide whether the extra benefits they expect are worth the input when compared with other means of accomplishing the same mission; to project for five-year periods the cost estimates of related military programs; to assess military power and the costs of military power by grouping tactical and strategic forces regardless of the particular military service that provide them. Now the Navy's Polaris-armed submarines are grouped with the Air Force land-based intercontinental missiles and bombers and are not budgeted separately under the Navy and the Air Force. The new Pentagon analysts seek to avoid serious imbalances in the defense program, such as bombers without enough bases and crews, fighter-bombers without ordnance and Army divisions without adequate equipment or airlift, all of which they claim has occurred in the preceding year.[3]

The preacher of the new economics at the Pentagon is Charles Johnson Hitch, a mild, phlegmatic Rhodes Scholar who spent twelve years with Rand. Hitch is author of *America's Economic Strength*.[4] and co-author with Roland N. McKean of *The Economics of De-*

fense in the Nuclear Age.[5] The latter book won the 1961 literary award of the Armed Forces Management Association and probably was responsible for Hitch's appointment as Assistant Secretary of Defense (Controller). It has been called the bible of the Pentagon, hailed by the new managers, but assailed by others as too mechanistic in its approach. Critics say it shows insufficient respect for the human factors that go into successful military defense planning. Hitch, appearing before the Senate Armed Services Committee for confirmation in his new post, quoted Job 31:35: "Oh . . . that mine adversary had written a book."

Hitch, fifty-two when he joined the Kennedy Administration, is older and milder than most of the defense intellectuals who have upset the old-timers around the Pentagon. He also has had some previous government experience. Slightly built, brown-haired, bespectacled, he is a native of Boonville, a small town on the Missouri River between St. Louis and Kansas City. He attended Kemper Military Academy in Boonville, received his Bachelor of Arts degree from the University of Arizona, took a year of graduate study at Harvard, went to Oxford as a Rhodes Scholar, getting his master's there. Except for a World War II intermission, he taught at Queens College from 1935 to 1948. During the war, he served on W. Averell Harriman's first Lend-Lease mission in London and in the War Production Board in Washington. He was inducted into the Army in 1943, assigned to the Office of Strategic Services and was discharged as a first lieutenant in 1945. After brief stints in the Office of War Mobilization, again at Oxford, and as a visiting professor at the University of São Paulo, Brazil, Hitch joined Rand in 1948. He was chairman of its research council when McNamara, whom he had never met, called him to Washington.

According to the Hitch-McKean thesis, national security depends upon many factors—the morale of a country's soldiers, the number and ingenuity of its scientists, the character and skill of its political and military leaders, its geographic position, "and even—in this nuclear age—the prevailing winds that blow across its expanses," but it also depends fundamentally upon economic factors. For example, if a commander has $10 million and Missile X costing $10 million provides the most speedy and powerful weapon for his purpose, then it is also the missile that most economically achieves that purpose. Economics provides a way of looking at the defense budget to permit choice. "Strategy and cost are as interdependent as the front and rear sights of a rifle," according to the authors of *The Economics of Defense in the Nuclear Age.* "It does not make sense to ask the correct position of the rear sight except in relation to the front sight and the target. The job of economizing, which some would delegate to budgeteers and controllers, cannot be distinguished from the whole task of making military decisions."[6]

The budget is the principal management tool in the Defense Department. While the separate military departments argue over the proper premises for national strategy, the budget is the one place where at least once a year all the varied programs of the Pentagon are brought together at one time. It is not only the instrument by which resources are allocated, but it is the instrument for controlling the program. When the world power structure shifted only slightly or when weapons technology developed slowly, military budgeting was little more than a problem of deciding how much, Hitch likes to point out. With the swift revolution in technology, the what factor—the sound choice of weapons systems in advance of their existence—assumes a key role in national security objectives. Yet, it is precisely in the area of key decisions about future weapons, around which much of the defense program revolved, that the Pentagon's previous financial management showed its greatest weakness, Hitch believes.

Past methods have not facilitated the relating of costs to weapons system, tasks and missions, he argues. For example, the defense policy-makers certainly must know the costs of military personnel, military construction, etc. But they also must know the cost of a wing of B-52 bombers over a reasonable period of years. Only then can the policy-makers compare the "cost effectiveness" of that wing of bombers with some alternative system for performing the same or similar tasks.

With this in mind, Hitch has developed budgetary categories that disregard the military services, but lump together, for example, B-52 wings, infantry battalions and combatant ships—together with all the equipment, men, installations, supplies and support required to make them an effective military force. He then estimates the cost for the total. "Economic choice in military affairs is a way of looking at problems and does not necessarily depend upon the use of analytical aids or computational devices," Hitch says, answering the critics who claim he relies on computers. He says: "These aids and devices are often very helpful in analyzing complex military problems. Even where they may not contribute directly to the solution, they may assist in thinking the problem through in terms of objectives and costs. In any case, mathematical models and computations are in no sense substitutes for, or rivals of, good intuitive judgment; they supplement and complement it."[7]

With these "supplements" the new managers at the Pentagon have tackled the costly tendency to invest in virtually every idea in missilry and nuclear physics that give hope of producing a wonder weapon. Many billions of dollars have been spent on weapons and equipment that later had to be abandoned. The Navaho guided missile cost 679.8 million before it was dropped in 1957. The Snark missile was perfected and declared operational even after it was considered obsolete. When canceled in 1962, it had cost $677.4 million. The Navy's Seamaster or flying boat cost $33.4 million before it was scrubbed in 1959. One of the first actions of the Kennedy Administration was to drop the project for a nuclear-powered airplane as a failure at a cost of about one billion dollars and nearly fifteen years' effort. The sustained effort was due largely to Congressional interest. The Eisenhower Administration made several moves to abandon the nuclear-powered airplane. Secretary of Defense Wilson called it a "shitepoke," a bird that could not fly. But fear that Russians might develop such a plane kept the program going. The respected magazine, *Aviation Week,* carried a story in 1958 that the Russians had flown an airplane with nuclear power.

Typical of the failures in foreseeing the entire operational picture in a new weapons development was the project Goose. This was to be a pilotless aircraft that would fly at about the speed of a B-52 bomber and appear on enemy radar screens as a manned bomber. The operational concept proved faulty and Goose laid a golden egg costing the government $80 million in three years before it was canceled in December, 1958.

The McNamara-Hitch cost-effectiveness technique rejects the duplicate or parallel approach which some military men, particularly in the Air Force, once hailed as a virtue. Where a development could add a unique and new dimension to military power—such as the H-bomb or the first ICBM—the incumbent defense managers say, the great costs and risks of dual approach were justified. But such instances were rare, they claim. At any rate, they insist that by conducting a lengthy "program definition phase" solely to define the purpose and possibility of each project before ordering large-scale development they can avoid the costly parallel developments such as Atlas and Titan, which cost $2 billion each; and such rivalries as shook the Pentagon—the Nike-Hercules vs. the land-based Talos; the Nike-Hercules vs. the Bomarc, the Thor vs. the Jupiter, and a host of duplications in all-weather fighter aircraft for relatively minor differences in individual service requirements.

McNamara's insistence upon a single fighter plane for use by both the Air Force and the Navy precipitated the great TFX controversy of 1963. Neither the Air Force nor the Navy was enthusiastic over the idea. Each had special requirements, the Air Force being concerned with weight and speed, the Navy with compactness that could be accommodated on carriers. The Air Force already had been required to adapt the Navy's F-4H for its purposes. But this time, as a follow-on weapon, the TFX was to be designed from the start as a jet fighter to meet the requirements of both services. McNamara felt that if he could get a single plane to meet the requirements of more than one service, he would save a billion dollars on this project alone and set a precedent that would bring savings with other weapons. More than a year and a half was spent in working out the designs.

The plane, although called a fighter, was to be heavier than a World War II B-17 bomber. The design was radical in many respects. The most intriguing was its retractable swept wings. On take-off, cruising and landing, the wings would be extended to permit slow flight, but when speed was desired, the wings would be drawn into the fuselage giving the plane a missile-like appearance for supersonic flight. Some concessions were to be made for the

Navy. For example, the nose of the plane might have to be placed on hinges, so that it could be folded aside to permit use of the elevators on aircraft carriers. Despite minor modifications, however, McNamara insisted upon a high degree of what he called "commonality." He did not want to support each version with costly separate banks of spare parts and maintenance shops. The technological unification effort in the TFX was as important as the controversy over the contract that illustrated the pressures in the military-industrial complex.

The changing pattern of military procurement and the over-all burgeoning of defense costs have been among the most serious problems faced by successive Republican and Democratic Administrations. Tanks, other vehicles, weapons and ammunition, plus various types of commercial equipment, constituted 50 percent of the military hard goods delivered in the fiscal year 1953, the last year of the Korean conflict.[8] By the time the Kennedy Administration took over, these items were only 12.4 percent of the total of prime contract awards. Missiles accounted for only .5 percent of the hard goods delivered in 1953. In fiscal year 1961 missiles took up 33.6 percent of the prime contract awards. Closely associated with this development was the fact that deliveries on electronic contracts in 1953 were 11.2 percent of the hard goods total, whereas by 1961 they represented 18 percent of the total. In other words, missiles and electronics between them took up more than half of the military hard goods total of contracts. Aircraft and ships were the only hard goods categories that showed little change in the relative share of total procurement from 1953 to 1961. Aircraft, 31.5 percent of 1953 deliveries, dropped slightly to 28.2 percent in 1961; ships (26.2 percent during World War II) were 6.8 percent in 1953 and 7.8 percent in 1961.

The relative stability in the proportion of airplane deliveries was not specially significant for the future, the Pentagon has warned. "It must not be assumed," an official report emphasized, "that these percentages can be projected indefinitely into the future with any degree of confidence. New strategic and tactical considerations may affect the relative emphasis upon these categories. Certainly some types or groups of items now in demand will decline in importance, and others will increase their proportionate shares." Significantly the report added:

Revolutionary changes in weaponry have been reflected, naturally enough, in manufacturing processes. Mass production items were a large part of the FY 1953 hard goods buy; but by FY 1961, these had dwindled, comparatively. Instead, the more recent emphasis has been upon research and development, and upon fewer, far more costly weapon units. Traditional metal fabricating processes are giving way to more intricate and sophisticated techniques. In consequence, blue collar workers are fewer, while scientists, engineers, and technicians multiply in establishments serving defense procurement needs.[9]

These changes have coincided with major geographic shifts in contract awards from region to region and between states. The most dramatic geographic adjustments can be found in the losses of the East North Central and Middle Atlantic areas, and in the large net gains of the West Coast and Mountain states. Michigan, with its auto industry, for example, obtained 10.5 percent of the military prime contracts during World War II and 9.5 percent during Korea, yet had only 2.7 percent of the smaller 1961 contract total. The states of Illinois, Ohio, Indiana and Wisconsin, combined, had 21.9 percent of the total in World War II, 17.8 percent during Korea, and only 9.1 percent in 1961.

It is hard to translate dollar prime contracts into employment figures. Different products require different numbers of workers. Also, extensive out-of-state subcontracting is not reflected in the official statistics. But it is evident nevertheless that the drop in annual prime contract awards in the East North Central area from $8.7 billion during Korea to $2.6 billion in 1961 has had a severe economic impact. Regardless of how computed, the loss of $6.1 billion a year in defense contracts has meant the loss of hundreds of thousands of jobs. It is not surprising, therefore, that many communities in that area have encountered recurrent unemployment problems. During World War II they contributed heavily to the production of wheeled vehicles, conventional ammunition and the weapons that bulked largely in defense procurement but which since have formed a relatively smaller share of defense requirements.

The Mountain and Pacific states, on the other hand, rose from 13.5 percent of the prime World War II contracts to 18.6 percent during Korea and 32.6 percent in 1961. The rise was clearly related to the vast expansion of missile and electronics procurement. The Middle Atlantic states—New York, Pennsylvania, New Jersey—had a smaller share of defense prime contracts in 1961 than in Korea, but the losses were relatively less serious than for the Midwest. The drop from 25.1 percent in 1953 to 19.9 percent in 1961 reflected gains in electronics and missiles, especially along the seaboard, that compensated for losses in traditional procurement, particularly in the western section of New York State. This illustrates within even a narrow geographical area the shifts that create job problems.

The rapid rise in missiles and electronics has provided firms in Massachusetts, Texas, Florida, California and Colorado with a higher share of defense contracts. An important factor here is that more than half of all missile awards and about one-quarter of all electronics awards in 1961 were for work in research, development, test and evaluation. And there is a strong tendency to concentrate such contracts in California and the coastal strip from Boston to Washington, D.C., near university and nonprofit research centers. Defense officials say that the contract patterns in research foreshadow continued important changes. Research contracts totaled $6 billion in 1961 and were expected to rise even higher in the succeeding years. Research contracts now comprise about one-quarter of all prime contract awards in continental United States. California alone had 41.3 percent of the research contracts in 1961. New York was second with 12.2 percent and together the two leaders accounted for more than half of these contracts. Only a dozen states held 90 percent of the research contracts, with the California and Eastern seaboards accounting for three-fourths of the total.

"This is of major importance," the Pentagon points out,

because any company which has conducted or managed the research, design, development and test work on a new weapon system—or a major component—and has assembled the engineering talent and experience for this purpose, is obviously in an exceptionally strong position to compete for the follow-on production contracts and for new developmental contracts as well. It is logical, then, that production contracts for the newer sophisticated items, which will figure in future procurement, may tend to be placed in areas where RDT & E effort has been centered. The point is reinforced by the fact that the development and test work represents a much larger share of some types of procurement than of others.[10]

Defense statisticians have pointed out that the areas that have gained a long head start in the new and expanding fields of missiles and electronics can look forward to economic benefits. These regions collect specialized scientific and engineering talent, specialized facilities, labor skills and production experience. Successful research and design lead to development contracts, which in turn create new research abilities. "The process is circular, and it regenerates itself," the Pentagon observes. A brochure entitled *Charter of Progress,* published by the Graduate Research Center of the Southwest in Dallas, Texas, and cited in the Pentagon study, commented:

Management planners, in considering sites for new or expanded facilities, have found that the availability of trained minds overshadows even such factors as the labor market, water supply, and power sources. The evidence is overwhelming: Route 128, encircling Boston; the industrial complex around San Francisco Bay; that related to the California Institute of Technology and U.C.L.A. in the Los Angeles area; and other similar situations are cogent examples of the clustering of industry around centers of learning. Such a migration arises from the need by industry for access to persons with advanced training who can translate the new science into vastly improved or wholly new products.

These comparisons show the profound changes in the economics of defense that are taking place in the efforts to satisfy what President Eisenhower once termed the "craving for absolute security." The government has undertaken certain measures to ameliorate the procurement shifts. Intensive studies have been initiated in several departments and agencies, besides the Defense Department, to study long-range military buying needs. One of President Johnson's first acts was to order an interdepartmental survey of the probable impact upon the economy of pending defense procurement changes, and he wisely included possible arms-reduction agreements as a factor. Yet, even with the admittedly faint, tentative moves toward arms reduction and control, the defense budgeting problem has remained the same as it was under the first Secretary of Defense, Forrestal: "How to provide enough for national security without its eating our collective head off!" A decade and a half later, President Kennedy observed gloomily: "There is no discount price on defense."

In 1964, after a publicized campaign of cuts in defense spending, President Johnson presented Congress with a budget calling for expenditures of $51.2 billion in the fiscal year 1965, still more than half the total Federal budget.

XVIII

──────────────────────────────────── ☆

From a Reporter's Notebook

I

"I didn't raise my boy to be a soldier."

—Old song

Perhaps the most annoying aspect of this country's military pre-occupation is the institution of compulsory military service, once an anathema to the American people. Foreigners settled in America to avoid military service in their native lands. Daniel Webster, in 1814, warned in Congress: "If the Administration has found it cannot form an Army without conscription, it will find, if it ventures on these experiments, that it cannot enforce conscription without an Army." His words were borne out in the draft riots of the Civil War a half-century later. The first peacetime draft in the United States did not come until 1940, and even then over the hesitation of President Roosevelt, who feared Congress would balk. A year later, barely four months before Pearl Harbor, the draft law squeaked through the House by one vote. After World War II, the draft was dropped, only to be reinstated in 1948 in a bitter nationwide debate. Following that, in an air of continuous crisis, the peacetime draft was renewed regularly with less and less argument. In 1963, it was barreled through the Senate in less than ten minutes.

There have been many complaints about the draft. The law requires all young men to serve, but there are so many exemptions and deferments that barely more than half of those who have registered serve. Most draftees consider themselves "suckers," and so do many who volunteer for other forms of service under the stimulus of the draft. This was brought out forcibly in the unhappy call-up of Reservists in the Berlin crisis of 1961. The complaints and criticisms took on the semblance of insubordination at some training camps. There were threats of strikes and lurid—but often all too true—stories issued to the press of poor facilities and individual injustices. It was reminiscent of what amounted to a national scandal in the Korean War call-up a decade earlier. At that time, between 600,000 and 700,000 World War II veterans were summoned while about 1.6 million qualified young men of draft age were not called. In the Berlin call-up only 150,000 Reservists were called, but at least 50,000 of them had served active duty periods while hundreds of thousands of others had not served and were not called. A college professor who had served two years as a draftee was called back for crisis duty. He wrote:

It is ironic that a 31-year-old college professor should be recalled to serve as a radio operator—a job I was schooled for in the Army but to which I was never assigned and have not practiced—while the Army reduces its draft calls. I left 110 college students. The Army refused to delay until the end of the school year, although the sidelight is that most of my students were deferred in order to attend my classes.[1]

General James A. Van Fleet's delicate description of the complaints as "pardon me bitching" seemed quite an understatement. Van Fleet had been brought out of retirement to serve as an adviser in the Reserve call-up. Whether the Reservists were right to complain, their attitude reflected the attitude of American youth involuntarily summoned to military duty, even in a "cold war" crisis.

The Defense Department argues that without the draft it could not maintain adequate levels of military manpower. But this assertion has not been tested in more than ten years. Moreover, the World War II "baby crop" is coming of age. Compared with 1,476,000 males who reached eighteen in 1962, statisticians expect 1,880,000 males to reach eighteen in 1966. Even the Assistant Secretary of Defense, Norman S. Paul, who spoke for the draft extension during Congressional hearings, told another audience that if only the prestige of military service were enhanced, "we could probably throw away the draft in short order and build the kind of volunteer-professional force we seek."[2]

In 1963 Representative Robert Kastenmeier of Wisconsin proposed the creation of a Presidential commission to analyze all tasks performed in military service, assess training methods, study the effects of the draft on the civilian economy and its psychological effects on the country and consider alternatives to the draft.[3] But few persons listened to him. Peacetime military conscription, a relic of the "Old World," has been maintained in the modern era along with the military-industrial complex. Having become accustomed to the draft, the American people have given up their historic opposition to it. As Alexander Pope said of vice,

> . . . seen too oft, familiar with her face,
> We first endure, then pity, then embrace.

I I

"Start Your Survival Program Today."

—Civil Defense appeal

Habituation to the "cold war," to the constant living with the idea that sudden nuclear war could come at any moment has been one of the numbing characteristics of the post-Korea period. The shelter program is an example. No amount of panic crying in the late fifties has succeeded in rousing the United States to programs of civil defense. Here and there puzzled local officials have carried out exercises in clearing the streets and shepherding children to cellars and under school desks. But most communities have wearied of "alerts." Sporadic crises have brought sporadic, halfhearted campaigns for building shelters.

When the Kennedy Administration took office, its determination to "do something" about the problems of government included civil defense. The Office of Civil Defense was moved from the Executive offices, where it had existed in obscurity and somnolence, to the operationally active Department of Defense. At the same time, the Berlin crisis, one of the first the new President had to face, brought an air of panic into his demeanor. In a gloomy television address to the nation, July 25, 1961, he warned of war, ordered the mobilization of 150,000 Reservists—a relatively small number, but enough to produce a jolt—and said: "I want to talk frankly with you tonight about the first steps we shall take. These actions will require sacrifice on the part of many citizens. More will be required in the near future. They will require of all of us courage and perseverance for many years to come." And he went on to tell of the partial mobilization. Not in many years had an American President talked so soberly of troops, and planes, and ships, and submarines, and tactical power and airlift and the readiness at all times "to talk, if talk will help. But we must also be ready to resist force, if force is used."

"We have another sober responsibility," the President went on, his young face knotted worriedly at the eyebrows. "To recognize the possibilities of nuclear war in the missile age, without our citizens knowing what they should do or where they should go if the bombs begin to fall, would be a failure of responsibility. . . . Tomorrow, I am requesting of the Congress new funds for the following immediate objectives: to identify and mark space in existing structures—public and private—that could be used for fallout shelters in case of attack; to stock these shelters with food, water, first-aid kits, tools, sanitation facilities and other minimum essentials for survival; to increase their capacity; to improve our air-raid warning systems, including a new household warning system now under development; and to take other measures that will be effective at an early date to save millions of lives if needed. In addition, new Federal buildings will include space suitable for fallout shelters, as well as normal use. . . . In the event of an attack, the lives of those families which are not hit in a nuclear blast and fire can still be saved—if they can be warned to take shelter and if that shelter is available. We owe that kind of insurance to our families—and to our country. . . . The time to start is now."

Thus were the American people, who had not fought a war on home soil for a hundred years, once again linked to the battlefield. The government brought out pamphlets for nationwide circulation, *Fallout Protection, What to Know and Do About Nuclear Attack, The Family Fallout Shelter, Family Shelter Designs, Fire Fighting for Householders, Emergency Sanitation at Home, Home Protection Exercise*. One item, entitled *Between You and Disaster*, explained how to stock essential supplies and urged, "Start your survival program today."

The reaction in the country was characteristically high-pitched American. Newspapers began covering the civil defense story and each published piece generated more activity. Again there was a spurt of community planning for civil defense. Wealthy citizens began building their own shelters. Commercial firms began offering shelters in various sizes, shapes and prices. Earnest persons providing shelters for their families noticed that some of their neighbors were not doing so and worried about poaching if nuclear war came. An enterprising builder near Chicago said he planned to build community shelters on a "key club" basis and would hire a policeman for each entrance to keep out nonmembers. A man building a shelter near Chicago said he intended to mount a machine gun at the entrance to shoot down anyone who tried to force his way in. In Las Vegas, Nevada, the head of the civil defense agency urged the formation of a local militia to repel a probable invasion by citizens from Southern California who, in case of nuclear war, "would come into Nevada like a swarm of locusts."

A nationwide moral argument ensued. Would it be right to shoot a man seeking entrance to a shelter? The associate editor of the Catholic magazine, *America*, said:

If a man builds a shelter for his family then it is the family that has first right to use it. The right becomes empty if a misguided charity prompts a pitying householder to crowd his haven to the hatch in the hour of peril; for this conduct makes sure that no one would survive. . . .

I doubt that any Catholic moralist would condemn the man who used available violence to repel panicky aggressors plying crowbars at the shelter door, or who took strong measures to evict trespassers who locked themselves in the family shelter before his own family had a chance to find sanctuary therein.[4]

When war did not come on the morrow, those who had not had a chance or did not have the money, time or other wherewithal for building a shelter, began to forget about it, and the civil defense program again sank in public apathy and distaste. Congress in 1962 refused to appropriate most of the money requested for the program. Assistant Secretary of Defense Steuart L. Pittman, a Washington lawyer who was in charge of the Office of Civil Defense, carried on bravely, but support for the program seemed to depend upon a state of panic, something the Administration obviously had no desire to maintain. The Pentagon itself took the emphasis off the shelter-building program and sought to compromise with a country-wide program of marking existing spaces suitable for shelter. Instead of a public campaign, the civil defense officials decided upon quiet negotiation with community leaders.

Every once in a while there would be a flurry of civil defense activity, as in the Cuba crisis. But the absence of panic gave the civil defense bandwagon no grid for its wheels. In May, 1963, the Oregon State Legislature voted to abolish the state's civil defense program following similar action by the city council in Portland, Oregon. As Congress began hearings on a $175 million request to expand the shelter marking and stocking program, the Pentagon's Civil Defense chief Pittman said gloomily, "The mood of the Congress is the same as the country. They would rather think of other things."

The civil defense hearings of 1963 began with a ninety-minute provocative staff report designed to summarize the most prevalent objections to civil defense. Congress, the report said, would have to answer this question: "Whether the prosecution of the currently planned fallout shelter program, or any extension or expansion of it, would work a cruel and dangerous deception on the American people; or would it, on the other hand, constitute the salvation of this country both for itself and as the leader of the free world."[5] The report then summarized charges that the civil defense program was technically and morally unsound: the shelter program posed insuperable problems for engineers; fire obviated the value of shelters; chemical and biological weapons would endanger occupants of shelters more than those who remained outside; there would be no meaningful survival after death; the sight of shelters would add to public anxiety; shelters were immoral because they encouraged selfish behavior; a shelter program might provoke war and discourage America's allies; it would impair the cause of peace by implying a resignation to war.

To all of these charges, civil defense officials had answers: there was enough engineering knowledge to build shelters; only six cities (not named) were potentially vulnerable to fire storms due to nuclear explosions; chemical and biological weapons were not "competitive with nuclear weapons as a killer of people"; the sight of shelters would not cause anxiety—for example, children in a completely underground schoolhouse in Abo, New Mexico, did not appear to be suffering from this precaution; as for selfishness and cowardice, Civil Defense chief Pittman said: "If it is appropriate to use moral epithets such as cowardly and selfish, I personally believe they are more aptly applied to those who loudly proclaim their willingness to lie down and die while our country is under attack."[6]

The testimony seesawed in violent attacks upon the whole idea of asking the American people to scurry into hiding when, after all, there was no place to hide from atomic holocaust, and support of civil defense as the only decent, sensible thing responsible leaders could do. As usual, like psychiatric witnesses at a murder trial, scientists could be found to take either side. When it was all over, after several weeks of hearings, the committee recommended approval of the program, more out of fear than conviction. "I won't play God," Representative F. Edward Hebert, chairman of the subcommittee, said. "I won't pass judgment on the lives of millions of people."[7]

But that was as far as it went. Again in 1963, apathy was so great and Senate resistance so strong that the bill was not approved by the end of the year.

III

"Alarmist cries about the lack of civilian control over the military, in our nation, deal with a strawman issue."

—ROBERT A. LOVETT, former Secretary
of Defense

Americans are prone to worry over the specter of military influence upon civil authority and to nourish their fears with examples around the world. There were five military coups or near-coups in 1960, prompting the *Times* of London to call it "a good year for generals." There were as many or more in 1961 and 1962. And the year 1963 turned out to be a superb year, by the *Times'* criterion. President Olympio of Togo was assassinated in a mixed civilian-military coup; military men ousted Guatemalan President Ydigoras; the Army in Syria placed the Ba'ath party in power; an Army coup in Turkey failed, but the Kassim regime in Syria was eliminated—and Kassim assassinated—by a mixed civilian-military group that was immediately confronted with an attempted Army coup but staved it off; Ecuadoran President Arosemena was deposed by a military junta, and this was followed by successive military coups in the Dominican Republic and Honduras that jolted Latin America. A military junta deposed President Ngo Dinh Diem and his brother Ngo Dinh Nu in South Vietnam, assassinating them. The coup was accomplished despite, and some say because of, the very large presence of United States military personnel in the country that was assisting the Diem regime in the war against the Communist Viet Cong.

Could such things happen in the United States? When President Kennedy was assassinated, one of Lyndon Johnson's immediate concerns was whether a plot was in motion. The President said "worldwide plot," so he apparently thought of some foreign rather than domestic enemy.[8] Yet even so cautious a scholar as Professor Morris Janowitz closed his social and political portrait of the professional soldier with a warning of possible feelings of frustration by military "absolutists" or "hard liners" if they found no outlet for their professional talent. Would high American officers, feeling frustrated by the prospect of a disarmament "deal" with the Soviet Union, attempt a coup?

That was the story told in *Seven Days in May*, an exciting novel, inevitably turned into a movie. "Democracy in the United States is so taken for granted," a book reviewer commented, "that a novel about its overthrow is good for shock value, if nothing else."[9] Brigadier General S. L. A. Marshall, one of the leading military author-journalists, was shocked. "In this book," he wrote angrily,

the United States military is caricatured as poor automatons—men who obey a superior's order unquestioningly, however lawless or treasonable, which is sheer poppycock. The implication is that the high command, given sufficient provocation, would act as irresponsibly as a junta in Lima. It is no answer to say that nothing in my 45 years of experience warrants such suspicion.[10]

The testimony of history and the evidence at hand are against the thesis of military usurpation of authority in the United States. In 1962, at the height of the military "muzzling" furor, former Defense Secretary Robert A. Lovett declared: "Alarmist cries about the lack of civilian control over the military, in our nation, deal with a strawman issue. They are concerned with a problem that does not really exist, and they are divisive and damaging by falsely implying that the military does not accept our historic tradition of civilian supremacy. Nothing could be more wrong. I have been with the military in three wars and have worked with them in other governmental capacities and I have never heard any military commander raise the slightest question at any time as to their subordination to civilian control."[11]

Is the precedent of history enough, however, in an unprecedented situation? A close look at the operations of the military establishment indicates that concern over militaristic seizure of power is an anachronism in the United States. For one thing, the unique American-style open political warfare indulged in by the military in advocating certain national security goals has served to provide an "outlet for frustration which, in other settings, had been the catalyst to set off an outburst of militarism." The American style, in which military officers are encouraged to speak out even on subjects that are not

directly related to their professional responsibilities, has served also
to identify them publicly with recognizable political attitudes even
when these bear no party label. This has made covert adventurism
on the part of the military a rather difficult prospect. Moreover, open
disagreements among the military leaders or, occasionally, as a group
opposed to the Administration inevitably have brought civilian intervention. In 1958 it brought amendments to the National Security
Act that diminished the military and increased civilian authority.

In fact, the increase in the size of the Department of Defense and
its statutory authority has created a new problem in military management. Instead of the old question whether military professionals are
talented enough to cope with over-all policy planning, a new one
underscores the paucity of civilian talent. "Charlie," Secretary of
Defense Lovett told the incoming Secretary Wilson in 1953, "Do not
be too critical of some of these men that are here to help you do this
job, because in some cases they are the thirty-third men I proposi-
tioned to come before I could get anyone."

Nevertheless, notably since the Kennedy Administration, civilian
experts of great talent have taken over influential positions, much to
the dismay of the uniformed military. Some military leaders complain
about these "computer boys," who, they say, are outweighing the
experienced military professionals in fields outside their competence.
But much of the complaint appears to stem from resentment that
these experts previously served the military services directly, whereas
now they serve the civilian channel of command through the Secretary of Defense. In the new military establishment, dependent upon
science and industry as never before, these experts in mufti exert
enormous influence over "purely military" judgments affecting training and armaments. At the same time, the size and complexity of the
modern military service have turned the uniformed leaders into
bureaucratic managers. The civilians have thus become "militarized"
and the military "civilianized." The distinctions between the aims
of the military and civilian officials have become so blurred as to
render meaningless the old-fashioned fears of military usurpation of
civilian control. By the same token, the argument raised in some
quarters that civilian echelons are "dominating the military" is
equally baseless. Under the Constitution, the civilian authority is

supposed to dominate the military so long as it remains responsible to the President, and he in turn is subject to the will of the electorate.

This does not mean that defense matters do not require continuous and alert scrutiny. On the contrary, they deserve increased attention. One of the dangers in the modern and vast centralized military establishment is the reduction of controversy within the bureaucracy. Increased and centralized authority in the hands of the Secretary of Defense is an aid to good management, but has as a drawback the possibility that all alternatives may not reach him, that the interpretation of facts may be tailored to his prejudices. Another danger is the absence of challenge by other elements in the governmental bureaucracy. Military requirements have become so complicated that even the members of the National Security Council can do little more than listen to the details.

Admiral Arthur Radford, who was chairman of the Joint Chiefs of Staff during the Eisenhower Administration, testified before a Senate subcommittee: "I suppose somebody in the N.S.C. could sit there and say, 'I don't think we need this many bomber squadrons,' but somebody else would say, 'What do you know about it?' " Before he became Secretary of State, John Foster Dulles warned against "excessive zeal to give the military whatever they professionally suggest." Theoretically, everything is supposed to be open to challenge "in the land of the free." But it is difficult to challenge military policies when they seem too complicated to understand. There is a growing tendency among Americans to overrespect the "experts," civilian and military, although a wise man once said that "experts should be kept on tap, not on top."

IV

"It would seem to me basic, all through history . . . that it's inherent in that Government's right, if necessary, to lie to save itself when it's going into a nuclear war. This seems to me basic. Basic."
—ASSISTANT SECRETARY OF DEFENSE ARTHUR SYLVESTER

Our nation is largely dependent upon private news media, especially the newspapers, for the conduct of government. In countries where there is no free press, it makes little difference whether the people know all or most of what is going on. A visible police power and clear instructions permit a despotic government to operate fairly efficiently. In the United States, however, a well-educated people and a traditional appetite for "news," whatever its nature, facilitate government discipline. They also require most citizens to be "up to the minute." A characteristic greeting is "What's new?" While some persons nervously profess an unwillingness to know what is going on at the Pentagon, that place is nevertheless a news center. With so many persons in the armed forces, with so many communities dependent upon military activities, the affairs of the Department of Defense are of interest to most Americans even when there is no crisis. There are many ways in which that interest can be met, and one way is not to put out any news at all. On the other hand, news is produced by staged public events, formal announcements of personnel appointments and transfers, troop shifts, weapons developments and contracts, inspection tours, draft calls, press conferences, single interviews and background meetings.

The background meetings are a particular art of government. One type consists of a meeting between a spokesman and the press, at which the material the official puts out may be used if his identity is shielded. It is not so nefarious a practice as it appears, since the information is usually more important than the source, who is acting on instructions from higher authority. There are background briefings at which the source is a high official who feels he can speak more freely if not identified. There are also some hush-hush backgrounders in which the source may not be identified and the material may not be used in its original form. This, in addition to broadening the outlook of the newsmen, is a nifty means of floating government ideas without pinpointing responsibility.

There are other means of getting the news. In addition to visiting officials at the Pentagon, reading announcements, attending press conferences and studying available literature, reporters like me on the defense beat in Washington follow the story wherever it leads. Thus we go to Capitol Hill and attend important hearings, particularly those of the Armed Services Committees, the Preparedness subcommittees, the Defense Appropriations subcommittees, and the

Investigating subcommittees. We attend the debates of military-oriented legislation in both the House and the Senate. We maintain contacts with such Representatives and Senators as have demonstrated a knowledgeable interest in defense affairs. We maintain contacts with staff members of important committees. We go to the White House and interview Presidential assistants. We try to get our questions in at the President's press conferences. We go to the State Department to learn what we can about the foreign implications of various military programs—NATO, Cuba, Southeast Asia. We even have an official contact at the Central Intelligence Agency, who usually can tell us nothing but tries to keep us happy. When one avenue of government is closed to us, we try another.

Other sources of news about the armed forces are the many private military organizations. We keep in touch with the individual defense contractors, many of whose functionaries are as knowledgeable as the men in government. We interview the members of private research organizations, many of whom are under contract to the government for special studies.

And yet we who work at it every day cannot be confident of keeping pace with the flow of news about national security. This is not surprising. High-ranking members of the armed forces admit that within a few weeks and months after retiring and not being privy to the classified information that was available to them during their active careers they are soon at a loss to make reasoned judgments on certain events. Under the circumstances, if a diligent press cannot keep up with the complexities of national security, how much greater is the responsibility of the government to preserve faith in its public pronouncements. Ultimately, regardless of how effective the press turns out to be, the responsibility for putting out news about the government, particularly news about the security of the nation, rests with the government.

And yet there appears to be some confusion on this score. Often officials charge that the news is managed by the press, by the editors who select the articles and give them certain prominence, by the publishers who refuse to print certain articles, by columnists who distort the facts to come up with biased opinions. Such officials ignore the fact, proved repeatedly in American public affairs, that the authority of government and its ability to create the news and influence its impact by consistent actions that reflect its talents and intentions are capable of overpowering the most recalcitrant press. As to the press as an institution, it can claim to know all that is occurring. And a good newspaper can learn and publish a great deal. But it must not dare to assume the responsibility that rests with elected officials. The press can be a goad, nothing more. The officials are accountable for their actions. That is why it is important for the press to cite sources, while the government's responsibility lies in the fact that it is the source.

The government manages the news simply by governing. It also has auxiliary weapons. The government is in charge, most of the time, of the timing of its own announcements and proposals. There is a qualitative difference in the announcements made by the President, a Cabinet member or some subordinate official. Frequently, statements intended to be announced at the Pentagon are withheld and announced by the President at his news conference. The government controls whether an announcement is made in the morning for the afternoon papers, the evening for the morning papers, before the close of the stock market or afterward, just before Election Day or afterward. The government controls whether an announcement is made formally to everyone, informally to a handful of newsmen or as an exclusive leak, not necessarily to a friend but to a correspondent regarded as the most effective medium for the purpose at hand. The government decides whether to tell a story in whole or in part. It decides whether to tell a story at the same time that another item has captured attention or to wait for a propitious news lull. It picks a holiday weekend when newspaper circulations are low and radio and TV audiences small or it times its announcements when public attention has been focused on a related subject. The government can twist its announcement on a technicality, fail or refuse to answer questions for a variety of professed reasons without once mentioning security. It can say a question is being studied, a study has not been completed, that the man who knew the answer is absent, that the official is in a meeting. The government can even tell a lie and the reporter who hears it does not know whether the lie is an invention of a subordinate official or has been ordered at the White House.

In addition to such techniques of news management, there are other, less pleasant methods. Government censors carefully scrutinize all publications and speeches by government officials, including military officers, to make sure that these conform to government policy. There is nothing essentially wrong in this as an instrument of government, but it took the Stennis subcommittee's military "muzzling" hearings to make a large number of Americans aware that censorship is not an institution peculiar only to foreign despotisms. (It is an American failing, however, that high-ranking officials, even officers in uniform, incessantly make public speeches and write articles for publication. The "muzzling" hearings brought out many inconsistencies in speech policy control that invited charges of political rather than national security censorship, no doubt because many of the statements could become politically effective. The point need not be belabored. Many of the officers needed to be muzzled.)

The government also has inhibited Pentagon officials' contacts with the press, insisting upon monitors in all conversations with newsmen, tapping telephone lines and sending agents of the Federal Bureau of Investigation to search out alleged security leaks.

Newsmen have been subjected to a technique of whip and carrot. The carrot is the prospect of an exclusive interview or scoop. The whip strokes range from a warning snap to a lash. A characteristic warning snap is to insinuate that publication of certain types of stories, if not an outright breach of security, might have harmful consequences for America or, even, to put it bluntly, for the Administration. This warning is supposed to inhibit the reporter and often does. One whip stroke that usually accomplishes nothing but aggravation is the practice of calling a newsman's editor or publisher to complain about a particular story. Editors and publishers as a rule stick by their reporters, but there are exceptions to every rule.

Other strokes of the lash include wiretapping, so that reporters can no longer be confident of the privacy of their conversations and, what is worse, callers can no longer be confident. The government can and does send investigators on the reporter's trail. Investigators have interrogated reporters in a usually fruitless effort to ferret out their sources. In at least one instance an F.B.I. agent interrogated a temporary appointments secretary of a newspaperman to find out whom he was seeing. The agent nearly frightened the poor girl out of her wits.

These things have been done in the name of national security. Officials are only too ready to say that such and such aspects of its Administration affect national security and the less said about it the better. Yet it is precisely in the realm of national security that the people must be better informed. Some said after the Bay of Pigs misadventure that it failed because too much appeared in the press. It failed because it was ill-conceived as well as ill-executed. If the press was guilty, it was guilty of not having published enough about it. In the Cuba crisis of 1962 it was perfectly evident that United States military power and not clever management of the news forced the Soviet withdrawal from Cuba. The Kennedy Administration actually gave out considerably more information than I believe would have been given out by its predecessor. And in one remarkable episode the Secretary of Defense conducted a lengthy background briefing at the height of the crisis and followed it up by a public press conference. In the meantime there were other informative meetings with the press in other parts of government.

But the Administration confused the situation with a series of minor distortions and stratagems that could hardly have affected the outcome but served to undermine its standing with the press. Some of the restrictions on press contacts were more severe than existed in World War II or Korea. Some of the day-by-day official statements were obviously inaccurate as well as incomplete. Afterward, the Assistant Secretary of Defense for Public Affairs, Arthur Sylvester, a former newspaperman, boasted that information had been manipulated as a "weapon" in the crisis; and insisted that in any situation threatening nuclear war the government had a right to lie in order to carry out its security objectives. This statement struck at the heart of the established American premise of the people's "right to know" the truth. It jeopardized the credibility of the government and the reliability of the news media in precisely the situation when it was most needed; that is, in a time of crisis.

To Mr. Sylvester's credit, he has sponsored some commendable innovations in news dissemination at the Pentagon, although these do not quite compensate for at least one Kremlin-style restriction. That is, an official monitor is supposed to be present even at interviews with the Secretary of Defense, a requirement that seems more derogatory of the trust responsible officials deserve than it is obstructive to the interviewer. Unfortunately, the callous public endorsement of the lie as a technique in national security was not limited to Sylvester. Very early after assuming control of the defense establishment, Secretary McNamara complained about reports of military weakness that appeared in the press. "Why should we tell Russia that the Zeus [anti-missile] developments may not be satisfactory?" the Secretary demanded. "What we ought to be saying is that we have the most perfect anti-ICBM system that the human mind will ever devise."[12] Such insensitivity to a policy of propaganda that would mislead the American people into a false sense of security was rendered ironic by McNamara's own repeated refusal to support military requests for production of the Zeus.

Thus, it appears that the government has a tendency to mismanage the news. In the Cuba affair, somehow, by working extra hours, drinking extra cups of coffee, munching extra sandwiches, we reporters got the story at great cost to our nervous systems in the tradition of American journalism. But the cost to the American government may have been greater.

The American people deserve better-managed news, that is, a coherent presentation of defense policies and programs. The furor that has been created over unnecessary lack of government candor has severely damaged the credibility of its spokesmen. The attempted justification by Sylvester that the government has a right to lie if necessary in a nuclear crisis is only superficially plausible. For American Government spokesmen are not supposed to be certified liars. The extent of a crisis and the desirability of a lie in any given situation are so subjective that they must not be used to make a principle out of a tactic. The government is expected to manage its affairs better than that. If the management of the news is a weapon of government in a time of crisis, then using it to tell a lie can only result in a self-inflicted wound.

V

"Uncle Sam has become a world-renowned soldier in spite of himself."

—GENERAL MAXWELL D. TAYLOR, chairman
of the Joint Chiefs of Staff

On June 5, 1963, General Maxwell Davenport Taylor, chairman of the Joint Chiefs of Staff, addressed the graduating class at the United States Military Academy at West Point. In keeping with his reputation as a scholar he drew his theme from a famous oration by Ralph Waldo Emerson before the Phi Beta Kappa Society in 1837. The Emerson speech was entitled "The American Scholar." In it, Emerson proclaimed to the academic world the emancipation of American scholarship from European influence upon which it depended since colonial days. "Our days of dependence, our long apprenticeship to the learning of other lands, draws to a close," Emerson said.

At West Point, 126 years later, Taylor called attention to the emancipation of American military thought from European bondage. Taylor did not proclaim it as an event of the day. The turning point had occurred in the Civil War, in the wake of which, he said, American military leadership became increasingly independent of the European tradition that had "controlled its thinking and limited the soar of its initiative." Since World War I, General Taylor continued, the American military had generated its own doctrine, devised its own strategy, produced its own weapons and developed its own relationship to civil authority, largely without benefit of the Napoleons or the Schlieffens of the Old World.

The professional achievement of the American military was all the more remarkable, Taylor pointed out, because it was made by men who had never had the benefit of experience in the command of large units, since the armed forces of that period had "woefully few" large units. Officers like General Eisenhower and General Mark Clark were fortunate if they obtained in time of peace the command of a battalion before receiving in time of war the command of an

Army or theater of war. Yet, in spite of "a monotonous life and the absence of challenge which is often conducive to stagnation of thought, such men learned to think in broad terms unrelated to their routine tasks and prepared themselves for an international role on the company drill field."

General Taylor then referred to the close association of the American officer with the scientist and engineer as they brought about "the greatest change in weapons since the invention of gunpowder —the introduction of nuclear arms and their missile delivery systems." He stressed the American military role as "adviser of civilian leadership" in fitting the new weapons to shifting defense requirements. He pointed out proudly that America's voice was being heard in Allied councils on the subject of proper methods for defense against aggression. Thus, General Taylor went on in his talk to the young cadets whom he welcomed in the "fraternity of arms," the United States military not only had achieved its emancipation from foreign influence; it had itself become an ascendant influence in the military affairs of the world.

This ascendancy was only imperfectly or reluctantly recognized at home, he said. America boasted of its wealth, size, scenery and climate; the American Scholar, the American Businessman, the American Scientist, the Yankee trader, but not the generals and admirals that had led vast forces to victory in some of history's great campaigns—the invasion of Normandy, the conquest of Japan, the liberation of Italy, the defeat of the Communists in Korea. The lands, seas and air space which they had conquered and the prisoners which they had taken "dwarf the deeds of the great conquerors which provided the familiar faces in the history books of our childhood," but "still no orations" were devoted to the ascendancy of the American soldier.

"Why?" General Taylor asked, and he answered: "We Americans are made uneasy by the responsibilities of military leadership. As a nation we are still prey to the clichés about men on horseback and of the dangers of the military in a democracy. We still have trouble distinguishing between what is military and what is militaristic; between what is peaceful and what is pacifistic. We must perhaps progress further toward maturity before there will be wholehearted acceptance at home of the continuing need for a large and respected military profession in the United States in the same way as there is need for a class of businessmen, professional men, scientists, clergymen and scholars. Uncle Sam has become a world-renowned soldier in spite of himself."[13]

General Taylor's distinction between "what is military and what is militaristic" calls attention to the definitions used by Alfred Vagts in his classic history of militarism. Vagts wrote:

The military way is marked by a primary concentration of men and materials on winning specific objectives of power with the utmost efficiency, that is, with the least expenditure of blood and treasure. It is limited in scope, confined to one function, and scientific in its essential qualities. Militarism, on the other hand, presents a vast array of customs, interests, prestige, actions, and thought associated with armies and wars and yet transcending true military purposes. Indeed, militarism is so constituted that it may hamper and defeat the purpose of the military way. Its influence is unlimited in scope. It may permeate all society and become dominant over industry and arts. Rejecting the scientific character of the military way, militarism displays the qualities of caste and cult, authority and belief.[14]

The distinction, as Vagts noted, is fundamental and fateful. Any honest appraiser will see that our military efforts thus far have been directed along the military way rather than the road to militarism. Surely we have armed only at great provocation and with considerable reluctance. But it is also evident that our military effort permeates our society in many vital aspects—its economy, its politics, its educational systems, its scientific inquiry. If we have not been victimized, with a few minor exceptions, by the showy appurtenances of militarism, this may be due not so much to national character as to changed conditions.

The usual stereotypes of militarism no longer apply in the United States, for the simple reason that many of the military criteria no longer apply to our armed forces. There was a time when the acid test of our military preparedness was war. We could rely upon a tradition of maintaining a small military cadre and, in a crisis, call upon our "Minutemen," our average citizens, who grabbed their fowling pieces off the mantel and rushed to punish the aggressor.

America, always "quick on the draw," could wait nonchalantly for the bully to make the first move. When there were no wars to fight, we were comfortable in the absence of military paraphernalia in our way of life and ridiculed the strutting military figures abroad. But the idea that powerful armed forces are not needed until the time of actual warfare has been discarded. The acid test of military preparation in the nuclear era is no longer success in war but its prevention. We no longer dare permit "a first move."

New conditions have created for the United States a new modern requirement of military posturing as well as power. For the military to serve as a deterrent, it must be credible; to be credible, it must be visible. The process of making it visible calls for reaffirmations and demonstrations of strength that have been alien to us in the past. Now, armed to the teeth, we wear a "military scowl," as Fred Cook aptly put it.

The national defense establishment is a civilian-dominated institution for practical as well as traditional reasons. Yet the United States could embrace militarism under civilian as well as military auspices. A few years before his farewell address President Eisenhower was asked at a news conference whether he would spend more money on defense if he thought, as some of his critics were saying, that the nation could afford it. "I would not," Eisenhower replied heatedly. He added that anyone "with any sense" could see that if military spending were not restrained, the United States would become a "garrison state," that is, one in which most of the nation's energies were directed to its own national security. As more than half the national budget in recent years has been devoted to national military security, the Eisenhower observation is still relevant. The margin of difference between a garrison state, even when created by civilian leaders purely out of concern for security, and a militaristic state embellished with a panoply of military customs and castes cannot be very great.

Of course, psychiatrists point out that the human mind guides one's perceptions along the path of one's expectations. This was indicated by an experiment in which, by means of a stereopticon, different pictures were shown to the right and left eye simultaneously. When a baseball player and a bull fighter were shown, Americans tended to see the baseball player and Mexicans the bull fighter.[15] In the same way, many persons regard our present mammoth military preoccupation as an instrument of the military, and thus an aspect of militarism.

What is significant, however, is not the personification of danger in military or civilian dress, but the identification of danger. The enormous range and complexity of our military effort represent a clear and present danger to our democracy, regardless of historic inhibitions against militarism in the United States. The precedents of history, after all, are supposed to be educational, but they are not insurance policies. If we should wake one morning and discover that we live in a militarist society, it will do us no good to demand compensation on the ground that this is unprecedented in our experience or that we thought we had carefully exercised civilian control.

On the other hand, to suggest that America's gigantic military orientation holds dangers for us is not to make a prediction. For one thing, I am not sure we want to retain naïve notions that military preparedness is an intrinsic evil. It is simply not true that stockpiles of arms inevitably lead to war. Most wars have begun when at least one of the combatants had no military power. The size of the military establishment of the United States is no more due to the ambitions of the military chiefs than the size of the New York and Chicago police departments to their respective chiefs of police. Nor will we be well served if we retain old stereotypes about military professionals, particularly the denigrating one about the "military mind." We should recognize that military men are inclined to exaggerate the efficacy of arms in the same way that diplomats become convinced of their finesse in negotiation and orators of their ability to persuade a crowd. While rejecting a conspiratorial view of American affairs, we should recognize that lobbies exist, that conflicts of interest arise, that the free enterprise system is frequently compromised and that political judgments influence every aspect of our national security, including the individuals in and out of uniform who are responsible for it.

For these reasons, we must challenge the judgment of the specialists in civilian clothing as well as the professionals in uniform. Ours must not become a technocratic society. It must remain a political society in which we strive for popular rule, not because it is always the best or wisest, but because in the final analysis it is the only kind of rule we dare to trust. Thus all the traditional arguments against military dominance must be broadened to make them arguments against bureaucratic dominance. The military establishment must not be an automated juggernaut whose operations we take for granted. We ought to raise hell with it constantly, ask questions, demand truthful answers.

The vastness and intricacies and awesomeness of our military structure must not numb us into silence. Some years ago Supreme Court Justice William O. Douglas said: "Today as a result of our military-mindedness, there is less room for debate—less room for argument—less room for persuasion—than in almost any period of our history."[16] In recent years, despite occasional flare-ups over details, the management of the American military effort has come under increasingly diminished scrutiny by the general public. In one respect, this is not surprising. National aversion to the use of military force has prompted most Americans to avert their eyes from it. But a society such as ours requires constant self-examination and reappraisal. We must also try to see ourselves as others see us. General Taylor has reminded us that we are world-famous soldiers. If this takes us by surprise, it is warning enough.

Notes

I. America's Military Posture

1. Author's interview with Mr. Hauck.
2. Senator Robert P. Reynolds, *Congressional Record*, August 7, 1941.
3. Testimony, Gilmore D. Clarke, August, 1941.
4. *Architectural Forum*, January, 1943, p. 46; *Architectural Record*, January, 1943, p. 63.
5. *Congressional Record*, October 1, 1942.
6. Congress passed a special law September 15, 1950, enabling General Marshall to be Secretary of Defense.
7. President Eisenhower's press conference, May 14, 1953. General Maxwell Taylor described in his book, *The Uncertain Trumpet*, how he was "cross-examined" by the then Secretary of Defense Wilson and similarly questioned by President Eisenhower on his readiness to carry out orders.
8. *The Chance for Peace*, Department of State Bulletin, April 27, 1953.
9. S. E. Finer, *The Man on Horseback*, p. 141. New York: Frederick A. Praeger, Inc., 1962.
10. Charles W. Bailey and Fletcher Knebel, *Seven Days in May*. New York: Harper & Row, 1962.
11. Eugene Burdick and Harvey Wheeler, *Fail-Safe*. New York: McGraw-Hill Book Co., 1962.
12. For example, Fred J. Cook, *The Warfare State*. New York: The Macmillan Company, 1962.
13. It is significant as well as interesting that as late as January, 1962, the origin of this fear was cited in Congress. Former Secretary of Defense Robert A. Lovett, called to testify on military-civil relations, said: "From the days of Cromwell, some of whose officers not only sat in Parliament but also dissolved it when Parliament failed to do their bidding, peoples whose form of government is based on Anglo-Saxon traditions and institutions have wisely insisted on separating military and civilian arms of government." Testimony, Senate Special Preparedness Subcommittee, January 22, 1962.
14. *Journals of the Continental Congress*, XXVII, p. 433.

15. *Journal of William Maclay,* as quoted by A. E. Ekirch, *The Civilian and the Military.* London: Oxford University Press, 1956.
16. Ekirch in his Introduction to *The Civilian and the Military.*
17. Harold Laski, *Liberty in a Modern State.* New York: The Viking Press, 1949. Quoted by Ekirch.

ii. On the Eve of World War II

1. Annual Report, Admiral William Leahy, Chief of Naval Operations, 1938.
2. Annual Report, General Malin C. Craig, Chief of Staff of Army, 1938.
3. Author's interview with Lieutenant General Lewis B. Hershey, January, 1963.
4. R. Ernest and Trevor N. Dupuy, *Military Heritage of America.* New York: McGraw-Hill Book Co., 1956. In a similar occurrence, a public furor developed in 1958 over a Rand Corporation study, financed by the Air Force, that included a discussion of methods of surrender.
5. "Old Sarge," *How to Get Along in the Army.* New York: Appleton-Century, 1942.
6. The indemnity was $1,945,670 for property damage, $268,337 for personal injuries, for a total of $2,214,007. According to W. Leon Godshall, in "Trend to War in the Orient," a chapter in the book, *The Origins and Consequences of World War II,* the Japanese Colonel Kingoro Hashimoto had been told to "clear the river," but it was not contemplated by his superiors that he would attack a foreign vessel and "genuine consternation" reigned in Tokyo. This is an interpretation that is consonant only with the notion that the Japanese were not yet ready for war with the United States. That they were determined to abuse the United States publicly was indicated by other events. Godshall himself recalls that a little over a month later, on January 28, 1938, a Japanese sentry at the Nanking Barracks slapped the American Legation secretary, John M. Allison. The Japanese Foreign Office expressed "regret" three days later. In August that year, Rear Admiral H. E. Yarnell was refused a request to send supplies to the U.S.S. *Monocacy* on relief work in the Yangtze near Kiukiang. The Japanese said that shore batteries might make a mistake or that a relief ship might strike a Chinese mine. But by that time the military officers in the local command had had enough of Japanese obstruction. Admiral Yarnell ordered the U.S.S *Oahu* upstream anyway. No "mistakes" occurred.
7. Louis Morton, "Interservice Cooperation and Political-Military Collaboration," in the book *Total War and Cold War.* Columbus, Ohio: Ohio State University Press, 1962.
8. Author's interview with General Wheeler, January, 1963.
9. Author's interview with General Taylor, January, 1963.
10. Kevin McCann, *Man from Abilene,* p. 65. New York: Doubleday & Co., 1952.
11. Kenneth S. Davis, *Soldier of Democracy,* p. 248. New York: Doubleday & Co., 1952.
12. James M. Gavin, *War and Peace in the Space Age,* p. 36. New York: Harper & Brothers, 1958.

13. Charles A. and Mary R. Beard, *America in Midpassage*, pp. 490-91. New York: The Macmillan Company, 1939. Beard was so enraged by the Naval Expansion Bill he appeared on Capitol Hill to testify against it.
14. James MacGregor Burns, *John F. Kennedy, a Political Profile*, p. 37. New York: Harcourt, Brace & Co., 1959.
15. Author's interview with Representative Carl Vinson, December, 1963.
16. Transcript, House Committee on Naval Affairs, June 23, 1939, p. 1628.
17. Author's interview with Admiral Anderson, January, 1963.
18. Author's interview with General Wedemeyer, January, 1963.
19. K. T. Marshall, *Together: Annals of an Army Wife*. Atlanta, Georgia: Tupper & Love, 1946. Author's interview with Louis Johnson, January, 1963.
20. K. T. Marshall, *Together: Annals of an Army Wife*, p. 41.
21. *The Secret Diary of Harold Ickes*, Vol. I, p. 700. New York, Simon & Schuster, 1953.
22. Robert E. Sherwood, *Roosevelt and Hopkins*, Vol. II, pp. 120, 123, Pocket Books edition. Original edition published by Harper & Brothers, New York, 1948.
23. Mark S. Watson, *The Chief of Staff*, Army Green Book series, Office of the Chief of Military History, footnote at bottom of p. 132.
24. *The Secret Diary of Harold Ickes*, entry for Sunday, September 18, 1938.
25. This version is based on both the original memorandum of the meeting by General Arnold and the more elaborate postwar version in his book, *Global Mission*. The original notes by General Arnold were filed with the Chief of Staff. They were declassified from "secret" at the request of this author, although their contents previously had been known. General Arnold, in his subsequent version of the meeting, described it as the "Magna Charta" of the Air Force. In his book, he put the date as September 28, the day before he was appointed Chief of Staff of the Air Corps to succeed General Oscar Westover, victim of a California plane crash. A check of the White House records by official Air Force historians revealed no such September 28 meeting. The editors of *The Army Air Forces in World War II*, Vol. VI, *Men and Planes*, p. 9, suggest that General Arnold may have gotten the dates confused. It is known he frequently attended meetings with the President. In his book he said the President's views at the meeting were "a surprise to all but Hopkins and myself." In his postwar version of the meeting, General Arnold included Secretary of War Woodring and Secretary of the Navy Swanson, but they are not mentioned in the original memorandum.
26. General H. H. Arnold, *Global Mission*, p. 177. New York: Harper & Brothers, 1949.
27. Author's interview with General Burns, February, 1963.
28. Author's interview with General LeMay, December, 1962.

III. The Call to Arms

1. *New York Times*, May 23, 1940; author's interviews and correspondence with Mr. Clark, March, 1963; January, 1964.
2. Mark W. Watson, *Chief of Staff*. Watson in a foonote points out that

the Chief of Staff appointment book notes that the two advocates of the draft bill saw General Marshall at 9 A.M. A 9:30 A.M. caller was Representative James Wadsworth, Republican of New York, an early supporter of the draft law who afterward introduced it in the House.

3. Eliot Janeway, *The Struggle for Survival*, pp. 140-41. New Haven: Yale University Press, 1951.
4. Author's interviews and correspondence with Mr. Clark.
5. Mark W. Watson, *Chief of Staff*, p. 192.
6. *Ibid.*
7. Television interview, American Broadcasting Company, March 26, 1963.
8. Henry L. Stimson and McGeorge Bundy, *On Active Service in Peace and War*, xxi. New York: Harper & Brothers, 1947.
9. *Ibid.*, p. 331.
10. *Ibid.*, p. 342.
11. W. W. Rostow, *U. S. in the World Arena*, pp. 49-50. New York: Harper & Brothers, 1960.
12. W. F. Craven and J. L. Cate, editors, *The Army Air Forces in World War II*, Vol. VI, *Men and Planes*, p. 307. Chicago: University of Chicago Press, 1955.
13. *Men and Planes* tells this story of industry reluctance. So does the Office of the Chief of Military History volume on the *Army and Economic Mobilization*, particularly the financing aspects.
14. *New York Times*, May 20, 1942, p. 10.
15. *Ordnance, Procurement and Supply of Munitions*, OCMH, pp. 9-10.
16. *Army and Economic Mobilization*, OCMH, p. 275.
17. Groves' letter to Chief of Military History, reviewing draft of *History of Military Construction in the United States*, July 22, 1955, as quoted by R. Elbertson Smith in *Army and Economic Mobilization*, OCMH, p. 287.
18. Army Service Forces, History of Purchases Division, OCMH, as quoted in *Army and Economic Mobilization*, p. 293.
19. *Ibid.*, p. 304.
20. Captain E. B. Perry, U.S. Navy, "Three Texas Mules and the Navy," *Naval Institute Proceedings*, December, 1959.
21. W. F. Craven and J. L. Cate, *Men and Planes*, p. 343.
22. Arnold Rogow, author of *James Forrestal, a Study of Personality, Politics and Policy*, New York: The Macmillan Company, 1963, has written a fascinating "psychiatric biography" of the man.

iv. Men at War

1. The visitor, Edward R. Murrow, did get to see President Roosevelt. Anecdote told by John Gunther, *Roosevelt in Retrospect*, p. 324. New York: Harper & Brothers, 1950.
2. *The War Reports of Marshall, Arnold, King*, p. 511. New York: Lippincott, 1947.
3. W. W. Rostow, *U. S. in the World Arena*, p. 38.
4. Samuel Rosenman, *Public Papers and Addresses of Franklin Roosevelt*, Vol. IV, p. 251, quoted by John Gunther in *Roosevelt in Retrospect*.
5. Samuel Rosenman, *op. cit.*, vol. for 1944-1945, p. 362.
6. Ray S. Cline, *Washington Command Post*, OCMH, p. 44.

7. Robert E. Sherwood, *Roosevelt and Hopkins*, Vol. II, p. 391. Bantam Books edition.

8. *The Memoirs of Cordell Hull*, Vol. II, pp. 1109-11. New York: The Macmillan Company, 1948.

9. Ferdinand Eberstadt, report on *Unification of Armed Forces*, prepared for Secretary of the Navy Forrestal, September, 1945.

10. Ray S. Cline, *Washington Command Post*, p. 19.

11. John W. Masland and Lawrence I. Radway, *Soldiers and Scholars*, p. 5. Princeton: Princeton University Press, 1957.

12. John J. McCloy, *The Challenge to American Foreign Policy*, pp. 36-7. Cambridge: Harvard University Press, 1953.

13. Author's interview with General Gruenther, August, 1963.

14. Author's interview with General Collins, August, 1963.

15. *The War Reports of Marshall, Arnold, King*, p. 106.

16. Leslie R. Groves, *Now It Can Be Told*, p. 4. New York: Harper & Brothers, 1962.

17. Ray S. Cline, *Washington Command Post*, p. 145.

18. *Ibid.*

19. Harry C. Butcher, *My Three Years with Eisenhower*, p. 178b. New York: Simon & Schuster, 1946.

20. Dwight D. Eisenhower, *Crusade in Europe*, pp. 94-95. Garden City Books edition, 1952.

21. Louis Morton, *The War in the Pacific: Strategy and Command; The First Two Years*, p. 253, OCMH.

22. Robert L. Eichelberger, *Our Jungle Road to Tokyo*, p. 21. New York: The Viking Press, 1960.

23. R. E. Dupuy, *Men of West Point*, p. 364. New York: William Sloan Associates, 1951.

24. Harry S. Truman, *Memoirs*, Vol. II, *Years of Trial and Hope*, p. 442. New York: Doubleday & Co., 1956.

25. Samuel P. Huntington, *The Soldier and the State*, p. 333. Cambridge: Belknap Press of Harvard University Press, 1957.

26. Hanson Baldwin, "The Military Move In," *Harper's Magazine*, December, 1947.

27. Robert S. Allen, "Too Much Brass," *Collier's*, September 6, 1947.

28. Walter Millis, *Arms and the State: Civil-Military Elements in National Policy*, p. 141. New York: Twentieth Century Fund, 1958.

29. Private correspondence with author.

30. Henry L. Stimson and McGeorge Bundy, *On Active Service in Peace and War*, p. 408.

31. General Omar N. Bradley, "Should We Fear the Military?," *Look Magazine*, March 11, 1952.

v. Science in the War

1. Quoted in Gordon Dean, *Report on the Atom*, pp. 247-49. New York: Alfred A. Knopf, 1953.

2. In March, 1939, Fermi pointed out to representatives of the Navy Depart-

ment the possibility of achieving a controllable chain reaction with slow neutrons or an explosive reaction with fast ones. (James Finney Baxter, 3rd, *Scientists Against Time*, p. 423. Boston: Little, Brown & Co., 1946.) Fermi sought government backing for his work but failed. (United States Atomic Energy Commission Release, *20 Years of Nuclear Progress*, March 15, 1963.)

3. Mark W. Watson, *The Chief of Staff*, pp. 49-50.
4. General H. H. Arnold, *Global Mission*, p. 166.
5. Robert E. Sherwood, *Roosevelt and Hopkins*, Vol. I, p. 189.
6. James Finney Baxter, 3rd, *Scientists Against Time*, p. 425.
7. Ernest C. Pollard and William L. Davidson, *Applied Nuclear Physics*. New York: John Wiley & Sons, 1942.
8. *The First Pile*, United States Atomic Energy Commission report, March, 1955.
9. Army press release prepared by Professor Henry D. Smythe of Princeton, August 12, 1945.
10. Article by John W. Finney, *New York Times Magazine*, July 10, 1960.
11. Fletcher Knebel and Charles W. Bailey, "The Fight Over the A-Bomb," *Look Magazine*, August 13, 1963. The article was cleared by U.S. Government agencies.
12. Dwight D. Eisenhower, *Mandate for Change*, pp. 312-13. New York: Doubleday & Co., 1963.
13. Leslie R. Groves, *Now It Can Be Told*, Foreword.
14. James Finney Baxter, 3rd, *Scientists Against Time*, Appendix C.
15. Letter to author from Dr. Vannevar Bush, April 10, 1963.
16. Vannevar Bush, *Modern Arms and Free Men*, p. 247. New York: Simon & Schuster, 1949.

VI. America's Military Outposts

1. Henry L. Stimson and McGeorge Bundy, *On Active Service in Peace and War*, pp. 553-54.
2. Maxwell D. Taylor told the story in conversation with author in Frankfurt, Germany, 1950.
3. Lucius D. Clay, *Decision in Germany*, p. 6. New York: Doubleday & Co., 1950.
4. Lyford Moore, "The Man in the Goldfish Bowl," *This Is Germany*, edited by Arthur Settel, p. 28. New York: William Sloane Associates, 1950.
5. Lucius D. Clay, *Decision in Germany*, p. 6.
6. *Ibid.*, p. 57.
7. Harold Zink, "American Civil-Military Relations in the Occupation of Germany," *Total War and Cold War*, edited by Harry L. Coles, pp. 211-37. Columbus: Ohio State University Press, 1962.
8. *New York Times*, July 30, 1947.
9. Harold Zink, *Total War and Cold War*, pp. 211-37.
10. Marguerite Higgins, "Obituary of a Government," *This Is Germany*, pp. 323-24.
11. Robert Haeger, "No More Conquerors," *This Is Germany*, p. 17.

12. Harold Zink, *Total War and Cold War*, pp. 211-37.
13. Robert Cochrane, "MacArthur Era; Year Two," *Harper's Magazine*, September, 1947.
14. Richard Rovere and Arthur M. Schlesinger, *The General and the President*, p. 89. New York: Farrar, Straus, 1951.
15. *Ibid.*, p. 90.
16. General Maxwell D. Taylor, Commencement Speech, West Point, June 5, 1963.
17. Juan de Onis, *New York Times*, July 21, 1962.
18. "Ten Nation Progress Report," *Army*, publication of the Association of the United States Army, Washington, D.C., July, 1963.
19. *Ibid.*

VII. Troop (Indoctrination) Orientation

1. Testimony, Senate Preparedness Subcommittee, April 4, 1962.
2. *Ibid.*
3. *Ibid.*
4. *Ibid.*
5. *Ibid.*
6. *New York Times*, April 13, 1961.
7. Author's interview with Assistant Secretary of Defense Arthur Sylvester, April 18, 1962.
8. Pentagon announcement, June 12, 1961.
9. Author's interview with Lieutenant General William W. Quinn, December, 1963.
10. Morris Janowitz, *The Professional Soldier*, p. 178. The Free Press of Glencoe, Illinois, 1960. Admiral George Anderson made a similar comparison in his speech to the National Press Club, September 4, 1963.
11. Testimony, Senate Preparedness Subcommittee, March 8, 1962.
12. Testimony, Senate Preparedness Subcommittee, January 30, 1962.
13. *Ibid.*
14. Report to the Secretary of Defense of Advisory Committee on Non-Military Instruction, dated July 20, 1962, released by Pentagon October 30, 1962.
15. Report of President's Committee on Equal Opportunity in the Armed Forces, June 21, 1963.
16. Memorandum to President by Secretary McNamara, July 26, 1963.

VIII. Research and the Federal Government

1. Text, *New York Times*, January 19, 1963.
2. "Partners in Search of Policies," *Educational Record*, American Council on Education, July, 1963 issue.
3. Harvard University, *The President's Report*, January 8, 1962.
4. Dr. Nathan M. Pusey, special report, *Harvard and the Federal Government*, September, 1961.
5. Dr. Nathan M. Pusey, Commencement Address at Harvard University, Cambridge, Massachusetts, June 14, 1962.

6. Joint release, Harvard and Massachusetts Institute of Technology, for Sunday newspapers, September 2, 1962.
7. *New York Times,* May 19, 1963.
8. Harvard *Crimson,* March 7, 1963.
9. *New York Times,* June 7, 1963.
10. Harold Orlans, *Effects of Federal Programs on Higher Education.* Washington: Brookings Institution, 1962.
11. "Ideas: A New Defense Industry," *The Reporter,* March 2, 1961.
12. Hearings, House Defense Appropriations Subcommittee, April 3, 1963.
13. Report to President on *Government Contracting for Research and Development,* White House release, May 1, 1962.
14. John H. Rubel, Assistant Secretary of Defense for Research and Engineering, before the National Securities Industries Association in Washington, D.C., March 13, 1963.
15. Speech before the American Management Association, Hotel Astor, New York City, October 6, 1961.
16. Testimony, Senate Select Committee on Small Business, June 6, 1963.
17. *Ibid.*
18. Testimony, Congressional Joint Economic Committee, March 29, 1963.
19. Speech, National Rocket Club Dinner, March 22, 1963.
20. *Review of Space Research, the Report of the Summer Study Conducted Under the Auspices of the Space Science Board of the National Academy of Sciences,* Chapter 16, p. 6. (NAS-NRC publication 1079, 1962).
21. As quoted by Lawrence Galton in "Will Space Research Pay Off on Earth?," *New York Times Magazine,* May 26, 1963.

ix. Free Enterprise and National Defense

1. Department of Defense estimate in response to author's inquiry, December 23, 1963.
2. *Business Week,* November 10, 1962.
3. Cf. Footnote 17, Chapter 1.
4. *Business Week,* November 10, 1962.
5. *Ibid.*
6. NBC White Paper, "Arms and the State," March 25, 1963. Author served as adviser for this TV program.
7. *Wall Street Journal,* April 3, 1963.
8. *Ibid.*
9. Examples provided author by Department of Defense, June 18, 1963.
10. Testimony, House Armed Services Committee, January 30, 1963.
11. Author's interview with Thomas D. Morris, Assistant Secretary of Defense for Logistics and Installations, March 5, 1963.
12. Speech by Dr. Harold R. Brown, Director of Defense Research and Engineering, before Convention of Armed Forces Communications and Electronics Association, June 12, 1962.
13. Claude Witze, senior editor, *Air Force and Space Digest Magazine,* September, 1962, issue.
14. *Ibid.*

15. Stanford Research Institute Report, Menlo Park, California, May, 1963.
16. *Ibid.*
17. Claude Witze, cited earlier.
18. House Defense Appropriations Subcommittee Hearings, May 6, 1963.
19. Testimony, House Defense Appropriations Subcommittee, May 17, 1963.
20. Walter Millis, *Arms and Men*, New American Library, a Mentor Book reprint, p. 274. Original edition published by G. P. Putnam's Sons, 1956, New York.
21. As cited by Seymour Melman in *A Strategy for American Security*, including statistical material from *U.S. Statistical Extract*, 1962; *American Machinist Magazine*, November 26, 1962.

x. The Military and Politics

1. Joseph W. Martin, *My First Fifty Years in Politics*, as told to Robert J. Donovan, p. 171. New York: McGraw-Hill Book Co., 1960.
2. G. T. Curtis, *Life of James Buchanan*, Vol. II, p. 48. New York: Harper & Brothers, 1883.
3. Warren Moscow, "Dewey Asks a Rise in MacArthur Role in the Pacific War," *New York Times*, September 14, 1944.
4. George Stimpson, *A Book About American Politics*, p. 518. New York: Harper & Brothers, 1952.
5. Richard Rovere, *The Eisenhower Years*, pp. 9-10. New York: Farrar, Straus & Cudahy, 1956.
6. George Stimpson, *A Book About American Politics*, p. 263.
7. Dwight D. Eisenhower, *Mandate for Change*, p. 5.
8. Harry S. Truman, *Memoirs*, Vol. II, *Years of Trial and Hope*, p. 187; Dwight D. Eisenhower, *Mandate for Change*, p. 7. It is interesting to note that President Truman in his memoirs leaves out the phrase of the letter which Eisenhower includes in his version, "in the absence of some obvious and overriding reasons."
9. Author's interview with Mr. Truman, July, 1963.
10. K. T. Marshall, *Together: Annals of an Army Wife*, pp. 17-18; see also W. W. Rostow, *U. S. in the World Arena*, p. 49.
11. Forrest C. Pogue, *George C. Marshall, Education of a General, 1880-1939*, p. 326. New York: The Viking Press, 1963.
12. White House memorandum, December 5, 1950.
13. President Kennedy's press conference, August 10, 1961.
14. *New York Times*, January 28, 1961.
15. *New York Times*, April 14, 1961.
16. "Right Wing Officers Worrying Pentagon," article by Cabell Phillips, *New York Times*, June 18, 1961.
17. Letter to Senator Joseph S. Clark, Democrat of Pennsylvania, from Major General Fred C. Weyand, Deputy Army Chief for Legislative Liaison.
18. S. E. Finer, *Man on Horseback*, p. 143.
19. Morris Janowitz, *The Professional Soldier*, viii.
20. *Ibid.*, p. 374.
21. Hearings, Senate Preparedness Subcommittee, January 23, 1962.

xi. The Military Lobbies

1. Karl Schriftgiesser, *The Lobbyists*, pp. 14-15. Boston: Atlantic, Little, Brown & Co., 1951.
2. *Ibid.*, p. 11.
3. *New York Times* text, President Eisenhower's press conference, June 4, 1959.
4. Address to Army War College, February 5, 1963.
5. Remarks by Lieutenant General Robert M. Lee, Commander, Air Defense Command, Air Force Association Reserve Forces Seminar, Las Vegas, Nevada, September 21, 1962.
6. Martin Company Release No. 3369, September 19, 1962.
7. Washington *Star*, July 30, 1961.
8. *Collier's*, September 16, 1955.
9. *New York Times*, April 3, 1963.
10. Major General Arno Loehmann, *Air University Quarterly*, Fall, 1961, p. 5.
11. Quoted by Loehmann in *Air University Quarterly*, p. 8.
12. Morris Janowitz, *The Professional Soldier*, p. 392.

xii. Questions of Probity

1. The general was Major General Bennett E. Myers, the Secretary of the Air Force was Stuart Symington. *New York Times*, November 25, 1947.
2. *New York Times*, December 5, 1960.
3. *Ibid.*
4. Testimony, House Armed Services Subcommittee, September 1, 1959.
5. *New York Times*, December 28, 1961.
6. *New York Times*, December 30, 1961.
7. Testimony, House Armed Services Subcommittee, March 9, 1956.
8. *New York Times*, June 5, 1959.
9. Hearings, Senate Permanent Investigating Subcommittee, July 25, 1955.
10. *New York Times*, April 9, 1957.
11. *New York Times*, August 15, 1957.
12. *New York Times*, October 19, 1963.
13. *New York Times*, August 8, 1963.
14. Testimony, Senate Preparedness Subcommittee, June 14, 1963.
15. *Organizing for National Security, Staff Reports and Recommendations Committee on Government Operations*, Vol. III, p. 64. Washington: Government Printing Office, 1961.
16. Cited in *Conflict of Interest*, Association of Bar of City of New York, 1960, p. 35.
17. *Ibid.*
18. Quoted in *Wall Street Journal*, February 28, 1961.
19. Debate, House of Representatives, June 2, 1959.
20. *New York Times*, June 6, 1963.
21. NBC White Paper, "Arms and the State," March 25, 1962.
22. *Ibid.*
23. Executive Order 10939, White House, May 5, 1961.

XIII. Fantastic Weapons

1. Brigadier General Homer A. Boushey, speech to Aero Club, January 28, 1958, Washington, D.C. Remarks published in *Army-Navy-Air Force Register*, February 8, 1958.
2. Dr. Lee A. Du Bridge, president of the California Institute of Technology, quoted in *Time Magazine*, March 31, 1958.
3. Eisenhower Message to Congress proposing space agency, *New York Times*, April 3, 1958.
4. Eric Burgess, *Satellites and Space Flight*, pp. 1, 134. New York: The Macmillan Company, 1957.
5. *Electronic Age*, house organ of RCA, Summer, 1962.
6. General Curtis LeMay, lecture at Assumption College, Worcester, Massachusetts, reported in *New York Times*, March 29, 1963.
7. W. E. Knox, president of the Westinghouse Electric International Company, *New York Times Magazine*, November 18, 1962.
8. Ed Rees, *The Seas and the Subs*, p. 81. New York: Duell, Sloan & Pearce, 1961.
9. Clay Blair, *The Atomic Submarine and Admiral Rickover*, cited by Rees.
10. *New York Times*, June 22, 1963.
11. James Baar and William E. Howard, *Polaris!*, pp. 136-37. New York: Harcourt, Brace & Co., 1960.
12. "The Vision of Greater America," *The General Electric Forum*, Vol. V, No. 3, July-September, 1962.
13. Hearings, House Defense Appropriations Subcommittee, May 6, 1963.
14. Others on the committee were Professor Clark B. Millikan, Professor Charles C. Lauritsen, and Dr. Louis G. Dunn, all of California Institute of Technology; Dr. Hendrick W. Bode, Bell Telephone Laboratories; Dr. Allen E. Pucket, Hughes Aircraft Company; Dr. George B. Kistiakowsky, Harvard University and later President Eisenhower's science adviser; Professor Jerome B. Wiesner, Massachusetts Institute of Technology and later President Kennedy's science adviser; Lawrence A. Hyland, Bendix Aviation Corporation; Dr. Simon Ramo and Dr. Dean Wooldridge, both of Ramo-Wooldridge Corporation.
15. Address to Air Force Association annual convention, Philadelphia, September 24, 1961.
16. Address to American Astronautical Society, June 6, 1963.
17. Speech by Major General Joseph R. Holzapple, May 29, 1963.
18. Speech by Lieutenant General James Ferguson to Aviation Writers Convention, Dallas, Texas, May 24, 1963.
19. Speech by Secretary of the Air Force Zuckert to Los Angeles Chamber of Commerce, November 16, 1962.

XIV. Choosing a National Strategy

1. Department of State Bulletin, January 25, 1954, Vol. 30, p. 108. Speech was January 12, 1954.
2. James Reston, *New York Times*, April 16, 1959.

3. Speech to Dallas World Affairs Council, October 27, 1957.
4. General Maxwell D. Taylor, *The Uncertain Trumpet*, p. 9.
5. Kahn used this phrase in two books: *On Thermonuclear War*, Princeton: Princeton University Press, 1960; *Thinking About the Unthinkable*, New York: Horizon Press, 1962. It is interesting that Khrushchev used the phrase in his July, 1963, attack on the Chinese and Kennedy quoted it.
6. James R. Newman, *Scientific American*, March, 1961.
7. Arthur I. Waskow, *The Limits of Defense*. New York: Doubleday & Co., 1962.
8. Richard Fryklund, *One Hundred Million Lives*. New York: The Macmillan Company, 1962.
9. Robert S. McNamara, Testimony, House and Senate Armed Services Committee, January, 1963.
10. Speech to Economic Club of New York, November 18, 1963.
11. *New York Times*, January 24, 1960.
12. Dr. Alain C. Enthoven, Deputy Assistant Secretary of Defense for International Security Affairs, in speech to Loyola University Forum of National Affairs, February 10, 1963.
13. Testimony, House and Senate Armed Services Committees, January, 1963.
14. Speech to Economic Club of New York, November 18, 1963.
15. Speech to American Society of Newspaper Publishers, April 20, 1961.
16. Major General Chester V. Clifton, *Hail to the Chief*, Army publication of the Association of the United States Army, January, 1964.
17. *Ibid.*
18. Speech to U. S. Army Special Warfare School, June 28, 1961.

xv. Disarmament

1. *New York Times*, September 7, 1929.
2. Burton J. Hendrick, *Life and Letters of Walter H. Page*, Vol. II, pp. 269-71. Garden City: Doubleday, Page & Co., 1924.
3. *Current History Magazine*, October, 1939.
4. *Economic Impacts of Disarmament, Report to the U. S. Arms Control and Disarmament Agency*. Washington: Government Printing Office, January, 1962.
5. *Ibid.*
6. Speech on the Senate Floor, October 5, 1962.
7. Henry S. Rowen, *National Security and the American Economy in the 1960s, Joint Economic Committee Study Paper*. Washington: Government Printing Office, 1960. Rowen was later appointed Deputy Assistant Secretary of Defense (Planning and National Security Council).
8. Speech, International Arms Control Symposium, Ann Arbor, Michigan, December 18, 1962.
9. Interview with a high officer who may not be named.
10. Major Reginald Hargreaves, "The Disarmament Myth," *Ordnance Magazine*, September-October, 1960.
11. "How Arms Control Doctrine Can Affect U.S. Strategy," *Air Force and Space Digest*, publication of the Air Force Association, Washington, D.C., December, 1962.

12. Lieutenant Colonel Charles M. Ferguson, Jr., "A New U.S. Military Philosophy," *Naval Institute Proceedings*, January, 1961.

xvi. The "McNamara Monarchy"

1. Paul Y. Hammond, *Organizing for Defense, the American Military Establishment in the Twentieth Century*, p. 4. Princeton: Princeton University Press, 1961.
2. Report of President-elect Kennedy's task force, headed by Senator Stuart Symington, December, 1960. Text, *New York Times*, December 5, 1960.
3. Hanson W. Baldwin, "The McNamara Monarchy," *Saturday Evening Post*, March 9, 1963.
4. Theodore H. White, "Revolution in the Pentagon," *Look Magazine*, April 23, 1963.
5. S. P. Huntington, *Soldier and the State*, pp. 452-53.
6. *New York Times*, March 16, 1962. Full text of Lemnitzer memorandum to McNamara, dated March 2, 1961, follows:

I have studied the draft of the department of defense directive in Space Systems Development and what follows are my personal opinions:

Time precluded a development of a view by the Joint Chiefs of Staff. Although the service chiefs will undoubtedly have their views reflected in the comments of their respective service secretaries, I feel that in general the Joint Chiefs of Staff should be given a full opportunity to study carefully matters of this sort which have far reaching military implications. In my opinion the new directive goes too far. It makes a change in basic policy whereas all that appears to me to be warranted at this time is an updating to meet those changes we can now foresee. I have reviewed carefully the existing directive, issued on 18 Sept. 1959 and believe that in the main, it continues to be a sound basis (on which to operate).

The current directive established the principle that under the overall direction of the department of defense, each service should develop those payloads in which it has a primary interest or special competence. Operating under this principle has in my opinion not resulted in waste, inefficiency, or lack of effectiveness. On the contrary, I believe it has contributed to a comprehensive, rapid and orderly development of the utilization of space for military purposes.

As Chief of Staff of the Army, I became intimately acquainted with the development of the communication satellite and in retrospect believe that the rather remarkable progress achieved could not have been possible if policy had not encouraged and permitted the army the degree of freedom it had.

I am quite sure this would apply equally to the Navy's development of the navigation satellite. . . .

(The new directive correctly recognizes that all military departments and the department of defense had substantial interests in space.)

However, the effect of these important concepts is lost, in my opinion, when they are relegated to the status of exceptions to rather than being within policy. I cannot demonstrate that maximum economy of defense resources might not be achieved by making a single service responsible for development of all space payloads, but I do feel strongly that such a move would result in our overall loss of effectiveness through failure to utilize to its full potential the initiative, background, experience, and brainpower available. We are just beginning to explore how to use space as a military working environment. We simply do not yet know what the full use of space will encompass and how the interest of the department of defense as a whole can best be served. Encouraging all services to develop space systems in which they have a primary interest or special competence is to me far the better way to use the resources we can allocate to this area.

I am confident that close department of defense supervision of expenditures can assure good economy and management.

7. *New York Times*, May 27, 1961.
8. Stewart Alsop, *Saturday Evening Post*, November 27, 1962.
9. Speech, American Society of Newspaper Editors, April 20, 1963.
10. *Look Magazine*, April 23, 1963.
11. General Thomas D. White, *Newsweek*, June, 1963.
12. Author's interview with Mr. Stahr, July 7, 1962.
13. President Kennedy's news conference, March 21, 1963.
14. *New York Times*, January 2, 1964.
15. General Maxwell D. Taylor, *The Uncertain Trumpet*, pp. 109-11.

xvii. Billions for Defense

1. Quoted by Senator William E. Proxmire, "Spendthrifts for Defense," *The Nation*, August 25, 1962.
2. House Armed Services Committee report accompanying H.R. 9751, March 7, 1962.
3. Dr. Alain C. Enthoven, speech before Naval War College, Newport, Rhode Island, June 6, 1963.
4. Clarendon Press, 1961.
5. Harvard University Press, 1960.
6. *The Economics of Defense in the Nuclear Age*, p. 3.
7. Speech, Armed Forces Management Association, Washington, D.C., March 1, 1961.
8. This and much of succeeding material is from *The Changing Patterns of Defense Procurement*, special study of Department of Defense, June 19, 1962.
9. *Ibid.*
10. I am keeping to 1961 for this comparison because it was the year used in the Defense study of 1962, quoted here.

xviii. From a Reporter's Notebook

1. Private correspondence.
2. Speech, Yale Club, Boston, Massachusetts, January 15, 1963.
3. Debate, House of Representatives, March 11, 1963.

4. This and other examples of civil defense reaction taken from *The Progressive Magazine*, article by Sidney Lens, February, 1962.
5. Hearings, House Armed Services Subcommittee on Civil Defense, May 28, 1963.
6. Testimony, House Armed Services Subcommittee on Civil Defense, May 28, 1963.
7. *New York Times*, July 25, 1963.
8. *New York Times*, December 24, 1963. Report of radio interview with Malcolm Kilduff, White House assistant press secretary, over stations of the Westinghouse Broadcasting Company.
9. David Dempsey, *New York Times Book Review*, October 16, 1962.
10. S. L. A. Marshall, book review, *The New Republic*, October 1, 1962.
11. Testimony, Senate Preparedness Subcommittee, January 23, 1962.
12. *New York Times*, May 11, 1961.
13. Speech, West Point, June, 1963.
14. Alfred Vagts, *A History of Militarism*, pp. 13-15. London: Hollis & Carter, 1959.
15. Jerome D. Frank, "Breaking the Thought Barrier," *Psychiatry: Journal for the Study of Interpersonal Processes*, Vol. 23, No. 3, August, 1960.
16. "Should We Fear the Military?," *Look Magazine*, March 11, 1952.

Index

About the Author

JACK RAYMOND, who has covered Defense Affairs for the *New York Times* for seven years, was born in Poland but raised in New York City. While in school he was sports correspondent for the New York *World Telegram* and free-lanced for other New York papers.

In 1940 he joined the *New York Times,* leaving to go into the United States Army in 1942. While in military service he went to North Africa for the *Stars and Stripes,* serving as combat correspondent in Italy, France and Germany. He was awarded the Bronze Star for the capture of four Germans while on a *Stars and Stripes* assignment. At the end of the war he was being held by the Russians to prevent his entry into Berlin.

Returning to the *Times* in 1945, Mr. Raymond covered Germany for four years, reporting such events as the last of the Nuremberg Trials, the formation of the West German Government and the Berlin Blockade. In Yugoslavia in 1952 he covered Tito's disagreement with Stalin, then the reconciliation with Khrushchev and the ouster of Djilas. In 1955 he was one of the first correspondents to tour the Iron Curtain countries; the next year he covered the 20th Congress in Moscow and traveled through Russia reporting on the de-Stalinization which followed. Later that year he went to Outer Mongolia.

At the end of 1956, Mr. Raymond took up his present assignment in Washington as the Pentagon correspondent for the *New York Times.* He lives there with his wife and two teen-age children.

Format by Sidney Feinberg
Set in Linotype Caledonia
Composed, printed and bound by The Haddon Craftsmen, Inc.
HARPER & ROW, PUBLISHERS, INCORPORATED